CW00832166

Why is there only one word for Thesaurus ?

being the Memoirs of David Watkin

For Sheila, on a
delightful, but rainy
afternoon. With my
kindest wishes,

David.

1st June '03
Brighton.

Published in Brighton
The Trouser Press 1998

Acknowledgements

*Designed by Rachael Adams in (Bimbo Severe),
AGaramond and Franklin Gothic on 90gsm Fineblade
Cartridge.
This book is published by Subscription*

ISBN   1 871966 44 2

The Subscription has been organised by Samuel Mullen at the premises of Holleyman and Treacher in Brighton, with the help of David Plumtree and Michael Kadwell.
Most of the blame for the enterprise attaches to Chris Mullen, without whom it is unlikely ever to have got into print.
Thanks also to Oriole Mullen, for taking a busman's holiday from marking children's exam papers, to check the manuscript.

The frontispiece drawing is by Dante Ferretti (his copyright).
The drawing on page 6 is by John Vernon Lord (his copyright).
The drawing on page 54 is by David Rees Davies (his copyright).

With grateful acknowledgments to Faber and Faber Ltd., for permission to print part of W.H. Auden's poem 'Josef Weinhaber'.
Every effort has been made to trace the copyright holder of Gavin Ewart's lines at the end of Chapter 32.

*Printed and bound in Great Britain
by Bookcraft (Bath), Avon*

List of Subscribers

A

Angela Allen
Daphne Anstey
Kenny Atherfold

Joe and Marsha Aulisi
Jane Austin, *three copies*

B

Roderick Barron, *two copies*
Tim Battersby
John Bentham-Dinsdale
Nick Benstead
Bianca Bevacqua
Yvonne Blake Carrettero
David Brass
Mike Brewster
Adam Brown
Barry Brown

Linda Brown, *two copies*
Luke Brown
Derek Browne
Robin Browne
Kevin Brownlow
Greg Bubb
Jon Bunker
Kerry Burrows
Tom Bussmann

C

John Calley
Robert Cameron
Patrick Capone
Richard Carlson
Gil Carretero-Estevez
Dennis Carrigan, *six copies*
Adele Carroll
David Carter
Toll Christie
Michael Clarke
Alan Clarkson

Bob Claydon
Mary North Clow
Sean Connery
Ann Cook
Mrs J.Cooke
Freddy Cooper
Anna Cottle
Barry Coward
Ron Craigen
Patrick Crockart
Adam Croft

D

John Daly
Jimmy Devis
Tim Dodd

Pete Doherty
Clive Donner
Diana Donovan

E

Frank Elliot
Julia Elton
Eton College, *two copies*

Peter Ewens
Anne Excell
Chester Eyre, *two copies*

F

Chuck Finch
Tommy Finch, *three copies*
Cary Fisher, *five copies*
Kevin Fitzpatrick

Barbara Franc
Kevin Fraser
Laurie Frost
John Fundus

Jürgen Flimm
Eddie Fowlie

Kenny Fundus

G

Dennis Gamiello
Andy Garcia
David Garfath
Michael Garfath
Jim and Margot Garrett
Jo Godman
Magdalen Goffin
Justin Grace

Sally Grace
Alan Grant
Jo Gregory
Grip House, *two copies*
Dick Guinness
Ritchie Guinness
Timothy Guinness

H

Gemma Hale
Nicky Hand
Heidi Handorf, *two copies*
Peter Hannen
Brian Harris
John Harris
Stuart Harris
Gordon Hayman
Llewellyn Hazel
Heritage Bookshop,
  ten copies
Joyce Herlihy, *two copies*
Charles Hewitt

G.Heywood Hill Books,
  three copies
David Hibberd
Paul Higgins
Phillip Hill, *four copies*
Dagmar Hirtz, *two copies*
Ian Holm
Hugh Hudson
David Hughes
Alan Hume
Simon Hume
Robert Humm
Gerry Humphreys

I

Imperial War Museum,
  Film Archive

J

Lili Jacobs
Steve Jaggs
Norman Jewison
Chris Job

Bill Jones
Jeremy Jones
Kenneth V. Jones

K

Chaim Kantor
Caroline Kean
William Kerwick

Beeban Kidron
Emma Kirkby
Gabor Kover

L

Brian Lake
Howard Lakin
Jim Lee
John Legard
Richard and Deidre Lester

Peter Levelle
Local 52 IATSE
Local 600 IATSE
Richard Loncraine
Sidney Lumet

M

Peter MacDonald
Ed Maggs
Kay Mander
John Manners
Dicky Marden

Andrew Mead
Joe Mendoza
Christopher Miles
Skip Millor
Hugh Mitchell

Barry Martin
Veronica Martin
Bill Mason
Timothy McAuliffe
Patrick McEnallay
Martin McKeand
Don McPherson

N

Liam Neeson, *two copies*
Sol Negrin

O

John O'Driscol
Ronan O'Leary, *two copies*
Harald Ortenburger

P

John Palmer
Luke Palmer
Panavision UK,
twenty copies
Uberto Pasolini
Yves Pasquier
Frank Paulin
Bob Paynter
Ron Pearce, *twelve copies*
Zoran Perisic
Tobi Pilavin

R

Hugh Ragget
Pam Rainsbury, *two copies*
Jocelyn Rickards
Brooks Riley

S

Gloria Sachs
David and Tracy Saltzman
Sir Sydney Samuelson
Nick Schlesinger
David Schulson
Monika Schwinger
Ted Scott
Dario Sedo
Peter Sellars
Mary Selway
Mary Shaw
Paul Simmonds

T

Natasha Tahta
Randy Tambling
Ronnie Taylor
David Thomas

Juliet Mitchell
Rainer Mochert
Ann Mollo
Nick Morgan
Mark Moriarty
Betty Mulcahy

Marc Neikrug
Ray Norris

Helen Osborne
Les Ostinelli

Pinewood Studios,
three copies
Pippo Pisciotto
Sydney Pollack, *two copies*
Ray Potter
Terry Potter
Mike Price
Noah Prince
Clive Prior
Sally Pumford
Sir David Puttnam

Pam Riley
Sheila Ritchie
Mostyn Rowlands

John Simons
Brian Skeet
Ann Skinner
Bob Smith
Stephen Smith
Roger Smither
Susan Starr
David Stephenson
Bobby Stilwell
Jane Stoggles
Tom Stoppard
Ann Sweeney

Alex Thomson
Martin Thompson
Phillip Todd
John Trumper

John Venables	V	Robin Vidgeon
John Victor Smith		
	W	
Eva Wagner		Eckhard Wendling
Ray Walledge		Bill Westley
Tony Walton		Tony Wilkins
Ben Weinstein		Paul Wilson
Lou Weinstein		Norma Winstone
Keith and Vivienne Welch		Charles Wood
Stephen Wellings		
	Y	
Young's Antiquarian Books		
	Z	
Franco Zeffirelli		Pinchas Zuckerman

This book has not known a publisher; not even a literary agent. It owes its existence to people good at giving, and caring - its impresario a teacher at the University of Brighton, one of its illustrators a Professor there, and its designer a former pupil.

It has been corrected (thank heavens) by a Brighton mother and schoolteacher, and administered by a Brighton schoolboy.

It has wandered into a neighbouring county westwards, to find the right printer, and up to London to get vetted by a lady solicitor who, halfway through an introductory phone-call, undertook to do so, "for a laugh".

Finally it wrote itself.

Like our Millennium House of Commons, it has a good balance of the sexes.

It is a child of love - some may think it a bastard - both words for the same thing, which is why we have a thesaurus.

NOTE

Since chapter 34 was written there has been a different government in this country, that has restored much of the support for a British film industry that its predecessor had removed.

DW March 1998

Chapters

"I am not sure that Browning was not right when he wrote,

'Grow old along with me !
The best is yet to be,
The last of life, for which the first was made.'

Let me assure the youth of this country that old age is the most splendid period of life, when we can contemplate the full maturity of what has gone before. Of course we all have regrets, but I believe you will find, like I do, that the sins for which one is sorry are those of omission, not of commission; not mistakes (he who has never made mistakes never made anything), but opportunities lost. Therefore I advise you all not to worry about getting rid of what is bad in you unless you can replace it with something better, otherwise there will be a vacuum, which is fatal.... Let your life be positive, never negative."

Ralph Vaughan Williams.

Childhood

If at all curious as to how self-absorbed you are, there is a kind of litmus test for egocentrics; simply start a book on some subject or other, anything you know enough about, and then see if it turns into an autobiography.

1

The era of British cinema documentary was launched (in a lot of water) by John Grierson with the silent film, DRIFTERS, for the Empire Marketing Board in 1928. It caused a sensation. Apart from newsreels, film cameras were not put in places where they'd confront much reality, let alone in a small boat at the height of a North Sea gale; the subject however, had not been selected for its dramatic possibilities. Right in character from the start, the documentary movement began by exploiting the vanity of its sponsors. There was no money to be had anywhere, until Grierson (who happened to have been on mine-sweepers throughout the 1914-1918 war) discovered by chance that the Financial Secretary of the day was the greatest living authority on the British herring industry!

In 1933 the unit moved to the Post Office, became the Crown Film Unit during the war, and in effect, finished up with British Transport Films after the end of it. Those final years were like a last Summer into Autumn; seasons full of delights and, as I had basked pleasantly throughout much of them why not write a short monograph about it all.

It didn't get very far ....

My birthday was on the 23rd of March 1925, a Monday, thereby securing the longest possible interval before the next visit to church. I was the youngest of four sons; there was a gap of two years between each of my elder brothers followed by an extended hiatus of seven, which suggests that the first mistake in my life was not my fault. A further distinction that set me apart from the others was that whereas they each of them managed comfortably on two nannies per childhood, I finished up with a total of fourteen. The reasons for this are now likely to remain obscure apart from one instance. My mode of transport at the time was an elegant and recognisable chocolate brown perambulator, lined out in black, a coffee silk canopy with a wide fringe, and four white-wall tyres completing its magnificence.

On apparent good terms with one of the fourteen

My mother's bosom friend, always referred to by my father as the pouter pigeon, was married to Did Smith the local jobmaster. They were childless but supported a family of three dogs - Chummy, a mongrel answerable to Did (who had no pretensions), a very stupid borzoi called Boris and a pekingese, Anna May Wong, answerable to Masie (full of them), who had named their house with the canine amalgamation *Chumboranna* in consequence.

Motoring her Hotchkiss past the Dane Park one bright day, Masie caught sight of the only chocolate and white-wall pram in Margate tied-up to the railings. She evidently did not perceive this as any reason to stop (even though park railings were for the most part uncluttered after the advent of universal suffrage), but on returning to *Chumboranna* she did mention it to my mother over the telephone. The explanation proved simple enough; the current nanny had a boyfriend with a motor bike, and, being a responsible girl, she had secured me in this manner before going for a ride on his pillion. Shortly afterwards she was replaced, so that accounts for one of them.

Then a story, which I find hard to credit, held that at a more advanced age, on returning from walks I would instruct the nanny to leave me at the main gate, making my own way to the front door while she dashed round to the tradesmen's entrance and through the house to open it for me. A passageway ran from one end of the ground floor to the other and the hazards encountered there were not only from nannies rushing along it to the front door. It led also to the drawing-room which in turn through some French windows gave onto the garden, where the lawn, if taken diagonally, was exactly 22 yards (the required length for a cricket pitch). One of my brothers, who fancied himself as a fast bowler, used to start his run-up to the wicket from just outside the kitchen, thence along the passage into the drawing-room. My mother and Masie were quite accustomed to this and sat unconcerned with their tea and curate's aid while he hurtled past; the latter by the way was an Edwardian three-tier cake-stand, not a choir-boy. It was excellent training in alertness for the batsman who had his first sight of the bowler as he burst through the French windows less than a second before delivery. It is possible that a collision with the fast bowler in this thoroughfare put paid to another of the nannies, leaving me stuck on the doorstep, but that is only a conjecture.

A member of the domestic household, not highly regarded by the nannies (who saw themselves as superior beings) but with whom I established excellent relations, was our cook-general. These were not as might be supposed military persons having culinary interests, but the British equivalent of what the French describe rather better as a "bonne à tout faire". They were also known as *maid*-servants, supposedly it was taken for granted that they wouldn't have time to spare for sex; ours certainly never had much (time that is). She occupied a small room up in the attic and never saw the inside of it from six in the morning til eleven at night because she was slaving away at cleaning the house as well as cooking and serving all our meals. In spite of this they were cheerful, good-natured girls and I greatly preferred them to nannies. They enjoyed few privileges other than being given my mother's cast-off dresses, which I never envied them, and the opportunity to chat with the various errand-boys who used to deliver their goods to the back door, which from the age of about ten onwards I certainly did. Cook-generals who were not Catholics had a slightly better time of it as they were not dragooned into attending church, where they were expected to sit right the opposite side from the rest of us; a segregation that seemed inconsistent with what was being dished out from the pulpit much of the time.

If, from their earliest years, you cram your children's heads with nonsense, you can expect a kick-back or two as a result. My mind had been bombarded with the Virgin mother of Christ at an age when I had no notion whatever about virginity and was not being given much by way of an explanation. A wish not to be outdone in this regard led me to assert, at a tea party she was giving for her non-catholic friends, that *my* mother was a virgin - causing her to choke on one of Bertha the cook-general's rock cakes and Masie Smith to pass a remark which looking back across the years was probably uncalled for.

I remember another time when my mother and Masie were engaged in a private tête-à-tête, in other words a good gossip together. They always employed initials instead of names when I was present, though I could never understand why since I knew perfectly well who everyone was. (I might have been less knowing in other areas as where an attempt to uncover the mysteries of sex by consulting the Catholic Encyclopaedia proved a complete failure). On this occasion the strongest disapproval was being levelled at two sets of initials because they were sleeping together.

" .... but how can they be doing anything wrong if they're asleep? "
The young are essentially logical. Barry, a friend of mine, was seventeen

before he realised that oral sex did not mean talking about it. More recently a praiseworthy attempt by one schoolteacher to forestall this particular area of misunderstanding with the aid of a Mars bar in a classroom demonstration caused a gigantic uproar from the Tory cabinet minister for education. This led to a good lady of my acquaintance being asked by her twelve year old offspring to explain oral sex. Being a sane woman who respected children, she did so without any fuss. He thought for a moment and then asked why the gentleman in the government was so upset.

" I'm afraid that's rather more difficult to explain, dear. "

As a child I suffered periodical attacks of asthma (strangely these persisted until I went into the army when the shock which that translation incurred brought them finally to an end). It would be quite awful for about a week, followed by ample compensation in the form of a week's convalescence away from school. I was just over one of these attacks when, on a summer's night, I suddenly awoke with a sense of something unusual. I could just make out in the dimness a small figure sitting beside my pillow, between me and the bedroom wall. It appeared that one question about our existence which had long been a puzzle was now explained, and I called out to my mother that I had just had a baby. This seemed to disconcert her more than it did the pet monkey that had escaped from its owner and climbed in through my bedroom window. However it made its way out by the same route, went next door and bit the headmistress of the local kindergarten, with whom I had many old scores to settle, one of which was making me sing "Where are you going to my pretty maid?" to a fat child called Yvonne O'Kelly. The worst of this was that I knew very well where she was going to - she was going to dress up as a fairy and dance around to Schubert's F minor Moment Musicale no 3 (which has almost ruined the piece for me for life). A lesser offence was hitting me with a walking-stick. From biting Miss Bell it went on to cause a grand uproar throughout the whole of Northdown Avenue. I thought it was an excellent monkey - it certainly knew the right people to bite.

Although terrified by the storm in the *William Tell* overture, I had an early liking for music which blossomed when a friend of the family gave me some records of Beethoven's 5th symphony played by the Vienna Philharmonic under Franz Schalk. The friend happened to be the local Catholic priest otherwise I would probably not have been allowed to keep them. That good man helped to shape the rest of my life, though not at all in the way his job intended him to. From then on I had no doubt that my previous intention to become an engine-driver (a common one in those days of steam on the railways) was mistaken. I wanted to be a musician, so I asked my father if I could have lessons, and a piano for Christmas. He was a man with highly developed selfish instincts and at once declared his veto on the grounds -

"Why is there only one word for Thesaurus?"

(a) I would make no money at it.

(b) I would make a noise in the house.

- both undoubtedly true, though which was uppermost in his mind is hard to tell. He even cast a more tolerant eye over my previous ambition.

"An engine-driver has to be a very intelligent man."

So that put the practising musicians of this world in their place.

Oddly enough he was not unmusical. I'd asked him what Wagner was like and when by chance someone switched on the wireless in the middle of the *Tannhäuser* overture he instantly said

"That's Wagner - he worked his violins very hard."

(not to mention his sopranos, I was later to discover). He also delighted in telling me about a stage mishap in *Maritana* so he'd actually been to an opera of sorts. I knew from my mother that as a young man he had sung the drawing-room ballads of the time, when everyone made their own music at home (who was making a noise in the house then?), and he still occasionally sang snatches to himself of such things as "The Roadside Fire" of Vaughan Williams in a pleasant light tenor voice that was always dead in tune. Once he suggested - and I was thrilled to share it with him - we listen to *Trial by Jury* together; but apart from that single time he never listened to music.

I got to grips with the remaining eight symphonies by turning the wireless very low and sandwiching my head between its speaker and a heavy cushion to prevent any sound from escaping - only a moderate achievement when placed beside that of Handel, whose father must have been a direct forerunner of mine; when Handel senior became aware of his son's aptitude he promptly cleared every musical instrument from the house. There were no wireless sets about at the time so the enterprising child smuggled a small clavichord into a room at the top of the house and without assistance of any kind taught himself to play it. Whether he took the precaution to stuff it with cushions is unrecorded by either Burney or Hawkins, but as someone who has been similarly placed I would surmise that he did. A third victim of this form of parental guidance, the artist John Vernon Lord, adopted a more scientific solution than either of us by running his fingernail inside the grooves of his mother's old 78s.

Just once - it was when Toscanini was here conducting the BBC orchestra - my father startled me by saying I could listen to the Sunday afternoon broadcast, for no other reason I soon discovered, than that it was a Mass. It was also the one piece of Beethoven I was not yet ready for (the D minor) and I wasn't having any; I went out and did some train spotting.

I was a "one off" so far as musical interests were concerned, and my father had nothing to worry about on that score (pun accidental) from anyone else in the family. True there was a drunken aunt on my mother's side who had taken lessons with Dame Clara Butt, but there clearly were not going to be any lessons for me. There were small chances of any

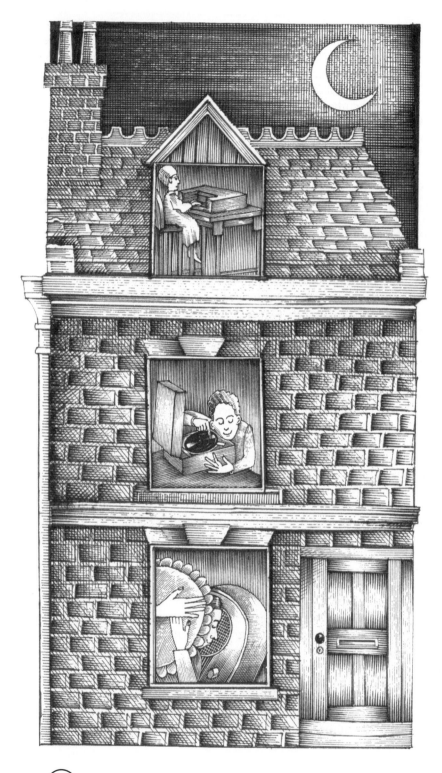

"Why is there only one word for Thesaurus?"

musical education to be had at school either, where it never got further than the class standing round a piano singing in unison ballads such as "The Ashgrove" and "Hearts of Oak" (a somewhat sylvan repertory). In another song the couplet -

" Each with his bonny lass
   A dancing on the grass "

earned me a reprimand for rhyming "lass" with the ensuing "grass" (the other way round seemed more suited to Yorkshire than Kent and would also involve shortening the "a" in dancing). This was my first encounter with "eye rhyme" and I thought it was cheating.

"Who is Sylvia? What is she?", coming after Yvonne O'Kelly's F minor piece, did little to advance the cause of poor Schubert, and as the questions posed about the young lady were not answered to my satisfaction I asked the music master to elucidate. Well known to be less interested in girls even than I was, he muttered something about two gentlemen of Verona and dropped her and Schubert in favour of Dr Arne and natural history.

There was an even more tenuous link with the musical world that I did not discover until long afterwards. Margate, between the wars, was littered with private schools where the middle classes could emulate their betters by boarding their children as far away from home as possible for the most impressionable part of their lives on the pretence that this, and the sea air, were in some way beneficial. The gymnastics training for these numerous establishments provided a full time job for an ex-army serjeant straight from the pages of Kipling - waxed moustache, ramrod back, and hard as iron. Although I never once saw him smile I neither feared nor disliked him, as many of the children did, I think because he communicated that feeling of security that comes from doing something superbly well no matter what it is; and I doubt very much if anyone else could have taught me to climb up a rope. To this day I am unable to hear the duet for counter-tenors in Purcell's "Come Ye Sons of Art" sung by the son and grandson of my old gym instructor without reflecting that if Serjeant Deller was not endowed with a sense of humour, nature certainly is.

Self education may sometimes result in incorrect assumptions being made, especially when it has to rely for the most part on announcements over the wireless. I was puzzled by the Vulgar Boatman and more than a little intrigued by the Griller Quartet. I had seen a picture somewhere of a vigorously bearded Joachim Quartet and wondered if this was perhaps an attempt to go one better. I don't think I actually believed there was a group of hirsute anthropoids grappling with late Beethoven, but they certainly figured in my delighted imagination together with another virtuoso from the animal kingdom who had concertised in the nineteenth century throughout Europe and America with the improbable name of Ole Bull - a sort of Orpheus in reverse.

Although curious over their rather odd name I had led too sheltered an existence to form any inaccurate assumptions about the Black Dyke Mills Band, but down at Margate harbour one afternoon I finally met up with the vulgar boatman; he was pissing over the gunwale into the sea while his companion lowered a bucket to the same spot and poured it straight into the deck cauldron where they were boiling their catch of shrimps; but Chaliapin's dismal old song about him every time you switched on the wireless remained a constant annoyance. Another time a splash of static radio interference obscured the announcer's voice at the finish of one rousing piece, leaving me confused as to the nationality of its author. The matter was cleared up, though with some loss of face, during the next singing class. The British Grenadiers died away and I raised my hand,

" MacManinoff, Sir, was he Scots or Russian? "

The northernmost part of these islands does indeed appear now and then to occasion misunderstandings; without having seen her name in writing, my brother Peter concluded reasonably enough that Molière was a Scottish lady, and quite recently a young friend of mine exploring the world of music wanted to know who Frazer Franck was. As for the Russians, Marmeladov's unavoidable associations with English breakfasts always had me in helpless giggles over *Crime and Punishment.*

Half a century later I was astounded to see a set chair next to mine displaying the name of the great Russian basso of my childhood years. Shortly thereafter an elderly actor sat down beside me and for an instant I thought the impossible had happened, for Fyodor Chaliapin, although more slightly built, looked very like the photographs I had seen of his father all those years ago. At an end of picture gathering I sat enthralled beside a window in Norman Jewison's home north of Toronto (nostalgically named Putney Heath Farms from the days when we were lucky enough to have him living in England) while Fyodor talked of his childhood home in Rome where MacManinov himself, a family friend, was a daily visitor as was also his fellow composer Prokofiev.

" I can remember my father pleading with him not to go back to Russia. "

Although I'd abandoned engine-driving as a profession I was still avidly enthusiastic about railways. All my holidays were spent at the side of the line where the beautiful, burnished locomotives were either friends from the local shed at Ramsgate, or (what made the summer holidays best of all) exciting strangers at the head of excursion trains from far away places.

At one point the line ran within view of the school playing fields. All that cricket in the back garden had done little to bring about any skill at the game, but once, when there was an epidemic of measles (which I'd already had), I found myself playing in the first eleven against a rival school. On the day in question I had gone in to bat and was being given centre by the umpire when a venerable 4-4-0 puffed past on a local passenger. Naturally I turned to look at it, which meant that the umpire,

"Why is there only one word for Thesaurus?"

who was engaged in giving me centre wicket (fortunately one of *their* masters), had to start all over again.

" What was it? "

After a bewildered second or two I realised that the enquiry came from the enemy wicket-keeper.

" An F1 - outside springs on the tender. "

I had started off a bit nervous but from now on the innings was a delight. I usually contrived a single at the end of the over so that we could have more time together, and only once did my new found friend refer to any outside topic,

" I don't want you to go, so please try to keep inside your crease or I'll get into trouble for not stumping you. "

Thanks to a passion shared (in company with Dvorak) for a beautiful machine, we had instantly become friends, but three wooden sticks stuck in the ground were our only sanction to be together. The young bow far too easily to convention, which is a pity as the sight of batsman and wicket-keeper swapping names and addresses on the pitch would have been a charming one; nevertheless I have clearly not forgotten him.

A similar thing happened at football. I soon realised that the position of full-back afforded interludes of relative calm, as opposed to rushing up and down the field all afternoon, and with a like-minded companion was engaged in so earnest a literary debate with our goal-keeper (a boy with a strange liking for the novels of Sir Walter Scott) that our side lost. Most of the blame was laid rather unfairly upon the enthusiast for the author of *Waverley* whose plight was aggravated by being known from then on as the ancient mariner, one of the full-backs - whom I'll leave you to guess - having recalled the second line of Coleridge's Rime,

" It is an ancient Mariner,
   And he stoppeth one of three "

Authority was greatly put out by an interest in literature at the expense of sport; to them the reading of any book that had not been set for an exam seemed unnatural and improper. On the other hand the biggest dunce would be cheerfully excused if at the same time he was "victor ludorum" - just what the Empire needed. In this they were almost certainly right, although their other favourite claim, that sports made everybody too tired to masturbate, was, I believe, quite fellatious.

Although I started out with a wish to conform and an inclination to believe what I was told, there did run, thankfully, a seam of perverse enquiry within this unpromising material. I can remember having to decide quickly whether or not to ask my father, who was telling me the story of Abraham and Isaac, whether he was prepared to kill *me* if God asked him to. Knowing what the answer would be, and that it was likely to be accompanied by a clip on the ear, I thought the better of it. That, however, did not stop me from deciding that anyone who applied those sort of tests to friendship was probably best avoided, a feeling strengthened later on by his subsequent conduct in the book of Job - giving people presents and then taking them back again. In fact the more I got to know about Jehovah the more he seemed a grumpy, vindictive old thing, always wanting his own way and acting like a spoilt child whenever he didn't get it - as Simon Raven was to describe him a quarter of a century later, a celestial bore. I wisely kept these ideas to myself for the most part, although some of the more innocuous had an occasional outing. One Wednesday before Easter, all the altar-boys, who were designated a passive role in the ritual washing of feet, were being admonished in advance to be sure to have nice clean extremities on the following day - this, reasonably enough, by the parish priest who had to do the washing. The giver of Beethoven's fifth was a much safer target than my dad,

" But surely if they're clean to start with there'd be no point in washing them ...? "

Logic and religion are uneasy companions. Fish on Friday was scarcely a privation with the best of turbot, halibut or Dover sole, and my father always took Marmite instead of the usual Bovril sandwiches (yeast as opposed to beef extract) to the office on that day of the week - "It makes a pleasant change".

The ten weeks before Easter you were expected to make a personal sacrifice, "giving something up for Lent" it was called. I'd had quite enough of going without chocolate for ten weeks at a time and announced one year that I was going to give up going to church; but it is part of the sad lot of childhood to be assumed to be joking when one is perfectly serious.

Living in Margate and working in London meant a lot of train travel, and I think it was to help pass the time spent on this journey that my father took to doing cross-word puzzles. He became very good at it and completed *The Times'* puzzle every day with no trouble at all. On Sundays he'd tackle a more difficult affair in *The Observer*, set by someone calling themselves Torquemada. I asked why and was proudly told that "He was the Grand Inquisitor". I said that perhaps he was but he burned people alive and it wasn't very nice to name a cross-word puzzle after him.

" That has been greatly exaggerated. "

" So nobody got burned at the stake? "

" Only stubborn heretics, and it was a long time ago. "

As if that made it all right. I knew of course that a stubborn heretic meant in fact anybody who did not agree with my father and that I was fairly close to being one myself, so I left it at that. What I did not know then, was that even while we were talking it was still business as usual - "About this time (the end of August 1936) a procession with the Archbishop of Toledo at its head marched through the streets of Pamplona carrying an image of the Madonna del Pilar. When it was over, the image of the Madonna was set up in the middle of the principal square of the town,

"Why is there only one word for Thesaurus?"

and the clergy were drawn up round it in military formation; after a short ceremony, sixty prisoners were shot to the honour and glory of the Virgin and the accompaniment of a peal of bells." (*Spanish Testament* by Arthur Koestler, chapter 5.) Even the chaste Diana of the ancient world was hardly as bloodthirsty a virgin. Alongside this the British hierarchy were a half-hearted bunch, and though there were Te Deums galore to celebrate the destruction of Spain's freely elected *socialist* government I don't remember anyone being shot.

This feeble behaviour on the part of the English Catholics was more than made up for in Rome after 1945 by the archbishop Alois Hudal, a close friend of Pius XII, who ran an escape organisation providing money, passports, passage from Genoa and jobs on arrival, for top-scoring Nazis like Franz Stangl (two million Jews), Adolf Eichmann and many others - "The Bishop came into the room, held out both his hands and said, 'You must be Franz Stangl. I was expecting you'.... he gave me a Red Cross Passport .... I said they made a mistake in my name but he patted my shoulder and said 'Let's let sleeping dogs lie - never mind'..." (Franz Stangl to Gitta Sereny). The Vatican knew all about the Holocaust almost before anyone else did, certainly from 1942, and kept a determined silence about it to the end; a single condom provokes a quicker response from the Vicar of Christ than six million Jews. The worst that can be said is that this doesn't surprise anyone. The Church's only serious rival in the field of Nazi rescue, the Government of the United States, were no challenge numerically, as they confined their benefaction to those whom they considered useful to them, like doctors who experimented on people, and SS slave-masters who were good at building rockets (they even re-wrote the files for that one).

Given his strong attachment to Rome, my dad's selection of a godfather for me had been oddly inconsistent. His choice fell on a non-catholic bachelor ex-mayor of Margate, C of E if anything at all, and, to judge from how he walked, as camp as Christmas. His explanation was always that Alderman Wood owned the largest jewellers shop in Margate and the objective was to secure a valuable christening present for me. To make sure of this he approached the Alderman at the end of the ceremony,

" You see we named the boy after you. "

" No you didn't; my name is Daniel. "

Whether this error had a bearing on the amazingly slender serviette-ring that arrived shortly afterwards I rather doubt. For me it has always been a providential escape - I should hate to have been called Dan.

Religious principles likewise never got in the way of using his social position as a solicitor, with a brass plate outside the house, to impose on the local tradesmen. When he had to go into the London Clinic for a time, my mother took over his affairs and found among other things that we owed the milkman £100. In 1935 that was indeed something - today it would be about two thousand pounds, which is quite a milk bill. When he died, my brother Peter, who was his executor, came across a sealed envelope among his papers which was addressed to my mother and marked "to be opened only in the event of my death". Scenting some unknown insurance policy that was going to provide wealth for us all, Peter hopefully opened it. What he found was a bill for two term's fees from my prep-school - "to be paid out of my estate as a matter of conscience". Peter did his best but the two old queens that ran Cambridge House (I remember *them* all right) had long since died, while the school buildings had been demolished and replaced by cheap housing. I still think fondly of my two terms' stolen education and wonder if I learned anything useful in them. What I do know is that if Cambridge House had been a Catholic school they'd have got paid.

The one time I remember him taking any real interest in someone else's affairs he'd have done better to mind his own business. He virtually drove a former nanny into suing her boyfriend for breach of promise, a ridiculous statute now done away with - "I know you've realised just in time that you hate the sight of me, but if you don't hang around despising us both for the rest of our lives, I'll take you to court".

As head of the family he at least distributed his selfishness evenly among all of us including my mother. Indeed, on the day of their wedding no sooner were they alone together than he gave her a solemn assurance that for the remainder of his life she would always come second. Somewhat taken aback she enquired who was the lucky individual that would come first - and was told that it was God. Her names were Beatrice Lynda but she was always called by the delightful (to me) abbreviation Trixie. Hers was a different character altogether and I am not sorry there is some of it to be found in me - bad as well as good. When I am impulsive or generous I know exactly where it comes from, also the seeds of rebellion. Though long suffering enough as a rule, she had nevertheless suggested on one occasion, when we were all being dragged out to Mass, that since he already had his reserved seat in heaven why not leave the rest of us alone? This took him by surprise; now and then she surprised me,

" The boy stood on the burning deck,
   His breeches wanted mending.
   The Captain shouted from the bridge
   Watch out if I catch you bending! "

Where she got that from I can't imagine.

There is a nice irony regarding my antipathy to the religion I was brought up in because without it I should probably not be here at all. Mine was a difficult birth and the doctor sought sanction of my father to safeguard her at my expense. He refused to give it and so we both survived. The day happened to be her birthday as well as mine and the fast bowler, on being taken in to wish her many happy returns, caught his first sight of me,

"Why is there only one word for Thesaurus?"

" Is that all you got for your birthday, Mummy? "
She probably thought it more than enough.

My father was the eldest son, and the youngest, my uncle Laurie, had been nobbled by a buxom Cambridgeshire barmaid when he was a young officer in the 1914-1918 war, thereby provoking outrage and disapproval from the rest of the family. I on the other hand liked Auntie Edie very much, and not only on account of her close resemblance to Oliver Hardy; she breathed a different kind of air and because children pick up this sort of thing easily I understood her better than the rest. My mother might have felt the same had jealousy not come into it. Edie having rightly decided that the Watkins were a bunch of "old sticks" (and because the youngest of them was infinitely more tractable than the oldest), was able to deal quite easily with problems which for my mother were insurmountable. For example Trixie had always wanted a motor car but this held no attractions for my father. It would be a much more awkward place for *The Times* crossword than the armchair in in the front room, also it would absorb money that would otherwise go into the collecting plate on Sundays. Edie simply went out and bought hers - Laurie, after a brief instruction on how to control the thing (there were no driving tests in those days), drove the family straight down to another product of Edie's enterprise, at Birchington-on-Sea.

One day, while he was at the office, she had quietly armed herself with a three-foot tape from her work-basket, got on a train to this pretty sea-side village, measured up a plot of land, and arranged for a bungalow to be built on it. The proximity of Birchington to us in Margate meant that these singular achievements were periodically brought home to my mother by Edie, Laurie, and an unwelcome brat of a cousin Mary (whom I was required to play with), driving up to the front door unexpectedly at teatime in the manner of visiting Royalty. Only in the realm of her imagination was my mother able to better Edie's Wolsley. There, there was always a Rolls Royce, although she would follow up these flights of fancy by saying that the only time she was ever likely to ride in one would be a hearse. Sadly this turned out to be true and, years afterwards, it was the moment when, at her funeral, I saw that the waiting hearse was a Rolls Royce that I was no longer to able to keep from crying.

While, at home, we drifted along with our cooks-general - serious Elsie giving place to her much jollier sister Bertha, followed by Ruby and finally Florence (these changes all accounted for by romance except for Ruby, who unquestionably was a blockhead) - Edie, always abreast of the fashion, got herself a girl from the Continent. Hildegarde proved quite satisfactory (and probably for even less than the £1 a week our girls got) except that on entering the mädchen's bedroom one day, Edie was confronted with a photograph of Hitler. This she turned face to the wall, without making any comment. Hildgarde would turn it back again, likewise without comment. The Führer must have got quite giddy with this first and silent battle of World War II, in which I have little doubt Edie was the victor.

By the time real hostilities began, Hildgarde was back home and no more was heard of her until a plea for help arrived in 1945.

" Well dear, I *know* she dropped bombs on us, but we can't let the gel starve ".

Food parcels were despatched, and if they included any of Edie's dandelion wine I am sure Hildegarde was quickly restored. Years later my aunt had her own reward, with one of those coincidences in which human life abounds. After Laurie's death, Edie, having a quiet break in Torremolinos (even Torremolinos was quiet to begin with) was approached by a lady in a restaurant,

" Oh Mrs Watkin, I recognised you by your voice ! "

At this point I am conscious that my account of my parents has come out slightly too kind to my mother, who among other things was a fearful snob, as well as too harsh towards my father, who was not without his good points even though they may not have sprung instantly to mind. After one of my brothers had read this chapter in typescript I sounded him about it,

" Let's think what was good about him. "

there was a prolonged pause and then we both started to laugh. He did inspire a mild interest in professional cricket, at a time when batsmen were committed to scoring runs rather than just staying at the wicket all day long and bowlers confined their objective to sending them back to the pavilion rather than into hospital. It was stylish and often exciting to watch.

I remember the first money I earned. My father had to check a legal document at Herne Bay and one Saturday morning took me along to help him. That was a treat in itself because of the train ride (there was a great racing stretch between Herne Bay and Birchington). When we got to the lawyer's office we sat in a room while I read from one copy and he checked the other. An oddity that struck me, apart from the extreme dullness of the text, was the total absence of punctuation. My father explained that no legal document ever had any because it alters meaning, and a comma could cause a disaster; so I learned the value of punctuation. When we had finished he gave me a bright new shilling.

Every Saturday we set out together across the countryside to St Peter's, lying inland from Broadstairs, where the village butcher, a Mr Creasy, made the best pork sausages ever for Sunday's breakfast. An objective redoubles the enjoyment of any excursion, also next door to this great butcher was a sweet shop where there was always a bag of toffees for me. Our path took us through some allotments and over an iron foot-bridge across the railway close to Draper's windmills and from then on ran parallel to the line all the way to St Peter's Churchyard, where my father said that all the occupants were deaf and dumb. He always made the same

"Why is there only one word for Thesaurus?"

jokes, which I didn't mind in the least, in fact I'd have been rather disconcerted if he hadn't. Should one of the Victoria to Ramsgates chuff along past us he'd take watch and chain from his waistcoat pocket and glance at it, not, I must add, to see whether the train was on time but to check that his watch was. Perhaps that will convey better than anything the different world of the 1930s.

It was while walking through these fields one springtime, that my father remarked that green was by far the most restful colour to the eyes and it has been a favourite colour to me ever since. This helps to balance one very distinguished colleague who so dislikes it that he refuses to fly Aer Lingus, and is said by industry gossips to have once fired a clapper-boy for bringing his tea in a green mug.

He also took me for the first time in my life to a cinema, The Lounge in the Northdown Road, which later became The Cameo. They had great names for cinemas in those days, many of them beginning with R - The Regal, The Rex, and a bit dare-devil, The Roxy (it only needed a few lamps to fail and it would turn into something quite different). My father had explained before we went that "this actor never smiles", which did not bother me at all, but nothing had prepared me for the alarming size of Buster Keaton's head on the screen compared to the two ladies seated in the row in front of us. Shortly after this my enemy Miss Bell put on a 16mm showing at the kindergarten featuring none other than Rin Tin Tin (an acting shepherd dog). By some ill luck the next day she eavesdropped on an unfavourable comparison I was drawing between that animal and Buster Keaton, so my first essay into film criticism got me into trouble.

Best of all, however, my father read to me every evening when I was in bed - *Treasure Island* of course, but mostly Dickens, and to that I owe a very great deal.

As for my mother's snobbery it began with a refusal ever to acknowledge that we resided in Margate, Kent. That had always to be elevated to Cliftonville, Thanet. She used to patronise the local house of haute-couture, which styled itself "El Donnée" but was in fact run by some people called Robinson. They dealt in what were termed "exclusive models" which meant that they were overpriced but there was only one of them. This came to grief one day when my mother and Maisy Smith met in the Northdown Road identically attired. Without exchanging a word, both turned instantly, rushed home and gave the offending garments to their respective cooks-general. I don't know if those two ladies ever met each other (they wouldn't have had much time off in which to do it) but I feel sure that if they did they'd have had the sense not to care.

Boyhood in Margate is actually the only time in my life when I really loved "going to the pictures". Inside the cinema it was dark and warm and safe, like snug in bed with nice dreams most of the time - the exceptions being love scenes and musicals (I did *not* like Busby Berkeley). As for the censor's idea that sex scenes are harmful to the young, I feel pretty sure I'd have been equally bored if there'd been two young men kissing each other. It's no fun to watch, any more than a banqueting scene has anything to do with gastronomy; the only danger to youth from sex on the screen is that it might put them off it.

My parents in 1946, forward focus, taken with the looted Rolleiflex

One day my father took me to Canterbury to see the West Indies play Kent. The visitors had to 'follow on' and when Kent got them all out again before lunch he suggested going to look at the cathedral. As we walked inside something happened that I can never forget. I looked up and was unable to breath - the sheer height of the perpendicular nave brought about a physical shock that was literally breathtaking. Such a thing has never happened to me since, and when years later I went back to Canterbury hoping for a repetition I was disappointed. By that time of course the cathedral, in relation to myself, was only half the size. So childhood ends.

"Why is there only one word for Thesaurus?"

School

My school could have been presided over by Dr Pangloss himself.

2

We were handed a great deal of partial information (partial in both senses) such as having the British Empire depicted to us as a kind of benevolent global nanny (which compared with the Dutch and the French it may have been). Not only did the sun never set on it (though it was soon going to) but in the school atlas it was arrayed in a colour that might suggest to a later generation of schoolchildren that we were all gay.

British justice was the finest in the world, though again we weren't told exactly what it was fine at. Some of those best qualified to provide an answer had long been stuck in a bed of quick-lime, a handy obliterator of evidence, great for delaying any grudging admission of having hanged the innocent. The plus side of this is that every time the Tories try to bring back capital punishment yet another embarrassing case of injustice turns up. There was a slight minus in 1965 when we finally had the grace to return the remains of the Irish patriot Roger Casement (hanged in Pentonville, 1916) to Dublin for a state funeral in Glasnevin cemetery, when it was believed just as likely that whom they actually got was Dr Crippen.

Incidentally if there were grounds to hang Casement then we should have hanged Edward Carson as well while we were at it, for gun-running in Ulster. He was the architect of all we still suffer over Northern Ireland, yet he is only remembered for prosecuting Oscar Wilde. Starting a civil war and destroying one of our best playwrights is a fair slice of havoc for one individual; to make matters worse his son was the Tory member for Thanet and my father used to vote for him.

One crafty dodge for smoothing the path of government is simply to reverse the meanings of words, like calling a grovelling apology a Royal pardon (how can you pardon people, usually dead, who did nothing wrong in the first place?) Pardoning surely belongs to the victims of injustice not to its perpetrators. If an enlightened parliament had not done away with capital punishment, the state would have killed at least twenty innocent people during my lifetime alone, and that's only the ones we know about. More ludicrous still is dishing out royal pardons to *our own* soldiers whom *we* shot (one at least barely seventeen years old), because they were stressed to breaking point by the barbarities of 1914 - 1918. Brenda would be better advised directing her pardons towards Douglas Haig (there's bound to be a statue somewhere - they could hang it round its neck) and his fellow *Donkeys*, so comprehensively described by Alan Clark (Hutchinson, 1961). It's not often I can recommend a book by a Tory minister.

A British judge and Master of the Rolls (some kind of chauffeur?) declared, on the outcry when four innocent people were found to have been wrongly imprisoned for nearly a decade and a half, that "if we'd hanged them 14 years ago they wouldn't be making a fuss now". True but it doesn't suggest much of a passion for justice. A safer claim to make with all those red skirts and camp wigs, is of the finest fancy dress in the world. Whilst on the subject, dragging up (apart from the stage, and the Chelsea Arts Ball), is usually suspect - whether it consists of aprons and rolled up trouser legs or red jackets gallivanting over the countryside, after some defenceless quadruped. The day I can only maintain authority by coming onto the set in a mitre, I'll give up the business.

Royalty did come in useful one December afternoon in 1937 when our end of term exams were brought to an abrupt end and we sat and listened to King Edward VIII on the wireless. That added "irrevocable" to my vocabulary, by the way; it was also a good time for the carol singers,

" Hark the Herald Angels sing
  Mrs Simpson's pinched our King "

By an odd coincidence, Edward's broadcast had interrupted an history paper on the Tudors, and I thought it a bit inconsistent of the Church of England, which had been founded with the single object of allowing the eighth Henry a divorce, to now create a fuss about its very own raison d'être. Yet, as in the case of Abraham and Isaac, I decided not to ask what would simply have been dismissed as an impertinent question. That adjective is a splendid case of what has just been said about reversing the meaning of words, and was used without fail whenever you really hit the nail on the head.

My favourite lesson was English. Each week we were given a subject on which to write an essay. You could always tell exactly the sort of thing expected of you, an expectation I took care on principle to disappoint. "Where there's a will there's a way" was clearly after a prose eulogy of

"Why is there only one word for Thesaurus?"

determination and resourcefulness; so I set to at some length about a family feuding over a legacy.

Indirectly this practice would end with a useful lesson for me. I made it a rule of the game that every essay must be interesting, it started after all with the advantage that the ideas were my own rather than those implied by the set subject; to be different just for its own sake would be silly. I used to get good marks, always best in English and way down in everything else. Only once, when "Where there's Muck there's Brass" sparked off two pages about Wagner conducting, was it suggested that I was trying too hard. Then overnight everything changed from benevolence to severity, with no marks at all; I had not altered in any way nor had the style of my essays. All that was different was the English teacher.

Whether this sudden migration from top to bottom of the English class had anything to do with it; or whether for some other reason which I never discovered (for I was no more unhappy at school than most boys are), there now arrived a strange interlude in my education. I was taken away from school and a private tutor found to come to our house every weekday. He was probably somewhat lazy; I have since come to realise that there isn't much wrong with that provided you use laziness creatively. After a modest tribute had been paid to mathematics (my most hated and worst subject) and French (almost as bad) we would sit in armchairs on opposite sides of the room and read through Shakespeare's plays aloud, he taking half the parts and I the others. It was the happiest and most wonderful experience.

" No profit growes, where is no pleasure tane:
In briefe sir, studie what you most affect ".
The Taming of the Shrew. Act 1, Scene 1.

At half past three he would leave me to my freedom and go to take tea with my mother. I did not realise it at the time of course but it is obvious now (and confirmed by my elder brothers) that he was having an affair with her.

This delightful state of existence for the three of us lasted for about a year, in which time we got through all the histories and all the comedies. Then, alas, he and my mother had a row and, narrowly missing King Lear, I got sent back to school. I certainly didn't catch up with him there; they avoided going into details about mad kings, whether they were Lear, George III, or Edward VIII. I did however renew acquaintance with Richard II and The Merchant of Venice, both of whom got me into trouble, the first for giggling at every mention of Bushy, Bagot and Green, and the second for doing the same over Antonio's line in the first scene,

" My ventures are not in one bottom trusted."

Even worse was suggesting that Shylock was really the hero of the piece. All these levities had been accepted quite naturally the year before and all survived my growing up (if that in fact ever happened) so perhaps they were meant to. It doesn't prevent Shakespeare (the greatest living playwright, to quote Ian Holm) from poking fun at the Jews, because his genius was that he was complete. One of the less obvious evils of fascism (whether right or left 'cos it's the same either end) is that it makes it difficult to be balanced about anything. Why shouldn't we laugh at the Jews or the Irish or Gays or Blacks? To laugh is not to sneer; anyone can laugh at me if they want - it's a compliment.

Another bizarre friendship of my mother's was with a Mr Chatterton. It was exercised for the most part in the remote, if not entirely chaste, arena of the Margate telephone exchange, of which he was the night supervisor. A prey to insomnia, she would talk for hours in the night-time (I think I believed that was why he was called Chatterton) and he would "plug her in" to any entertaining conversations that came along. This placed her pretty high as an authority on local gossip, and it was an innocent enough form of eavesdropping compared with what is carried on by the British establishment today. She assured us all over breakfast one morning that Vic Oliver, a stand-up comic married to one of Churchill's daughters, who was playing at the Theatre Royal, was on excellent terms with his wife (for one evening at least). He was Viennese, Jewish, and musical. "I will now play 'The Kitten on the Keys' by der Pussy" was his kind of thing. The old man is said not to have been all that pleased about the match. When asked at a Chartwell gathering which leader in the last war had he most admired he surprised everybody by citing Mussolini.

" He had his son-in-law shot. "

Back at school a second unusualness happened, or rather didn't happen. I never ever sat for an examination. I can remember saying that I simply did not wish to compete with anybody, but how I managed to maintain such a sensible attitude up to the age of seventeen and a half in an education system based solely on the arid notion of rivalry I have no idea; possibly the war helped. So the two factors in my upbringing which did me the most good were certainly unorthodox then and are probably illegal now. I still know that competing is not for me and have never done it.

We have an Establishment that only feels safe with conformity and so always frustrates the true point of education - encouraging people to think for themselves. The trouble with me, I was told, was that I had too much imagination (is that possible?). A young friend of mine once carried home a school report regretting that,

" Andrew is more interested in the world outside the classroom. "
It can't have been difficult, but good for him all the same. Yet another, Sam, at the age of twelve, was complained of for disrupting religious instruction by asking questions (they must have been hard to answer). His father visited the school and found a nice but dazed teacher,

" Sam appears to hold God in contempt. "

"Why is there only one word for Thesaurus?"

Unfortunately contempt, like its counterpart respect, has to be earned by the recipient - so if anyone's to blame it is God and not Sam! The poor boy had chronic difficulty satisfying his teachers,

" Who sang "I'm Dreaming of a White Christmas? "

(the question raises doubts as to the value of the curriculum)

" The Klu Klux Klan. "

" Incorrect, it was Bing Crosby. "

Not much difference from my day; we were given a poem by Ralph Hodgson.

" See an old unhappy bull,
Sick in mind and body both,
Slouching in the undergrowth
Of the forest beautiful ..."

" Sir, is this about a violinist? "

(Ole Bull had been dragged into a recent essay)

" That's enough! "

I'm sure it was.

Towards the end of 1939, after massive pestering of my parents, I got to my first orchestral concert; I refuse to count Herbert Lodge and the Margate Municipal Orchestra playing Edward German on the Oval bandstand. Lodge (an ex-bass player, like Koussevitsky, but that was the only resemblance) wore his hair in the manner of Leopold Stokowsky and corsets in the manner of Dr Malcolm Sargent. Nevertheless my first proper concert (in Margate's Winter Gardens) was a bit strange, with a conductor I hadn't heard of (Karl Haas) playing a composer I'd not heard of either (Carl Stamitz). According to the programme the band were refugees, Czech I think and mostly very young, who had just arrived in this country. I believed they had just stepped off a fishing boat at Ramsgate, and indeed they certainly looked like it, but their playing sounded glorious to me, and it probably was. In a way that now seems clear, that concert signalled the beginning of the upheaval my life was entering into, along with theirs, and with the rest of Europe.

As well as affording a diversion from examinations the war also helped the musical side of things. In 1940 we moved from the coast and spent the war years nomading about the home counties, first in Maida Vale, then Reading and finally Bushey, so I was able to take myself off to concerts, most of them with the wonderful Henry Wood, one of the greatest conductors of all time and certainly the most underrated. A Brahms Haydn Variations, taken from a tape circulated privately for a number of years among Toscanini's adherents and attributed to him and the Brunswick company, proved upon examination to be a Decca recording by Wood and the Queens Hall orchestra. This error has been widely construed as flattering to Wood, but listening to the performance suggests rather that it was a compliment to Toscanini.

Our temporary domicile in Maida Vale was a residential hotel in

Clifton Gardens where another aunt of mine lived. This one was non-alcoholic, had taken no lessons from Clara Butt, and was secretary to one of the partners of Cartier in Bond Street - a pugnacious and entertaining character named Etienne Bellenger. As the firm's arbiter of bad debts Mr Bellenger followed two courses of action; if the person concerned was royal, titled or "well connected" they might run up bills until kingdom come; if on the other hand there was a hint of the parvenu a different line was taken,

" Tell the bitch to pay ".

In the early days of the war there had been an amusing cash transaction. A refugee lady, dressed like a tramp and consequently unlikely to have been extended any credit by Mr Bellenger, walked into the showroom carrying a battered suitcase and asked what they had in the way of diamonds. Having made her selection she opened up the case, which was naturally stuffed with currency, and grabbed the salesman by the arm,

" The British Navy - it will fight? "

" Yes, yes, the British Navy'll fight all right. "

Most of the other property in Clifton Gardens was owned by the Church Commissioners, who numbered among their tenants a colony of up-market prostitutes, the Archbishop of Canterbury having the same unconcern as Mr Bellenger as to where his money originated. I had only the vaguest notion of what they were doing, thought they brightened the street up considerably, and couldn't see why they should be sniffed at by all the other residents.

By this time sex was becoming an all round puzzle to me because the only side of it that had so far managed to arouse my interest was getting yelled at by one's guides to morality because they considered it to be "unnatural". The only practice, or lack of it, pertaining to sex that seemed thoroughly unnatural to me was celibacy - which the extraordinary religion of my father esteemed above everything else. If my very nature was fundamentally at odds with religion I was not devious enough to effect a compromise. Soon I should have to choose.

"Why is there only one word for Thesaurus?"

A Digression

There used to be a deplorable custom of starting off autobiographies with an account of one's ancestors, as if it were not fortune enough finding someone prepared to sit down and read about you, let alone your dusty old forbears.

3

However one of mine was such a lad that a piece about him may actually liven things up a bit.

Sir Edward Watkin, Bart, was a railway magnate in the days when trains were the new great way of getting around, and he controlled several of the more important companies by the light-hearted expedient of riding roughshod over the other directors.

In those days one of the top jobs on a railway was that of the CME or chief mechanical engineer, and finding himself with a son of restricted ability who was desirous of such a post, Sir Edward set about creating a vacancy on the South Eastern Railway, of which he happened to be the chairman.

That railway's CME at the time was an eminent engineer named James Cudworth and it was the principal job of CMEs to design the railway company's stud of iron horses in which, provided those machines managed to drag their trains about successfully, they had much glory. Without a word to anyone (and certainly not to Mr Cudworth or any of the South Eastern directors), Sir Edward ordered a batch of express locomotives from a firm of private builders to the design of the CME of another railway with which he was involved, an engineer rivalling in distinction poor Mr Cudworth, named John Ramsbottom. The first Cudworth learned of it was on the way to work one morning when his train drew into the platform of the local station behind a shining new engine he knew nothing about, and his first act after Mr Ramsbottom's unwelcome machinery had whisked him up to his office was to send off his resignation to the company chairman, who was neither surprised to receive nor reluctant to accept it. I leave you to guess who was the South Eastern's next CME.

As well as the South Eastern, Sir Edward was chairman of the Manchester, Sheffield and Lincolnshire Railway (known by some as the Money Sunk and Lost) and also of the Metropolitan line in the capital. If he could bring his provincial railway into London, which he eventually did at Marylebone as the Great Central (the Money Sunk & Lost thereby becoming the Gone Completely), he would be able to run trains on his own metals straight from Manchester to Dover. But he was something of a visionary and saw further than others did, as far as Paris in fact, and he started to dig the channel tunnel in 1881. After about half a mile he was brought to a stop, not by any geological obstruction but by Parliament which, seeing invariably less far than anyone else (the end of its nose or the next election whichever is the closer), is the very opposite of visionary. The scare at the time was that a tunnel would open the way for some future enemy to invade us all, and the evidence of the Parliamentary Committee of Enquiry makes interesting reading. Opposition came, not from the army (who sensibly observed that the sooner this enemy, whoever he was, got his troops into the tunnel the sooner we could let the sea in on them), but from that service with a vested interest in the Channel which might be compromised by any subaqueous means of crossing it. In other words it was strongly opposed by the Royal Navy.

"The Railway Interest"

It took them a hundred years to catch up with where he'd left off (even then using the old tunnel as a test bore) and by that time they had done away with his direct line from Manchester. What would the old bugger have said I wonder? One thing he'd have noticed at the final opening

"Why is there only one word for Thesaurus?"

would have been the resumption of a practice that must have ceased when he was still a young man a century and a half ago, that of posh people sitting inside their own carriage anchored onto a flat wagon - this time none other than Vicky's great, great grandchild, Brenda herself, in her Rolls Royce.

From beneath the surface of the planet he later aspired in 1889 to rise well above it with a tower at Wembley Park that would be higher than that already completed by Monsieur Eiffel in Paris (an intended 1200 feet as against the 984 of Eiffel's construction). In a speech referring to the scheme, he is reported as saying his mottoes had always been "Never be beaten" and "Never admit defeat", but in spite of these alas not always sustainable sentiments and although the Navy obligingly did not object to anything so far inland as Wembley, "Watkin's Folly", as it came to be called, failed to get more than part of the way up through running out of finance.

His artistic perceptions may have been less keen than his industrial ones, to judge by the one painting he owned that we know about and considering some of the people that were painting away throughout the last third of that century. When he died in 1901, his son (the Cudworth replacement) sold the family mansion, Rose Hill, to the City of Manchester,

82

DESIGN No. 37.

The First Prize of 500 Guineas was awarded to this design.

A. D. STEWART, M.Inst.C.E.,
2, Queen Square Place, W.;

J. M. MACLAREN and W. DUNN, A.R.I.B.A.,
21, King William Street, Strand, W.C.

whose Social Services Department used it as a home for deprived boys (deprived of what?). "Icebergs", a 5 x 9 ft canvas painted by F.E.Church (1826-1900), was left behind in the house through being incorrectly labelled as the property of a Mr Watson. It ended up in use as a dartboard by the new residents, who perhaps had more enlightened tastes in art. By 1979 the place needed a lick of paint so the matron of the establishment bunged their dartboard into Sothebys, where it fetched a gigantic sum from the Dallas Museum of Fine Arts.

Towards the end of his life the old boy built himself a chalet at the foot of Snowdon. The mountain was his last obsession; he had a strange love for it and in the manner of some lovers sought to keep the object of his affections to himself. He could not buy a whole mountain but he did start purchasing parcels of land around its base, intending when the circle was complete to prevent anyone else from going up, or so it has been suggested; though if that is the case why did he make a path to the summit (still marked on ordnance survey maps as the Watkin Path) that was opened by his mate Gladstone with a tremendous fuss on 17th September 1892? Victoria's unfavourite Prime Minister (he never bothered to flatter her) got on top of a great glacial-worn rock, named after him ever since, and addressed a crowd of 2,000 farmers, shepherds and guides who were thereby inspired to sing a lot of Welsh hymns. Then alas the last bit of his friend's path defeated him. "People atop the mountain, muffling themselves well, awaited with impatience. At last a cluster of tiny specks far down, were made out to be the Premier and his party. Slowly - very slowly indeed to the watchers - did they seem to come upwards, until at a point below the deep grade to the summit they paused. Then there was a sign of hesitation, which a glass showed to be the holding of a conference. A long pause succeeded, and then amid outspoken disappointment Mr Gladstone was seen to turn and descend."

I discovered all this by chance while shooting a documentary for the Duke of Edinburgh Award people, about some unlucky children struggling around the Welsh mountains in hopes of meriting the ducal approbation (which Mr Gladstone certainly wouldn't have got after turning back). Edward's chalet had been burned down just a year before by some Australian tenants with an oil heater, but I was able to wander around in the garden and picked up a piece of the local slate that had been part of his mantelpiece.

His second marriage was to a widow of ample means and shortly after it took place the following poem made its appearance.

> From Snowdon's breezy summit
> To Dover's chalky strand,
> He carries us the slower
> Of any in the land.
>
> He bores the Channel Tunnel,
> He builds the Watkin Tower;
> But neither helps his income
> Like Mrs Ingram's dower.
>
> He'd blacken Kent with coal-pits,
> And cave St John's Wood in,
> But these are merely trifles
> In his career of sin.

"Why is there only one word for Thesaurus?"

For he doth run the Underground
In whose mephitic air,
The gasping, choking Londoner
Doth think of him and swear.

A nephew, also named Edward, was the manager of the Hull and Barnsley Railway for many years. By the time I made his acquaintance he had retired to live in Eastbourne - not that I ever set eyes on him, but as Uncle Edward (he was actually my father's uncle) he undeviatingly sent £1 on my birthday and another at Xmas. When he died, my mother, well knowing what Edie would be up to, urged my father as head of the family to go at once to Eastbourne and make his presence felt. He was far too indolent to put himself to any such trouble, which needless to say, was not the case with the Sevenoaks branch. Edie had Laurie down in Eastbourne before you could say Jack Robinson, and in due course the Wolsley drew up outside our house. Aunty Edie, who had secured to herself all of Uncle Edward's silver, paintings and much more beside, delivered a homily to my mother about it being one's duty to keep family treasures intact, and handed over a few pieces of electroplate. I loved every minute of it, and when they had gone couldn't resist quoting from a popular song of the time,
    Edie was a lady
    Though her past was shady, (Barmaid from Bottisham)
    Edie spelled class
    With a capital K.
That, and the loud evidence that the departing Wolsley was badly in need of a decoke managed to elicit a reluctant smile from my mother, who recognised Edie's achievements and grudgingly applauded them.

"Why is there only one word for Thesaurus?"

The Army

The time was approaching when I could expect to be called up for the armed forces, and I thought that this unwelcome event ought to be postponed for as long as possible.

4

Apart from anything else, I could foresee that someone who was annually petrified by the affable celebrations of November the fifth was unlikely to be much use on the field of Mars.

It is perhaps as well that I did not then know about Lytton Strachey's adroit reply (he was gay) during the 1914-18 war when a conscientious objector's tribunal asked him their stock question -

" What would you do if a German soldier was about to rape your sister?"

" I should interpose *my* body. "

A fair response to a society that would dish out a prison sentence for sticking anything into a young man; unless of course it was a bayonet in which case they'd give you a medal.

However at this stage of the war the Royal Navy found itself acutely short of junior officers and had started up something called the "Y" Scheme, an advance recruitment plan to select suitable young candidates before call-up. We were warned at the outset, as though it were a disadvantage, that if we put down for this there would be a ten months delay getting conscripted due to a training backlog. Since this would give them the best part of another year to get their war over without hurting me in the process, it seemed on the contrary to be very attractive. So down went my name and 1943 became my Indian Summer of freedom.

In the end, of course, the day of reckoning arrived and I was required to appear before the Lords of Admiralty to be interviewed. It had now become necessary that the Navy should be given some good reasons for not taking matters any further and with this in the front of my mind I arrived neat and clean at Cockspur Street where I was sent into a room that was quite empty except for a long oak refectory table, a solitary chair in front, and what appeared to be four admirals in full costume seated behind. On the table top was a group of small models of warships such as were then for sale in all toyshops under the brand name of "Dinky Toys".

What followed would certainly have delighted W.S.Gilbert and if I did not have any clear idea how to deal with my situation then, one was about to be handed to me.

" So you want to be a Naval Officer, young man? "

" Yes Sir. "

" Sit down. "

An arm wreathed in gold moved to indicate a large battleship among the Dinky Toys.

" What ship is that? "

The absurdity of a group of senior officers (if gold thread is anything to go by) at the height of the war playing Dinky Toys with the likes of me gave a welcome boost to my sagging confidence.

" A destroyer Sir. "

An incorrect reply but one which provided some cover to any charge of my being frivolous, since the vessel in question was certainly able to destroy most things that got within range. This however proved an unnecessary precaution - he was very polite.

" No, that is a battleship. Now what is this one? "

He pointed to an aircraft-carrier. Stronger measures seemed called for.

" A submarine Sir. "

That will bring down the wrath of ages I thought, but I had not understood the good manners by means of which elite bodies deal with outsiders. I was not, to their great relief, in the Navy yet and therefore neither entitled to nor worthy of their displeasure. It was suggested by the leading admiral that someone who had taken so little trouble to become acquainted with HM's ships might not be regarded as a suitable officer cadet. He added without a trace of irony that he was sorry I should be disappointed.

On the fourth of February 1944 I was required to present myself to the British Army at Bury St Edmunds. Without question the army did me a huge amount of good but the first weeks on this obverse side of life were a horrendous time. I was born with many blessings and one of them is a hopeless memory for the bad things; my mind retains only a bare outline without vividness, whereas all the good stays as clear as a spring morning. Those early weeks in the army, however, manage to pass through these happy filters of the mind and I can still experience the despair that I felt then at my loss of freedom, and also my disbelief when I discovered that some of my new companions considered themselves better off and welcomed the change in their lives. I may have been denied a piano but

"Why is there only one word for Thesaurus?"

I'd escaped most other forms of deprivation and could not understand their willingness to exchange freedom for a straw palliasse, army catering, and being shouted at.

When we had been reduced to a set of numbers and names on a list, a sergeant commenced enquiries as to our religious beliefs. Being a W affords a certain amount of time to consider and when he came to me I had decided that I was an agnostic.

" Wot? "

" Agnostic Sergeant. "

" There's two religions in this army, C of E and RC, so which is it? "
There had been a Phillips earlier on who'd taken a while to decide; and I remembered from school how, thanks to my father's insistence, I'd been spared all those sturdy Protestant hymns first thing of a morning (so that even late in life I thought "Gladly the Cross-Eyed Bear" was a child's story book). I thereupon opted for RC, and all I regret missing as a result was one padre's hour that everyone seems to have enjoyed. After exhorting his youthful flock to shun all pre-marital sex the warlike cleric asked if there were any questions.

" But if you don't 'av a bit beforehand, how d'you know she's got one?"
A very sensible precaution it seemed to me.

The first pay parade I was handed some money by the Company Commander so I thanked him politely. A pair of cold blue eyes looked steadily into mine,

" Don't thank me, thank King George. "
Before I had time to enquire of either of them why out of a week's pay of £1 I had only been given ten shillings I was hustled away by the serjeant-major, so I asked him instead.

" That pays for the blanket you'll be buried in if you get yourself killed."
If any who came through the war without availing themselves of this considerate provision imagined that on getting demobbed they would be reimbursed for the unused blanket they were in for a disappointment; however by that time I had sold enough blankets on my own account to cover both principal and interest.

It would be hard to find a more perfect example of our engaging national habit of naming things by the exact opposite of what they actually are than the private soldier. There is absolutely no privacy to his life whatsoever; he even has to shit in company, though I took to using the officer's toilets very early on and was only apprehended once,

" Got caught short, Sir."

" Don't let it happen again."
Casualty is further word that has had its meaning conveniently reversed - there is nothing casual about getting killed. It is a tinkering with the language for which euphemism really is too mild a description. Another, "sectarian killing", is a favoured way of distancing religious murder from

religion.

Cars and washing machines are acknowledged to break down occasionally, but for computers the verb is not "to break down" but "to go down". I was quite astonished the first time I encountered this usage (at an airport, needless to say), but I suppose it's better to be sexy than merely inefficient.

"Field Sports" attempts to suggest that it is in some way sporting for a lot of dim-witted dogs followed by a bunch of even more dim-witted humans, to chase a fox across the landscape, tear it to pieces, and smear its blood all over any children in the vicinity.

Again, our Overseas Dominions changed into a Commonwealth almost overnight without regard to the wealth of its black and yellow constituents having little in common with that of its white ones. Even the War Office (a perfectly appropriate name for the place) now calls itself the Ministry of Defence, though here it must be admitted that for a few weeks the description was accurate, in so far as their last flat-out war was launched in order to *defend* Mrs Thatcher from losing an election. Sadly it worked.

Cousin to this quaint habit of inverting definitions is that of declaring the inevitable to be illegal. Thus it is out of order to suggest that anyone is telling lies inside the House of Commons, where they do little else; and you can land in gaol for contempt of a judiciary that does nothing much to engender any other sort of response.

In early December we sailed from Folkestone in the SS *Canterbury* and landed at Ostend the following morning, straight onto the oldest train I have ever seen, and trundled up to Louvain. Exploring my first Continental city I was accosted by a boy of about twelve in quest of English stamps. I had not imagined what opportunities the liberation of Europe had opened up for young philatelists, but fortunately did have a couple of letters from England in my pocket. I was taken home in triumph and soon became a sort of honorary member of his family. Madame Graftiaux was particularly heartening because she was an almost perfect Walloon equivalent of Auntie Edie. My school French had a splendid time of it and I learned, through gales of laughter from Madame Graftiaux, that "J'ai assez mangé" and not "Je suis plein" is the proper way to decline a second helping of Sunday lunch. Young Eduard became very attached and showed me everywhere. Passing a pile of masonry that must have been either a cathedral, or a town hall at the very least, I asked what had happened (it was miles from any military target).

" It was the Americans - they were always doing it."
a pause
" If an *American* soldier asks, then my parents say it was the British. But I tell you the truth."
(Either that or he was an even smoother liar than Mum and Dad).

From the all-pervading warmth of Belgium, France was very different.

Stuck in Villers-Bretonneux (already an ex-battlefield from 1914-18) the only thing to do on a Sunday was trek to the nearest town, Amiens, though always under strict orders for never less than three together because isolated British soldiers were constantly being set upon and killed by the recently liberated populace (you'd be far safer in the occupied areas of Germany).

After many vicissitudes not worth recording, and on the evening before my twentieth birthday, the army finally made the discovery (long after I had) that I was not fighting material and sent me off to the Brussels Garrison. As the regiment I was leaving went straight into the Rhine crossing, that was about the best birthday present of my life. Good fortune did not end there either because I fell straight into a job as the regimental quartermaster's clerk, not to mention that the quartermaster-serjeant, Les Wright, had been butler to Lady Cunard before the war and I was thrilled to meet someone who'd had day to day encounters with Sir Thomas Beecham, even if they were only in the capacity of a butler.

From then on life took off. Concerts at the Conservatoire, opera at the Monnaie; I even tried out straight sex with a couple of charming girl prostitutes (not at the same time). One of them was doing it to build up some finance before getting married,

" Does your boyfriend know about this? "

" Mais oui, it was his idea. "

I might have suggested that the boyfriend should make his own contribution to the fund raising, but I was not forward enough in those days.

One day Copeland, a Jewish boy from my training battalion, turned up in transit. With the astuteness of his race he had calculated that his life was worth a bullet wound in his foot, and had made the transaction. He told me that Greaves had been killed, a shy, gentle, boy who, like me, would have been useless in a fight.

" Left, Right, foreskins tight
  And bollocks to the front
  We are the boys who make no noise
  We're always after cunt.
  We're the heroes of the night,
  And we'd rather fuck than fight .... "

The song lapses into coarseness at this point so I have not quoted it in full, but the sentiments expressed seem admirable to me and as it was popular with the only people who defended society's values at any risk to themselves it might be better sung at the Cenotaph than what is usually on the programme. When Michael Foot was howled at because, as Leader of the Opposition, he sported a type of donkey-jacket on Armistice Day, he was closer than anyone else to wearing what many had worn to Armageddon - dark suits and top-hats were the uniform of those who sent them there.

Another art-song, or lied, of the time (sung to the tune of Colonel Bogey) was recalled startlingly to mind many years afterwards with the release, by Gorbachev, of information about the remains of the Führer, which had been a heavily guarded secret ever since the Russians had dug them up in the Reich Chancellery garden in 1945. Their autopsy disclosed that the body had only one testicle (a detail no one could have ascertained in his lifetime since even his own doctors were never allowed to examine him that closely).

" Hitler has only got one ball ..."

Whether the British army was equally prescient with the rest of the lyrics cannot be known for certain, though I think it is unlikely.

" Göering has two but they're too small,
   Himmler
   Has something simm'ler
   But poor old Goeballs has no balls at all."

This affords something of an easy transition to the next topic - an honoured army ritual, the FFI inspection by the medical officer once a month. The letters stood for "free from infection" and the affair was a sort of military fashion parade. While the MO sat in a suitably low chair everyone else had to file past lowering their trousers in salute while he took a bored look for signs of crabs, scabies or VD. One of the perks of being on the QM staff was that we only had to send a single representative each time, which brought the indignity down to only once a year, if that, and my being responsible for keeping the roster made sure that myself was never on it.

One day the regimental cobbler came in looking somewhat crestfallen and asked for a word in private.

" I'm down for the FFI tomorrow - can you take me off it 'til next month? "

I adopted a fatherly attitude and said kindly that if he'd got a dose it wouldn't go away of its own accord and why not report sick today? Then he couldn't be done for concealing it - a couple of penicillin jabs and he'd be as right as rain.

" No it's not that, Corp, I aven't caught anything ..."

he lowered his voice confidentially

"... it's just I went with this girl last night and right in the middle of it she bit me. I don't want the MO to see 'cos it's obvious like ".

I had never heard of anything like this before.

" Christ! You won't be seeing *her* again then ".

" Tonight actually "

Totally bemused I reached for the list and substituted the armourer's assistant, a mild lad unlikely to raise objections and fairly certain not to have been bitten by anyone.

Every week there was a clothing exchange. The squaddies brought in their worn clothing and got issued with new. You were supposed to check

"Why is there only one word for Thesaurus?"

that the items were well worn before exchanging them, but it seemed churlish to be too exacting. It would also have run counter to our own interest because by the end of the week there was a three-ton lorry load of used clothing to be taken down to the ordnance depot at the Midi station. The three-tonner would pause outside while I went into a hut to get the vouchers signed, then it would bypass the entrance and drive off to its weekly rendezvous with the black market. I was disconcerted only once during these operations when an attractive offer was made to throw in the lorry as well, and I had to explain that, without wishing to give offence, in this instance I would rather err on the side of caution as suspicions might be aroused if I returned to barracks on foot.

To keep up a supply of new gear for friends and also for bartering purposes, the clothing ledger entries had to be modified after they had been initialled by the QM. This was effected by a discreet application of Milton (the bleach not the poet) to remove the fresh ink, restoring the buff colour to the paper with cold tea and then, when all was dry, putting in figures that corresponded better with what was left on the shelves. It was after I had made rather a mess of this on one occasion that Les employed an expression that I have taken to ever since,

" Fuck a stoat! "

something he may have picked up from Lady Cunard, or more likely from her daughter.

All this more than paid for the sex education and opera tickets. It was also nice to be able now and then to reduce some of the hazards of kit inspection for others, remembering how I was once informed, on being found short of several items at one of these ceremonies,

" You'd lose your bollocks Private Watkin, if they weren't in a bag ".

When Les returned to civilian life his place was taken by a chilly individual, albeit one whom my mother would have called a better educated class of person. He was more educated all right - he asked me if I'd help him sell some insulin. At one stroke an innocent game turned into something nasty; I hated him, didn't touch his insulin, and was glad when he in turn got demobbed shortly afterwards.

The resident soprano at the opera-house was a Madame Prick. Her name, doubtless highly respectable in Belgium, was a source of endless delight for the British Army as it was constantly appearing all over the city on hoardings proclaiming

" *FAUST* - PRICK " and so on.

Also to be seen everywhere were premises that displayed signs bearing the letters PAC, which in service parlance stood for Prophylactic Aid Centre. These were small medical rooms where servicemen were given contraceptives beforehand, and could go for an anti-septic clean up afterwards. It didn't sound at all attractive and I never myself entered one. The name however became indelibly associated in my young mind with venereal disease and it never occurred to me that prophylactic could mean protection against any other ailments.

One evening the field telephone rang and when I picked it up the QM was on the other end. There had been a bad accident to a Canadian leave train in Germany, gear was strewn all over the place and there would be a load of kits arriving at the Midi station about one in the morning. I was to take a 15cwt truck and pick them up as soon as they arrived. The QM, an old soldier, was quite specific,

" Make sure you only sign for *damaged kits*, 'cos that's what they'll be when BAOR get their hands on 'em - and I'm not having it blamed on us ".

I took Taffy, the storeman, along and we picked the stuff up. Once back inside the stores, any kits that remained intact were quickly brought into line with the rest and in the small hours of the morning something like a miniature Witches Sabbath was in progress with the two storemen dancing about exploring the hoard in front of them, Taffy all warm human sympathy whilst rifling their gear,

" Those poor bastards -- here *I'll* 'ave that. It's dreadful to think of look you; unlucky buggers -- cor, *exactly* what I'm after ... "

There was an astonishing profusion of contraceptives, not much call for prophylactic aid centres with Canadians, I thought, but there I was wrong. Taffy, who had abandoned an attempt to cram his feet into a pair of dancing shoes several sizes too small for them, but with all other requirements of his foreseeable future catered for, sat quietly amusing himself nosing through pay-books (every soldier's combined identity card and service record). Suddenly he leapt up, yelping like an excited puppy, and came bounding over to show me the recorded total of one individual who had contracted gonorrhoea eight times and syphilis twice. It was certainly impressive, breathtaking in fact - he must have had little time left over for anything else. My sole acquisition was a Rolleiflex camera, which was to bear interesting results later on, being the start of any interest I've subsequently had in photography.

Due, I believe, to having to get out of our barracks before another became vacant, the early summer of 1945 saw the regiment dispersed in the countryside to the south of Brussels. Our company was billeted in a tiny village called Virginal Samme, a name that intrigued the British Army almost as much as Madame Prick had done.

There is a shot in Jacques Tati's JOUR DE FETE taken from very high up looking down into a valley where the village band is marching along while the postman approaches them from behind on his bicycle. The only sound is the loud insistent buzzing of a wasp and all the comedy is in the gestures, first of the postman, and then, as he overtakes them, you can follow the trail of the insect from the rear to the front of the band. VE Day in Virginal was delightfully warm and sunny so I decided to spend it quietly with a book in the back garden of the house where I was billeted. From there could be heard just such a band marching round and round

"Why is there only one word for Thesaurus?"

the village and outlying fields. They confined themselves to one tune the whole day long which the entire village sang with them.

" Ils sont foutus, on ne les vera plus,
Les Fridolins sont partis pour Berlin.
Churchill s'en va, avec tous ses soldats,
Pour flanquer à Hitler un coup'd pied
Dans le derrière. "

At each of the numerous cafés en route they would pause and take refreshment for about half an hour, then the procession would resume its course. After each of these breaks, lapses in intonation were more pronounced, and as the day wore on a newcomer to the scene might have believed he was hearing a piece by Charles Ives or, come mid-afternoon, Schoenberg. It is rare to partake in festivity at a stage removed from it, where the entertainment may be enjoyed without the bother. The music that drifted on the evening air into my garden was of such a kind that it's a pity there wasn't a sound crew about.

Virginal Samme, Belgium.

8th May 1945

I ls sont fou - tus on ne les ve - ra

plus les Fri - dol - ins sont par - tis pour Ber -

- lin Chur - chill s'en va av - ec tous ses Sol -

- dats, pour flanqu - er à Hit - ler un coup'd pied

daus l'der - rière .

ORDER REF: 12640

Just prior to one of my leaves home, an officer's camp-bed, turned up in the stores. It was a splendid affair and brand new, with sturdy dark green canvas and beautiful polished wood that telescoped neatly inside its own miniature kit-bag. I'd no use at all for a camp-bed but it was a nice thing and I took it with me. I had not seen Laurie and Edie since the war started, and so was delighted when they drove over one day to see us. At tea, Edie was regaling us with accounts of her house parties for Mary's friends (Mary being now of an age to have friends who were doubtless more fun to play with than I had been). Everybody, it appeared, had a great time on these occasions (a form of diversion that, with my father around, no one in our house would know much about), and guests never really minded having to sleep on the living-room floor afterwards. This was too good an opportunity to miss, and I asked Edie if she would like to buy a camp-bed that happened to be on the market. My mother was truly horrified, considering it pas de rigeur to sell things to one's relatives - but Edie already had her purse and money out,

"The boy is the only Watkin with a scrap of sense, Trixie dear."

Army administration allows two regimental officers other than the Quartermaster to indent for specialised stores for their own departments; one was the transport officer and the other was the medical officer. The removal of our regiment from Belgium into Germany coincided with two occurrences; one was the posting to us of a new medical officer, and the other was a spectacular rise in the incidence of VD. The new MO was a young man, and such an offensive one that he succeeded in making himself unpopular with every rank in the battalion. One of the first sweeps of this new medical broom was to display a huge graph outside the MI room showing the weekly VD figures. These undulated gently along the bottom of this chart of amatory misfortune until shortly after our arrival in Hamburg, when an extra sheet of paper had to be added at the top.

Fate decreed that at this point, in consequence of a mistake at the ordnance depot, a consignment of eight very large metal drums containing a protective for motor mechanics against dermatitis was delivered to the quartermaster instead of the transport officer. Knowing they were not for us, and seeing PROPHYLACTIC OINTMENT in large letters on the side of each drum, I innocently sent them over to the MO who, thinking the QM was having a public joke at his expense, flew into a fine rage and there was nearly a fight in the officer's mess. Mess waiters in a conscript army are not always men of the highest discretion and by morning the QM found himself the hero of a delighted battalion. He was a regular soldier, up through the ranks, and really really nice. We had the same third-form prep-school sense of humour and he'd been suitably appreciative when I spotted, on a list of Polish DPs employed to clean barracks, that there was a Mr Pisarski working for us (in this respect we were both in more illustrious company than either of us realised - Churchill having expressed the hope barely six months earlier that the Greek Prime Minister, a General Plastiras, didn't have feet of clay). His reaction therefore came as no surprise.

" You're a right cunt Corporal Watkin. I wouldn't be without you for anything ".

The move into Germany had involved returning much of the QM stores to Ordnance. This meant a corresponding surge in my own marketing activities. On our last day in Brussels I had on my hands a stack of leather from the regimental cobbler. It was too late in the day to get hold of any transport, which meant throwing the wooden cases over the barrack wall at an appointed hour of the night into waiting hands on the outside. My punter had mentioned that he was out of ready cash but

"Why is there only one word for Thesaurus?"

would send the money to England. It seemed highly improbable to me so, as there was nothing I could do, I quickly forgot about it. However when I got home on the next leave there was a letter with a Newcastle-upon-Tyne postmark containing a cheque. It taught me to think better of people. Finally it is really true to say that the principal motivation for these goings-on was excitement and the fun of it; the pocket-money was secondary to that, if only by a margin.

After Brussels Hamburg was a pretty grim affair. Most of the town was destroyed but there was a large garrison cinema in the centre and by this time German civilians were allowed inside. When at the end of the programme "God Save the King" came on they were the only ones standing up, while the royal gentleman's uniformed subjects made a dash for the exits. This elicited a series of exhortations in part one orders deploring the bad example being set to the Germans. In truth of course authority had got it wrong as usual. With their glorious disregard of anthems the British civilian army was setting the best possible example to a nation that had "stood up" too readily and for too long. Governing powers never see far beyond their noses. I have often thought, when they banned Leni Riefenstahl from making films (a director of genius, like it or not) it would have been smarter to give her a crew, and pack her off to film Auschwitz, if only to give TRIUMPH DES WILLENS a proper ending. Incomplete as it stands, a prelude only, it would then have been quite a film; when she made it in 1934 the set hadn't been built.

Talking in 1994 with a Brighton organist and music teacher, I discovered that we had both been in Hamburg at the same time almost half a century before. More sensible than I, he had risked a visit to the Speckstrasse, situated inside the red light district and heavily out of bounds to troops (presumably on account of the MI-Room graph) and there he had found an old man digging among the debris that was about all that remained of the city after the attentions of our Mr Harris.

Asked in halting German if he knew the whereabouts of Brahms' "geburtshaus", the old fellow nodded and going further along the street until he stood over another pile of rubble, pointed silently to it. It must have been a touching moment - the young soldier and the old man - but these sentiments were soon diverted as I tried to imagine my acquaintance, had he been caught, explaining to his CO that he had gone to the Speckstrasse in quest of Brahms and not of its current attractions. I went on from there to consider, had his plea met with success, whether this would have led to an upsurge of interest in Brahms among the rank and file of the British army.

"Why is there only one word for Thesaurus?"

The Southern Railway Film Unit

*The yawning gap between army and civilian life can be
summed up in the contrast between the first Regimental
Quartermaster-Serjeant I served with, and the last.*

5

L es Wright had been an easy, charming, good-looking ex-butler and I
was sorry when he got demobbed. RQMS Crisp, who bore the
appropriate Christian names John Thomas, was none of these, though he
was pleasant enough. Being a regular soldier he lived in married quarters
(the schedules for which were a comedy in themselves i.e. below the rank
of Colonel you weren't allowed a carving-knife or a chamber-pot). One
day, while unpacking a couple of his boxes that had arrived from England
I came across a Collins Classic of a Dickens title inscribed "To the dearest,
lovable and adoring wife from her husband - J.T.Crisp. WO II (Warrant
Officer 2nd class)".

It was nice finally to escape back into the comparatively sane world of
Les Wright.

On release from the army in October 1947 it was too late at the age
of twenty three to pursue a career in music. I decidedly did not want to
work in an office and thinking the film business might be fun set about
joining it. This got an instant rebuff from the trade union concerned,
which did not consider that four years spent defending *their* freedom
entitled me to any of my own where choosing a job was concerned; the
sort of thing that only stiffens resolve and, however flippant the original
impulse may have been, I was now determined on it.

My father and uncle were both solicitors for the Southern Railway,
whose offices were at Waterloo Station. I remember as a child coming
home from church where a sermon had been preached on the text "Be not
solicitous .... wherewith ye shall be clothed" (Matthew VI, 25. Luke XII,

22.), full of concern for the head of the family and urging a change of profession. He was not without a sense of humour and indeed was more amused than the situation seemed to warrant one Saturday lunchtime when a client, lured by the brass plate, who had just sworn an affidavit on the New Testament, turned out to be Jewish. My offer to run down the street and bring him back was not however accepted.

One of his more interesting cases was where a gentleman, happening to sneeze while he was in the public convenience on Waterloo station, his false teeth flew out and fell into the urinal. They floated along to the end of the channel where they disappeared for ever because a grille that normally rests on top of the drain (for the set purpose of rescuing dentures and perhaps other things) was not in place. On these grounds he sued the railway company for negligence; I do not know with what success.

At all events my uncle Laurie found that there was a small unit of four people making documentary and training films in the nether regions of Waterloo Station, well beneath, in every sense, the notice of any trade union; whereupon my father set up his Blickensderfer (the oldest typewriter in the world) on the dining-room table and dashed off a letter to the company chairman. "I can get you in there" he said, "you might as well learn something while you are waiting". I think it was the first time I saw him put himself out for someone else, and was really touched by it.

So began a very happy first year; there was Basil, a busy but sensible boss, a gay script-writer, and best of all, old Tom Heritage. He was well named. The only real railwayman among us he had started on the Brighton line as a boy in the uniform grade, i.e. the lower orders. He finally landed up as our projectionist and used to travel all over the system showing training films to staff in a railway carriage that had been converted into a cinema. This was known as the cinema coach and in it Tom took a serious proprietorial interest - about which more later.

My task the first day, and for about a week thereafter, was to sit at a flat-bed, winding through reels of old material from the vaults - much of it dating from the silent era and therefore shot with an open gate (that is with the picture occupying the whole space between the sprocket holes, part of which now accommodates the sound track). One fascinating sequence of shots was of a four-funnel ocean liner leaving Southampton and I did my best with a magnifier to discover the name. There were only five vessels with that number of stacks, and two of them came to a notorious end, for she was either the *Aquitania*, the *Mauretania*, the *Lusitania*, the *Olympic* or the *Titanic*. Now alas we shall never know, as that material also disappeared under water, when the vaults beneath Waterloo station were flooded in 1955.

After a few days of this my left thumb and forefinger were cut to bits from winding films through them, but it had been a very sensible beginning - learning how to handle film, and what happens when you

"Why is there only one word for Thesaurus?"

drop the centre out of a thousand foot roll.

I was terribly self-conscious the first time I went with Basil to set up a camera in public (the York Road as it happened), and recall being told roundly that if I was embarrassed that easily I'd better get out now. He was right but he needn't have worried, I soon overcame my shyness and by the next outing (the Hungerford Bridge) I was enjoying myself.

Amid great excitement one day a new piece of equipment arrived - a sound recorder. This was before the days of magnetic tape and the cumbersome machine achieved its results by cutting them into a wax-coated aluminium disc. Its first task, or more likely a try-out, was to record the arrival of the *Queen Mary* in Southampton docks; a choice that suggests a lowish estimate of its powers, since failure to register what was modestly called "the ship's whistle" would not auger much success at picking up any other sounds, stentorian being quite inadequate to describe the blast that diminished whatever surrounding hubbub there might be to a stunned silence. The new toy was next called upon to create a sound impression of a bus crash for the railway St John's Ambulance first aid classes. This was the greatest fun and the first time that I realised I was in a job where you actually got paid for larking about, something that as a child I had had to do for nothing. The four of us gathered in the Old Post Office Yard, throwing sheets of corrugated iron on the ground and jumping on them, smashing plate glass and screaming and yelling for all we were worth. In some ways I don't think I've ever been that happy since.

Our little unit came under the wing of the Public Relations and Advertising Department upstairs in the station offices, whence everybody would crowd into the small theatre below the arches whenever there was a first run through of one of Bobby's commentaries. These were one-off affairs because afterwards drastic changes had to be made before final recording could take place. For example in a travel film about the river Thames, over a shot of two youths in swimming trunks lying on the river bank, "... Runnymede, the birthplace of English liberty, where the English still take liberties with each other - especially at week-ends ...". The only other samples I can now call to mind were in a catering film called SERVICES RENDERED where a young commi-chef putting some basins into an oven is asked "What's in *your* pudding, little boy?" (that actually survived in the finished film), and also of the Charing Cross Hotel, which had its own carpenter's shop where we were told "... most of the time is spent replacing springs in beds from the bridal suites ..." - that one did get changed, to something about mirrors broken over the heads of erring husbands. He certainly seemed to have something of a preoccupation with sex.

There was no gay liberation movement in those days and Bobby was an eye-opener for me. There was a less attractive side to him; he was given to writing letters to *The Times* (seldom a good idea). One of these I remember called for the introduction by his employers of "Men Only" compartments on their trains. In those days a number of compartments on all trains were reserved for "Ladies Only", and admittedly these rarely housed more than a sprinkling of stern matrons, even during the worst of the rush-hour when all the rest of their sex elected to join the standing crush with the rest of us. The letter was amusing enough, but it made me uncomfortable because on this occasion Bobby was probably in earnest. However I certainly found his openness and honesty about himself very refreshing. Everyone, including Basil who commuted every day from respectable Haywards Heath, found him great fun and only Tom used to qualify his amusement,

" It's disgusting really you know. He had a good education (it happened to be Lancing), but that's often the case with the higher class of people - you never find that sort of thing with the working man. " Unfortunately for this theory Bobby's tastes were obviously such that I was sure quite a number of working men must have had a very good time with him. When I pointed this out it was the closest dear Tom ever came to disapproving of me.

All day long music was played over loud-speakers spaced up above the vast concourse of Waterloo station. There was an announcer's box high up in the roof where a girl sat with a microphone, a turntable and a pile of 78rpm records, like an Olympian disc-jockey. The Public Relations Department decided that appropriate variations in the kind of music played would ease the flow of people about the concourse and the film unit was instructed to conduct experiments. The task fell to Bobby and one afternoon as the rush-hour crowds built up he set about it very simply. He planned to make a sudden switch from Handel's Largo to the Tritsch-Tratsch Polka of Johann Strauss. I was posted down on the concourse with instructions to note carefully any changes that took place. When the moment came nobody took the smallest notice so far as I could see, nor did they shortly afterwards when the music was interrupted by Bobby's honeyed invitation -

" If the young sailor standing opposite platform 9 will come to the foot of the announcer's box he will find something to his advantage. "

I began my career with chronological exactness on the first of January 1948 (in those days a holiday only in Scotland) and three months later, on April 13th, shot my first piece of film in rather interesting circumstances. All the others were out on a job and I was left guarding the unit's sanctum inside some arches underneath the station and giving onto the Old Post-office Yard in the York Road. Close by was an hydraulic lift by which rolling-stock from the Waterloo and City underground railway was raised to the level of the main line and so to Eastleigh for repairs. While some wagons were being shunted onto this device the hydraulics gave out and the lift started to descend, dragging the rest of the train plus the engine (an M7 0-4-4 tank no 672) along with it, at which point the

"Why is there only one word for Thesaurus?"

driver and fireman promptly mixed metaphors and abandoned ship. Disturbed by the most almighty crashing and thundering, I grabbed a Newman Sinclair and took some shots of no 672 looking like an upside-down Hornby toy at the bottom of the lift-shaft.

When the others came back everybody was pleased and excited until word very quickly came down from above that my negative must be destroyed unprocessed - an early lesson for me that the truth is seldom popular in official circles. However it was not long before my second solo exercise took place. There had been severe flooding on the Edinburgh route with sections of the main line washed away, and a film had been quickly put together. All that was needed to complete it was a background for the titles, so I was dispatched to the RAF memorial on the Embankment to film some floating debris on the Thames (easy enough to come by even in those days). Apart from nearly getting arrested by a nosy policeman all went well and this time I not only made it to the developer but was actually used behind the imaginative title FLOODS IN THE NORTH.

This first year at work I lodged with Edie and Laurie at Riverhead just outside Sevenoaks. My cousin was now a companionable and shrewd young lady, though potty about horses (same as Brenda) which Edie, busy forgetting humble origins, regarded as a mark of gentility. Although never within striking distance of Trixie's snobbish potential, my aunt did carry domestic pride to uncomfortable lengths, particularly as regards her *linen* chest. Convinced that fine Irish linen was certain indication of a person of quality, she made sure this piece of furniture meant just what it said, and anyone unlucky enough to have slept between linen sheets will know that they are not only stiff as a board even before one has spent a night in them, but are still chillingly cold in the height of summer. It was the prospect of a second winter looming up that caused me to leave Riverhead and go into digs with a policeman's family in Wimbledon Park.

Mrs Rhodda had three young children and no pretensions to gentility whatever. Her youngest, a Shirley Temple-like five year old, stood regarding me eating my supper one evening with large cornflower eyes.

" Mr Watkin. "

" Yes dear. "

" You're a cunt. "

(I wondered which of her brothers was reading Chaucer).

" Did you hear what your daughter said? "

" Child's bleeding right an' all. "

I was sorry to leave Mrs Rhodda but Bobby's lifestyle had expanded my horizons and I doubt if even she would have appreciated strange young men staying the night.

All the while I was writing to 2 Soho Square (union HQ) asking to be let in, which of course got nowhere. Then something happened. The Labour government of the day had been elected on a programme of nationalisation which included the entire transport system of the country - railways, road haulage, canals and docks. These all came together under the aegis of the British Transport Commission which decided from the start that films should play a large part in unifying the different branches of the country's transport, and Edgar Anstey, who was an experienced documentary producer, got the job of forming the unit that came to be known as British Transport Films. A stipulation of the Nationalisation of Transport Act of Parliament was that no employee of any of the former undertakings should either lose or be forced to change his job. This meant that the union found itself with a splendid new haven for a great many of its members, but which at the same time contained four who were not of the fold and could neither be sacked nor removed elsewhere. As a result I received two letters from Soho Square in the same week. The first stating bluntly that they weren't going to give me a ticket, and the second urgently requesting that I apply for one at once. I can't remember if they were both signed by the same person but it is nice to think so.

Curiosity as to what the future held in store was heightened when we were given the job of recording a sort of accession speech by Edgar, who arrived wearing the expected grey suit relieved by a pair of unexpected bright pink socks - a daring colour in those days although the implications were confined at that period to politics, not sex. I felt we were in with a chance. Our disc recorder was trotted out for the third and last time in its brief career, and after the trumpetings of the *Queen Mary*, and the turmoil of our faked bus accident, the calm wafflings of Edgar about the "efficacy of film" must have come as a peaceful end to it.

Within days of it being established we received our first and only directive from the new Transport Commission. It was typical of such bodies and fetches us incongruously back to Tom and the cinema coach. Some civil servant had decreed that all shows given in the coach must now commence with the running of a National Anthem trailer. Tom was outraged. Not that he was unpatriotic - it would have been hard to find anyone more respectful of the British crown than the Edwardian Tom, but he could not understand what asking God to save the King had to do with asking engine-drivers to save coal. Things *may* have been aggravated by the fact that his reels were already made up and there was no room to join anything more on the front; when he tried to do that it fell off the spool all over the floor, so Tom went off to his coach that evening in an ill humour. He returned the next morning his usual happy self however,

" When they heared the roll of drums at the start they all stood up in the beam of the projector. "

There's not enough height in a railway carriage for national anthems.

The day finally came when we left the arches below Waterloo station for ever and became absorbed into the new organisation. What for me was a springboard into the future was sadly not so regarded by any of the others to whom it was an unwelcome intrusion into their world. They

"Why is there only one word for Thesaurus?"

British Transport Films production no.1 "Transport", Waterloo, 2nd August 1949.
L to R: David Watkin, Ron Craigen, Basil Sangsten, John Shearman (covered) and Bobby Arlen.
(The slate no. is one short of a remark from the latter).   *Photo: National Railway Museum*

refused to oblige the union by joining its ranks, displaying at the same time an admirable independence and an astonishing lack of common sense. In accordance with the Act of Parliament they neither lost nor were obliged to change their jobs; the jobs simply became backwaters within the organisation.

The first picture with my new trainee's ticket was on a grand scale with a sound camera, a real actress (Barbara Lott), and the eminent director J.B.Holmes. It was virtually a small feature film, fully scripted, about life in Southampton woven around the docks and shipping. Jack Holmes was a charming gentleman, with a slight, rather attractive stammer that disappeared completely when, occasionally, he read the commentaries for other people's films - or as in this one, played a small part as a night-school teacher. That scene was my first time putting the board in with synch sound, and a right balls-up I made of it. As, still floundering about, I'd almost got it right, Jack himself came to the rescue by announcing "after false start" (necessary for the poor editor to sort out the mess). The first time I was helped out of a hole by a director - but by no means the last.

Shooting began with a night sequence of a pilot bringing the 40,000 ton liner *Andes*, ex Buenos Aires, into port. I was very impressed and when she was safely berthed I told him so. He was a modest man.

" I just stand on the starboard wing (of the bridge) and watch two street-lamps in the Terrace Gardens - when they are in line with each other I blow the ship's whistle and the tugs do the rest. "

Some weeks later we were set up for a night scene in the very same Terrace Gardens. Ritchie, the cameraman, had deployed a couple of 150amp arcs and several 5ks about the place and I wondered hopefully if the *Andes* was due in.

Her captain was a rather irascible man, though this may have been because I burned some holes in his deck with a fog canister that decided it was a Roman candle and shot up a shower of sparks instead of the anticipated smoke. (It spoiled Ritchie's shot at the same time and he didn't make half as much fuss). The old man had a liking for gin, a beverage that used to render him more disagreeable than ever. The third officer, a young man about my own age, explained that they always knew when to expect the worst because the gin acted as a solvent to whatever fixative the skipper employed to hold his dentures in place. (Perhaps it was he who had suffered the mishap in the Waterloo station toilet).

If Bobby Arlen had clarified my ideas about sexual emancipation, Jimmy Ritchie did much the same with regard to socialism. Hotel breakfasts seated between Jack Holmes scanning *The Times* and Jimmy waving the *New Statesman* (much better then than now) were heady affairs and I used to revel in it. The Americans in particular came in for a lot of stick (apart from Gregg Toland, Ritchie had very little time for them). In the course of a discussion about how varied national character was reflected in ships, someone observed that the S.S.*America* had by far the most mellifluous siren of all.

" Well nobody would deny that they can make a noise successfully. " The differences were certainly obvious enough - the French Line by miles the most stylish, Cunard orderly and above all quiet. When either of the Queens was leaving, apart from three shattering blasts of the siren to warn that she was under way, you would not be aware of anything happening. On the other hand United States Lines, as Ritchie was quick to point out, always departed in an aura of hubbub and panic, crew members rushing up gangways adjusting their clothing, shouts, whistles, chaos. One voyage got no farther than half-way down Southampton Water before a propeller fell off the mellifluous *America* resulting in an humiliating return to port with the passengers transferred to hotels to wait for berths in other ships. As we were shooting in the wheel-house of the *Queen Elizabeth* at the time I was prompted to enquire of her first officer,

" What do *you* do when a propeller drops off? "

He replied very much in the manner of Jeeves addressing Bertie Wooster.

" Propellers do not drop off this ship, Sir. "

This was the occasion of my first ever focus-pull, on a 75mm lens

"Why is there only one word for Thesaurus?"

bringing the Commodore of the Cunard Line to the front of his bridge to take an 83,000 ton ship out. My main concern at the time was not so much getting the shot right as how to ask him to do it again if I didn't. The next focus job was in the customs shed in the midst of chaos; at least there'd been none of that on the bridge of the QE. This time I certainly did need a second take, and Gracie Fields was very sweet about it,

" Are y'alright now luv? "

1950 was in the last hey-day of the big liners before air travel became widespread and most of the nine weeks of filming was spent on board those wonderful ships or the tugs that nursed them in and out of the port. I was thus introduced into a world of romance and luxury that I have never seen anything near the like of since. Both that world and my little film unit were at the end of their lives. When the shooting was finished a meeting took place to decide on a title for it. The one chosen, OCEAN TERMINAL, was the most commonplace. The best to my mind was FOUR TIDES (the Isle of Wight divides the waters of the Solent so that Southampton has four tides in 24 hours instead of everywhere else's two). Because of the great Cunarders *Queen Mary* and *Queen Elizabeth* someone suggested PORT OF QUEENS. There was a flash of the old Bobby ...

" Portsmouth perhaps, Southampton - no. "

Poor Portsmouth; while making THE BOYFRIEND in the old theatre there Ken Russell had occasion to ask one of his actresses, who had a dangerously possessive husband, to stop fucking the camera department trainee, for his own safety and the general benefit of all concerned. He was told by the lady that she would lay the whole of Portsmouth if she had a mind to. Lunching with Max Adrian I said perhaps the whole of Portsmouth might not wish to be laid. Max was inclined to agree,

" From what I know of it, she'll find one or two pockets of resistance."

"Why is there only one word for Thesaurus?"

British Transport Films

In the course of my duties as a twenty-four year old messenger boy I was constantly carrying cans of film around London.

6

Although all filmstock had long since been coated onto a perfectly safe cellulose tri-acetate base as opposed to the high-explosive cellulose nitrate of earlier times, needless to say the regulations of London Transport had never been brought up to date; all film therefore was banned from the Underground and had to travel by taxi. It wasn't long before I adopted a procedure of my own for transporting film cans about, which was to wrap them in a copy of *The Times* newspaper, take them on the Tube, and charge up the taxi fare to the petty cash. I became so accurate at gauging taxi fares from any point to point in the London area that I was consulted by everyone in the unit, the understandable exceptions being the unit accountant and the boss, Edgar Anstey.

Another of my perks was to drive people down to Beaconsfield for music recordings. The day of the session for a film about the Channel Islands, I had the composer Malcolm Arnold as a passenger together with the conductor John Hollingsworth, a splendid musician underrated by a lot of people including Beecham who couldn't resist commenting that "Conductors are Bourne not Hollingsworth" (a bit of period ephemera that reminds us not only of a vanished department store, but also that T.B. wasn't always as funny as he thought he was). John and Malcolm were close friends rather in the lively manner of Peter Warlock, E.J.Moeran and Constant Lambert, and I treasure the memory of a jolly lunch at a pub in the village. So jolly indeed was the lunch that by the time we got back to the studio it was suggested that I should conduct the LSO; lacking the self-assurance of Edward Heath I declined the offer.

Edgar's secretary at this time was a girl named Hester Green, somewhere between Myrna Loy and a captain in the Women's Land Army, whose interest for me lay in her membership of the Royal Choral Society. Her particular idol was Victor de Sabata, who appears to have succeeded in charming lady choristers to an even greater extent than Flash Harry himself. Walking one morning from Piccadilly underground to our premises in Savile Row and calculating how much I could charge for the taxi fare, I happened to glance into one of the tailoring establishments and saw the Maestro in person, presumably in the market for a suit. When I got to the office I put my head round Hester's door and told her whom I'd just seen. With a yell of "Sab!" that would have put her in the back row of any choral society with serious pretensions, she hurtled past out into the street, leaving Edgar to get on with the day by himself. But Hester's best claim on posterity is that she is the first-hand source of a Beecham story that is outside the canon and had indeed taken place only the day before. They were rehearsing a Handel piece, *The Messiah* I believe, with the customary harpsichord continuo jangling away underneath the rest of the fabric. Sir Thomas stopped,

" I can't say I care for your instrument Mr So-and-So. It calls to mind a resolute attempt to copulate --- inside a bird-cage. "

Although I cared little for the new Festival Hall, concertgoing at this time was OK. Josef Krips had the London Symphony orchestra and once you got used to the conductor looking like Mr Pickwick everything was fine. Work of course interfered at all the worst moments. In 1952 I planned to stand, overnight if necessary, for the second of Toscanini's only two concerts in England after the war, but the travelogue we were shooting in Devon overran by a day, and the maestro had to give place to a fish auction in Brixham. Nonetheless fate isn't always unkind; I'd successfully made it to Furtwängler and Myra Hess four years earlier, so if it had to be only one concert out of the two at least I got it the right way round.

One of my first jobs, as a third camera assistant, was to be my only experience of the original three-strip Technicolor. This was a process as interesting as it was cumbersome, involving three separate rolls of film passing through the camera together. Personally I have found threesomes to be unsatisfactory affairs - one member, in my limited experience, tending to get left rather out of things. However the photographic variety seemed to manage well enough; two of the emulsions being run face to face in what may be described as missionary fashion, and the third at right angles through a prism. Here analogy breaks down.

Each strip of film was sensitised to a different colour and the three resulting black and white records were then used to make prints in exactly the same way as is used to reproduce coloured illustrations in books. There is a gentle irony attached to all this because a print could be made today of a three-strip picture of the 1930s which would be as pristine as

"Why is there only one word for Thesaurus?"

the original, whereas one taken from the more modern process dating from the mid-fifties, where the dyes are incorporated in the emulsion, would be faded and dull. It is often the case that people who initiate a thing care enough about it to get it right, and it is those who come along afterwards and "improve" (which usually means making it more convenient for somebody, often an accountant) who manage to get it wrong. Place a page from a Gutenberg Bible beside one from any 19th century book and the browned and crumbling relic will not be the one made in 1455.

To return to my part in the proceedings, this consisted solely in filling forms, one oblong folio for each shot, detailing the colour of everything in sight from the sky and the grass to the leading actor's face after lunch. Three-strip afforded an uncanny degree of colour control and my job is supposed to have originated because of a picture shot on location in southern Ireland, where the letter and phone boxes are painted green. After a titanic struggle the exhausted laboratory sent back the first batch of rushes with them as red as ever, only to get a rough bollocking by way of thanks.

Technicolor three-strip was developed and patented by a scientist, unable to spell correctly and of a retiring disposition who, perhaps due to an attraction of opposites, had married a strong-minded wife with a liking for brash colours. The name of this Pre-Raphaelite lady was Natalie Kalmus and it appears on every three-strip picture as colour consultant, consultant in this context being a euphemism for dictator. It might be interesting to print a few of these movies with a somewhat calmer palette but it probably would not suit them.

There were two cameramen on the staff at this time. Ron Craigen was a careful, precise man with an overriding interest in the mechanical side of things, while the other, Jimmy Ritchie, was quite simply a born cinematographer. Edgar shrewdly appointed the first to be chief cameraman of the unit since Ron would be less easily wooed away from his beloved equipment than someone who might have been one of the great feature cameramen of his era, and probably knew it. Edgar would thus avoid the possible annoyance of having to find a new head for the department.

When my trainee period with the union came to an end I was placed with Ron as his permanent assistant. Of course I wanted to go with Ritchie, although in fact I was probably better off as things were. If a fault occurred I had a boss who was completely happy taking the camera to bits - something I was quite incapable of doing; moreover alongside a talent bordering on genius there is a tendency to imitate, whereas watching Ron I was not inhibited from considering, sometimes at least, how I might do it differently myself; surely a better upbringing. Shifting around because of holidays I did the odd picture with Jimmy anyway and so got enough insight into the other approach, and it was to him that I went for advice seven years later when I got my first break as a cameraman. This finally happened because of the efforts of a very remarkable director named John Taylor. In the face of stern opposition from the conservative elements in the office - which amounted to just about everyone - he managed to cart me off to Blackpool to photograph a 16mm film called HOLIDAY.

At the age of sixteen John had been Robert Flaherty's assistant shooting MAN OF ARAN, where, on top of everything else, he developed and printed every foot of the film in a hut on the island. That *was* in the days of nitrate stock (as nearly related to gun-cotton as makes very little difference) despite which the "island laboratory", as the hut was called, relied on three Valour paraffin stoves to supply heat for drying the film. I don't know if John ever contemplated the hazards in this arrangement, but I'd be more interested to know whether Flaherty ever did.

Flaherty's first major documentary, NANOOK OF THE NORTH, about the lives of the Innuits in the North Hudson bay area, was sponsored by the fur traders Revillon Frères (not very wild-life friendly by today's standards). Engaged in cutting the negative, back in New York, while smoking a cigar, he blew the entire film and himself out of the cutting-room window into the street. It may seem surprising for a director to be cutting negative, but it was fairly common in those days for one of two reasons; either to save money, or, more likely in Flaherty's case, as the one sure way to secure final cut. Undaunted however, like Carlyle after a discriminating housemaid had burned the manuscript of his *History of the French Revolution*, he just went back and did it all again. At least in Flaherty's case we can be glad that he did, but I don't know how Revillon Frères felt about it.

I once asked what "old Flaherty", as John always referred to him, had been like.

"Well he was a very violent man. If a magazine jammed he would take it from the camera and dash it onto the rocks."

There had also been a brand new telephoto lens poised axe-like in the air, that was only saved by the nimble sixteen year old jumping up behind the

"Why is there only one word for Thesaurus?"

director and swinging on the other end of it. I don't think as an assistant I'd have been quite up to "old Flaherty".

John also told how the publicity department, in a fit of zeal, got themselves a huge basking shark (I hope suitably embalmed) for display in the window of the Gaumont British office in Wardour Street. They then discovered it was too big to go in the window, so they cut twenty four inches out of the middle and joined the two ends together (nothing has changed much).

After the war John was producer in charge of the Crown Film Unit until he had a row with his brother-in-law, not surprisingly since the brother-in-law was John Grierson. In 1953 John's own company, Countryman Films, made the documentary film THE CONQUEST OF EVEREST, and he told me an interesting fact about the final assault on the summit, of which there is no film record. Sixteen millimeter film (although serious mathematicians would probably quibble about it) is half the size of professional 35mm stock. It clearly made a lot of sense for home movies but was often employed on documentaries without any valid reason. Being half the size it was obviously half the price, which of course appealed to accountants and production managers, but as I have always been ready to point out, if directors would only shoot half the amount of unnecessary material that some of them love so inordinately we should finish up in the same place only with much more pleasing results. 16mm in consequence has always been fair game for the sallies of cameramen who actually care what goes on the screen (a greater number than might be thought).

There are however certain circumstances in which the use of 16mm is justified and the top of Mount Everest would seem to be one of them. Unfortunately, throughout the two months of the expedition, Tom Stobart, as a result of constant ribbing for humping the Newman Sinclair about all the time rather than take the other "neat little thing" out of its box, had seen fit to express himself forcefully on the subject with the result that when it came to the final two-man assault on the summit, where every ounce of weight was important, Hillary refused to take it.

" It's been called a ridiculous toy ever since we started out so why on earth should I carry it now? "
It may have been an excuse, I'm sure Hillary and Tensing had enough to contend with, but as John said to me with a rueful smile,
" It's a pity cameramen can't keep their fucking mouths shut. "

As a freelance director John had made a number of films for Transport and I'd worked on some of them as an assistant. He always had about him a quiet serenity to balance his good-natured cynicism; when someone asked him why he wanted me for Blackpool - "...well it will annoy everybody for one thing...". He was the sort of person who made you think - that is how I should like to be. An attribute I learned from him was how to use four letter words, among the oldest in our language, with

John Taylor with Self in 1990   Photo: Keith Hamshere

charm - "Hello you old cunt" was a greeting reserved only for people he really liked, and since knowing him I've been able to employ these poor maligned little fellows as freely as I've wished, though under no circumstances ever with any ill nature. That is how crews know if I'm seriously annoyed with them; *then* I never swear. There is no such thing as bad language - only the bad use of it, and I'd be all for putting a stop to that.

In fact it is these prim taboos that are the real evil. D.H.Lawrence knew it was the taboo itself, and not its object, that we should worry about, because ".. the result of taboo is insanity". The current media fashion, short lived I hope, is to substitute a noun, "bonk", for the verb "fuck". Everybody knows exactly what is meant - it even has the same sinister number of letters - but somehow *now* it is all right! And so a useful word is lost to the language, and you can no longer give anyone a bonk without a misunderstanding. It really is such nonsensical childishness.

Another aspect of John was that of the naturalist, and I remember one halcyon day during THE ENGLAND OF ELIZABETH, a remote sea shore on the west coast, John, in no hurry about shooting, wandering at low tide, looking into rock pools and describing a traditional way to catch lobsters by poking a stick into their lairs; because lobsters combine stupidity with stubbornness (one can think of parallels) they never let go once they have laid hold and are pulled out of the water, supplying their own hook as it were. It is called diddling, with the first i pronounced long.

Both sides of John emerge in a tale told by Rory McLeod, a delightful person who survived a brief spell as my assistant to become a cameraman himself and went out with John to get a shot of some adders for a nature documentary. The artists were relaxing inside a pen outdoors and appeared so comfortably asleep that John suggested lunch. Halfway through the ale and sandwiches Rory glanced into the pen and remarked that two of the snakes were fighting. John quickly grabbed the camera and started shooting,

" Actually they're fucking, but trust a Scotsman

not to know the difference. "

I did not properly understand the reversal stock that was to be used for Blackpool so I sought out Jimmy Ritchie and asked him. Reversal is a kind of film that, by some conjuring of the black arts, creates its own positive instead of going via a negative like everyone else; don't ask how, this is not that sort of book. To this day I still find it hard to evaluate the brief twenty minutes or so which followed. Clearly and concisely he disposed of the reversal problem, said two utterly simple and revealing things about lighting and then,

" .... most important of all never worry about the results. Do all the right things; then go back over it and make sure that you've done all the right things - then forget about it. Next day if there's anything wrong don't blame yourself; don't blame anyone else; find out why so it doesn't happen again. "

Complete sanity and I never forgot it.

It was all very much to the point so far as Blackpool was concerned. Part of the problem with reversal is the absence of anything like the exposure latitude there is with negative emulsions. It is used a lot by stills photographers who cope by means of bracketing - that is making two further exposures one stop either side of what is judged to be the correct one. This expedient can hardly be applied to movies. A director may go through a number of takes before he gets the performance he wants, and the reason behind the tradition in the camera department of getting it right every time so "they need never go again for us" is because sod's law will contrive that, get it wrong but once and it will be the take that was best for everybody else.

The next difficulty with the stock was that instead of going to a laboratory in the normal way it had to be sent back to Kodak who were the only people that could process it. Unfortunately they tended to get a different colour balance each time, so the only way to ensure that the complete film would match was not to send anything in at all until the six weeks of shooting was over and then process the whole lot at the same time. This was not too much fun for anybody, but for me it was quite bizarre. It meant that on my first picture as a cameraman I could not make a mistake, and that if I did nobody would find out until it was too late. I dealt with this potentially stressful situation by deciding, as I needed the money, to go ahead but with the resigned acceptance that my future career would lie inside the cutting-rooms. I even asked John to write to the BBC and set me up an interview. He understood perfectly, was vastly amused at my way of inspiring the director's confidence, and gave me a glowing recommendation to the BBC for use should the need arise. With this escape hatch in the back of my mind I was able to relax and get on. There was even an occasional twinge of regret, because one has such fun on a picture, that this was to be my only experience of it.

John's letter was never posted.

Among those who appeared briefly in the Blackpool film were Arthur Askey, the singer Alma Cogan (the poor girl was grossly overlit by me), Charlie Cairoli the clown, who I was pleased to see had a signed photograph of Barbirolli in his dressing-room, and Stanley Matthews the footballer. Although I took a mild interest in cricket I did not know much about the world of football. We had been allowed to set-up in one of the grandstands where we obstructed the view of a number of regular supporters, though I was too concerned at getting my part right i.e. staying with Matthews, to be aware of their displeasure. When the two teams ran onto the field I asked John which of them was Blackpool, which caused a few murmurs, again unnoticed by me until I further enquired which player was Stanley Matthews. John managed to calm them down after a bit and in fact my second enquiry turned out to be quite unnecessary when they started to play - he stood out at once. It was magical to watch and I was carried away by him - time ceased to exist. Afterwards he proved to be a modest and good man, concerned for the welfare of players who in those far-off days were poorly paid and when finally they had to go were just "given a gold watch".

Edgar promised Ritchie, who was getting restless, a break to direct and so I took over THE ENGLAND OF ELIZABETH with John Taylor again. It is nice to have one's name on the same picture as Vaughan Williams although on the only occasion when I should have met the great man I was sent off to get a shot of a train or something. Par for the course (I don't play golf but learned this expression from my electricians who all do), and I never much minded missing garden parties at the palace (twice); but VW was one of my heroes. It is part of the price one pays for going up in the world; if I'd still been chauffeuring people to music recordings I'd have seen him. It appears to have been quite a session as at one point the old man, who was no lightweight, tipped too far back in his chair and was only saved from disaster by Edgar making a dive and grabbing him.

Somebody that I did meet on the film was the founding father of documentary himself. John Grierson was married to John Taylor's sister and we drove down to their farm, Tog Hill in Wiltshire, to shoot a fiery beacon for the Spanish Armada. I remember sitting in a very spacious room, a converted barn I think, with a staircase at one end at the top of which was a door. Grierson came in through this door talking, descended the stairs talking, shook hands, sat down opposite and continued talking for about an hour and a half then retired up the stairs talking and disappeared through the door.

My first ever lit interior turned out modestly enough to be the nave of King's College Chapel in Cambridge. There was a fair sprinkling of deans, proctors etc but their attention was soon diverted away from me by the sight of Arthur Green and Fat Mac (Donald) of Mole Richardson processing down the aisle arm in arm as bride and groom, Arthur being

"Why is there only one word for Thesaurus?"

the bride as I remember.

Happily I was now able in small measure to repay some of my debt to Jimmy Ritchie. The next film for me after THE ENGLAND OF ELIZABETH was his first picture as a director, and it turned out to be a very charming one. It was about a railway orphanage in Derby run by a lady who reminded you of Margaret Rutherford. She truly understood us all, children and grown-ups alike, and loved the children as they did her. I had never found myself in such a happy place and when I said so to Jim it must have stayed in his mind because THE HAPPY PLACE became the working title (though it finished up as CARE OF St CHRISTOPHERS). She encouraged the children to keep their own pets-

" It's very good for them to manage things entirely on their own and I try never to interfere. There was a boy who kept pigeons, a bright nice boy. After a time he started to sell them to people outside - nothing wrong in that at all but then they started to come back - pigeons *do* you see, and then he would sell them again. I thought well if people are foolish enough .... but in the end I had to put a stop to it. "

Every evening we took the children up to bed. They would take a flying leap into your arms to be carried to the dormitory. The confidence and love they poured out was a great gift to the spirit but it was also heartbreaking. Frank Brice used to call her Mrs Fizackerly. I don't know her real name but she was a great woman.

It was with Ritchie that I first encountered the phenomenon of directors working themselves into a kind of frenzy of enthusiasm (rather like witch doctors) that was disproportionate to anything warranted by the subject. On getting up to Killin to start work on THEY TAKE THE HIGH ROAD, a mild documentary about lorries ferrying cement for building a hydro-electric dam up in the mountains, I was told eagerly,

" It's THE WAGES OF FEAR without the nitro-glycerine. "

I could see what he meant and said so; I could also see that THE WAGES OF FEAR without any unstable explosive about would be a rather dull film, but did not say so. I'm sure it turned out all right within its limitations - most things do.

It was while on another picture in Scotland that a very strange and wonderful thing happened to me. The director's assistant went completely mad. Though uncommon this is not strange and wonderful, but it meant the director, Ken Fairbairn, and my own assistant had to leave me with the camera on a hillside to film a sunset while they took the poor man to a hospital. After an hour or so the awesome stillness and wild beauty of the place had cast me into an almost trance-like state. Then suddenly a piper started up from the far side of one of the hills, music I had never heard before, I suppose a pibroch, that continued wild and beautiful through time that for me had ceased to exist. I have never been enchanted so, and couldn't bear the thought that sooner or later it would end; and this from an instrument that I normally detest. How much was due to the music and how much to the loneliness I do not know, but I learned then that the bagpipes is an instrument of distance and space and have stopped being rude about it.

Ken was a nice man; known as "Twitcher" because of a tendency to be hyperactive, he was also small in stature, resulting in most of his set-ups being done on the baby-legs, which was a bit trying. He wrote his own scripts for the most part; one that I did for him about the lost luggage office was called A DESPERATE CASE. Another about incoherent station announcements had a similarly apt title to begin with: GET LOST! but Edgar made him change it.

There was one other favourite director - R.K.Neilson Baxter. Rod Baxter was a most urbane, civilised and charming man. He directed UNDER THE RIVER, a film about the making of the Severn Tunnel, based on a book by Thomas Walker published in 1888. The tunnel is subject to the incursion of a massive fresh water spring and at Sudbrook, on the Monmouthshire side of the river, six Cornish beam engines had been pumping out an average twenty five million gallons into the Severn every day since 1886. If all six were to stop the tunnel would be completely flooded in a couple of hours. They hadn't stopped of course, and in fact nothing at all had changed for over sixty five years; it was an extraordinary stepping back in time. The whole thing suited us both and was a joy from beginning to end. I did several pictures with him and it was always the same. He once paid me the staggering compliment of saying that I was the English Bert Haanstra. He knew Haanstra well, they were good friends, and I greatly valued his saying it.

Another of Rod's pictures was about the then new roll-on roll-off ferries. It involved numerous trips on the *Bardic Ferry* from Tilbury to Antwerp and thence via Aachen and the Brenner down to Milan. On the first trip our German contact, whom we had never met before, stood punctually awaiting us at the appointed rendezvous, the Opernplatz in Frankfurt-am-Main. As we got out of the car facing the desolate shell of their once beautiful opera house (still in ruin in 1957), Rod asked me very quietly,

"Did we do that?"
Friends may be out of sight, but they are seldom out of mind, and I certainly remembered young Eduard Graftiaux and Louvain.

"No, no - the Americans."

We had been allotted a Customs official to steer us in and out of Tilbury each time. He always wore the same dog-tooth jacket and grey flannels like someone out of Motor Sport, and was also always completely sozzled like an alcoholic version of Ralph Richardson. If the latter was an act to put smugglers off their guard it was a very consistent one.

The *Bardic* ran a steady traffic in Swiss watches which used to travel in the ship's engine room because it was the only place on board where there was enough noise to drown the chorus of ticking; they certainly

"Why is there only one word for Thesaurus?"

never had the least trouble with our dog-tooth jacketed acquaintance. The same picture also had a couple of short scenes with dear old Ralph Michael and Richard Pearson, whom I would meet up with later in HOW I WON THE WAR.

Stewart McAllister has a book to himself (*Portrait of an Invisible Man* by Dai Vaughan, published by the BFI in 1983), but there is a reason to mention him here. He managed to upset just about everyone at Transport (he could certainly be abrasive) but he was unfailingly kind to me; though we did fall out just once. I was sent to get a high speed shot (1000 frames per second - which means

Mac, at 25 Savile Row, with the Burlington House clock (used for checking the infinity mark on lenses) at the far end of the street.
Photo: National Railway Museum.

rushes go on for ever) of what happens inside incorrectly loaded goods vans when they are rough-shunted in marshalling yards. This technique for putting goods trains together quickly is to uncouple one or more wagons and give them an almighty shove so that they hurtle off on their own and collide more or less violently (depending on the skill of the engine driver) with whatever train they're allotted to. The instant they have cleared them, the points are switched over just in time for the next lot to be sent off to another line of trucks bound for somewhere else. It sounds like great fun if you don't have to do it every day.

Down in Battersea yard I took note of the assembled props: heavy bales, oil drums, steel castings, carboys of suspicious-looking liquids - the lot, and judiciously set up the camera well braced off at the back of the van facing forward - so that on impact all the stuff would be thrown away from us. When he saw the rushes Mac was quite specific,

" Och ye fucking idiot, why didna ye set up the other way? "

" What and have it land all over the camera, not to mention us? "
Thinking about it now he was probably right - impractical, but right.

In 1941 Mac became involved in an amazing collaboration with the best of all British documentary directors, Humphrey Jennings, that continued until Jennings' death in 1950. It was often said that the partnership was not a real one and that everything came from Jennings. I didn't believe it and long afterwards when I met Jennings' daughter

Charlotte she confirmed,

"If there's one talent Dad didn't have it was for editing - he'd have left everything in. "

It accords exactly with what Mac used to tell me gleefully of immense rows, with Jennings insisting upon restoring Mac's excisions, followed by Mac quietly going back in the middle of the night and taking them out again. Each time film was joined during editing, two frames were lost that had to be replaced by white spacing; given natures of such evenly matched stubbornness it's a wonder their cutting-copy did not ultimately consist entirely of blank spacing (a possible advantage when it came to showing to clients).

Their masterpiece, on which in unique equality Mac shares the director's credit, is LISTEN TO BRITAIN; the finest documentary ever made. In it there is a sequence of a National Gallery concert with Myra Hess playing Mozart's G major concerto, K 453. Humphrey originally intended a Bach piece and it was his young assistant Joe Mendoza who suggested the concerto. Myra thought it a lovely idea but hardly possible,

" We would need to have a platform for the orchestra. "

As Joe said - at 19 you'll do anything; he got the Crown unit construction department to build a platform and went round to Harrods and persuaded a carpet out of them. We were a different nation in 1941. Imagine Harrods, or anyone else today, giving a carpet to a 19 year old boy who wanted to put on a Mozart concerto to make people cheerful. That was the first orchestral programme at the Gallery, until then there had been only recitals and chamber works; thereafter they kept their platform until the end of the war.

It was Myra who asked Queen Elizabeth to appear in Humphrey's film and when the audience had left after the concert she returned to the gallery.

" Where do you want me to sit, Mr Jennings? "

It is the job of chroniclers to rescue what would otherwise be obscure forever, and it is said that Humphrey, who could be careless about his clothes, directed the whole of this scene with his flies open. We therefore cannot be certain if Queen Elizabeth and Kenneth Clark are smiling at Mozart, or at the director's trousers. Libby, Myra's niece, is inclined to favour Mozart because whenever the Queen was sitting for a portrait, Myra would go to the palace and play for her, so that she would look relaxed and happy.

We have digressed a bit from McAllister to the Queen Mother, but to return to him, I have met with two men in this business who quite simply loved films more than the rest of us do; one was Eddie Fowlie who will turn up in a later chapter. Mac was the other.

Sadly few of these films stand up to the passage of time, mainly because they have to bear the incubus of a spoken commentary. It is as if no audience could be relied on to keep their eyes open and must be told,

"Why is there only one word for Thesaurus?"

in phrase after stilted phrase, what they can very well see for themselves if they are looking at the screen. Certainly a reason why LISTEN TO BRITAIN stands up across the years is because, for once, its sounds and images are left alone. Try putting a commentary over them and see what happens.

A DIARY FOR TIMOTHY at least had the merit that the words had been written by E.M.Forster - they end with these lines,

" ... and so, dear Tim, what are you going to do ... are you going to have greed for money or power ousting decency from the world as they have in the past? "

Mrs Thatcher would have been nineteen years old at the time. History lays out a curious pattern of parallels and coincidences,

" And what rough beast, its hour come round at last,

Slouches towards Bethlehem to be born? "

When Yeats wrote those lines Hitler would have been about the same age - the stepping off point. Needless to add that I am quite aware that to place Hitler and Mrs Thatcher in the same context is unfair to both of them.

By the time of the Festival of Britain film, FAMILY PORTRAIT, all was lost and we were back with what John Legard, an editor from Crown and Transport, aptly described as "the illustrated lecture". Interestingly Mac had told John the commentary was first recorded by Laurence Olivier but that the result sounded so flat and dull that they had done it again with somebody else. It is possible, unkind people might even say understandable, that Larry was bored; but it might be amusing to lay his recording, if it still exists, against the picture and take another look. A determination to sound keenly interested renders the outcome less attractive as a rule, and Larry may have been right - he was a crafty old sod who usually knew what he was after.

"Why is there only one word for Thesaurus?"

The Electrical Gentlemen

Cameramen control their end of things by a sort of combined operation; on one hand the camera crew whom he shares with the director, and on the other the electricians who are his alone.

7

Except for the studios, who had their own people, all the electricians were supplied by Mole Richardsons. The Moley Men as they were called were a remarkable breed, Olympian drinkers (whose work remained unaffected by it) and unique humorists who adorned the set like a chorus of silent clowns.

An illustration from my days as an assistant took place one evening on Victoria station where Ritchie was photographing the departure of the night sleeping car train to Paris. One of the station porters got into conversation with the sparks and confided that seeing all the lights recalled for him the far off days when he had enjoyed some success in the music halls.

" I used to be on the boards myself. "

The Moleys expressed wide disbelief and without exchanging so much as a glance with each other a space was cleared and a 150amp arc wound to the top of its stand, spotted and tipped down, creating a circle of light on the platform.

" We can't believe that. "

" Give us a demonstration then. "

The stationmaster, a high dignitary in a top hat and swallow-tail coat, arrived on the platform to behold one of his porters executing a dance figure in the manner of Fred Astaire in and around the Luis Vuiton hatboxes to the applause of the Moley Men and surprised looks of the first class passengers.

With a decline in the fortunes of Mole Richardson and a rise in those of the Lee brothers, the Moley Men became an extinct species, drifting and dispersing like the morning mist. It was probably as well. The new boys from Lees were just as much fun and just as good electricians - only the baroque element had gone, like the change from a tiger to a domestic cat. During the power-cuts of the late 70s a Lees crew on their way back from a job stopped at a candle-lit pub, unloaded some 2Ks from the truck, started up the genny and had drinks on the house for the rest of the evening. It would have been a rash publican who entered into that sort of arrangement with the gentlemen from Moles.

Just one Moley Man survived for many many years, like the last Dodo. This was because he acted as guardian and sole operator of a unique and very special lamp. There used to be two sizes of arc follow-spot: 120amps and 250amps. The 120s were rather small beer, but the 250s would make anything that's around today look silly. On a lonely eminence above the lot of them however, was one solitary 300amp device, so sexy that it had to be water-cooled while in use, and these ministrations were always presided over by the last of the Moley Men - a gentleman named Bert Monk.

Part of the Musketeers films of Richard Lester was shot in Franco's palace of El Pardo, north west of Madrid. The old tyrant had a set of apartments in a closed-off wing, and nearer to where we were shooting (next door in fact), an audience chamber or throne room, quite small, without a stick of furniture of any kind apart from a pompous gold throne covered in red damask. I wanted to put a spotlamp in there to beam through a small window (rather like a projection port) into our set. This idea got a flat no to begin with, but after I had stressed that there would be no film crew invading the sanctum - just a little lamp with its minder - somehow or other it was allowed. Perhaps the word Monk helped to pacify them.

All the way from England came my Trojan Horse and its ostler to be admitted to the holy of holies, *and locked in*. Bert, being a thorough professional, set about checking everything, and to satisfy himself that the water seals were a good tight fit - removed them. Unhappily someone outside the building had just turned on the tap. I could hear muffled cries of

" Turn the water off, you Spanish cunts! "

but it took a while before someone with a more sober disposition than I, got the message translated and relayed, and in the meantime the water pressure being quite high, the red damask finished up a bit of a mess.

It isn't every day one can piss all over the throne of a Fascist Dictator, and so far as I am concerned Bert Monk went out of my life on a tidal wave of glory.

It was a practice among the fraternity at one time to re-connect the wires to the electricity meters in their homes over the week-end so as to reverse the polarity. The meter would then adopt a subtracting instead of an adding role, reducing the amount of current shown as used but not by enough to give the game away, and since no one was going to call to read the meter at a week-end there was no risk of discovery. One of my gaffers suffered a heart attack on a Monday morning while driving to work, and sadly died in hospital the following Wednesday. Come Saturday there was a phone-call from his house,

" Can you send one of the lads round, the meter's still going backwards."

I think he would have been happy with that.

As orchestral musicians are the soundest judges (pun unintentional) of a conductor's abilities, or the absence of them, so are electricians of cameramen. Praise from them is worth the having, and they are never fooled-

" ... we got to the location so I just put up a 10k as a work-light, and this man rushed out with his meter. "

It is quite chastening to hear about someone faster than I am.

The staff electrician at Transport was Frank Brice. He had been with the original Post Office Unit and described how the first generators they got were the discarded engines taken from the scrapped Barnes Wallis airship R100. He had worked on what must be the most famous documentary of them all, NIGHT MAIL, for which W.H. Auden had written the words and Benjamin Britten the music. It was in the days before mechanised arc lamps and it was necessary to keep the correct gap between the carbons by hand feeding them. There is a scene where the train climbs over the Pennines at Shap Fell in the middle of the night and Frank had deployed a long line of 150amp arcs in a field alongside the track (I should think at about ten yards apart). He was on his own and so had to run from each lamp to the next adjusting the gap until he got to the end of the line and then hare back to the beginning and start again. I love the thought that that shot is only on the screen because one man was running up and down a field.

Frank was a splendid electrician and gaffered most of the jobs that I did while I was at Transport. One of these was a film about what happens on the London Underground between the last train at night and the first one in the morning. It was directed by a very distinguished documentary director named Ralph Keene. "Bunny", as he was called by his contemporaries (but never by me), was a very nice man but he would have been described by my mother as "highly strung". This manifested itself one night when we were shooting outside Baker Street station. At around three o'clock in the morning a van drove past and bundles of newspapers were slung out onto the pavement. The headlines landed uppermost and it appeared that we and the French had forgotten all about manners and taken ourselves into Suez without being invited. Ralph got very excited and said that the unit should wrap and we should all go home.

Shooting a training film (drivers converting from steam to diesel).
Ritchie standing behind me, and Frank Brice with his hand on a pup.   *Photo: National Railway Museum.*

" That fool Nasser. World events are taking place - we can't stand here."
I pointed out that we had just spent about two hours lighting the front of
Baker Street station plus half the Marylebone Road, and after a bit
managed to calm him down sufficiently to finish the night's work.
Afterwards he confided to me with great charm that at the time of
Dunkirk he had been filming up in the Potteries for Basil Wright.

" Basil couldn't understand why I immediately brought the unit back
to London - quite annoyed he was. I can't help having a sense of
proportion - great events and a piffling little film. But Basil never
understood it. "
Frank understood all right. A couple of hours into the following night's
work he drew a newspaper from his pocket, shaking his head and looking
very grave.
" The world situation's pretty bad Guvnor - don't you think we should
go home? "

My own sense of proportion was developing a more practical side. It
was clear from the start that a film shot is only a photograph and that no
photograph is worth any risk to life or limb - mine or anyone else's. Over
years of working in various industrial locations it was noticeable that the
less imaginative directors were the most inclined to take risks. They felt
sure that no one had ever put a camera *there* before, which was probably
correct - no one else had been silly enough. The truth is that a long lens
from a safe distance may be more effective on the screen than a wide one

"Why is there only one word for Thesaurus?"

dangerously close.

The pursuit of safety by means of long lenses occasionally yields unexpected results. I was having to film the Royal Agricultural Show in Dundee while it was getting a visit from the Queen Mother. Our production office in London had neglected to seek permission from the Scottish Office and this meant that I was getting chased all over the place by a disagreeable man called Mr Mackenzie. About the middle of the afternoon the Queen Mother, attended by her steward the Earl of Airlie, an august dignitary in full Highland costume, settled in the middle of an otherwise empty grandstand to watch some performing sheepdogs. I put on a long lens and crouched down at the bottom of the stand where I was shielded from Mr Mackenzie by the barrier. This provided a low angle shot of the lady and I was busily filming it when the Earl was called away for some reason. He rose and excused himself with a profound bow which replaced the Queen Mother on the screen with a dusky demonstration that nothing is worn beneath a kilt. This unique transition shot from the Queen Mother's face to the Earl of Airlie's arse was never used. It is the way of editors, with films as well as books, to leave out the interesting parts (apart from anything else I should have liked Mr Mackenzie to have seen it). They did exactly the same with another shot of mine. I was sent out to get some stuff of the railway station at Woking and managed to find them one angle featuring a fortuitous juxtaposition of two adjacent hoardings. The one on the left carried only the giant letters VD with, very much smaller, the address of the local clinic, while its neighbour simply bore a familiar slogan of the time, " I Got It at the Co-op. "

The same modesty and reserve which the Southern Railway had displayed with regard to no 637 at the foot of the Waterloo and City lift-shaft was adopted by my new employers in the case of all subsequent mishaps encountered while running their railways. Only once, in August 1955, did pride overcome reticence when a new system of hydraulic jacks was being put to use, for the first time, to extricate a large express locomotive from a field of Brussels-sprouts near Rugby in which it unexpectedly found itself. When we arrived on the scene it certainly represented a fine old mess, but work was being carried out with admirable quiet and efficiency under the supervision of the District Running Inspector, a railwayman of the old school whom I took to at once. During a lull in the proceedings I asked him how it had all come about.

" Oh that's easy enough up to a point; there's a 15mph limit on that curve and he came round it at 60. Beyond that we'll never find out because he and his fireman were both killed. Not that we'd know in any case - they'll never say what really happened. "

This was said more with kindness than reproach, and he went on,

" Just once I got the whole story and that was because I was there before he'd had time to gather his wits. Purely by chance I was at a place where the main line runs through the centre of a marshalling yard where goods trains are shunted and made up. I saw that a train was signalled and also that there was a light engine waiting to cross from one side to the other. Suddenly the signal came off allowing the light engine to move across the track right in the path of the oncoming express. There was no collision because the engine completed the move with a couple of minutes to spare, but because of what is called "interlocking" what I had just witnessed could not possibly have taken place. Whenever the signals are cleared for the main line the points and signals for anything to cross it are automatically locked - it would be impossible for the signalman to move his levers. I ran to the box where my surprise appearance gave the man on duty such a shock that I got the truth out of him. He had worked the same signal-box for the past 30 years and in the course of that time had discovered a way to beat the system. Due to slight wear in the linkage he found that by half pulling on one lever while reaching out and kicking another with his foot he could actually pull off the locked signal with his other hand. He had kept this genie inside its bottle for a couple of years but it had nagged at him more and more until he had felt impelled to try it just the once. It was a Sunday, it was quiet, and there was sufficient time for the move before the other train arrived. "

I think my friend contented himself with providing a ticking off, knowing that there was one signalman at least with whom this sort of aberration would not happen again.

Around lunchtime we were rather surprised to see Mac sauntering through the Brussels-sprouts. He had been spending the week-end at Llandudno and wanted to play with his all stations pass. It was then possible to go by train cross-country from almost any point in Britain to any other, without going into London and out again. It was quicker and more interesting, but that was before a Minister of Transport, associated with a large road building company, had finished destroying half the country's rail network. It was a bit barefaced, even for a Tory, and, considering that one freight train with a single power unit is equivalent of about a hundred juggernauts polluting the planet, not very ecologically responsible either. Naturally he preferred a properly subsidised railway system for his own use, and on completing the havoc here Ernie Marples removed his money and himself to France for the rest of his days.

There was no facet of British life, from stately home to steel-works, that I did not experience at close quarters during this period, with the happy exception of coal-mining. Fortunately for me the Coal Board had its own unit with a gentle old cameraman named Cyril Arapoff, who compensated for his sojourns below ground by photographing ballet dancers when he was above it. There were several nicely produced books of the work of this mild Stygean Degas.

I might find myself inside a factory in the Midlands for as long as a week or more observing people engaged in a routine that would dominate

"Why is there only one word for Thesaurus?"

them relentlessly for years to come while I had the comfort of knowing that in a day or two I should be somewhere else, and whatever the hardship, discomfort or excitement was, it would be different. It was a feeling akin to that, which few will admit to, when someone dies; whatever sadness is alloyed with satisfaction that oneself is still alive. There were constant insights and amusements, as in a canning factory in Dundee where a confiding foreman who was looking after us pointed to some steaming vats containing sugar and water.

" That's for the tinned fruit. Peaches cost more than syrup so you'll get mostly syrup in a tin of peaches. On the other hand the syrup costs more than rhubarb does so there'll be stacks of rhubarb and not much juice with it."

I am often reminded of this principle as it becomes ever more difficult to get a straightforward ice cream unencumbered with pulp from a jam makers or sweepings from a chocolate factory.

Back at 25, Savile Row there was always a pleasant element of eccentricity somewhere about, usually in the adjoining offices of the head of the camera department, Ron Craigen, and the boss of the cutting rooms, Stewart McAllister. Both had a child's fascination for new gadgetry of any kind, and certainly in Mac's case it could be as remote from anything to do with film-making as it liked. He had the first ever nylon suit which always, right from the start, looked completely crumpled as though he had slept in it. He wore it every single day quite assured that it couldn't wear out and he need never buy another.

Nylon suits do not appear to affect editors who wear them in any way that is perceivable on the screen whereas, at least in one instance, Ron's enthusiasm led him to construct, with some ingenuity, an electric motor that would take a full 100ft of 16mm through a Kodak Cine Special camera instead of the very limited run of its own clockwork drive. This he did for the specific purpose of obtaining uninterrupted colour shots of the Coronation Procession from the vantage of Charing Cross railway bridge. Unfortunately when the day arrived there was such an endless multitude of guardsmen tramping down Northumberland Avenue that Ron's motor got extremely hot and seized-up solid just as Brenda was in the offing. In consequence I was a bit preoccupied and don't recall seeing her at all; the memory that persists is of Churchill, who looked like a marshmallow in fancy dress.

Their most resolute enterprise, to my mind, was in the early 1950s when electric razors were something of a novelty. On a short trip to Paris Mac and Ron carted a rotary converter (something to do with electricity, largely constructed of lead, approximately 2 x 1 x 1 feet and weighing about 10 cwt) onto the Night Ferry because the electricity supply on that train was unsuitable for shaving. These shifting enthusiasms led at one time (while I was still his assistant) to Ron bringing a rug-making machine wherever he went. Thankfully he carried it himself, though on location in Tewkesbury I remember being asked to his hotel room and to hold both forearms apart supporting skeins of wool while he wound them into a ball. I was already quite good at this having had to perform the same service for at least two of the nannies, though it is a skill that, despite a long career in films, has not been called upon since.

One December I attended a union meeting. This was very unusual because these affairs always took place during the lunch hour, which time I invariably went home a mere three stations away on the underground. The shop steward was a nice man - "You really ought to come once in a while". On this particular occasion my friend was out all day doing the Christmas shopping so there was no lunch to go home to, and it was flattering to note the satisfaction caused by my Prodigal Son appearance among them. The meeting opened and launched straightway into the question of the unfortunate plight of certain earnest ladies who found themselves lodged inside Holloway women's prison throughout the festive season on account of a doubtless worthy protest in which they had engaged.

I suppose I had naively expected to hear about such relevant matters to trade unions as pay or working conditions and in consequence sat silently bemused for quite some time while a discussion took place about Christmas puddings. These were to be sent to solace the good ladies in their sojourn behind bars. Matters are seldom expressed briefly at union meetings so I have made a précis rather than give a full account of all that was said.

" How many; one each? "

" Large puddings are better value. "

" Yes brother Washbourne, but would the prison authorities allow them to share out the larger puddings among themselves? "

Here indeed lay a difficulty as no one present had ever been inside to find out what Christmas pudding procedures are followed in H.M. prisons.

" George Elvin (the General Secretary) might know. "

" What was he in Holloway for? "

Although I asked this in all innocence there was an indecorous titter from one or two of the more frivolous brothers. It was then decided to approach the Home Office and find out; but that was not by any means an end of it. Which make of pudding ought we to send? One suggested Foster Clarke's, another that there was more fruit in Peak Freans, which was countered by a dark hint that the treatment of union representatives in the latter's factories left much to be desired. It was at this point that I intervened a second time to suggest Fortnum's, Jackson's Piccadilly, or at the very least Harrods, since the gentlewomen in question probably came from commodious houses in Hampstead and would be quite unused to anyone else's; and, apart from any of that, if they decided to go on a hunger-strike Christmas puddings would be an embarrassment. The only time I ever addressed a union meeting it ended with the complete

"Why is there only one word for Thesaurus?"

overthrow of the proposal; not so much as a mince tart received sanction. Afterwards the shop steward took me quietly aside and suggested that in future it might be better if I went home to lunch.

Among my presents that Xmas was an electric tooth-brush which turned out to be a rather silly affair. The main drawback to this species of oral vibrator was that the batteries did not last very long and always gave out when you were in a hurry. This brings us back to Harrods. In their chemist's shop I was being served by a very engaging young man and, noticing a display of them, I asked him if there was a mains operated version. Apparently there had been but the line was discontinued after a customer had electrocuted himself whilst cleaning his teeth in the bath. This was absurd enough to cause me to laugh and seeing that we shared the same deplorable sense of humour he decided that he could do better.

" I've not been here long or I probably wouldn't be telling you this, " he giggled, " the older ones won't talk about it. "
(One of them must have.)

" You know in the banking hall there's all those oil paintings of the directors? "
(I did indeed.)

" Well the wife of one of them came in here with a prescription for a cold, and we made it up wrong and it killed him. "
He ended with a note of pride -
" One of our own directors. "
If all their salesmen were like him I would shop in Harrods more often.

The subsequent history of the trades unions in this country is appalling. Built with devotion and sacrifice to look after working people at the beck of unfettered employers, they ended up in 1979 by destroying socialism in Britain. A brave attempt by one courageous little woman to bring them into reasonable order (Barbara Castle's "In Place of Strife", stamped on by her cabinet colleagues) proved their last chance to regulate themselves, and when they were wiped out of existence by a very different "little woman" it almost served them right. Unfortunately it also set film technicians back where they started - being screwed by the management.

A justification often made for the ensuing reduction in the size of crews, and working whoever are left for ridiculous hours, (that it assists films that would not otherwise be made), is rarely true; what it does assist and encourage is massive incompetence - directors can flounder about for hours at no additional cost. None that appears on a balance sheet at any rate, though for the last four hours of a sixteen-hour day there will probably be about half an hour's real work done. I deliberately slow up after a point, not because I'm bloody minded but because otherwise, sooner or later, I'll make a mistake. After a couple of weeks the whole unit loses its edge, and one day somebody will kill themselves driving home half asleep (shortly after this was written somebody did).

It is tragic, because this business must be one of the very few where you actually get paid money for playing at make-believe, and staying a kid all your life. It requires serious ineptitude to turn something so immensely delightful into a distressing experience for everybody. It would be worth years in a film school for young people to spend a few hours on a set with someone like Sidney Lumet. To start with he respects everybody on the crew and moreover understands what they are doing just as well as they do; driving to work one morning on CRITICAL CARE he was praising the work of Dona Granata, the costume designer, and I remarked upon her unusual practice of actually *thinking* about what she was doing.

" And feeling, and caring", he smiled, ... "all the good things".

In the Autumn of 1995, 3-30pm was a sort of enchanted hour in New York, at which Sidney would finish the day's work on NIGHT FALLS ON MANHATTAN at the same moment that a certain other movie

"Rapid Sid" is on the right of the picture.   *Photo: Adger W. Cowans*

shooting in the town was about to turn over on their first shot. It was not that "Rapid Sid" was slipshod in any way, quite the reverse; he has done his homework, won't shoot anything he doesn't need, and what he does need is all the better for being done by people who are fresh, relaxed, and enjoying themselves. The more alternatives somebody shoots the less they are doing any directing at all; the decisions are just being deferred. Much of what passes for film making at the time of writing is a profound insult to common sense, and the dispatch of a few Christmas puddings to North London would now be a small price to put a stop to it.

"Why is there only one word for Thesaurus?"

Leaving Transport

I started to find towards the end of the fifties that I could be setting up the tripod in much the same place that I'd set it up seven years before (almost as though the holes were still there) and it seemed time to move on.

8

There were several factors but the catalyst turned out to be Joan Littlewood. She was just about to direct a film and for some reason came to see Edgar. Hugh Raggett, an editor friend, very much bolder than I was, waylaid her as she was leaving and asked her out for coffee with myself and my assistant, a lively young mind named John Burrows. She took a shine to us and after a few more coffee sessions was determined that I should photograph SPARRERS CAN'T SING and that Hugh should cut it.

In the theatre she was a great originator, and a resourceful one when required. Brendan Behan, with *The Hostage* still unfinished, was unable to write while he was sober but at the same time would soon be dead if he started to drink. Joan bundled him into a small boat and put out to sea where rolling about in the swell induced feelings close enough to inebriation to make him completely happy; in this way she got the rest of the play out of him. However she had no experience nor understanding of the established procedures for making films, and no reticence about her opinion of those who did. Her producer Donald Taylor (no connection with John - except the tenuous one that *Donald* married Grierson's sister and Grierson married *John's* sister!) had been around for a very long time and was quietly laying his plans to control this madwoman; plans in which, as I can perfectly understand, we were to play no part. Anyone in his situation with a large amount of money to protect would wish to surround her with experienced people, and in his view that was certainly not us. However he kept quiet about it and I was taken on. In fact I was not quite so innocent as he thought I was and had concerns of my own about some of her declared intentions. There were to be no close-ups,

" I want to see all my actors together - not piecemeal. "
Obviously this is what happens in the theatre, but I feared it would be disastrous in the cinema. She was in fact right in one respect that I did not understand until, years afterwards, Frankie Howerd could not be persuaded into a close-up for a commercial we were doing,

" Comedy doesn't work in close-up. "
A moment's thought and of course it doesn't.

Nothing I *said* to Joan made any difference so I decided to *do* something. Let her choose a scene out of the script and we would shoot it her way - then she would see. What I ought to have done was shoot the scene fully but put all the cover shots out of the way and let her try to cut the thing without them. I was young however, with plenty to think about other than politics. So ironically it was my very attempt to guard Donald Taylor's interests which gave him the perfect excuse to fire me, which he promptly did, putting Max Greene in my place. Not that it mattered; as he did it by telegram on the Saturday before starting shooting on the Monday it was obviously prearranged and he'd have soon found a pretext if I hadn't supplied one.

I was prepared at the time to accept that he could have been justified in putting stolid old Mutz with her, except of course that it's pointless buying a Ferrari in order to stick a governor on it; the cinema has a long record of hiring people for their originality and then wanting them to be ordinary. As it turned out his tactics succeeded in wrecking the picture a lot more effectively than anything I could have done. Far worse, Joan was put off having any more to do with films. She was just ahead of her time - another year or two, and working with different people, might have seen some amazing things.

During our short time together we were looking for set-ups by the observatory at Greenwich and I said why not stick the camera on the meridian for a lark.

" You're nearly as bad as Brendan. We brought *him* up here, and when we showed him the meridian he pissed on it. "

Edgar was splendid. When I first told him I had been offered this feature to photograph he had said, with a great deal of wisdom and kindness,

" Don't give your notice in. I will arrange unpaid leave while you go off and shoot your film. Then you can come back to us for as long as you want; there's bound to be an hiatus before something else comes your way. "
So I just went back a bit earlier than expected, with some useful lessons learned. Getting fired in this game doesn't cause the harm that people think it does - there can't be many of us it hasn't happened to at least once; and certainly, if anyone doesn't want me, I don't want them !

Charles Potter told me long afterwards that Edgar had got Donald Taylor into his office and dressed him down.

In his way Edgar was a great man, but it was in the political not the creative world. He could persuade the sceptics of the value of films and defend his unit from all attacks, but the more imaginative an idea the more certain it was that Edgar would oppose it. Perhaps he was simply anticipating our Philistine sponsors and heading off difficulties for himself in advance, but it could be very disappointing.

A bare week before London's trams would disappear for ever Edgar's henchman Ian Ferguson told John Krish,

" John, old love, you're not doing anything on Saturday night I hope, because Ed wants you to be set up inside the New Cross depot from about nine. The Chairman of London Transport is going to be there to watch the last tram drive in and shake hands with the driver. You'll have four hundred feet" (about four minutes) "so you'll be fine."

Notice it is not the trams that are of interest here - just some old chairman making a speech. Edgar refused to sanction any other coverage, sensing perhaps that people so ashamed of their past as subsequently to bulldoze the Euston Arch would not be susceptible to tram-nostalgia. John, for his part, believed a film *must* be made and with the connivance of Edgar's assistant producer, John Shearman, purloined 2000ft from the stock cupboard, and I clearly remember giving them my short ends to help eke it out. This was an act of some altruism as these were a marketable commodity (anything less than 40ft was useless in a magazine and, if black and white, could be sold to photographers in Oxford Street).

So for that last week Krish and his cameraman Bob Paynter forged ahead in defiance of the production office, without a camera car and carrying all the equipment on and off buses. With the trams at the knackers and John's material safely in the can, Edgar was persuaded reluctantly to put it together. From there it went on to become the first Transport film to be selected at a festival and win, and to be one of the first to get theatrical distribution; at the time of writing it is still on permanent show at the Transport Museum. This lovely one-reeler carries Edgar's name as producer; but one of his best and most popular pictures was shot in spite of him, and though *The Elephant* may never forget John Krish, Edgar never forgave him and John did not work for Transport again until after Anstey's retirement.

He was then called back in 1978 because they wanted a short film to persuade children from getting injured or killed on the railway lines, and from throwing stones and other missiles at the trains in retaliation. John gave them a sardonic piece about a school sports day held on a railway track, with prizes for the greatest number of injuries sustained. Intended as amusing enough to retain the kid's interest and bloody enough to put them off further trespassing, THE FINISHING LINE was rejected by a large majority of teachers because it shook up the children (as it was meant to). So a product that did its job successfully was speedily withdrawn and replaced by a vapid admonitory film that probably had every child with any spirit climbing the nearest embankment.

Michael Clarke, another director at Transport, told me how he had made a thoroughly unsentimental film about Wales that showed the country opening up to new industries and using a short sequence of a miners' choir singing Handel's "All we like sheep" in such a way as to imply that they would no longer be endlessly shepherded down mines and into steel works. He had then gone off to do something, for an outside sponsor, in the Middle East and returned to find his picture re-cut, music from the Messiah plastered indiscriminately over the sound track, and everything back in cosy old Wales. It may be that Michael's irony was lost on his producer, but it is also likely that, as boss of the largest surviving documentary unit, the old Edgar had a more careful eye to the sensibilities of our masters than the young one who had made HOUSING PROBLEMS and ENOUGH TO EAT. Even without Edgar it was quite common for pictures to be interfered with in the cutting rooms - documentary films being naturally vulnerable in this respect, and one certain way to upset a director was for editors to claim, as they frequently did, to have "saved the picture on the cutting bench".

Edgar's selective obtuseness could not always be ascribed to looking over his shoulder at the sponsors; Rod Baxter's film about the Severn Tunnel is an instance. When the workings were inundated by an underground spring in 1880, the terrified workmen left hurriedly without closing the door behind them (they had probably not had nannies to inculcate this important habit in early life) and as long as it remained open the pumps could not make any headway. The door was 1000 feet up a tunnel full of debris which no diver could climb over dragging an air hose after him and the whole enterprise was only saved by a man named Lambert carrying his own supply of oxygen "in a knapsack" - the first time ever this invention was put to use. Siebe Gorman the makers of the equipment, still flourishing in 1958, were keen for us to re-enact the scene in a tank they used for training divers, equipped with observation windows - I wouldn't even have to get wet. One shot of a dim figure making his way over a couple of upturned skips and some baulks of timber, would have brought the whole film to life, but Edgar set his face against it from the start. It wasn't even going to cost him - Siebe Gorman were *giving* it to us, but he had I think a somewhat puritanical approach to "documentary"; Siebe Gorman's tank was not the real thing - that was OK for "features".

All considered I still believe on balance that Edgar was a good boss. Without him I don't think the unit would have survived; indeed after he went it didn't. I could not have had a better upbringing. I learned to improvise rapidly and to make do; yet if a job required any big tools they would be provided. I once asked to have eight brutes,

"Why is there only one word for Thesaurus?"

" Can you do it with six? "

" Of course I can. "

Also to be flexible in order to survive, never to compromise on fundamentals but when obviously defeated to give in gracefully.

More than thirty years after the Donald Taylor debacle, in the summer of 1994, I was very touched by a television documentary about Joan, and phoned-up someone who always knew her whereabouts.

" I'd like to send her a note. "

" Don't. Go and see her - she's staying in Victor Spinetti's house. "

I strolled down to Devonshire Place. Inside, a lady wearing the inevitable peaked cap sat on a sofa.

" Come and sit down, dear. "

She turned and looked at me.

" I was right. I knew you were good. "

It may not be overmodest to record this but it was such a great thing for me, simply because she was speaking from a time long before I had done anything for her to go by.

Although there was now no free pass into the great wide world to be had from SPARRERS I knew I'd soon have to leave in any case; outside I was quite unknown and as long as I stayed I could do nothing about it. While still at Transport I had done two things which were to prove helpful after I'd left - one in the short term, the other very much in the long term. The first resulted from Kodak bringing out a new colour film stock which I needed to test. I always regard tests as tedious affairs and suggested to Edgar that while I was at it I would make him a short film; let him choose a subject for me (like the school essays). He promptly suggested a large railway station. When I pointed out that John Schlesinger was down at Waterloo doing exactly that, all he said was that it might be interesting to have two points of view. At the time I simply thought it a bit odd but over the years I have come to appreciate the subtlety of Edgar's mind. John would be bound to hear about what was happening and I may have been Edgar's grain of sand in the oyster shell, especially as John had been offered my services to photograph his picture but had declined them on the grounds that anybody who was on the permanent staff of a place like Transport couldn't be much good, and had insisted on someone from the BBC (as if that was any better). Anyhow I chose to steer well clear of Schlesinger and went off to Paddington with John Burrows. The basic idea was to show things both as abstract forms and as they are ordinarily seen. It must have been the most economical picture ever made since I only ever did one take and every shot was used. This was not done on account of cost, I just like to work that way.

When I was teaching myself photography by doing stills I never made more than one negative for each subject. It is a case of deciding what you want beforehand as opposed to firing off 36 exposures and hoping that one of them will be a picture. Many years later I met Norman Parkinson and happened to mention this. He then told me about the time he spent as Cecil Beaton's assistant. Cecil would take his time arranging everything as he wanted it, the shutter would click, and Norman would start putting the camera away.

" But Mr Beaton you've only taken one photograph? "

" We only want one. "

I doubt if Myra Hess was ever called in on these occasions. There is probably a Webern piece brief enough, but the sitter might not be looking relaxed and happy.

Hugh Raggett cut Paddington Station together using some music by the Modern Jazz Quartet and the result was a sort of seven and a half minute TV commercial. When I showed it to Edgar I got told off. He didn't think it was a film at all, and I had been grossly extravagant printing everything in colour. Just how I was supposed to test a new colour stock by printing everything in black and white he was not able to tell me. The cutting copy lay untouched the rest of my time there and when I left I showed it around to anyone I could get to look at it. All my early freelance jobs I got on the strength of it and it was probably the saving of me.

"Why is there only one word for Thesaurus?"

Early Commercials

The second of the two things that happened just before leaving Transport which were so helpful afterwards, arose from a visit to Kenwood House one Sunday afternoon and seeing there a painting of a girl by Vermeer of Delft, himself a cameraman of sorts.

9

She was in a room lit by a single window plus whatever light would have been reflected naturally from the walls and floor. It is the only time ever that I have thought about a painting in relation to what I do (a sort of pretension I much dislike), but it did happen this once. I was doing a picture with Rod Baxter about London Transport at the time, called ALL THAT MIGHTY HEART, and there was a domestic scene with a housewife in Welwyn Garden City hoovering her front room before setting out on a Green Line bus to go shopping. Thinking there might be some Vermeer-like fun to be had with this (by aiming a single brute through the window and letting reflected light do the rest of the work) I ordered a pair of best quality, double-bed sized white sheets, which somehow arrived without question, and it all went well. The next day rushes were everything I'd hoped for.

Shortly afterwards, inside a bus repair depot, I asked Frank to set a 10k for me. No sooner was it switched on than smoke began to come from the housing. Frank, looking a bit upset, ran over and switched it off. He offered no explanation until later when he told me that he had hidden my sheets inside it prior to taking them home. Now they were ruined and I felt very sorry for Frank, in fact for the next few days I tried not to use any 10ks so as not to remind him of his loss.

Now that I knew the idea would work I kept it in reserve for when something needed to look beautiful in that particular way. In fact I didn't use it again until after starting on TV commercials, when I trotted it out on a scene with some young children, where once again it looked good.

By this time I was helping to stock up the linen-cupboards in quite a number of electrical households.

Long after reflecting sources had been absorbed into an overall lighting technique I reverted to the old "keylight filler and back" for a shot of a TV newscaster, which would certainly have been lit that way, and asked my operator what he thought of the result.

" It's a bit like Basil Emmott. "

Known as "Burn 'em up Basil" on account of a tendency to overlight his actors, Emmott enjoyed, oddly enough, the distinction of having photographed Grierson's DRIFTERS - so he must have been a good sailor at least.

Richard Lester, Madrid, 1973.

Among those early commercials was a Shredded Wheat film for Richard Lester, again with young children, so out came the sheets for another airing. Richard was pleased with the result and asked if I would like to do his next picture. There was a scene in it that took place in a white room, walls, floor, ceiling, everything. It was almost a law that anything that was white on a film set had either to be painted grey or else dipped in tea. An unnecessary sanction relicted, as these things usually are, from a time when it actually made sense (perhaps from the days of orthochromatic stock). I had never bothered with it and said that *of course* he could shoot in his white room. Possibly if I had spent all my time in features these traditions would have been more ingrained and I might not have questioned them; who knows? Richard then said that he was about to do some commercials for Lyons Quick-Brew Tea with Barbara Mullen. She lived in Dun Laoghaire in a house with an all white kitchen where we would shoot one of the commercials and find out what happened. I already knew Barbara because she was Mrs John Taylor - I was back with

"Why is there only one word for Thesaurus?"

old friends again. The white kitchen was fine in rushes but unfortunately in those days TV transmissions were guarded by a kind of Cerberus who would not allow such things under any circumstances; knobs were quickly adjusted, the white walls became grey, and Barbara looked like the black Madonna having a brew-up. This did not please anyone very much, apart from John of course who was vastly amused. Richard and I were both handed memos laying it down that for TV we should operate on the same principle as a chessboard i.e. equal areas of black and white. While it is true that video-electronics are not good at accommodating a wide contrast, as we shall see in a later chapter, I doubt if it was ever quite as primitive as that.

I began my freelance career just in time to work with two of the great operators of the 1940s and 50s, Gus Driss and Jeff Seaholm. Gus, by the time I knew him, had been ruined by drink. Jeff's work on the other hand remained flawless, though it must be admitted that he suffered fools a bit less gladly after lunch. He always wore a silk scarf tucked into an open-necked shirt and when lining-up never used the view-finder. He would just stand, feet slightly apart, leaning forward from the waist with his hands tucked into pockets of immaculate dog-tooth check. "Forty", he named the lens, and the grip, always at his side at these moments, extended two fingers holding a piece of chalk. By the time it hit the ground, leaving its tiny mark, Jeff had walked away and was back talking quietly to me about a French commercial where they had pronounced his name so as to rhyme with Guillaume. That was the set-up and it was never wrong. The story is told of a commercial set in a dentist's surgery with a black and white tiled floor. The tiles were in fact a patterned paper that had been pasted down, which meant that the heavy dentist's chair, once set in position, could not be moved again without ripping it up. Jeff, hands in pockets, leaned forward looking intently at the empty space before him and indicated a spot.

" The chair goes there. "

The art director, fresh from television, rushed over.

" No, no, we must wait for the camera. "

Without pausing to look round Jeff said quietly,

" I am the camera. "

He could be pretty ruthless with incompetents but he was invariably kind and charming towards me, which was a great compliment, and I took pains to deserve it. He was also the only operator that always called me "Sonny" and I think the only one I'd have wanted to.

Camera operating at that time demanded a level of expertise that seemed uncanny to a newcomer. This was on account of something called parallax - not the poem by Nancy Cunard but the name for a simple law of nature: that two separate objects cannot occupy the same exact position in space. One example of this is seats in opera houses, but it also applies to the film being exposed and the viewfinder, only one of which can be exactly behind the camera lens. It is obviously preferable to have the film behind the lens and locate the finder slightly to one side. This did not matter much until an actor came close on a lens such as a 50mm or 75mm, when if the operator could see him at all it meant that there would only be a photograph of one ear. This conflict of interests has since been resolved by sticking a piece of mirror on the front of the shutter with a prism at right-angles to it, but in those days operators took it all in their stride and made the correct allowance without thinking about it.

Skill of this order is awe inspiring to the young and it's to be hoped that they end up acquiring some of their own. If I pride myself on anything today it is that no electrician ever has to move a lamp unnecessarily on my behalf. Paul Wilson, an operator of a younger generation than Jeff (in fact he is the same age as myself), worked on Hitchcock's last film in this country. The next time we were together after that I asked what he was like.

" He was an old man and never got out of his chair. He'd ask what the lens was and then tell me exactly what the framing would be on the actors as they or the camera moved about the set. He was always right and if anything went slightly amiss during a take, before I could tell him about it - he told me. "

Paul remarked about this facility to Hitch who replied that he'd had to learn the lenses when he was young because Jack Cox (a great English cameraman of the 20s and 30s) would never let him look through the camera.

Sod's law for film sets decrees that however much time has been spent hanging around doing nothing, the moment activity and concentration are called for coincides exactly with someone thrusting a cup of tea and a bacon sandwich at you. Paul remarked on this when an exasperating instance of it happened to him, and the next afternoon at a quarter to four an assistant came up and said Mr Hitchcock wished to see him in his trailer - they were in Pinewood and the director's caravan was parked outside the stage. Inside Hitch was presiding over some Crown Derby, cucumber sandwiches, and a Dundee cake.

" I heard what you said yesterday Paul, and you were right. Today we'll both take our tea in peace, on condition that you don't talk about the film. How many children have you got? "

In the event, good family man though Paul is, they ended up talking about trains, both being railway enthusiasts. After a bit this was interrupted by an anxious first assistant,

" We need Paul on the set. "

" Paul - is having - his tea. "

It made me think of Tony Richardson, except of course that they would not have been discussing trains - more likely someone on the unit.

Another wonderful operator of my own generation was Alan McCabe. He and Paul had been a pair of young tearaways in earlier times but, whereas Paul settled down and became respectable, Alan stayed a roving vagabond of an artist all his life. He would be at home anywhere, was a splendid cook, and there was a slight air of mystery about him, exemplified by being always on time to the minute although he never wore a watch. When we had known each other for a number of years he once said

" You know, you and I have worked together on two films that will be classics of the cinema. "

He meant CHARGE OF THE LIGHT BRIGADE and CATCH 22, and perhaps looking back he was right; but then, Alan himself was a classic of the cinema.

A favourite manoeuvre of his was to take the Chapman crane right to the top and sit quietly above all the bustle in the set, and out of my reach to tease him. However the fact that the smallest detail never escaped his eye was something in Alan that I was usually able to exploit. One day in Merton Park we had a clapper-boy who was very new to the job and correspondingly anxious to please. I sent him to the studio restaurant with instructions to bring back a pot of coffee and a porcelain cup and saucer. Standing just underneath, where, although he would give no sign, Alan could not fail to see, I held the cup and saucer while the young man deferentially poured the coffee. He did it very carefully but, due to a flaw in design, the lid at the last moment fell into the filled cup with disastrous results. The poor lad was just about to dry me off with his handkerchief when the voice drifted down from above,

" You can do all my pictures from now on, Barry. "

Hopefully the last two stories will reassure everybody that due attention is paid to our staple beverages on British film sets.

Alan used to say that I reminded him of Pennington Richards and although this was a strong advance on Basil Emmott it still made me a bit nervous. I had met Penny Richards just once, sitting in awed silence in the theatre at Beaconsfield while he gave Ken Cameron (looking like a sprightlier version of the Earl of Airlie) an account of a visit to a friend's country cottage; after a drink or two he had gone into the garden and eaten all of his host's roses. It struck me at the time as eccentric behaviour on a level with biting people while having sex with them, and whenever Alan made this comparison, which he did quite often, I imagined someone sitting on a lawn surrounded by denuded rose bushes and worried that I fell short of what was required to live up to it; I also thought it would've been fun taking Penny to the Chelsea flower show. He'd then changed the subject to a running bet carried on with his current director; if he used more than three lights he had to pay the director, less than three and the director paid him,

" I was lagging behind until this scene that cried out for only a single lamp; after that he gave up. "

so I think I can see what Alan had in mind.

By this time I had spent about three years on commercials. There was one I remember (because it taught me a valuable lesson) where the art department had built a living-room set in Twickenham Studios. A pair of chairs which ought to have been Mies Van Der Rohe turned out unfortunately to be somebody else's and by 8.30am the department responsible had gone scurrying off in quest of the right ones. The rest of us carried on with the usual preparations but eventually everything was ready and we all stood about waiting for the chairs to arrive. Richard and I were talking together when he paused to look at his watch, turned to the first assistant and said that we would start shooting. I was puzzled by this as the correct chairs had not yet arrived. He then explained that if he waited any longer he would go into overtime that was not in the budget; the chairs had been worth waiting until 11 o'clock, but not beyond.

I always looked forward to the jobs with Wynne Films in Brighton, a self-contained little company with its own studio in a converted church in St Nicholas Road (it's nice to see the converting going the other way now and again). They were a delightful outfit, as anything with Jewish/Irish overtones has to be - the former supplied by the owner brothers and the latter by the production side, Paddy Nolan and his young assistant Pat Cahill. They also had one of the best camera operators, Cyril Gray. Cyril had one fatal flaw - half a glass of lager and he was beyond control. So long as he stayed in Brighton it was OK; he stuck to lime juice at lunch, and I declined all invitations to "stay on for a bit" when we wrapped. He was on first name terms with the entire Brighton police force from the frequent occasions when he was their overnight guest, as well as the taxi drivers who would always "see Cyril home" on those occasions when he wasn't.

The company also owned a small hotel in Rottingdean, where visiting actors or directors who needed to stop over were accommodated. The establishment is alleged to have supplied other forms of accommodation as well. Don Higgins, who had been an agency person before he became a director, said he was once offered a dissolute sojourn in Rottingdean in return for a batch of soap commercials. Much to my annoyance, at the very time I came to live in Brighton, Wynnes removed themselves to London, and the church reconverted to auction rooms. They seem not to have prospered in Dean Street; perhaps they'd underestimated the importance of Rottingdean.

There is a sad postlude to all of this. There was a girl in the early 70s (the date not her age) who combined writing historical novels with running a small second-hand bookshop in Kemp Town. She was having a good deal of trouble with her publisher, who wanted more feminine interest in her magnum opus on William the Conqueror than history has provided. While I was going through her shelves one day, somebody came in selling cheap ball-pens and suchlike. I could hear an amusing dialogue going on behind me and joined in a couple of times over my shoulder.

Weeks later I called in again to enquire after William the First.

" That man who came in last time you were here knew you. "
I was floored - if only Cyril had said who he was. He has been dead a number of years, but any Brighton taxi drivers who know what I work at, will still ask if I knew him.

The Common Market got away to an early start for some of us and by the end of the 60s I'd been invited to most of the countries of Western Europe. My first commercial in Germany took me by a strange chance back to the great Hanseatic city where I'd spent my final year as a soldier and which I'd last seen setting out from Altona station on the journey to the demobilisation centre in York. In a large area of wasteland known as the Heiligengeistfeld, a massive World War Two bunker and gun emplacement, Hochbunker, still dominates the skyline of the St Pauli district. With at least twenty feet of reinforced concrete around, above and below, some sensible person had decided that it would make an excellent film studio, and indeed for the sound department at any rate there could not be a better. Like a new boy at school I walked onto the crowded stage and was greeted by Fritz Mathies, one of Germany's most talented commercial directors, with a warm smile and a sweep of his hand,

" We built all this to keep you out, and now we are happy to invite you in. "

Two friends of mine Don McPherson and Nick Benstead had started a company which they called Radio Pictures (complete with the RKO Radio mast for its mascot). One of their films was for a DIY electric drill which, after boring through the living-room wall, reveals the kingdom of heaven on the other side of it. The set for this was conceived (like its prototype) on a very grandiose scale and designed for one of the large stages at Pinewood. But, as with an earlier light-bearer, Radio Pictures were cast into the exterior darkness to fall steadily downwards, by way of reductions in the celestial budget, until, with better luck than Lucifer, they managed to halt their descent at a small studio opposite Barnes Pond. Here there was space for only half a dozen angels and all rays of heavenly light had to be contrived by stretching pieces of fuse wire across the matt-box and cross-lighting them. However the camera lied quite happily and nobody knew any different.

An endearing thing about the steam locomotive used to be that a measure of skill on the part of its driver and fireman would bring out a corresponding improvement in its performance. The machine encouraged the best in the men, who in their turn brought out the best in the machine. Whatever hard discomfort there was on the footplate, they had a pride in their craft of a different order from what is derived from sitting in the cab of an electric vehicle turning the power and the brakes on and off. The same thing is true with arc lamps, which call for skill and care in order to make the light that in all other lamps arrives (or doesn't) with the click of a switch. In Munich at the start of one job I was enchanted by the sight of one of my sparks perched on top of a pair of tall steps burning a brute as ably as anyone could wish. In the ordinary way that is to be expected and does not give rise to enchantment but on this occasion the electrician was about twelve years old, if that. He turned out to be the son of the generator driver and did splendidly throughout the entire morning up until just before lunch when, spotting the approach of a sturdy hausfrau, he made a rapid descent, though sadly not rapid enough to save his Dad from a telling off.

Another job in Munich was rather more strange. We were in a doctor's house in the wealthy suburb of Grunewald and, when my side of things was completed, I wandered into the next room where there were some bookshelves. There is an irresistible fascination for me in a line of books, for one thing they tell you so much about their owner. What these had to impart was equivocal to say the least. To start with there were about a dozen Nazional Socialist Arbeits Partei booklets dating from 1931, followed by *Mein Kampf,* then a couple of biographies of Mr Nice-Guy himself. One was the standard work by Alan Bullock but the other, a massive volume, was by a German author. I took this down to look at and found that on the front endpaper someone had written "Ünserer Führer" below which, in two columns, about eight people had signed their names. This looked like going one worse than the family Bible but then, incongruously, its neighbour on the shelf turned out to be the *Diary of Ann Frank.* The high spot though, was a children's book published in Munich in 1939 called *Mother, tell us about Hitler.* There were illustrations of a Fagin-like character with a beard and skull-cap removing the last stick of furniture from a dismayed family of Aryans, and a pretty little Hitler Jugend getting beaten up by a band of very unattractive Communists. The owner of the house was not at home but I doubt whether meeting him would have told me any more than his books did.

In the world of commercials the absurdities of film making are compounded by those of advertising; a strong mix, especially when attempts are made to reconcile the latter with a code of ethics. An obsession with purity has always troubled the English, and soap and washing powders figured largely among the products receiving our attention. One such TV spot was of three small boys playing together. The mother of one, by means of the product, has clothed him in a shirt of dazzling white. The other two are presumably illegitimate because their shirts are noticeably less white and not dazzling at all. I said that this effect could be easily obtained by dressing these two in shirts that were pale grey. The advertising people were truly horrified at this, declaring that it was unethical; a stronger light must be arranged to fall on one than on the other two. I pointed out that photographically the two things were exactly the same, but for ethical reasons the clumsier method was adopted. I was quite happy to do what they wanted, especially as I was able to show them

"Why is there only one word for Thesaurus?"

that in fact the whitest shirt on the set was being worn by our focus-puller, a dapper youth named Spratling.

The finest washing-powder spot of all, however, was of a round table discussion chaired by a disc-jockey of the time called Tim Gudgin. A dozen housewives were gathered from all parts of the British Isles and six camera crews assembled to film them. Mr Gudgin got them going as to why they preferred the product to all other brands and six cameras churned away in the hope that the ladies would say something of interest. One of them did,

" .... it's the only one that gets the stains out of my son's pyjamas .... "
Editors again being what they are this was not used.

Just as my first appearance on a cinema screen had been the title background for the documentary FLOODS IN THE NORTH so my maiden appearance in the feature world was with the title backgrounds for somebody else's film - Ted Moore's GOLDFINGER, one of the Bond movies. Working on commercials for Hugh Hudson I had met a most original and inventive graphic designer named Robert Brownjohn. BJ as he liked to be called (either because he was an American or wished to be thought one) came up with an idea of projecting clips from the film onto the naked body of a young lady entirely covered in gold make-up. He was given one of the Twickenham stages for a week and told to go there and direct it himself. He then very kindly asked me to join him.

This was my first experience of any kind of process and I thought quite carefully about it. The only problem I could foresee was that the blue arc-light of the projector would, like an alchemist in reverse, transform gold into silver. This could be easily prevented by a standard 85 correction filter, and having done this amount of homework I arrived on the stage at Twickenham full of confidence and calm. This was just as well, as I was confronted by a process technician strutting about the stage like a farmyard cock, festooned with light-meters, and telling everyone else on the set how to do their jobs. Luckily I did not allow him to interfere with my side of things and quietly stuck to what I'd already decided. The next morning the otherwise perfect material was badly unsteady and all had to be re-shot owing to our voluble friend having failed to check his print sprockets. He then blamed the laboratory.

BJ was like an excited child and taking alternately one colour of pills for up and another for down from a Georgian silver snuff-box. He was continually exhorting the crew to get a move on, but they were far too fond of him to mind and simply carried on normally. I was standing next to him during an unusually quiet spell when he clicked a stop-watch that he had in his hand and shouted at the crew to hurry up. He then looked at the watch and turned to me,

" I've been timing myself to see how long I could keep quiet but it's no use - I'm a born leader ... "
As he said this he seemed suddenly struck by an amazing idea

" ... you know what I've just realised? I'm in charge of all these people - one, two, three ..... "

I got called away before he had finished his head count but he soon came over, awed and delighted, and gave me the total.

In 1963 Christopher Miles directed a short film at the old World Wide studios in Chancery Lane. THE SIX-SIDED TRIANGLE parodied

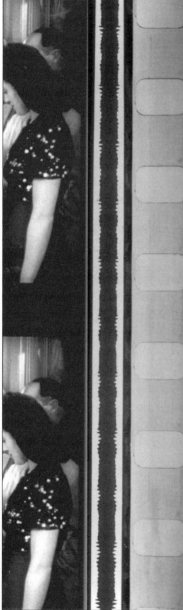

Optical sound-track.

fashions in the cinema by representing the wife and lover interrupted by husband situation six times over; French - Godard, Swedish - Bergman, British - Asquith (anybody for tennis), Italian - dolce vita, Japan - Kurosawa, and to begin with, Valentino's silent sheik. The Bergman skit, at least, was a clear success because the Swedes insisted on its removal before allowing the five-sided triangle to be shown in Sweden - you can take the piss out of the Italians, the French, and the Japanese, but not us! Christopher had his sister, Sarah, doing the wife, and Nicol Williamson overdoing the lover. At least I'd got my show reel out of British Transport Films for nothing; poor Chris had had to sell his flat.

The sets were cleverly done by Bernard Sarron, starting off a career-long love/hate relationship with the art department, with love. I had a glorious time mimicking other people's lighting styles, and for Rudolf Valentino tried to copy something else as well. Film stock in the silent days was all orthochromatic, only sensitive to the blue end of the spectrum; it simply did not perceive red at all, so that if a red and a black object were photographed side by side the red would come out the more intense black of the two. It had long ago disappeared, giving place to panchromatic emulsions with much broader sensitivities. However, magnetic recording had not reached the cinema yet, sound tracks were still recorded photographically, and I

"Why is there only one word for Thesaurus?"

discovered that sound stock was still orthochromatic. It was very slow, needing masses of light, but I have seldom been put off by those considerations. When the time came it was a trifle disconcerting to find that Bernard had dressed the entire set with velvet hangings, cushions and carpets in all shades of red, but luck held as usual and it all came out quite convincing.

There is an interesting aspect to photographic, or optical sound, as it was called. The old editors were so skilled in handling it that instead of running the sound through the moviola together with the picture, they just held it up to the light and read it. I can remember watching fascinated while Mac, engulfed in celluloid, would run it through his hands like a seaman preparing to throw a rope, and pick out the single word on which he wanted to cut.

Finally, in October 1964, before embarking on the first feature film, my thoughts went back twelve years to a day on a canal tow-path in the Midlands when I was assisting Ritchie. Two untidy kids were observing us with keen eyes.

" That's not clever what you're doing - I could do that. "
Jimmy finished the shot, cut the camera and locked it off.

" You're absolutely right it's not clever at all. What *is* clever is to get someone to pay you to do it. "

"Why is there only one word for Thesaurus?"

The Knack, and the Beatles

One benefit that I gained from this first film was that it disposed once and for all of any idea of having an agent.

10

Because his first feature is so important to a young cameraman production companies are sparing of their munificence; to their mind he's lucky to be doing it. That's fair enough and Woodfall were probably more fair than most. Nonetheless £100 per week in 1964 was less than I would have got doing commercials. Richard Lester therefore offered the loan of his agent and gave me a number to call. "Leave them to me", I was told, and when the gentleman phoned back about a week later he certainly sounded pleased, "I've got them up to £110 for you". The mathematics were not difficult even for me - without an agent £100, with an agent £99; it suggested that I didn't need one, it was not as though he'd found the job in the first place. But there is a greater advantage in not having an agent than merely saving his ten per cent, which is that there is nobody touting you around to half-interested directors and producers. People who phoned me had only their own motivation to do so.

You may have noticed that entering the world of feature films coincides with the first mention of serious money in this narrative. That is natural enough, money plays a different role where features are concerned - they are expected to make it. Now there is a snag as regards the good management of resources on a movie and it is that what may look like perfectly good sense on paper can add up to total nonsense on the floor, and I was about to witness a fine old example of it. Woodfall's production manager was a rather foolish man, Leigh Aman, who because he'd inherited the title of Lord Marley in 1952, was constantly mocked by

Tony Richardson - "What has the noble Lord got to say?" But all that I was to learn in the future.

Quite appropriately, Leigh's single moment of success (the one time somebody didn't listen to him when they should have) had nothing to do with films. He was returning from the US on a Boeing 707, in the early days of the big jets and when Northolt was London's second airport, used only for European flights like a sort of little brother for Heath Row. After a glance out of the window to look at England, always a welcome sight to a returning traveller, he called the stewardess and asked her to inform the captain that he was making a wrong approach.

" We are going into Northolt."

The space waitress disappeared up front but soon returned with a reassurance that,

" Our pilots know what they are doing."

" Well I can promise you this one doesn't - I flew from here all through the war and the runway's too short for one of these."

I remembered driving to Beaconsfield for a music session and passing underneath the the wing of a giant aircraft that had barely managed to stop short of the A40 dual carriageway. It had stood there looking embarrassed for a couple of weeks until, by stripping everything out, they were able to lighten it enough to fly off to the right airport.

Because it was my first time, Leigh would not allow me to have the camera operator I asked for and, unwilling to risk the sort of obloquy that had been heaped on BOAC's unfortunate pilot for ignoring it, everyone was now heeding Leigh Aman's advice like mad. So instead of Paul Wilson I was given somebody quite inexperienced who undertook the task for £5 a week less money. He was naturally slower, which put time on the job; and an optical blow-up, required to remove a microphone that was upstaging the actors, not only degraded the scene, but cost more than had been saved by not having my choice in the first place. Had "the noble Lord" been made to look an idiot in consequence, something might have been learned, but nothing would link the loss of money, time, and the quality of the film to him - it would simply be blamed on the unit. Of course this sort of silliness doesn't happen when there is a production manager, and there are some, able to understand that decent looking pictures are not by nature in conflict with decent looking accounts.

In this instance it made even less sense because after the large profits from many of their films, especially TOM JONES, Woodfall, for tax reasons, needed to do a film that would lose money. They may have thought the combination of Richard and myself a sure way to bring this about, but when the attempt ended in failure and the picture made another enormous gain Tony Richardson suggested to Oscar Lewenstein, whose production it was, that I should have a percentage of the profits. Oscar, never an open-handed soul, thought that would never do.

" If David had money we wouldn't be able to get him when we wanted

"Why is there only one word for Thesaurus?"

him."

To think that having money would prevent anyone working for people they liked strikes me as odd now as it did then, but I suppose it is natural for communist millionaires to have odd ideas. He was small and slight in stature, bearing an uncanny resemblance to Bertrand Russell; Wolf Mankovitz once wickedly described him as a sabre-toothed mouse. Though I liked Oscar and he was tireless in what he did for the theatre (films not so much) he certainly had a reputation for being unlavish. There is a famous entry in Joe Orton's diaries, when he and Kenneth Halliwell stayed at the house in Shoreham, lamenting that they were never offered a cup of tea the whole time they were there. Shortly after *The Orton Diaries* were published I ran into Oscar in a local bookshop.

" Why didn't you give them a cup of tea, Oscar? "

" They could have had one, they could have had a cup of tea - they didn't ask for one. "

When a film finishes shooting there is always an end of picture party, but somebody at Woodfall had the bright idea that this time a party should be held at the beginning, a day or two before the start of shooting. (That alone would have paid for my operator come to think of it). For my first entrance into features, where I was quite unknown to everyone, I had no mind to go on display and said politely that I would not be coming. This had Richard on the phone,

" You must come and get to know everybody you'll be working with. "

" You don't get to know by going to parties - after the first day's work we'll know each other all right. "

I went to the end of picture party instead.

We had a scene outside the Albert Hall where a rally of Tolen's admirers is taking place. It involved a large crowd of young girls all in identical costumes of a dazzling white material, what little there was of it. Throughout the morning, whenever a door into the hall was opened, faint snatches of Handel would drift out so there was obviously a rehearsal going on. Towards lunchtime we were set up outside the artist's entrance with a milling throng of our extras when Sir Malcolm Sargent emerged. I'd often seen this very assured musician on the concert platform but this was the first time I'd ever seen him disconcerted (again pun accidental). Just for a moment he thought they had gathered to see him; he was still more put out when he realised that they hadn't.

A few days into the shooting the sound mixer, an enchanting man, asked me if I had managed to fuck anything up yet.

" I don't think so. "

" Well should you happen to, let me know whereabouts, then when we get to it in the rushes I'll turn the sound all the way up and they won't notice. "

" That's very kind. "

" Not at all, you can do the same for me; if there's a bad patch of sound, run through the focus on the projector - it's just as effective."

Dicky Bird died as the result of a completely unnecessary accident on a picture. He used to send me postcards from time to time; the last one read simply,

" How are you? I'm still getting away with it, Dicky. "

As this book will continue to show, the film business is an odd affair; after waiting years to do a feature I was suddenly confronted with a choice of two at the same time. Stanley Donen was going to do a picture with Sophia Loren and Gregory Peck and wanted to meet, so one evening I went along to his home in the Bayswater Road opposite Hyde Park. Stanley came into the room wearing a pair of purple velvet slippers with a large SD embroidered on each foot in gold thread. On a previous interview where gold thread was involved I had not taken the job; there was also an atmosphere of "de haut en bas" that I was not keen about. Mainly though, it just seemed a bit too soon to embark on something like this with two actors, nice though I knew them to be, who were both at an age when they would be concerned about their looks. Richard heard about it and said that he had intended to ask for me on his next film which was to be with the Beatles. When he added that *they* didn't give a toss about how they looked, he was echoing my own thoughts, so there was nothing left to be said other than thanks. Donen's producer got quite annoyed when I told him.

" People in your situation don't turn down a picture with Donen. "

" Someone in my situation just has. "

" Well you'll never work with him from now on. "

Years afterwards when I was asked if I was available for a Donen picture I was busy and had to say no - so he was right.

My second film started off with some shooting in the Bahamas, at that time still a British colony. I remember a birthday party given for George by an unattractive Swiss doctor friend or satellite, which gave an insight into the behaviour of the four boys - that whenever it was deplorable there was probably a good reason. Came the moment to cut the cake, they went completely wild, slashing it to pieces like a quartet of maniacs. There was a very nasty edge to it that disgusted me and I said so to Richard. He explained that at the last moment they'd found out it had only been laid on for a publicity stunt, decided enough was enough, and were making sure it couldn't be used.

The trip out to Nassau had been on a charter 707, which landed in the small hours of the morning at Kennedy airport for refuelling; everyone had to get off the plane and go through the US immigration, though goodness knows why since we were getting straight back onto it. Trooping aboard again, Richard seemed more amused than annoyed at having had to sign a declaration that his son Dominic was not a communist ; Dominic was three years old at the time and as Richard said "at that age everybody is".

The four Beatles shared a gargantuan zest for just about everything, it was like being with four boisterous and precocious children. They suffered, for the most part admirably, the constant intrusions of the public with what is best described as good-natured rudeness. Sunday in the hotel there was a serve-yourself buffet and I was standing in the queue behind the four lads. Next to them an American matron unfortunately provided an opening by saying to Paul

" You're Paul aren't you? "

" John. "

she addressed John,

" Then you must be Paul. "

" George. "

" Well but you're all so young, I wouldn't like to tell you *my* age. "

in chorus,

" We'd HATE you to tell us your age. "

How the four of them managed an identical response, unrehearsed and completely together I cannot explain; I can only suppose it had happened before.

One evening during dinner a small package was handed to John which turned out to be the first copies from the press of his second book, *A Spaniard in the Works*, and they were handed around the table for us all to look at. I've never had any qualms about asking an author to sign one of his books for me but this seemed rather close to asking an actor for his autograph and I hesitated too long over it. Richard was less diffident and John wrote something in one of the books and handed it to him; later when he came to look inside he was a bit surprised to find an inscription "... from George" - but only a bit. Curiously a third book, of political opinions, was never published, although proof copies dated 1972 are known to exist.

My first encounter with John had certainly supported the idea that the Beatles did not care how they would look on the screen. Each time that I went anywhere near him with a light-meter he quietly told me to fuck off, testing as children and animals do, where the boundaries lay. The first couple of times drew absolutely no reaction but the third time I said to him that I was paid to photograph a wide variety of objects - two years ago it might have been a railway train or a power station but at the moment, among other things, it happened to be his face; it was all the same to me. After that we got on very well. He had a rare and enviable independence of mind. One mealtime there was an argument about the exact meaning of a word and one of the discutants claimed the authority of the Complete Oxford dictionary.

" So? Some feller wrote that."

Our first set in Nassau was in the grounds of the native hospital, whose buildings consisted only of some straggling wooden huts. While we were laying a track (which took so long it was the last track ever in any of

Richard's pictures), the boys wandered around inside only to be appalled by everything they set eyes on; dirt and neglect, the patients lying on straw in the stifling heat without any water to drink. Now oddly enough the Beatles were always an object of fascination to those people who regard themselves as the English upper class (invariably to be seen looking inane in countless photographs within the pages of Tatler) so at the end of the first week a banquet was held at Government House. Mr Lennon was placed next to the Governor and right away enquired of that worthy when he had last paid a visit to our hospital. John was able to project his voice, without a hint of shouting, into the far corners of any room he happened to be in, and although the crown's representatives are skilled at brushing awkwardness under the table cloth, this time it didn't work, John was like a ferret with a rat.

It must have been a long while since anything as good had happened out there; 1943 probably, when Alfred de Marigny had suggested to a previous incumbent (and it's uncanny how like John this sounds)

" If you were of any consequence you wouldn't be presiding over this pimple on the arse of the British Empire. "

That had been occasioned by the then governor, the Duke of Windsor, interesting himself, too much rather than too little, in black people by diverting their water supply into the swimming pools of the white and wealthy. This led the unreasonable blacks to die and become ill. Marigny was alarmed at the prospect of an epidemic and his protest probably owed more to self interest than it did to altruism. Either way his reward was to be framed for the murder of Harry Oakes - two birds with one stone since the governor had one person to protect and another on whom to be revenged.

Back in England we went down to Cliveden, the stately home belonging to Lord Astor, and where the Profumo affair had all begun a couple of years earlier. This noble Lord, true to form, wished to meet the Beatles before shooting started and all the crew stood in the great hall while the old aristocrat tottered down his marble staircase. John was very polite.

" I must say it's a fair pad you've got here, Lord Asthma. "

At Lord Asthma's suggestion those on the unit who felt themselves able were invited to race once around his carp pond for the prize of a bottle of vintage champagne. I wondered if this was a diversion that was always offered to his guests, and tried to imagine Christine Keeler and Mandy Rice-Davis chasing Mr Profumo around his lordship's carp. The contest was won with ease by the four Beatles, although in what order I do not recall. They however declined his lordship's Dom Perignon in favour of a sniff each from his oxygen bottles. Whether this request was granted I do not know.

At this period I was passing through a phase of tactile and olfactory inquisitiveness and, although oxygen bottles did not interest me, I used

"Why is there only one word for Thesaurus?"

to feel and smell the bark of trees and on picking up a new book would bury my face in its pages. Directors are observant beings and Richard had noticed this habit of mine. For one of the Cliveden scenes I thought about using a gauze, I can't think why - it must have been a joke of some kind. I hate diffusion and so never carry any nets or gauzes with me; then I remembered that the current Lady Astor had previously been Bronwen Pugh, a well known fashion model, so I went across and asked her if she could lend me a black silk garment of some sort. She was very obliging, went off to have a look and appeared a few minutes later descending the grand staircase waving a pair of black silk knickers which she handed to me with a gracious smile. This caused Richard to offer a really unnecessary admonition.

" Smell those and you're off the picture. "

HELP opens with the Beatles throwing darts at a cinema screen (had they hailed from Manchester and not Liverpool, I might have suspected them of being former inmates of Rose Hill) and as darts, obviously, won't stick into a translucent screen, rear-projection was ruled out, leaving front projection and blue-screen to choose from. The respective masters of these techniques were both employed by the Rank Organisation based at Pinewood and in all innocence I said to get them down to Twickenham and help us decide which to go with. They did that all right; as soon as they saw each other there was a stand-up fight from which the blue screen oracle was ultimately forced to retire from the field.

By now my lighting techniques had made me an object of derision with the more conservative practitioners of the craft: "who's this young upstart that aims his lights away from the actors?" One day at Twickenham I found my director talking with a tubby, baldish gentleman whom he introduced to me as Otto Heller. Almost at once Richard was called away; Otto looked up at a large white reflector hanging over the set and observed charitably,

" Is a gimmick, you won't last. Your director now, *he* has talent. "
I said I was glad somebody had it. In the event what didn't last was the ridicule (gradually replaced by imitation) and I still rather miss it.

While in Austria for a skiing sequence we all had a day off in Salzburg. I went in the morning to see Mozart's house and had just left there when I ran into our American producer, Walter Shenson, with his son, a quiet little boy of about ten or eleven. Big Walt was his usual affable self.

" Hi, say do you know where Mose-art's house is? "
I told how to get there.

" It's his first time here and all he wants to do is see this Mose-art's house. I've got a nutty son. "
He shook his head and walked away leaving me to remember Beethoven scratching his way through an old wireless speaker into the mind of a boy much the same age as Shenson's kid. And a large cushion.

I was to get a further uncanny reminder of those days of my pre-war childhood a few weeks later. Between pictures I was happy to return to TV commercials; apart from being enjoyable they afforded some useful independence - it wasn't necessary to do a rubbishy film just because there was nothing else. One of these spots was set in a lorry driver's cafe down on the old Great West Road just past London Airport.

My mother's best friend, of much earlier standing than Maisie Smith (although built upon similar lines) was Gwendolyn Ida Palmer Cotton. Called Gipsy because of her initials, she was, although no relation, always Auntie Gipsy so far as I was concerned. She and her husband came to stay with us every summer, a visit always welcomed by me as she was good fun and never departed without giving me half-a-crown. Their arrival one year serves as a fine example of how children contrive to get themselves completely misunderstood. Very excited and hoping they were here for a long stay, I greeted her on the doorstep,

" Hullo Auntie Gipsy, when are you going back? "

Her adult mind at once drew the wrong inference and she was mortally offended. I was ignored for two weeks and, when to all round relief they departed, there was no half-crown.

Perhaps she was now feeling a twinge of remorse on the other side. There used to be students patrolling the sands at Margate carrying cumbersome post-card size reflex cameras. They took pictures of everybody and the next day these were displayed in racks each bearing a number, you then went along and ordered what you wanted. Back in the lorry driver's cafe on the Great West Road thirty five years later I had finished my part of things and wandered round the set looking at the dressing. Suddenly I was staring at an old post-card photograph of a lady in a deck-chair. It is a Margate Corporation deck-chair, the lady is unquestionably Gipsy, and the bucket and spade close by are certainly mine. My immediate reaction was of considerable relief that no one on the unit would see their cameraman wearing a sailor suit; the photographer must have been a feature operator - he had framed me out.

On another job in Stratford-on-Avon, for some reason the whole unit had dinner together and were ranged on both sides of a long refectory table. I was sitting at about the centre on one side, directly facing the gentleman from the advertising agency, who I noticed had been drinking a little. Suddenly in the middle of dinner he asked if I had any children.

" No. "

" Are you married? "

" No. "

" Are you queer? "

" Yes. "

This shut him up as I'd thought it would and the silence that followed was swiftly broken by my gaffer electrician, Roy Rodhouse.

" Well he don't tell lies anyway. "

I remembered from 1943 that interviews conducted across refectory

"Why is there only one word for Thesaurus?"

tables were liable to consist of silly questions. So I had landed squarely outside the closet; I had been a half-hearted occupant anyway.

"Why is there only one word for Thesaurus?"

How I Won the War

*The next picture with Richard was called HOW I
WON THE WAR. He had really wanted to do Catch
22 but Warner Brothers were hanging onto the rights.*

11

Charles Ryan's HIWW was an English book that with elements added from *Dingo*, by Charles Wood who wrote the screen-play, had much the same underlying idea. In it Michael Crawford leads a platoon of soldiers through World War 2 getting one of their number killed in each campaign. Contemporary wartime black and white newsreels were cut together with our own material and the completed scene was then tinted a specific colour (Dunkirk - yellow, Arnhem - blue and so on). Instead of disappearing, the dead soldiers keep their places in the platoon, never speaking, and each with his battle-dress dyed the same colour as the scene in which he has been killed.

It sounds cumbersome but it works, moreover it introduces us to Denis O'Dell. He was Richard's producer, Irish, quick-witted and charming, which was a great help with our armed services who might not have given us much in the way of assistance had they known more about what we were up to. One necessity was to borrow a squadron of tanks and surprisingly, after the War Office had been sent a truncated version of the script, these arrived. We started off, as is often the way, shooting the last scene in the picture first and right in the middle of it their Brigadier turned up unannounced. Out to see for himself what we were getting up to with his tanks, what he in fact saw was Michael Crawford leading his platoon of polychrome ghosts across the Rhine bridge.

Brig   " Good God ! What on earth's that? "

Denis " A test for Technicolor, Sir. "

Another requirement was a landing-craft for an invasion scene to be shot on a beach in the south of Spain. Philip, our art director, a young man on his first film, had been shown a very nice one in Cadiz without anybody mentioning that, due to lacking most of the hull below the water-line, it had been sitting comfortably on the bottom of the harbour for the past twenty years. Perhaps they were making up for what we did to their king's beard some time before; at all events Philip (ours not theirs) soon found out when the time came to sail the thing round the coast to Almeria. While a conference was taking place as to the best way to film an army being put on shore without any boats our director glanced out to sea and noticed some warships on the horizon.

" What's that? "

" The American fleet on manoeuvres. "

" Get Denis .... "

The American Admiral was very nice and said that anything was alright by him so long as we got an OK from Washington. When Washington cabled a firm refusal, Denis somehow, after several "pink gins all round" in the wardroom, managed to persuade the officers on board the flagship that Washington had in fact said "yes".

And so for a day we had the illicit use of an LCT and two destroyers belonging to someone else's country. It is the only time that I ever saw Denis looking worried.

" Just be as quick as you can, Richard. "

During the German part of our filming John Lennon arrived at the remote inn on the Luneberg Heath where we were all staying. His role as a British army private called for some curtailment of his hairstyle and while this was being effected, Denis's son Sean, who was fifteen at the time and must have been reading Alexander Pope, strolled into the room and picked up one of the fallen locks.

" John, will you sign something to say that this is your hair? "

" No - but I'll sign something to say that it *was* my hair. "

As well as John's hair Sean was given a part in the film. Michael Hordern delivers a long and disjointed monologue in a 1914-18 dug-out with Sean as a little cadet singing "Keep the Home Fires Burning".

The day before we were to do this, someone from construction remarked that he was relieved now they had finished the set.

" Why - it can't have been that difficult? "

" No it wasn't, but halfway through, a squadron of tanks arrived and started firing 18-pounder guns only twenty yards away, and now they're at it all day long. "

" Have you mentioned this to Richard - there's about eight pages of dialogue? "

Came the day and the noise was indescribable. Long afterwards, while grading the finished film, I said to Richard that they had done an amazing looping job with that scene.

" There wasn't any looping, we used actual sound. "

" But .... "

" Michael's concentration and timing were so good that wherever we lost words behind the gunfire we were able to drop them in from another take and they always fitted. "

That gives an insight into the professionalism of actors, or some actors at least.

"Why is there only one word for Thesaurus?"

Peter Brook

The word genius has been misapplied so often that it has become almost impossible to use it at all, but if it belongs anywhere perhaps it is with Peter Brook.

12

His stage production of the *Marat Sade* with the Royal Shakespeare Company was to be filmed at Pinewood studios with Michael Birket producing, and I was asked to photograph it. Meanwhile Woodfall were setting out to make a trilogy of three short stories, each with a different director; Lindsay Anderson THE WHITE BUS, Tony Richardson RED AND BLUE, and Peter a slight comedy, written by himself, for just two actors. Oscar Lewenstein fancied the idea of my doing all three of them, to which end I was taken to lunch with Lindsay. He was fascinated by my documentary past and we had a great time talking about Ken Cameron and Grierson and the rest; he then went off and used Miroslav Ondricek, whom he had wanted in the first place.

I had a lot more lunches with Lindsay later on when he was playing opposite Gielgud in CHARIOTS OF FIRE. Hugh Hudson and I invented a simple game of introducing somebody's name into the conversation. With Lindsay this was like dropping a sucking pig into a tank of piranha-fish; whosoever, they were instantly torn to shreds. We planned for me to eat one day at a different table, to see what happened when Hugh mentioned Watkin, but never got around to it (the outcome was quite foreseeable anyway). It must be stressed that none of this could ever be a reason for not liking Lindsay, he was much too real for that.

Peter's story was based on an experience he'd had while rehearsing *Boris Godunov* at Covent Garden. Boris Christoff, disliking some piece of direction he'd been given, had stormed off to his dressing room. Peter, knowing that all the dressing rooms had speakers in them so that singers could always hear the stage and thus not miss their entries, quietly put the understudy into one of the great moments in Christoff's part, leaving operatic vanity to do the rest. The singer returned, pushed the poor understudy aside, and took over "in mid-note".

THE RIDE OF THE VALKYRIE had Zero Mostel playing an opera singer summoned from Vienna to replace a sick Wotan at the Royal Opera House. His plane arrives so late into Heathrow that he decides to change into his costume in the back of the limousine, chauffeured by Frank Thornton, that is taking him to the theatre. With the camera occupying the place of the front passenger seat, Peter had a platform fixed outside so that he could watch his actors through the window. There was a heavy blizzard at the time and I expressed some concern that a man of his age should be thus exposed to the elements. He smiled and asked how old I was.

" There you are then - we're the same age. "

" When is your birthday? "

Even the day was the same.

Everything went well to begin with but it wasn't long before Zero began to expand his performance. Nothing surprising about that except to Peter, who took him aside and suggested quietly that he was overacting. Zero's reaction to this was similar to that of Boris Christoff; though he didn't storm off his affections were a bit estranged. He had once suffered an injury to his legs in a road accident and they occasionally gave him trouble. At one point in a rehearsal he rather abruptly asked Peter to get him a chair. Apart from looking round for an assistant to go and get one Peter took no notice and Zero yelled at him,

" Brook you're *unreasonable*! "

There was not the slightest reaction from Peter and everything carried on as before. I don't remember whether the chair arrived or not.

Later in the shooting Peter asked for some small thing or other which was no problem at all, but I couldn't resist it

" Go on like this and I'll have to tell you you're unreasonable. "

" Ah, you know what that was worth - two days good behaviour. "

Working with Peter is as though never before was there any such thing as a film camera to tell a story with. His mind is completely open and in no way conditioned by established practices, though he understands perfectly what they are, as well as the commonly good reasons on which they are founded. It is very refreshing and we should all do it once in a while, like a spell on a health farm.

Towards the end of the little film with Zero, Peter was talking about our crew and which of them he wanted to take with him on MARAT SADE. It made perfect sense until he came to our nice but unassertive continuity girl.

" Why Pamela? "

Peter lifted both hands,

"Why is there only one word for Thesaurus?"

" She never says a word. "

He then went on to explain how, when he was making THE LORD OF THE FLIES, he had taken his cast of 12 to 14 year olds to a quiet tropical island for the whole of the summer holidays, and to help keep them amused had given them their own 16mm camera. One day they came and asked him what all this "continuity" was about. "Well", he explained, "suppose we took a shot of you walking down your High Street at home, and then we took another shot of you walking down the same street but you had a cat on your shoulder; the second shot would be out of continuity with the first one". They went off, happy with this comprehensive explanation, and eventually showed him a film they had made themselves, in which every shot was deliberately out of continuity with the one before it.

" It really was very good. "

While we were doing the final scene, on the stage of the Royal Opera House, Peter suggested that I should light a play for him. Nothing ever came of it and that is almost certainly for the best. Stage lighting is a specialised craft and the theatre is full of talented and imaginative people exercising it. Such did not appear to be the case with architectural schemes however, and when invited to undertake the lighting scenario for a water theme-park being constructed at Thorpe near Chertsey, I agreed to it.

There are no committees anywhere near a film production - otherwise nothing would ever get done properly, so I was unprepared when asked to go along and explain my ideas. The main surprise was a hirsute individual who had come in from Rotterdam. This Karl Marx look-alike was introduced as "a lighting designer who has done this sort of thing before". He certainly had and confirmed it at once by countering every suggestion of mine, even the most ordinary, with a more commonplace alternative. Nobody else said a word, but the architect looked embarrassed. After a bit I told them they were clearly under a misapprehension that I took part in competitions - this was not the case. I then went back to Brighton and sent them a bill, which they argued about paying.

THE RIDE OF THE VALKYRIE was never shown. Peter was too involved in the MARAT SADE to see it through the cutting rooms himself and the task fell to Lindsay who self-effacingly edited his own film to 45 minutes and cut Peter's down to seven. The other two were released on their own.

MARAT SADE is based on a historical fact. While in the insane asylum at Charenton, the Marquis de Sade had produced plays with his fellow inmates which were given in the bathhouse of the institution before an audience composed of the governor and his friends. In the theatre the proscenium is the natural division between the audience and the players but Peter was anxious to avoid anything that would turn the film into merely a photographed stage production, so he devised a simple solution by dividing the Pinewood set into two halves separated by a grille of iron bars.

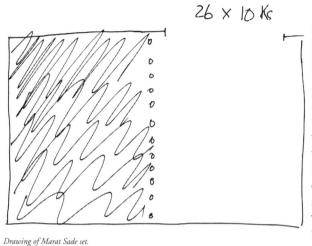

26 × 10 Ks

Drawing of Marat Sade set.

I had realised from the start that it would be impossible to light every set-up and finish the shooting within the schedule that we had, which was three weeks. It would not be difficult to light in a way that would allow Peter to go in any direction without making adjustments but that kind of lighting soon gets boring; however his iron bars gave me an idea. In the theatre the bathhouse set was all white tiles and this was to be retained at Pinewood, so I asked for the audience side of the bars to be painted completely black. That gave us an oblong set divided into two equal squares, one white and one black with the bars in between. Then as a single light source to serve both halves I had the art department build a giant translucent screen along the whole of one side of the white square at right angles to the bars.

Once the set was up I walked over it with an old Pinewood gaffer, Tommy Heathcote, and explained that it needed as much light as possible to come through the tracing-paper screen but that also I should be able to look at it from any position inside the set without seeing one hot-spot from a lamp - the screen must appear completely even. When I returned four days later it was done perfectly (using twenty six 10ks), the only lighting used throughout the film. This now meant that Peter could put his camera anywhere inside the set, pan it around in a complete circle and all the time he did so the character of the light would be changing. Without regard to the distance anyone might be from the "hot wall", as it came to be called, the entire film was shot at the same exposure, 2.5. A practical result of this was that if anyone were to walk from the centre of the white square to the centre of the dark (assuming he was able to get through the bars) he would photographically disappear, which was handy for the sound mixer as it meant that he could set up permanently, always see what was going on, but even when he was in the shot never be seen himself.

As a result of these efforts I now had nothing to do for three weeks.

Peter suggested that we should have a second camera on an Elemak, then I could get cover material all the time. The cast had played the thing together for over two years, so even if the main camera was only concerned with one actor, all forty of the others continued with whatever they would be doing at that moment; that was the RSC. One day Peter came over and asked how I was getting on.

" Fine. "

" Well if any of them start acting let me know and I'll come and put a stop to it. "

A few times in the course of the play an inmate breaks down and goes berserk until the guards catch up with him. The day it was Robert Lloyd's turn to run amok we were visited by a film critic of some note. As the shot ended, Robert, duly clubbed, fell with both his arms spread out. The excited journalist came over and said what a significant image of the crucifixion and how brilliant of Peter to have thought of it. When he was out of earshot Peter sighed and folded his arms together.

" Now I suppose I shall have to ask Robert if he can manage to fall down like this. "

One day we had a visit from Charlie Chaplin, the only time I saw him in person, and it was a bit of a let-down. He came on the set and stood beside Peter for one take, at the end of which he started to clap - one pair of hands breaking the silence. It was condescending, embarrassing, and quite awful.

On the last day of shooting, the "happening" as Peter called it, when the inmates riot and smash up the set, he came to me carrying an Eymo (the tiniest hand-held camera) saying he planned to use it himself when things got going.

" I'll just hold it without looking through. Any operator, good or bad, will automatically compose the image, and I want one that *isn't* composed. If I ask Jim to do that he will *arrange* what he believes is a random image, but it won't be; no eye can ever stop itself from composing."

This shook me a bit, not because of the idea itself but because it had also occurred to me in the past and I'd never done it. However irritation at being pre-empted soon gave way to smug satisfaction at being in such good company.

The riot scene was the first time it was necessary to see the audience, thus we had a crowd of professional extras from the FAA (Film Artists Association), persons who enjoyed a reputation, deserved or otherwise, for sometimes seeming less than 100% wrapped up in the task before them. Certainly arriving after three weeks of the discipline and concentration of the RSC was unlikely to show them in their best light. We all knew what to expect except Peter, who I felt certain had never encountered them before. He could scarcely believe it when he did. He called them all together, lectured them, and told them they were unprofessional. That was as surreal as telling Zero he was overacting. Yet just as a great conductor can transform a band of blasé orchestral players, so did Peter get all that he wanted from his FAA crowd.

MARAT was my first picture in one of the great studios. It was rather satisfying that it should be Pinewood where, on an errand for Ritchie to collect some $1/2$ blue filters (Pinewood used to dye their own) ten years before, I had first set foot in one of those legendary places and wandered, awe-struck, down the road that runs along the back of the main stages. They'd been shooting a new version of the man with the gong on C, the same stage that MARAT would occupy, the door was open and as I was peering inside Harry Waxman came out and walked past; the first time I had seen a real feature cameraman and, bless him, he certainly looked the part.

Tony Richardson

My first picture with Tony was made in France with an entirely French crew apart from myself and the editor.

13

Oscar Lewenstein had discovered an original screen-play written by Jean Genet many years before, to while away one of his sojourns inside a French prison, that Genet himself had entirely forgotten about. When invited by Tony to do some more work on putting it into shape he agreed but asked, not only for a staggering amount of money, but that it should be paid to him in advance. The "in advance" stipulation caused more anxiety than the amount did, and it was even suggested that the gentleman might, so to say, take the money and run. However Tony persuaded United Artists and a cheque was issued. The following Monday morning at 9 o'clock sharp he arrived at 11a Curzon Street and set quietly to work in as amiable and co-operative a manner as anyone could wish. Tony was delighted. On the Tuesday the same thing happened but on the Wednesday the great writer did not appear. Scouts were sent off to comb Silverstone and Brands Hatch (he was having an affair with a British racing driver at the time) but to no avail, they never saw him again. What did eventually come to light was a copy of a note to the young man saying, "Cheque's cleared - you can buy the car."

Genet's tale unfolds in Correze, one of those regions of rural France that have helped to bring that nation's agriculture into such dubious eminence as a liability for the rest of Europe; a place grown into wild decay and returned to the terrifying dominion of Pan. I am not given to undue sensitivity as a rule but the feeling was uncanny and all-pervading. This overripe neighbourhood very soon provided an instance of my new director's fascination with life forms that some of us find unattractive.

There was a mound of brushwood where I wanted to put a lamp, so to start things off, I picked up a couple of pieces and slung them aside. The electricians piled in with splendid energy, but after a minute or two scattered in all directions yelping French epithets, having just uncovered a rather large viper. Tony was quite put out,

" Why are they making such a fuss? They've driven it away - I wanted to touch it. "

" Suppose it had bitten you. "

" Well that's its nature. "

It must have been this strange wildness in the place that caused Tony to decide quite early on to have only the actual sound of nature, and no music at all to support his picture. It was done for him by a very special recordist, Peter Handford, and led at one point to a typical exchange between them. Tony had asked for the sound of bats to be laid over one scene, and Peter had explained that the frequency of bats' sounds is so high that it cannot be recorded on film. Even if it could, most people in a cinema audience would be unable to hear it.

"Well I'm most disappointed in you, Peter, why can't you invent something?"

This part of France is visited in summer by itinerant Italian wood-cutters, one of them in the company of his 14 year old son. He sends the boy to the village school where a repressed, spinsterish teacher has already taken note of his dad.

The film's misfortune lay in what is the lurking ruin of a great many movies - not getting the right cast. With Jeanne Moreau already fixed, Marlon Brando was keen to play the Italian but his studio had him under contract for one more year and refused to release him. Tony was reluctant to wait that long, mainly because he wanted to be making films, not sitting about, but also because it would then encroach on the preparation period for the epic CHARGE OF THE LIGHT BRIGADE. So he cast around and alighted on Ettore Manni, whose only fitness for the part of a wood-cutter seems to have been that he was a wooden actor. Tony said "If he looks right I can make it work"; well he was going to find out about that later on.

MADEMOISELLE was my first encounter with the ultra-wide screen format using anamorphic lenses, sometimes referred to as "scope". It is a process that I have come to dislike but at that time it was certainly intriguing. There was an interesting difference in that (unless you were cross-eyed) you would be unable with any comfort to see both ends of the screen at the same moment. In other words, for the first time, you would be composing pictures not within a frame but within a space; so I suggested to Tony that all the movement of a scene should be carefully arranged inside this space and that the camera would never move. It might help the austere style that had already been set for the picture, which was in black and white, and, as already explained, would have no

"Why is there only one word for Thesaurus?"

music.

Tony agreed and in fact the only person not pleased at the idea was the French camera-operator who, having panned and tilted his way through all Alain Resnais' pictures, felt that his talents were being neglected. At least it meant that the operating lay within my capabilities when I had to take over for the last two weeks because he wanted to go off and start another picture with his true master. I don't know if he'd be pleased or annoyed to find that in Tony's autobiography, *Long Distance Runner*, Fabers have credited him with the photography of the French language version - an interesting distinction since the only difference between the two versions is on the sound track. That's books on the cinema for you, though I expect it's *nothing* to the mistakes in this one.

The two language idea yielded hilarious results at the time due to all the French small part actors having to learn their English lines phonetically, the theory being that their lip movements would then allow them to be re-voiced later on. Unfortunately French is the language above all others where the stresses can be relied on to fall in the wrong place, whereby "What are you going to do about it?" emerged as a pair of triplets "WOD OO GOAN / DOO BOW TIT". With ardent Gallic bit players, scenting international renown, hurling this sort of thing at each other, it is a pity United Artists didn't come out with a "phonetic" version. We could credit the clapper-boy with the photography for that one.

This is probably as good a place as any to deal with that vexing nuisance the aspect ratio. This technical-sounding name means only that the picture is the wrong shape for television and in this respect MADEMOISELLE is in the demonstration class. When she turned up on video thirty years later the carefully arranged placement of images no longer existed, in fact one close-up with Jeanne on the edge of screen left, had me wondering why they had put in a shot of an empty landscape. It was at that moment that I feared what was going to happen to Gilles de Retz. This is a sequence where Jeanne goes wildly deranged in the classroom as she describes the paedophobic activities of the Marshall of France.

Diopter is a nice Greek name for a supplementary lens attachment that brings the focus down to a point only a few inches away. Due to the extra-wide format of "scope" it is possible to confine the close-up attachment to one side of the picture only ; this is called a half-diopter (a good example of it is Milo's egg in CATCH 22). Because the edge of the glass shows up as a strange unfocused vertical bar down the screen one always tries to lose it against a vague background, usually a bright sky. This time however it was the edge of the diopter that would make everything work. In a close-up Jeanne turns profile to camera and, as she does so, shifts very slightly sideways so the edge of the diopter pulls out the back of her head as though drawn by a magnet (one of Picasso's or Braque's ladies had the same trouble as I recall). It was an astonishing exercise of control by

Jeanne; however in this instance video, which would certainly have lost the thing outside the left of screen, was pre-empted. She and I needn't have bothered in the first place - a shot like that is a challenge to any editor and it had landed on the cutting-room floor years ago.

In ordinary wide-screen pictures, or "1.85 to 1" as it is called, there is a space at the top of the frame where no one may put anything (be it lamp or microphone) because although not seen in the cinema, it will disobligingly re-appear on the tele. Apart from handicapping the sound crew, it is obvious that a composition that fits two quite different shapes will, for that reason alone, be one with very little to say. It would be nice if somebody made up their mind; but no, for the past forty years there has been one frame for cinemas and another for television which of course actually means no frame for either - so there can never be properly effective use of composition, which is fifty percent of the power of any photograph.

Troubles with the French did not end with a deprived camera operator; another crew member proved sufficiently unsatisfactory for me to fire him, which brought the entire unit out on strike. Tony was magnificent. We sat it out for a week, after which, amour propre being satisfied, Albion was allowed somebody who could actually do the job.

My gaffer, Eli Fontanil, was a delightful character. Rubicund and happy, he approached me each morning reeking of garlic and proffering a glass filled with red ink.

"Prenez un coup d'rouge Monsieur David."

He and his crew were altogether splendid and I felt merged for the time being in the great tradition of French cinema. The only thing I found seriously disconcerting was that the entire crew expected to shake hands before starting work. This habit, taken over the whole period of shooting, must have added at least a day to the schedule and, as I disliked being made to act like the Queen Mother at a flower show every morning, I resorted to getting out of Tony's car with both hands deep in my trouser

pockets (which is not as easy as it sounds) and keeping them there for the first couple of hours.

By the middle of the picture (and owing much to the wartime efforts of Madame Graftiaux) my French was more fluent than it had ever been and I was constantly trying to use it more

The last B & W movie, when it was legitimate to wear a pan-glass.

idiomatically. Early on I had asked them what word to use for saving a lamp and was given the verb "soulager". One day I thought I would use it reflexively so instead of telling Eli to "soulagez les arcs" I shortened it to "soulagez-vous" which unfortunately meant something quite different. I was also to learn that "trouvez-vous un trou" was not the way to ask him to find a gap in the trees for one of the arcs.

All the while Mademoiselle is growing increasingly frantic over her wood-cutter, his offspring is building up a pretty strong crush over her. This, it hardly needs saying, is not reciprocated; in fact every time the object of her desire displays his total lack of interest in the lady she is more and more horrid to his unfortunate son. Eventually the lad is to be seen sitting in class sheltering a baby rabbit inside his jacket, intent on presenting it to her as a token of his devotion. But that particular day she is nastier to him than ever so that he runs out of the school in tears and dashes her present against a wall.

The unit were living in the village of Tarnac, most of us in the local estaminet, Tony in a house he had taken nearby, where I used to go for dinner every evening; and it was here that I had my first glimpse of the ways of directors. Keith Skinner, who played the boy, would be in a state of nervous apprehension every evening until he had ascertained that there was no rabbit-dashing on the call-sheet for the following day (this because Tony had told him he was going to have to do the scene with a live rabbit), and although he always bounced straight back into the lively, happy adolescent the moment he knew that it wasn't, it all seemed a bit unnecessary so I tackled Tony at dinner.

" ..... if he does it with a live rabbit it will either look nothing at all or it'll be so unpleasant that you won't be able to use it. "

" If he thinks that's what he has to do he'll play the scene better. "
Looking back I think it was not the one scene but all of them. At all events when we finally got there it was Keith's last day, and the props handed him a dead rabbit.

One week-end Oscar Beuselinck (Woodfall's lawyer) arrived with matters for Tony to deal with. Unfortunately the only time that I met Oscar B he must have been under sedation of some kind because he behaved quite normally, thus I can give no account of him worthy to stand beside what the reader will find on page 31 of *Kicking Against The Pricks* by the other Oscar (Lewenstein) or in John Osborne's *Almost A Gentleman*. Suffice it to say that Tony did not always find him attractive. When I arrived for dinner Oscar had just left and Tony was playing with his two year old daughter Tasha.

" We're going to drop the bomb on Oscar B. What are we going to do?"

" We're going to bomb the horrible man. "
A very articulate two year old. Vanessa, hot foot from Aldermaston, tried to remonstrate,

" You're teaching her wrong ideas. "

Tony looked enquiringly at his offspring.

" We're going to bomb the horrible man. "

Vanessa attempted to level the score a week or so later by announcing her intention to take the infant Joely along on her forthcoming cultural visit to the People's Republic of China.

" You can't look after my daughter, chasing around China! "

" She'll be fine in a People's Crèche. "

Lucky for Joely, Tony managed to prevail.

By now he had taken something of a shine to me and wanted to put me under contract to Woodfall to do all his pictures. My own instincts suggested otherwise, so I gave him a polite no.

" But I want you to do THE SAILOR FROM GIBRALTAR. "

This was a Marguerite Duras story, again with Jeanne Moreau (which ended well up the list of Tony's disasters). I said again that if we did too much too soon we would get tired of each other, or rather he would get tired of me, but that I would be thrilled if he still wanted me to do THE CHARGE when it happened. As I would not change my mind Tony resorted to guile and I arrived at the house one evening to find Raoul Coutard (a French cameraman in fashion at the time) sitting opposite me at the dinner table. Tony launched at once into his favourite game of setting two people at each other.

" Raoul has this wonderful new technique for matching scenes when the sun goes. It's quite marvellous. "

Coutard, who only spoke French, then said, what everybody already knows, that in black and white photography extending the development time increases the contrast so all you need to do when the sun disappears behind a cloud is push the contrast up, carry on shooting, and the scene would match. I pointed out in my halting French that doing that would hardly put the shadows of the trees back across the road. He shrugged his shoulders,

" Stories are more important than pictures. "

I smiled as sweetly as I could.

" Perhaps you should be a director then. "

Tony's evening was complete.

Another guest at about this time was the playwright, David Mercer, who was working on the script for the ill-fated SAILOR. He enlivened dinner one evening by saying that any scenes involving copulation should always be played for real. When I suggested that this might present a problem in the theatre when there was a matinee to be followed by an evening performance I was accused of being a Tory. I think the topic may have arisen because of Tony's concern about the ending of MADEMOISELLE. She takes an evening stroll in the direction of the woods and of course encounters none other than Ettore Manni. They then set out on an all night sexual Marathon through moonlit woods, byres and hayfields - every act more bizarre than the one before it. Tony

"Why is there only one word for Thesaurus?"

had already on several occasions remarked that these scenes were crucial, "If they work, the film will work". When it finally came to begin shooting them Tony approached me early in the evening.

" How many times do you think he fucks her during the night? "
Nicely brought-up English boy that I was, I ventured a cautious "Three". A couple of hours later he took me aside again.

" It's all a disaster! "

" Why? "

" You know what I asked you earlier. Well I've been round the unit and got some *very peculiar* answers. "

" Like? "

" That silly young third assistant said seventeen, and someone else said they do nothing at all. "

" Who was that? "

" That fool Ettore - that's why it's a disaster. "

When we made MADEMOISELLE Tony was at the height of universal renown from the success of TOM JONES and the two young assistant directors were determined to make an impression on him. An earlier scene in the schedule was set in a farmyard which our deranged schoolmistress has caused to become flooded to some depth with extremely dirty water. The state of the water was accounted for by the presence in it of every kind of animal to be found in a farmyard - cows, horses, pigs, geese et cetera, all thrashing about for dear life, with prop men firing shotguns into the air to increase the panic and chaos. In the midst of all, these two ardent youths, clad in wet-suits, were busy demonstrating their dedication to the cinema. Tony was standing beside the camera on top of a rostrum.

" Pierre, move that pig further into picture! "
The two wet-suits were now engaged in a desperate, spluttering struggle with a frantic sow twice the size of both of them put together. I looked up at my new director - he was shaking with delight.

You could never fool Tony for one instant; he had a sharp understanding of humans and when once somebody asked why he'd never done a space movie,

" I only know about people, and I've never met anyone from Mars. "

His fascination with mankind, love is not quite the right word, lies behind another incident at about this time. He had no need and certainly no inclination to make any TV commercials, but the more he turned down their offers the more desperate the advertising agencies were to get him. One day he suddenly phoned and asked if I was free on certain dates to do a commercial with him.

" That's a bit of a climb down. "
Tony never excused himself but came close to it for once.

" They're out of their minds what they've offered for a four day shoot - it'll pay for a swimming pool at Nid du Duc. "

This was Tony's village in the South of France and the pool was going to be a major construction exercise due to the nature of the terrain.

A week later Tony called again to say the job was off. There had been two scenes only, one involving some schoolchildren and the other the crew of an aircraft carrier. Because the product was being marketed both sides of the Atlantic it was explained to Tony at a meeting with the agency that he must not show American children or British children, nor American or British sailors, but "something in between". He stood up, said quietly that they had hired the wrong person, and left the room.

"They're very weird - they couldn't understand why anyone would walk away from so much money."

Well they had stumbled on an amazing and wonderful person, and a director of such talent that his neglect in later years was one of those sad misfortunes that afflict this wayward industry of ours.

Tony died of AIDS in Los Angeles in November 1991. There is one story about him that I will add here as a tribute to his generosity and caring for other people in this same wayward industry. Ken Loach was part way through shooting a film for United Artists on a modest budget when they decided that they did not like what he was doing and closed him down. He showed what had already been shot to Tony, who was about to start a picture for the same studio with Richard Burton. Tony persuaded UA to allow Loach to finish his picture by cross-collateralising it with his, that is if it lost money they could recover it out of Tony's profits (in those days pictures with Burton didn't lose money). The Loach film was called KES and it did very well, by which time everyone had persuaded themselves that they'd believed in it along - like Edgar with John Krish and London's trams.

LAUGHTER IN THE DARK was less fortunate. Burton was going through a phase of deliberately arriving late on set (perhaps he thought it didn't matter that much since he was too drunk to work anyway). The day on which, finding that due to a miscalculation he was about to arrive on time, he ordered his driver to go round the block for half-an-hour, Tony fired him. It was typically courageous and benefited both Burton himself and the next director he worked for, but it was LAUGHTER IN THE DARK and not KES that lost its money. That evening Elizabeth asked Tony to dinner, which was fine - they had known each other a long time. Because the British quarantine laws would have parted Elizabeth from her dogs the Burtons sailed their yacht up the Thames and anchored in the Pool of London. During dinner Elizabeth announced that Richard would come back and behave himself. Tony explained that there was no question of altering his decision and another actor was already cast, whereupon Elizabeth started screaming at him. The best expedient in such cases is a quiet exit but this is unusually difficult if you are on a yacht in the middle of a river. Tony had to stand on deck with Elizabeth yelling abuse through the cabin window while they got a boat out for him.

"Why is there only one word for Thesaurus?"

A significant film that would never have been completed without Tony's support was IT HAPPENED HERE, made by a couple of young hopefuls, Kevin Brownlow and Andrew Mollo. It is one of the best British films I have seen but too honest and altogether grown-up to get them very far. Kevin has taken to writing books on the cinema better than anyone else ever has, which may be great, but as a director he is a sad loss.

Tony's views on the British Royalty may easily be imagined and he had allowed them to become widely enough known among film crews for everyone to be surprised one morning at finding a photograph in their newspapers of a banquet, given for the Queen by the Reagans during a visit by her to the US, with Tony seated next to the lady in question. Speculation was rife, as the saying is, and had perforce to remain so. Long afterwards, however, I went out to Montreal for THE HOTEL NEW HAMPSHIRE and, knowing my Tony, made no reference to the matter for about seven weeks. Then one morning in the car without any preamble

" Well, what did she talk about? "

" She asked about Moustique. Margaret has a place there but it's "not on" for her to go, and she wanted to know what it was like. "

He learned subsequently that it was Margaret, whom he knew, that had suggested him to her sister after a phone-call asking for anyone who could give her a break from statecraft for a couple of hours. It was an ideal choice, although he had very nearly not gone along; it only happened that there was nothing else that evening and curiosity, always a powerful mover with Tony, got the upper hand. When he got there he was more than surprised to find where he was sitting.

" What else? "

" I asked her - how can you manage to go on doing this sort of thing, and she said very simply that she had made a deal with herself early on that for nine months of the year she would do whatever 'they' wanted and for the remaining three she would do what she wanted, which was to live quietly in the country. "

He came away liking her, ".. at least she's a professional".

Tony's dinner with HM was a better success than Richard Lester's luncheon some years before in the 1960s. These functions were, and probably still are, based on the principle that, by inviting people without a single notion in common, no alive idea can invade the arid boredom of the proceedings and the conversation will confine itself to completely safe topics such as the weather (though with the environment under threat from commerce I'm not sure even that is a bland enough subject any more). Richard put on his best suit for the occasion (I think it may have been his only one), in green velvet with a pink frilly shirt, and arrived at the palace simultaneously with the Chief Metropolitan Policeman in a contrasting blue and silver costume, who made desperate attempts to lag behind in the corridor so that it would not appear that they had arrived together. Not surprisingly Richard found the lady nervous and uncomfortable.

"Why is there only one word for Thesaurus?"

The Charge of the Light Brigade

THE CHARGE OF THE LIGHT BRIGADE went into production with an unlooked-for financial albatross round its neck.

14

The details of this particular military fiasco had been served up in readable form by Cecil Woodham-Smith and published with the title *The Reason Why* in 1953. The rights to this book belonged at the time to the actor Laurence Harvey who wanted to be given a lot of money for them. Woodfall decided that by discarding the title they could safely ignore this wish on the common sense grounds that there can hardly be any copyright on historical fact. A habit of mine that could be relied on to bring out the worst in all fourteen nannies was to contradict, but that is exactly what some old judge, unmindful of an upbringing so far in the past, took it upon himself to do - declaring that these particular facts had sprung to light only as the result of original research. (This may have been the occasion of poor Oscar B's visit to Tarnac when it was planned to drop the bomb on him). The upshot was that they not only had to pay Harvey for the rights but also, at his insistence, to give him a part in the film.

If actors dislike their ownership of books being ignored, directors certainly don't take it kindly when they cast themselves into other people's pictures. It had so happened that after riding unscathed the entire length of the "valley of death" Lord Cardigan was surrounded by a party of Cossacks whose officer, a Prince Radzivill, on riding up recognised him from their having previously met in London society. After a friendly chat Cardigan was allowed to trot back down the valley to his own lines. Tony, resolved that Laurence Harvey was never going to appear in his film, decided that this short episode could be dispensed with and so cast him as Radzivill. For most of the time, when it came to shoot the scene, the camera was not even running. As the role of Radzivill had formerly been allocated to John Osborne the whole affair succeeded in annoying just about everyone concerned in it.

An early suggestion of mine for the battle scenes did not receive the serious consideration it merited, through being mistaken as frivolous. Cannonballs were solid affairs which did *not* explode with fire and smoke when they landed, and could even be dodged by those observant and nimble enough. My idea was that replicas made of marshmallow inside a thin outer coating of liquorice, lobbed into shot by Roman style catapults from just outside the frame, would not only look realistic in flight but be soft and light enough not to harm either man or horse if they hit them. Indeed if pink marshmallow were used they'd go "splat" on the side of a horse very effectively. It may have been a mistake to add that there was likely to be a shortage of sweets for the camera crew in Turkey. No sooner did someone propose raspberry cream as an alternative filling than I realised the discussion was back in the territory of Xmas puddings for Holloway ; but the idea had been at least partly serious to begin with.

There was a last minute obstacle before we were able to commence shooting. The first Sunday afternoon after the unit was assembled in Turkey two of the younger actors went for a stroll in Ankara's answer to Hyde Park and, on reaching the Serpentine, were suddenly confronted with the spectacle of a well-dressed family man throwing stones at some frogs. With a wholly admirable zeal or, as Tony expressed it, "full of frog love", they remonstrated with the gentleman who responded by challenging them to a duel. This they gaily declined to accept and continued their walk, only to find the next morning that their bellicose paterfamilias was one of the officers in charge of the Turkish cavalry (the use of their cavalry had been our principal reason for going to Turkey in the first place). The army had been insulted, its ancient right to hurl stones at the smaller amphibians questioned and until honour was satisfied Tony would find it difficult making a film about a cavalry charge without any horses. Tony pointed out that he would be faced with a similar difficulty if two of his actors were dead. The question however was soon resolved, as are most questions, especially in Turkey, by a transfer of cash (another slice of the budget) into the officer's mess fund.

THE CHARGE was a period picture, but set at a time when photography was already in practice, although only just; Roger Fenton had been to the Crimea and made pictures of the British Army in camp there. The Newman Sinclair camera which belonged to the little Southern Railway unit in 1948 had carried Ross Xpress lenses in beautiful heavy brass mounts. I remembered that when we were absorbed into British Transport they were replaced by the much harder looking Cooke Speed-Panchros. I felt certain that those Ross lenses would be much closer to what Fenton had used and by searching through endless dusty corners in

camera workshops managed to assemble a workable set. Having found the lenses the next thing to do was to put them onto a camera and here also I was in luck with the standard camera at the time, a BNC Mitchell. Again the picture was to be shot in "scope" and the Panavision system as it then was had a separate anamorphoser which we simply mounted in front of them. I say simply but it caused severe difficulties for the camera mechanic and also for the crew who had to work with an unwieldy piece of equipment. In fact by the time we arrived in Turkey to begin shooting only the 75mm would fit on the camera. Typically, Tony was perfectly happy to make things work with only one lens if that would help the look of the film, so when the 50mm was ready we gift-wrapped it.

" Tony, a present for you. "

He was delighted, unwrapped it , and then very nearly dropped it.

" It's only a fucking lens - you said it was a present! "

A lens consists not of one but of several pieces of glass called elements, each of which in a modern lens is coated with a substance that enables light to pass cleanly through it; but with a Ross there is a fraction of light that gets scattered every time it hits an element so that the image is undergoing a progressive change during its passage through the lens until it reaches the film. The result of something happening *inside* a lens is different altogether from the blanket effect of diffusion placed outside it; unexpected and delightful accidents happen. The really wondrous images are always the outcome of some kind of accident; the only clever part is first, to create situations where they are likely to occur, and second, make sure to use them when they do. There is a good illustration of both from the storming of the Heights of Alma, for the wide shot of which the camera was set upon a tower. Now it is possible to decide upon a lens, and the composition, to rehearse the movements of the crowds of actors and extras, and to wait until the sun is in the right direction. But no one can arrange that smoke from explosions and the currents of air swirling between the hills will form themselves into the best mobile Delacroix as the scene progresses. However the air of general satisfaction at rushes was rudely disturbed when a foreground explosion was seen to dislodge a flag (that had been set to keep the sun out of the lens) which put in a sudden appearance as a black triangle at the top right hand corner of the screen. It seemed the only hope of rescuing this amazing shot from the cutting room floor would be to say something right away, so I suggested that the offending flag was actually quite unimportant. All this did was to turn the mutterings of woe to cries of ridicule, but, fortunately, Tony shared my unorthodox priorities.

"David's right, of course it doesn't matter. Who cares about an old flag?"
All of a sudden - no one.

There were some interesting people thrown together on THE CHARGE. The horse-master on the picture, Dicky Graydon, was also a well known stunt artist. Earlier in life he had combined the avocation of amateur jockey (known in equestrian circles as a gentleman rider) with that of a successful cat-burglar (as a child I had always taken this to mean someone who stole other people's cats) which I suppose is as good training as any for a subsequent career as a stunt man. He was wise, and very kind. When we got to Ankara he found there was a young Englishman serving eight years in a Turkish prison for getting caught with six ounces of cannabis. Dicky used to go round the unit collecting money from us and he and Corin Redgrave visited the prison every week-end with food et cetera.

Sir John Gielgud had some dialogue to play while seated on horseback and as he was extremely nervous about it, possibly from some previous experience, it fell to Dicky to find him a docile mount. The best candidate was an equine geriatric who, Dicky assured Sir John, was scarcely capable of movement.

" Then why is he flicking his ears? "
In fact Dicky's concern, which he kept to himself, was mainly with preventing the horse from falling asleep. I know that I frequently go to sleep on film sets and no harm has ever come of it, but I do not have a leading actor sitting on my back at the time.

Not all the cast were nervous of horses. On Sundays Tony, Jill Bennett and others used to take a picnic and ride with Dicky into the countryside. When he suggested to Jill that she should practice riding side-saddle (as she would have to do in the film) he was given a quick refusal.

" No fear, it's a lot more sexy this way. "
There were two people in the related departments of art and props who could not have been more unlike. The designer Lila de Nobili was a true artist of considerable standing in the theatre and opera house. This was to be the only occasion she worked in the cinema and I had to set my regret at not working with her again against the privilege and satisfaction of having done it once. She was an unworldly lady (even to the extent of trying to return part of her salary to a startled accountant because she

"Why is there only one word for Thesaurus?"

didn't think she was worth it) and, apart from that momentary distraction, entirely absorbed in her work.

A scene with a lot of crowd action may easily take the best part of the day to arrange, dressing and positioning groups of people and working out all their moves. We set up the Hyde Park military review in a wet field down at Aldershot. As well as all the extras there was a large contingent of the Household Cavalry mounted in review order. To have broken them for tea would have caused chaos so instead the catering truck, a large motor lorry with *Phil Hobbs - Location Caterers* in blue letters along its maroon sides, drove into the centre of the shot and got busy dispensing tea to the mounted troops. It chanced that at this juncture Lila, sensibly attired in Wellington boots, asked if she might look through the camera. When she did so she became very excited and seized my operator by the arm -

" That truck must be painted, it is a terrible colour for the scene. "

The next location after Aldershot was a ballroom in Carlton House Terrace; the first morning there Lila, was still wearing the Wellington boots.

The property master was one of those people we imagine to have been around in former times but to have died out in ours; in other words he was an immense personality, completely larger than life. Straight out of the pages of George Borrow, Eddy Fowlie was a true Romany Rye with imperial features and a flowing mane of white hair. I had worked with him before and been mildly surprised the first time I saw this rough-hewn individual drive up to the location, park his Rolls Royce and set to work. I soon learned that the Rolls was quite famous, having previously belonged to David Lean. David adored Eddy and gave it to him at the end of LAWRENCE OF ARABIA. I think the explanation of this close relationship between two such widely different men was that Eddy, as I mentioned earlier, overwhelmingly loved films. On his last film, A PASSAGE TO INDIA, David made Eddy his producer, and so set the seal on an amazing partnership.

In the MUSKETEERS with Richard Lester there is a scene where Michael York, dressed for the first time as a musketeer in his new velvet suit, emerges from the tailor's house into a crowded street market and gets barged against by a rat-catcher with a bunch of dead rats. Eddy had excelled himself with that street market ; there were stalls with every kind of produce, the right kinds of straw and filth all over the place, in fact a very triumph of realism. Unfortunately, just this once, Eddy had forgotten something - the dead rats.

" Eddy, where's the rats? "

" Someone's stolen them off the prop truck. "

(improbable this)

" Eddy, we've got to have rats. "

Eddy beckoned to two small Spanish kids whom he had enlisted, fetched out a wad of pesetas and told them to buy some guinea pigs and hurry back.

" May we keep them after the filming, Signor? "

Eddy mumbled an affirmative. In no time the boys were back and Eddy retired with the goods into the prop truck, wrung their necks, fixed a length of string where the tail should be, dusted them over with Fuller's earth, and we shot the scene. A week or two later there was a pastoral setting and Eddy was standing patiently playing a hose over some ducks to get them to stay put for the shot; both parties were enjoying themselves. Richard noticed me watching this and remarked that Eddy loved animals.

" What about the guinea pigs? "

" Ah, but he loves films more. "

One morning Eddy remarked how he enjoyed his porridge for breakfast. In the wilds of Madrid they had never heard of such a thing and I said how much I'd love to be able to do the same. A few days later Eddy told me there was a package marked for me in the production office. There was indeed and a very large one containing enough Scotts Oats to provision a regiment.

" Fantastic Eddy, how did you manage it? "

" Put it down to men sinking in a marsh. "

(there was actually a scene where that is supposed to happen).

Eddy was the kindest and most obliging of men but one thing he would never tolerate was any invasion of his domaine; no one was allowed anywhere near the props. No one that is until Lila. Like the three youths in the burning fiery furnace she would enter and leave the prop truck unscathed, without even the mildest complaint from Eddy. It was strangely moving to see the respect each had for the other. His jealousy of his department under all other circumstances was exemplified when we came to film the survivors of the Light Brigade dragging themselves back down the valley after their disastrous charge up it. Tony suggested combing the hospitals of Ankara for people with missing limbs.

" ... put them in costume and blood them up - it'll be a nice day out for them, and it will be good for the scene. "

The search was only too successful, some of the men having lost both arms and both legs. As mentioned just now, laying out a large scale action scene takes a very long time. The third assistant controlling the section of crowd with these unfortunate people was a careful and sensitive 18 year-old named Dusty Symons and he became very concerned about their discomfort in the intense heat with all the Turkish dust and flies. He was just having them carried into a nearby patch of shade until closer to the time of shooting, when Eddy happened to pass by.

" .... leave *them* alone - those without arms or legs is props, they have to be lifted on and off. "

One evening after work the first assistant, Clive Reed, asked me to go

"Why is there only one word for Thesaurus?"

with him and Tony to look at a farm which they wanted to use as a location. They had seen it the day before so they sat in the car when we got there saying that the location was just the other side of a ha-ha wall. I jumped straight over the ha-ha into the jaws of a large and disgruntled dog which they knew about but had forgotten to mention. I managed to escape but on getting back to the car found that it had bitten through a vein in my arm from which blood was spurting out like a fountain. As we drove back to Ankara and the doubtful ministrations of a Turkish doctor, Clive put a tourniquet on my arm in the back of the car - Tony observing from the front seat that,

" It's a pity the make-up people aren't here - they could see what it really looks like instead of that fucking stuff they keep putting all over the actors. "

He wasn't entirely joking; Tony liked reality a lot. A moment before turning over on David Hemmings' final shot in the picture, a close-up as he gets shot from his horse while trying to head off the Brigade, the camera operator asked the actor if he'd be kind enough to blow his nose. There was an agonised cry from Tony -

" I wanted that! "

" It looked disgusting. "

" Nothing human is disgusting. "

Terence actually - "humani nihil a me alienum puto", but the crew thought it original and were mightily impressed. I had no strong views on the matter but thought it was inconsistent in that case to want another take when Howard Marion Crawford's false teeth shot out in a close-up of his "view hulloos" at the battle of Alma; I suppose false teeth don't count as human.

When my arm had been fixed up, the unit nurse said they'd have to watch the dog for signs of rabies. The treatment in those days was an extremely unpleasant series of fourteen injections into the lining of one's stomach, but if the dog stayed OK for six weeks then that would not be necessary. A week or so later she came and said that as the dog had died they would have to begin the injections. I was in the middle of a day-for-night sequence, which was just as well as I had to concentrate on that, which gave me time to think. First of all I decided to make quite sure and asked Neil Hartley, the producer, to drive over to the farm himself and find out what had happened. We were just finishing the day-for-night when Neil drove up.

" The dog's fine - I don't know where that story came from. "

Tony said,

" I put it out - I wanted to see what you'd do. "

On large scale pictures where there is a lot going on it is useful to have an extra camera assistant to act as a kind of aide-de-camp. The idea does not always commend itself to production managers but I've done it on three pictures: CHARGE, CATCH 22, and THE BOYFRIEND, and in each case they saved the production their cost many times over. On CHARGE the post was filled by a lad named Robin. Quiet, beautifully mannered and splendid at his work, Robin was like the head boy at school. In Turkey he used to wear immaculate khaki-drill, and he always stood to attention when talking to Tony.

Our department was further augmented by a body of Turkish porters who were a great help in carrying all the equipment about. One of them had his son with him, a boy about twelve years old, and to amuse themselves the camera crew appointed this kid to stand behind my chair with a large golfing umbrella stuck in the ground. The way to deal with this sort of joke is of course to ignore it, but that was difficult the first time I tried to take a light-reading; as I reached out my hand into the sunlight he at once followed with the umbrella keeping me constantly in the shade; however it made everyone else happy.

The great battle scenes would find Robin and myself with the 600mm lens comfortably ensconced in some coign of vantage well away from the rest of the unit, and particularly from the special effects with all their noisy explosions. In the long hours of setting up (while Dusty was engaged in edifying exchanges with the property master), Robin and I relaxed in camp chairs under an awning, with cooling drinks to hand, and had the most delightful talks together. While waiting for the battle of Alma to start he unwisely told me how as an infant during the war he had been evacuated to a cottage on the Badminton estate where the old Queen Mary, of the toque and pendulous bosom, had been a fellow evacuee. From the big house she would emerge, when the mood took her, to enact Lady Bountiful around the estate, in the course of which she did on occasion dandle Childe Robin upon the royal knee. A few days later Tony was enjoying a good baiting of the camera department and without pausing to think I interposed,

" You ought to have more respect for this camera crew ; one of them has been cradled in the arms of Queen Mary. "

" Oh really, which is that? "

It was too late and I knew there was no way out, at which point right on cue the victim walked into the group.

" Oh Robin, I can't stop thinking of you - full of all that royal milk. "

While we were shooting in Turkey a war started between Egypt and Israel (at which point Ralph Keene would certainly have brought us all home). The unit was extremely partisan for the Israelis, possibly because the sound crew, apart from an outlying Irishman, were all Jewish, and six days later the Israeli victory was greeted with great jubilation by everyone, though with some concern on the part of sound maintenance who was anxious about his tree. On the way back to the hotel with Tony and the first assistant Clive Reed, Tony wanted to know why the unit was making so much fuss. This inspired Clive to treat us both to an account of his early youth as a Merchant Navy apprentice when frequent passages through the Suez Canal had unfortunately caused him to hold the Egyptians in low esteem ever since.

" They're all lazy, dirty and inefficient. "

Tony sighed,

" Well Clive, this world belongs to the lazy, dirty and inefficient just as much as it does to the busy, clean and organised. "

Today on a planet that we have poisoned and saddled with nuclear materials which the scientists who produce it have no notion how to dispose of, we may have to revise our ideas as to who are dirty and inefficient.

The first day of the landing sequence, which was shot on the Black Sea coast, I was careful to put my jeans back on after a sensible amount of exposure to the fierce sunlight. Unfortunately paddling about in the surf all day long you aren't aware of what is happening to the tops of your feet. The next day I was hardly able to walk and in the evening, desperate for a bath, I contrived by resting both heels at the end where the taps were and supporting my weight with both arms to lower myself in, leaving the sunburned feet out of the water. Never having got into a bath this way before, I was not at first surprised when all the water flowed up to one end and covered my face; perhaps that happened with this mode of entry. However when the next moment it had all removed itself to the opposite end leaving me high and dry, I realised that I was dealing with my first (and I hope last) earthquake. Thinking there might be better places than the eighth floor I paused only to put on a dressing gown before joining the throng on their way downstairs. Some of the younger actors had grabbed at the chance to make a nude entrance and our descent was quite a jolly affair. By the time we reached the ground floor it was all over and no one had been hurt, but realising that there had been a serious disaster somewhere in Turkey that would be in the news everybody sent off reassuring telegrams to their homes.

The next day Tony and I were driving to the set.

" It is very presumptuous sending all those telegrams as though people were interested. Did you send one? "

" Yes. "

" What did you put in it? "

" All is well, love, David. "

" That was very mischievous, it could cause a lot of harm. "

" I don't see what. "

" Another earthquake. "

I have already explained that our reason for being in Turkey in the first place was that they were one of only two countries left whose army still had a practical cavalry arm (the other was in North Africa where the terrain bore no resemblance at all to the Crimea). Interestingly the horses were all American, having been a part of Lease/Lend, and they were now getting a bit ancient. One died of old age, the only casualty we had on the picture, and Tony told Eddy to put it out in the empty valley where I could go out and shoot some evocative pictures. I suggested that Robin should do it.

" No, I want your eye. Shoot some stuff and then let Eddy smash its skull with a sledge-hammer and do some more; it'll be very good. "
I remembered Keith Skinner's rabbit.

" In that case definitely Robin. "

" Why? "

" Well - that sort of thing isn't really me. "

" Oh, what *is* you ? Julie Andrews I suppose. "

Robin went off with a camera and his is the final shot in the picture. I learned later from Kevin who edited THE CHARGE that there were a number of other Julie Andrews minded souls about, including the cutting rooms. Tony however was insistent. Kevin himself was certain it would be removed by the censor; this was not an innocuous shot of starving children that could slip by the animal loving English without a fuss. However someone was watching over Tony the day the censor Trevelyan came to view it. Kevin sat next to him in the theatre and as the offending image was about to arrive John Trevelyan glanced down at his notes. When he looked back up to the screen it was passed - and so was the film.

Towards the end of shooting, the crew decided that they wanted to give Tony a present, and a discussion as to what it should be was taking shape along lines similar to the Xmas puddings for Holloway argument described in an earlier chapter. Just why earnest deliberations about proposed gifts should trigger a Pavlovian response in myself to make frivolous suggestions I do not know, but remembering a couple of incidents during MADEMOISELLE, I said "Why don't you buy him a snake?"

The following day I discovered too late to put a stop to it, that someone had gone up to Harrods and come back with a pair of pythons. As it turned out Tony was delighted (although Jan, his driver who was given the task of feeding them live mice, certainly was not). The couple were given a free range of Tony's office at 11a Curzon Street, where visitors half way through a meeting would suddenly spot them gliding across the bookshelves - Tony taking no notice at all and relishing every moment.

It was in Curzon Street, before the snake era, that I once found him with Samuel Barber and Gian Carlo Menotti, who were on the way home from a holiday in Morocco. My impression of Barber was of a quiet and charming man. Menotti clearly possessed neither of these attributes although in their place he did appear to have a sharp enough tongue and was employing it to berate poor Sam, who had formed an attachment to an Arab boy and wanted to take him back to the States. Tony, as always in any human situation, combined understanding with good sense.

" I mean, you know, I think he's right Sam. "

It was once claimed by someone - "Where two or three are gathered together ... there am I in the midst of you". It was certainly true of Tony. If two people who knew him met, it would be a very short time before they started talking about him. But here let him have the last word,

" You're thoroughly slap-dash Mr Watkin, it's just that I happen to like things slap-dash. "

"Why is there only one word for Thesaurus?"

Catch 22

*Every film that I have worked on except CATCH 22
has been to some extent restricted as to the amount of
money there was to make it with, and the comforting
fact that this picture brought to light was that having
too much money can be a lot worse
than having too little.*

15

That should not really have been surprising because without any restriction there can be no shape and every step of a creative process is choosing one word, one note, one line or one colour rather than a thousand others. Thanks to my background I don't think there was much waste in my department but in many areas indulgence really got in the way; it's so easy to believe that because something is there it has to be used. This was best exemplified at the very end when, while the cutting-room wallowed in endless changes of mind, Robert Altman went into Mexico, made use of all our sets and shot MASH, which went out on release and completely pre-empted CATCH 22 before it had opened.

My presence in Hollywood was not exactly welcome and in the normal course of things would not have been tolerated. It came about because two thirds of the shooting was outside the US and the remaining studio work could just as easily be done in England. Paramount Studios was quiet at the time and wanted the film, moreover nobody was saying no to Mike Nichols. He had made only two relatively small scale pictures, WHO'S AFRAID OF VIRGINIA WOOLF and THE GRADUATE, but both of them had grossed profits of such magnitude that Paramount had no mind to deprive him of anything on the next one.

My first Hollywood encounter took place during preliminary meetings over here while giving their production manager, Jack Corrick, a lift to Elstree Studios (to get him aquainted with front projection, at that time unknown to them). Driving through north London we passed a betting shop.

" Do you play the horses, Dave? "

" Oh no, the rushes take care of all my gambling instincts."

There was a worried silence for the rest of the journey, but at least it stopped him calling me Dave (a detestable abbreviation). Where names were concerned Jack had an entertaining habit of getting everybody's wrong in some way. Clive Reed, the ex-Merchant Navy apprentice from the previous chapter, was invariably addressed as Clove, and I will leave you to work out who Vinni Manilli was.

When we started shooting in Mexico, the rushes, shown on a portable machine inside a Nissen hut, looked absolutely terrible; but that sort of thing never bothers me so long as I know the negative's OK. I was being splendidly looked after by Giff Chamberlain and Fred Detmers at Technicolor LA who were quite happy about things and when everybody went on complaining I told them to go up to Los Angeles and see the stuff properly projected. They insisted I went with them and I made it a condition of joining this unnecessary excursion that the Lear Jet they had hired must be rigorously searched for arachnids before take-off (it had stood out on the open runway overnight). John Calley our producer agreed,

" There's nothing worse than a Big T at 38,000 feet. "

I must have made some progress since 1961, because it came out later that America's version of Donald Taylor already had their Max Greene equivalent waiting for a phone-call to take over. This explained what seemed at the time to be rather fulsome apologies when everything came up looking gorgeous, as with Giff in charge I had known it would - a moment of rather more triumph than I realised. Meanwhile back in Guaymas my camera assistant had stripped down the projector and found a wire gauze stuck inside the optical system. Similar sabotage attempts of varying ineptitude were to continue over the next eight months. There was also a constant whispering campaign, if whisper is the right word, that Mike was subjected to and he would relay their mundane recommendations for my conduct of affairs, which naturally I declined to adopt.

I think you always sense the point where you *know* you cannot interfere with the truth of what you are doing. It becomes more clear and precise the greater the worth and integrity of the thing you're working on; with a piece of old rubbish it hardly matters. Up to now, with people like Richard, Tony and P Brook there had never been any conflict. One evening Mike asked me to take a walk with him before night shooting started, and laid out for me the Hollywood consensus about lighting movies which he "kind of went along with". CATCH 22 was a watershed for me if you like because it was absolutely clear what I could not bring myself to do. I explained this to him, that I was 6000 miles away from home, and life was too short for both of us to be disadvantaged. I'd happily stay on until he found someone he would feel good with, and then we could part liking each other. He went to his camper and I went to the set, scenting already the English countryside. But it was not to be; Mike came up about twenty minutes later,

" You're a strangely reasonable man, I think we'll stay together. "
After this he took to calling me Bartleby. By a kind stroke of fortune I had just read the *Piazza Tales* on the flight over and so knew what he was talking about.

This seems as good a place as any to say that from the very beginning I have shot all my films for an audience of one, namely the director (though some may be surprised to hear so). That is entirely natural and I never thought about it - like a girl wishing to please a lover. If she is a sensible girl that does not mean doing everything the lover wants and there, again without needing to think about it, I have been protected always by a deep respect for celluloid. Later on in the movie, Mike was telling us how strange they all found the Brits. When contemplating my removal, he had asked Alan how long it would take the crew to adjust to the replacement.

" No time at all - we'd all be on the plane with David."
This was incomprehensible to Hollywood !

Orson Welles arrived to play General Dreedle, and his first day with us was scheduled to do a scene where the crews are being briefed prior to setting out on a raid. We started off with the usual wide establishing shot of him, Richard Benjamin, Marty Balsam, Buck Henry and Austin Pendleton. Ready by nine o'clock we then spent until lunchtime trying to get beyond Orson's first line. Each time he would dry, stop dead, apologise most affably and start again. I was surprised that a legend of the cinema didn't seem able to manage a line right, at least I was until after lunch when it became clear enough. Mike abandoned the wide shot and went instead into Orson's close-up. The first take of this was as clear and incisive as the message to Mike that Big O was not going to say any of his lines in a wide shot with four other actors.

It is still a mystery to me why so good an artist should feel any need to outshine whoever else he was in a scene with, to the extent of screwing it up if a fellow actor was playing too well for his liking, but that is what Orson would do day after day with every trick that his thorough understanding of film technique put into his hands. For example there is a shot where he is met by Buck Henry and Marty Balsam as he steps down from an aircraft. There is some dialogue, at a certain point in which the three of them suddenly set off into a very fast and very long tracking-shot. As this involves a sharp pull-away it is necessary for the grip pulling the camera dolly to have a precise cue. That is quite easily done by selecting a given word in the dialogue; unfortunately it was Orson who had the dialogue at that particular moment.

" I will move on *'and'* OK? "
In take one Buck and Marty are obviously doing too well to please Orson

so on "and" he stays where he is, by which time the camera is way down the track and it looks as though it's the grip's fault.

The very next set-up was a group shot with Buck, a slight figure, standing behind and to one side of Orson. He had only one line to say but Big O obviously considered it one too many and had only to shift his weight onto one foot for Buck to be completely covered. Mike had learned by now and gave up after a couple of tries, but Buck signed to him to go once more. When the unwanted line arrived he made a giant leap and said it in mid air ; not usable but very amusing (except to Orson who couldn't see why we were all laughing).

The crafty bugger even tried to rope me in on one occasion when he wished to avoid something Mike had asked him.

" It'll be bad for David. "

" Very considerate, thank you Orson, but I'll be fine; Mike can be my guest. "

Finally Mike resorted to a rather feeble

" Oh let's shoot it, I probably won't use it. "

" Some drunken cutter'll use it. "

Mike scanned a group, standing at the back of the set, that included our editor.

" Sam, have you met Mr Welles? "

While lighting the inside of Major Major's office one morning I sensed a fervid excitement among the American crew and eventually a flustered key-grip rushed into the hut,

" D'ya wanna meet the Duke? "

For some reason Norfolk was the first to spring to mind but I quickly realised how many there were in Debrett and asked him to be more precise.

" The Dook - the big guy - John Wayne. "

" He's an actor isn't he? There's enough of them around as it is - let's get on with the set. "

" If he met you he might want you to do a picture with him. "

" All the more reason to get on with the set. "

At lunch I asked John Calley if Wayne was a friend of Mike's.

" Hell no, he's a monstrosity - way to the right of Attila the Hun. "

It transpired that Wayne, who at the time was seeing some heiress who happened to own the particular tract of Mexican desert that included our location, simply got into a plane and landed on our runway, not considering anything in the way of an invitation to be at all necessary. The Hollywood crew all worshipped cravenly - like having the Pope drop in on a convent. I doubt if his failure to meet me on this occasion had much to do with Wayne's resolve not to miss his chance the day he observed Noel Coward sitting in a Hollywood commissary . The Duke ambled over and introduced himself.

" Mr Coward, I'm John Wayne. "

Noel seized the outstretched hand and patted it reassuringly,

" Of course you are, dear boy, *of course* you are. "

I have never been the least concerned about screen credits (the size and duration of one's name on a picture) but my feeling, that if something is good enough they'll find out who did it and if it isn't then why tell them, was not shared by any of my colleagues in California. Several enquired if I had negotiated my credit satisfactorily and I merely thought them unduly nosey about my American Express account. When the picture finished I understood rather better. There was one department head, our second unit director, who was so out of touch with the rest of us that any of his stuff in the picture would have stuck out like a sore thumb. When I drew attention to this, I got told severely that Bundy was Hollywood's greatest son, and was referred to the chariot race in BEN HUR.

" That was Yakima Canutt. "

" No, no, it was Bundy. "

After four months of incompatible material had accumulated Hollywood's greatest was quietly removed and someone else took over. It was not a question of incompetence, just that Bundy's considerable competence was relentlessly focussed on another era of film-making. Nevertheless, regardless of the fact that nothing of his was in the finished film, the screen credits bore exactly what Bundy's agent had negotiated for him.

A few years later I sat at lunch next to Charlton Heston, who had played the title role in BEN HUR, and enquired about the chariot race.

" That was Yakima Canutt of course. "

" So I thought, but they kept telling me.... "

" Oh Bundy was there alright.... "

I never worked with Yakima, but someone who did described him as "unassuming", not an affordable attribute for a Los Angeles agent.

Several pictures on, something much worse happened, again a Hollywood man but this time the designer. He was rightly fired after the first week and on being told his only reply was,

" You understand my name will still be on the picture. "

I asked the producer why they had taken him on in the first place.

" Well we thought he'd done a good job on another movie, but now we find out that he was fired off that as well."

They are so different from us, no wonder we can't understand. If I was fired off a picture, however much or little of my stuff was used, that is the only time I *would* take an interest in the credits - I'd not allow my name anywhere near them !

One of the things that Bundy had been unwilling to do was to photograph anything against the light. Clearly raised in the Box-Brownie tradition the sun shone relentlessly on his camera-operator's shoulder blades. One day in the theatre, after some forty-odd minutes of stuff that looked as if it came straight out of a different movie, there was about fifteen seconds where the film was left running after the camera plane had peeled off at the end of a shot - suddenly fifteen seconds in the right light. It seemed an opportunity to get through to Bundy and I grabbed it.

" Bundy - that's terrific, it's absolutely beautiful. I can't think why you shot the other three quarters of an hour. "

Outside the theatre the delightful John Calley put his arm round my shoulders.

" Go easy on Bundy will you? "

" John - I was charming to him. "

" Well let me know if you're going to be vicious. "

There were certainly some amazing people about. Meta Rebner, the continuity girl, must have been close on seventy. She was a forceful Southern lady who had enjoyed the favours of no less a writer than William Faulkner and would broadcast this undoubted fact every possible chance she had. Although after a time this got a bit tiresome I liked old Meta who was a kind of transatlantic feminine counterpart of Eddy Fowlie. I remembered that she had worked with Tony Richardson when he directed THE LOVED ONE in Hollywood and the next time I saw Tony I asked him how he'd got on with her and had she by any chance mentioned Faulkner. Tony said she certainly had but he'd decided to put a stop to it once and for all by kidding her that he'd met several girls who'd also been Faulkner mistresses.

" Yes, but he didn't fuck the others! "

Paramount Studios employed two eighty year old process cameramen whose job it was to line-up and prepare any back-projection shots in advance. They were both named Ed but that is where the likeness came to an end. Ed Schneider was a quiet old man who almost never spoke, which was offset by Ed Hammerass who almost never stopped. One day I wandered onto their stage to find the projector some thirty degrees out of alignment with the camera, an error so elementary as to defy comment, and I drew it to their attention without making any.

" Schneider and I have been in this business sixty years - that's a hundred and twenty years' experience, how many years have you got son?"

I suggested that a hundred and twenty years' experience of doing something the wrong way might be less use than he seemed to think, to which he replied with no relevance that I could discern,

" Remember that I vote for the Oscars. "

There was certainly a grand preoccupation with prizes among these people. I was twice accosted while walking between stages in Paramount studios by complete strangers for no purpose except to inform me that they were Bud or Hank Such-and-such-a-body who'd got an Oscar for this or that film. They then went happily on their way, no reply apparently being called for in these one-sided encounters. You can have enough of almost anything and when told by someone on the unit that my gaffer would probably get me an Oscar if I'd only let him light the set instead of telling him what to do, I mentioned that although less prestigious than its American counterpart there was in fact a British Film Academy whose award was held by one of the English crew, and named the clapper-loader.

" Really - for loading? "

" More the tea, actually. "

Auntie Gipsy sitting beside my bucket and spade has shown what mute reminders may lie concealed among the set dressings, and I experienced a similar jolt in Doc Daneeka's office one morning from what appeared at first sight one of those albums that were given away by the tobacco companies before the war to house sets of their cigarette cards. The blank spaces in this booklet however were waiting to be filled by its owner with a series of personal initiations --

My first day in the army

   "   "   serjeant

   "   "   buddy (careful!)

   "   "   time overseas

and from here relentlessly onwards to

My first wound

(did any obsessive collector shoot himself in the foot rather than leave this one blank?). There was a final glorious caption awaiting completion by next of kin (which is perhaps better than being charged for a blanket). I handed this astonishing item to Mike who asked the second unit to shoot a couple of inserts in case he found a place for them, and with his customary unerring instincts the egregious Bundy turned in several thousand feet of it resting on a red velvet cushion, lit by a guttering candle.

There was a number of very large scale exercises in CATCH 22 and the largest that involved process, in that or any other film that I've had a hand in, was when Yossarian realises that they have been sent to bomb a town of no military importance and at the last moment drops the bombs harmlessly into the sea. Mike wanted to do this without any cuts - to open close on Alan Arkin through the perspex nose of the plane, widen to include the pilot and co-pilot, and finally all the way out to reveal the whole aircraft with the squadron flying behind. It was a choice between blue screen or front projection, both of them costly since it involved suspending an entire B25 bomber inside a stage. The plane itself was so heavy that an inner wall of scaffold tube had to be built around the stage to carry the lighting because the roof could not support any more weight. Front projection was well in advance of blue screen at that time so that was what I chose to use. (For the technically interested the shot started at 250mm and ended on 25mm using the whole length of a 10 to 1 zoom. The screen was 80 feet across, and the stop was 12.5).

It is obviously undesirable to have a B25 in a Paramount stage with both engines going flat out, even if in the circumstances it was at all likely to remain there for long; so my crew came up with twelve polished metal spindles turned quite slowly by an electric motor, in place of each propellor. This was after a Hollywood specialist, "the Doc", had been called in and handed a high fee for suggesting we shoot a long dialogue scene at eight frames per second!! We shot a quick test on the spindles to see if they would work, and for no other purpose, so everything else was left alone. The shot came on the screen with the rushes the next day looking exactly what it was supposed to be, the answer to a query not an advertisement for the camera crew. This was the signal for the anti-Brits to go into action once more and the following day, tagged onto the end of the rushes, was a process shot from a film they had made about Pearl Harbour. It depicted a Japanese plane without any perspex on the cockpit-cover in a steep dive, firing guns from which the smoke curled upwards in delicate ringlets. It was a ludicrous shot but arguably better than my test. Unfortunately for them Mike did not see rushes that morning and so missed this gentle hint. We made our shot the same day and achieved the only kind of success there is with a process shot - you could not tell it was process. When the lights came up I reminded them that there was something they had wanted Mike to see the day before. There was total silence at this and in spite of all my promptings the shot from TORA,TORA could not be found.

Sometimes farce and tragedy are no distance apart. By the time that Johnny Jordan, the air-to-air director/cameraman whom I had wanted in the first place, arrived in Guaymas to replace Bundy, the main unit was on the point of moving to Rome. Both Mike and I explained that Ferrara (the bombs in the sea shot just described) was going to be done with front projection and therefore was not on his list. But with us six thousand miles away somebody anxious for a pat on the head had other ideas and Johnny was told to fly the shot using doubles for the three actors. This was intended to present Mike with a fait accompli and pressure him into abandoning the costly studio version. It was a silly feeble piece of chicanery that was alas to prove far more costly. Something went wrong during the first attempt, Johnny was thrown from the camera plane at 4000ft and killed, while attempting a shot that would never have been used.

Similar politics had already caused a near disaster. Hungry Joe standing on a raft in the sea to photograph McWatt's plane gets sliced up by the propeller, leaving just his legs standing. It may appear to be difficult but in fact there is a very easy way to do this. A shield with two hand grips at the back to cover the top half of the body, and covered on the outside with front projection material, could be held by the actor against a waistband of make-up blood. With a brute positioned just above the camera on the shore the density of the shield could be matched to that of the sky beyond it. The actor could then dance a jig for as long as he was required to, provided he kept face-on to camera, and finally fall off the raft backwards. It was perfectly safe and completely effective, its only drawback was that it had been suggested by me. The special effects department had built a dummy that could be blown in half by an explosive charge and to my disbelief this method was insisted on. I have never seen anyone cut in half by an aeroplane but I do not believe their demise would be attended by an orange flash and clouds of black smoke, whatever they'd had for breakfast. I said this with due modesty and diffidence but to no purpose, and several ludicrous attempts were made. Finally a hand from the disintegrating dummy got lodged in the tail-plane and the pilot nearly crashed into the sea. Only then, faute de mieux, was my idea adopted and within twenty minutes the shot was made that is in the film.

Unfortunately his demise is about all that remains to be seen of Hungry Joe in the movie although we shot a lot of material of him taking flashlight photos around the base. I had thought of a device to make these more fun because what usually happens is that the flash affects only a single frame or else is hidden behind the shutter in which case nothing is seen of it at all ; editors then splice in a couple of frames of clear celluloid, resulting in something that passes for a flash about as successfully as printing everything blue convinces anyone about bad "day for night". I asked my crew to synchronise a distributor from an eight cylinder motor car so that it would fire off eight magnesium flash bulbs bang in the middle of eight consecutive frames. The Heath Robinson machine they came back with worked a treat, expanding the flash like stretching a piece of elastic. The best part was that the picture never disappeared during the flash - the image continued on the screen, but for one third of a second it was of surreal brightness. If Hungry Joe was in the shot the second of the eight bulbs was screwed into the flash attachment of the prop camera he was holding. Mike then wanted to take it a stage further so that the actor could replace the bulb and take a second picture without cutting the shot. My crew obliged him with a control box having a two-way switch and a firing button. It is usually a mistake to let directors have buttons in their hands because they get carried away watching the performance and in this case Mike forgot to release it after the first flash, so that the instant the actor put in the second bulb it went off in his hand, taking the skin off his fingers. Perhaps he played the piano or the violin because he got rather upset; but no matter how successfully an actor may portray a secondary character in a movie, to address its director as a dumb mother-fucker, with however much justification, is unwise. Mike cut his scenes out of the picture, and my eight-frame flash joined the growing list of ideas that never reach the screen.

Although by the time we got to Hollywood itself the unit had been together in Guaymas and Rome for nearly six months, permission was refused for the two junior members of my crew to work inside the unholy city. The BAFTA award loader was packed off home, but Mike, who may have guessed what was coming, insisted that the focus, Peter Ewens, remain in LA "on holiday" (rather like enforced rest in the army).

The script calls for Alan Arkin to go from his station in the nose of the aircraft to the dying rear-gunner in the tail section. To do this he must crawl snakelike through a two foot square passageway the entire length of the fusilage, climbing up over the bomb bay and down again en-route. This was our first task inside a Paramount stage.

The camera needed to track backwards about two feet ahead of him where there was barely room enough for a wild Arriflex and certainly none at all for anyone to operate it. Nelson Tyler, the designer of camera mounts for aircraft, had prepared a remote camera head fixed to an arm passing through a self-sealing slit to a normal geared head on a Chapman crane running along the outside, thus anticipating by many years the remote control systems of the Hot Head and Louma Crane. Unlike those however the video guidance for the crew was so blurred an image as to be all but useless, particularly for focus.

This state of affairs led to my establishing what I believe to be an unchallenged hat-trick by firing the focus-puller on each of my first three consecutive days in a Hollywood studio. The fourth day Peter's 'holiday' was interrupted and he was allowed to attempt what we were all assured was an impossible shot. But whereas each of his predecessors, relying on a perfect excuse, had not bothered themselves - Peter quietly observed what was going on, crawled behind the camera himself a couple of times, had a quiet word with the actor and got perfectly acceptable results. Eventually, of course, the cutting-rooms got to work and chopped the thing up into shorter sections (probably rightly - it was interminable) but at least Peter was allowed to finish the picture.

My belief from the early documentary days that danger contributes nothing became an axiom on CATCH 22. In the very first week we were quietly filming Richard Benjamin on top of the control tower which stood beside the runway. The second unit had been in the air and the whole squadron was coming in to land. From an excess of bravado they were doing it in far too close a pattern and one aircraft lost control through being caught in the prop-wash of the one in front. It came hurtling towards us, well below the height of the tower we were standing on, weaving alarmingly. On the ground people were scattering in all directions but interestingly all the ground-staff who understood about flying ran towards and not away from the sick plane ; that way the crash happens behind you. There seemed no way that it could avoid hitting the tower but at the last moment one of the spluttering engines fired up and the wing tipped just enough to clear us by about two feet. This experience was sufficient for me from then on to retire to a distance whenever planes were performing on the runway. When the time came to film the mass take-off of the squadron, eight camera positions had to be chosen. I only

"Why is there only one word for Thesaurus?"

took any interest in one of them, since clearly I should have to be in attendance somewhere, and soon had it worked out that that the only direction these things could be relied on not to travel was backwards. So the main camera was set up on the longest possible lens (an 800mm) at the back of the runway, where by luck it secured on of the best remembered shots in the picture. By guile out of cowardice.

One day in Oblatt's, the diner just outside the gate of Paramount Studios in Marathon Avenue, I was introduced to the great American cameraman, Harry Stradling. He had just got in from shooting in Brighton, and we were soon agreed that we were in a crazy business - here was I six thousand miles from home, filming in his town, while there he was six thousand miles from home filming in mine!

There is a custom in Hollywood that the chief electricians do most of the set lighting (leaving the cameramen free to poke their noses into the operator's job), and my Gaffer, a very good one, had tried without success to continue with this arrangement on my picture. Due to a perception blind-spot, he had not given up the attempt for eight months. When there was only about a week to go I thought I'd try some comforting words, "Never mind, Earl, you'll soon be back with Jimmy Wong Howe." Because I'd never known him get emotional over anything, his response surprised me rather - he spat on the ground,

" That's the only one that's worse than you. "

Dear Earl, he's been so nice to me since.

CATCH 22 was my first job in The States and I started off with the natural assumption that at least we had the language in common. That of course is wickedly deceptive because although you may be employing exactly the same words they do not always convey anything like the same meaning. Meanness is not parsimony for instance, and when Mike Nichols said that something I'd done "killed him" I was astonished to discover that it meant he liked it; and although enough of a linguist to explain to a startled native that the camera crew were only laughing because in England, "fanny" is at the front, Mike in turn needed assistance with "not half".

" Does he mean yes or no? "

His habit of calling all the actors "mothers" after every mistake they made puzzled me for a bit (there was nothing that I could discern as motherly about any of them) until I realised it was short for "mother-fucker". The Oedipal implications of this form of address are erroneous. The expression has its origins in slavery; black children applied it to the slave-masters simply as a straightforward description of what they were doing most of the time.

There was one quiet moment when I asked Meta if she had such a thing as a rubber, and she was further put out when the BAFTA Award clapper-boy (who occupied the chalet next-door to hers) offered to knock her up on a morning when we were given an early call. Finally it is important to bear in mind when asked if you would like some coke, that you will not necessarily be handed a drink; and should your dinner guests ask if they may wash up, not to construe this as an offer to do the dishes.

Long after I believed myself too well grounded in the vernacular for this sort of thing to happen there was a recurrence in 1992 on a picture in Utah. The very first day we were in a town called Ogden and the chief electrician, whom I had barely met, launched with no preamble into an encomium,

" While you're here you must see the Browning exhibit ..... "

Amazed for a moment, having always imagined they went to Italy, I then felt further surprise that a Hollywood gaffer could be that heavily into Browning. In fact of course there was nothing untoward at all - I was merely thinking about a poet while he was talking about a gun.

"Why is there only one word for Thesaurus?"

Ken Russell

After eight months of the world according to Hollywood it was good to get back home.

16

England was never fresher or greener. Not only England but Pinewood, Ken Russell, and THE DEVILS. Ken phoned seeking reassurance that the subject did not give offence. Apparently it had to a number of people and there'd been difficulty in crewing some departments.

" I promise there'll be nothing in the film that is not documented historical fact. There's no point otherwise. "

I'd read the book when it came out in 1952 and felt sad that people who'd work without demur on almost any rubbish could stumble over an honest account of Christianity's way of behaving throughout the ages. When later I came to know Christopher Isherwood quite well I once confessed that I'd found Huxley's novels impossible to read.

" Oh yes, he wasn't a novelist. The great thing about Aldous was that he had a noble curiosity, he would never rest until he had established the clear truth about whatever interested him. "

As on THE CHARGE OF THE LIGHT BRIGADE I was in luck with the designer. Impressed by a *Don Giovanni* at Covent Garden, Ken had given THE DEVILS to Derek Jarman, whose highly stylised designs at once set off an idea; if he would incorporate some heavily barred openings in his sets for the convent, I could emphasise the feeling of imprisonment by casting shadows of the bars across the walls and floors.

It was inside one of these that an interesting event took place. This particular set was the shape of a large semi-circular tunnel, or Nissen hut, with grilled openings in the roof only. The lighting, comprising twelve brutes and thirty 10ks, was all from above and outside the set. A scene between Vanessa Redgrave and Murray Melvin was taking rather a long time and the studio firemen, whose job it is to patrol the gantry with their thermometers, had all of them gone in a comradely manner to take tea together. Things went on so long that one of the brutes ran through its carbons and had to be switched out in the middle of take twenty something. This of course made it NG and the spark on the lamp quite rightly shouted to the gaffer, Johnny Swann, what had happened. This brought Ken bounding out of the set to deliver an all round bollocking in his inimitable style.

" ..... it doesn't *matter* what happens, I don't care if the roof caves in - no one's to make a sound until I say cut! "

Halfway through the following take the sprinklers came on and water descended in torrents like a tropical downpour. It requires only one drop of cold water to cause a 10k bulb to explode like a bomb (and there were thirty of them). The electricians took the quickest way down which was to jump through the ceiling openings into picture behind Vanessa who throughout all the uproar continued to play the scene without any interruption in her dialogue. Ken and I met laughing at the door of the stage,

" You'd better go back in and say cut. "

I learned some while after writing this that the esteem in which I held Derek had not been at all mutual, when someone drew my attention to a passage in his own book, *Dancing Ledge*,

" Rushes .... Ken sits at the back with the lighting cameraman, Watkin (I've corrected the spelling) who usually gets his way. Watkin, who always wears plimsolls, reminds me of a bad-tempered sportsmaster. One expects him to take out a whistle and blow it. He doesn't like me very much ... "

It was amusing of course but I was sad that he thought I didn't like him when I did, and eventually I wrote and said so.

Continuity Ann Skinner's sympathetic aspirations did not always accommodate the wise maxim that charity begins at home (distance perhaps lending some enchantment to things), she was nevertheless a nice liberal girl. There had been disastrous floods in Pakistan and Ann thought to shame the unit into giving to a relief fund by inviting Ken (whom she barely knew at that stage) to open it with a generous contribution as soon as he walked on set the first day of shooting.

" Fuck off. "

She looked at me.

" I agree with the director. "

" If we don't give something they'll all die. "

" But if we do give something they'll all come over here. "

That had been impossible to resist but then naturally we all did give her something, I don't know about Ken. A week or two later a yacht belonging to our Prime Minister (Sailor Ted) was wrecked in a storm and scattered in bits all over my local beach at Brighton. I told the loader to

"Why is there only one word for Thesaurus?"

Prospect Cottage · Dungeness

Dear David ·

Many Thanks you[r]
for your letter my God all
those Deni Days wars
blooming. Ken swearing ·
floors blooming and crows
drowning. It was great to
hear from you at least I got
the frame's right! actually
now all happy memories
my garden blooms

Derek J

cut a slot, like a money box, in an empty film can, with a label, *Morning Cloud II*, and place it prominently on the camera dolly. Ann soon came along.

" I *will* give you something if you promise he'll be on it when it sinks."

A rather endearing habit of hers was to develop a sort of school-girl "crush" on every director she worked with (again I'm not sure about Ken) whether it was Warris Hussein, Sir Dicky, or John Schlesinger. I once interrupted an eulogy on the latter by suggesting that, though good with his actors, John had no visual sense.

"How can you say that ?"

"He never asked me to do a picture."

In the course of the film there are three exorcisms each more frenetic than the one before, so it was necessary for me to know which we were doing.

" Is this the second orgy? "

Ken was delighted.

" Exorcism; that was a Freudian slip! "

He very cleverly cast professional dancers as the nuns for these scenes of abandoned depravity. Completely naked apart from a blanket each, these very lovely girls wandered contentedly about the stage until on "action" and a deafening playback of *Rite of Spring* the blankets dropped and they cavorted about in a most suggestive manner. On second thoughts explicit is probably a better word. Half way through the first take I noticed a group of electricians open mouthed, their faces were quite as entertaining as anything else that was going on. Before the end of the morning, however, they were back to the sports pages of their newspapers, displaying the healthy sanity that is normal to our natures when they are left alone.

For one of these scenes I had made use of an old army search-light, quite startling if you're not used to it. After the film was over I had a telephone-call from Vanessa. I get along well with actors as a rule but it is not usual for them to phone up.

" There's a meeting at Alexandra Palace on Sunday, can we have that search-light of yours? "

I told her who to get on to.

" One other thing, do you know any electricians who would work on Sunday for nothing? "

Here I was unable to help. It is not difficult to smile at Vanessa sometimes, but always with affection and respect. She has great courage and is more often right than she is given credit for.

The next year, by way of a change, Ken asked me to do THE BOYFRIEND, which he started off in true fashion. Parallel with the romance of Twiggy and Christopher Gable there was a more lurid affair between Georgina Hale and Antonia Ellis. We shot endlessly on this until one day Justine de Villeneuve, who was managing Twiggy at the time, got wind of it, said he could not have his artist appearing in a film with lesbians, and threatened to pull her out. Ken, well enough used to censorship on moral grounds, acceded with surprisingly good grace when it suddenly arose from expedience. Perhaps he'd already tired of the idea, it wasn't much of a loss.

The scene where the star, having broken a leg, comes back-stage on crutches to bitch her understudy, gave Ken the clever idea of casting Julie Andrews, who had been the star of the original stage production and would thus, in a sense, be playing it for real. However it came to nothing and we had Glenda Jackson instead.

The scheme for THE BOYFRIEND was to contrast the frayed and

shabby little provincial company's production, with the lavish Busby Berkeley imaginings of Mr De Thrill. Tony Walton (I was continuing my lucky spell with designers) worked out the sets accordingly - the humble ones for the stage of the Theatre Royal in Portsmouth, where we began shooting, and the Busby Berkeleys for Elstree Studios. Then something happened. Another MGM picture went out of control and over budget to such an extent that the studio came down and took half of Ken's money away to make up for it. That meant that some of the grand sets which had already been built for Elstree had to be pollarded to fit into the theatre at Portsmouth and of course immediately fell between the two styles, neither provincial enough for the one nor lavish enough for the other. Unfair perhaps but there is more than one way to make a film and Ken adapted. Near the end of shooting they told him there was no money at all to build the set for the last remaining musical number.

" Well it's supposed to be inside a Hollywood studio so we'll just use an empty stage up at Elstree as the set. "

Turning a handicap into an asset is great fun; the lamp store at Elstree turned out to be an Aladdin's cave stacked with lighting gear stretching back into the era of silent films, so it was possible to light the scene with every kind of arc that would have been used at the time (150amps, 120amps, 65amps, duarcs and even a Camden 1000 roaring away in the background), moreover they were such fascinating props that they could simply be left in shot whenever it suited us.

Ken takes a baroque glee in everything that he does; it is impossible for him to put anything dull in front of a camera. If it's over-the-top it's OTT better than anyone else.

Our production manager was an old antagonist and friend named Harry Benn. He chanced to walk in while I was estimating the lamp requirement for a musical number involving a long track from one end of the stage to the other. The set was deep blue and silver; moonlit, with everyone except Twiggy in silhouette, and it cried out for arcs. I had just paced it when Harry appeared.

" Know what you're doing here? "

" Yes Harry, sixty brutes. "

" What ? That's nonsense, there aren't sixty brutes, nobody uses sixty brutes! "

" Harry, if Bob Krasker was doing this picture he'd have a hundred brutes " (this was true)

" That's why he's not working. "

" Harry, if he's not working I'm sure he would let us have sixty out of his hundred brutes. "

There is nothing like a musical for establishing records. On another set Ken looked pensively up at the rail.

" How many 10ks have you got up there? "

" Ninety. "

" Put ten more up, go on. "

" Ken, that'd be cheating, I don't need them. "

We filmed one scene for THE DEVILS on the western shore of Wastwater in the Lake District. By the time we had finished it was approaching dusk and as Ken's white Rolls Royce began the steep climb away from us up the hillside the Ride of the Valkyries blazed out of its stereo system, echoing across the lake from the screes on the eastern side and back again out of the surrounding hills. A spectacular exit from a location and I hope a suitable one from this chapter.

"Why is there only one word for Thesaurus?"

What might have been

During my brief spell with SPARRERS CAN'T SING, Donald Taylor remarked that films were a "cup and lip" business.

17

As at the time he was setting out to fire me the first chance he got, this may have been intended to prepare the ground. It is nonetheless true, and everybody's career will include a fair number of "might have beens". SPARRERS was only a "might have been" so far as it involved me personally - this chapter is about the ones that never got made at all.

Firstly there was Ionescu's *Rhinoceros* for Woodfall, with Tony Hancock playing Berenger and Zero Mostel Jean, for some reason re-christened Hugo in the script. It would have been glorious to work with Zero again. He was declared un-American, a distinction owed to having been godfather to Paul Robeson's children. I grant that the original idea behind godfathers (a solemn promise to ram religion into harmless youngsters) is not very nice, in which respect, for a black kid to have a Jewish godfather seems less subversive than most. At any rate being un-American meant that Zero had plenty of time to paint. Joan Littlewood always said the period of his ostracism was the happiest in his life. I had missed him also when MADEMOISELLE got in the way of A FUNNY THING HAPPENED ON THE WAY TO THE FORUM, doubly sad because on that film I'd have met with Buster Keaton - it would have been nice to have told him how he'd put me in trouble with Rin Tin Tin and Miss Bell.

The director for RHINOCEROS was Alexander McKendrick, a man of immense charm and courtesy. Once he got onto a set however, he was reputed to become unreasonable and although I never got as far as a set with him in order to test this for myself, I may have witnessed something of the sort at one of the meetings regarding the final scene. In the script there was a fight between Berenger and his friend who has just turned into a rhinoceros, leaving him the last human on earth. Sandy wanted to shoot this on location in Harrods and as Woodfall had secured the cooperation of Chipperfield's Circus, he wanted to do it with Gus. Gus was the circus's fully grown rhino, and his keeper did not altogether share Sandy's enthusiasm.

" But you've told us that Gus is tame. "

" Well tame with a rhino ain't the same as tame with other hanimals Sir, it is much less so. And 'e wouldn't even be that in a place 'e wasn't used to. "

" How long would it take him to get used to a strange environment? "

" Three or four weeks. "

Sandy was quite relieved.

" Oh that's all right then, we'll leave him in Harrods for four weeks before we shoot. "

He then went on to talk about something else which I was unable to follow because I was still occupied with Harrods. It might be that after Tony Richardson's pythons they would take a rhinoceros in their stride, but it seemed doubtful and I could imagine all those Kensington and Knightsbridge ladies casting looks of austere disapproval at poor Gus wandering around getting used to his new surroundings. In the end the picture was abandoned on account of the nervous collapse, not of Gus but sadly, of Tony Hancock.

At one point in the mid-sixties I was getting incessant phone-calls in the small hours of the morning about a projected version of *Jane Eyre* that was going to be directed by Andy Warhol. The more I found out about this projected exercise the more it seemed to be one not to do, and after a while managed to fob them off with someone else, Chick Anstiss, who got all the small hours telephone calls thereafter. It finally came to nothing anyway, for reasons subsequently disclosed by the writer (a Mr Ronnie Tavel, not Miss Brontë) -

" I wrote the whole script of JANE EYRE BEAR, which was a three-hour film that never got produced because the guy who was supposed to put up the money came in throwing guns around and shooting at the ceiling at ten o'clock in the morning."

(after lunch would have been OK?)

" I knew he was drunk because I'd had breakfast with him ... I thought, Well he likes me but ... something's going on here that's too weird. "

I felt pleased with my instincts, it would have been a touch too weird for me also. I later discovered that Andy was a good friend of Don McPherson (chapter 9) though, according to Don, this was after he had calmed down a bit. When Don was leaving New York to come and work in Europe, Warhol gave him a cake covered with his own decorations surrounding the valediction "Don Voyage" - unfortunately for the art

"Why is there only one word for Thesaurus?"

world they ate it. I caught up with Jane in the end, but by that time she was in the hands of a quite different director.

Possibly because of the similarity in subject to THE CHARGE OF THE LIGHT BRIGADE, Stanley Kubrick asked me to go and see him regarding a film about Napoleon. This doesn't quite qualify as a "might have been" because I never intended doing it - Stanley, always his own photographer, would interfere; and although he was kind enough to say that with me there he wouldn't be tempted to, I didn't believe him. A pity as I liked him very much and we met in MGM several times just to chat together.

There was a recruiting scene in THE CHARGE that was lit to quite a low level; once we had shot it, they took the camera around doing hand-held cut-aways of people in dark corners, and since none was of vital importance I let them carry on and just followed, taking readings after they'd finished instead of the more customary procedure of doing it beforehand. Just as well because in some cases there was no reading at all; yet in rushes it was some of the best stuff I'd ever seen. Telling Stanley about it and that of course one could never put a sequence so near the threshold of the film and risk a thin negative (the worst sin of all) he had an immediate answer - relate a polaroid exposure to the film in the camera and if the polaroid is OK then the shot will be; a sensible solution for rare occasions. He then indicated a row of metal filing cabinets covering an entire wall of his office.

" They contain a polaroid for every set-up in every one of my movies." Outside the window was a bright and sunny summer's day.

" But Stanley, without getting out of this chair, let alone touching a meter, I can tell you it's 12.5 out there. "

" Always take a polaroid. "

This rather supported my instinct not to get involved. The strange part is that cameramen who began their careers with Kubrick continue to litter the set with polaroids for the rest of their lives. As I was leaving he said,

" You know a lot about photography. "

I am not sure if this is the case; I am quite sure however, despite his obsessiveness, that no one can know more about it than Stanley.

The fate of UP AGAINST IT, a screenplay written by Joe Orton for the Beatles, is a sad one. The idea of the Beatles being too straight-laced for Orton is difficult to imagine but, for whatever reason, they hated it. So somebody decided to turn the script into a musical with Mick Jagger and The Rolling Stones. One lunch-time in the restaurant at Twickenham studios Joe Orton failed to arrive for his first meeting with Richard Lester. Phone-calls to his house were not answered so Oscar Lewenstein's driver was sent over to Islington and it was he who found the bodies.

With everything set to go and only a few weeks before shooting, a quick decision was made to do THE BED-SITTING ROOM instead. The only "might have been" about that picture is the entire last reel of it.

This film about the aftermath of a nuclear war is a grim depiction of a maimed planet; only in the last reel is there a rebirth and the world becomes green again in a kind of idyllic epilogue. By a misfortune the laboratory in Los Angeles doing the bulk release prints had a snarl-up which destroyed the whole final reel of original negative - a bit of a disaster since the only part of the entire picture that has to look gorgeous now comes from a dupe.

Peter Brook's astonishing production of *A Midsummer Night's Dream* was all set to be filmed in the same way that we had done the MARAT SADE only to have the finance removed at the last minute because

"... some Peter guy's already done this show" (it was Hall); "another Peter'll confuse 'em" (how about calling him John then?) This sort of detail seems to unsettle Hollywood; when Alan Bennett's *The Madness of George III* became a film it had to be called THE MADNESS OF KING GEORGE or the public might think it was a sequel (one would imagine that of all people the Americans would know about George III).

Hollywood reasoning that leads to a *favourable* decision may be equally beside the point. After one of his pictures had made them a lot of money Ken Russell was invited to LA to discuss what he would like to do next. Ken, who always has a dozen different ideas for projects, went through all of them but without arousing any interest.

" Isn't there anything else you'd like to do? "
Ken thought for a moment.
" I could make a film about Tchaikowsky."
" Who's he? "
Wisely Ken said nothing about music,
" He was a homosexual who married a nymphomaniac."
" Right - we'll do it."

Franco Zeffirelli grew up in Florence and has a very real love for it. When the Arno burst its banks and flooded the city in 1966 he dropped whatever he was doing and joined with other volunteers cleaning the corrosive silt from paintings and books (and also making a film of it). He described to me how they would take the books apart, washing and laying to dry every page separately. He had considerably more success rescuing Renaissance literature than he did in securing the rights to his own script about his home town, and it is unlikely that it will ever be made. THE FLORENTINES was the story of four years during which two men were invited by the Grand Duke of Tuscany to come to the city and work. One of them, an old man, was to make a statue, while the other, a youngster, was to do a painting. Both men were gay, and each disliked the other. At the end of four years the painter produced a large statue, and the sculptor (who was a bit of an all-rounder), came up with a rather small painting; a bonfire, not of the vanities but of Savonarola in person, was thrown in to enliven it all. It would have been uncommon to have David and the Mona Lisa as the two principals in a movie.

Other pictures that would have been fun to do again include a project of Franco's, *Dante's Inferno* in 70mm, designed by Danilo Donati, and Tony Richardson's *I Claudius* with Albert Finney. Tony intended shooting Claudius in the exact locations where the events happened without regard to their present varying degrees of ruination, relying on the truth of the place itself instead of building a replica (however historically accurate). The idea was typical of Tony, and I'm sure it would have worked.

We had recced the Forum together and one morning found ourselves inside the Pantheon, the only Roman building still with its original roof, the great bronze dome with its centre open to the sky. When the new religion got a hold it vandalised the city for materials to build its own temples and the only reason the Pantheon has survived is that they turned it straight into a church without knocking it down first. Tony said that he intended to shoot all the scenes inside from low angles, and without thinking I asked why. He swept his arm above the heads of countless priests, nuns, and American tourists to indicate the ring of altars and statues of saints that surrounded us.

" So we can miss all this fucking stuff. "

The Catholics could be relied on to bring out the best in Tony. On holiday in Portugal with Jeremy Fry, he had taken along his current boyfriend, a pleasant Latin American called Richard. The country is littered with churches (dripping gold filched from Richard's forefathers), such a glut in fact that the final basilica proved one too many for Jeremy,

" You go, I'll stay with the car. "

In the gloom Richard chattered away in Portuguese to the curator who insisted they must not go without seeing the crypt, where they housed one of their top saints. Behind heavy bars in a golden prison cell lay a blackened skeleton in full bishop's gear, mitre and the lot. The verger had things to do, told them to let themselves out, and left them alone. Tony pushed against a golden door, which should have been locked but wasn't, and thus encouraged, put his hand up the bishop's robe, helped himself to a shinbone, rearranged things, and with an extra tibia stuffed in his sock they went out to Jeremy asleep in the sunlight. He woke up with an object being thrust into his hand,

" Jeremy this is for you, we didn't want you to miss everything. "

Tony was again involved in a project with Harry Saltzman for a film about Nijinsky and there was a clear enough explanation why he didn't do that one. He wanted Lila to design the picture and Harry Saltzman wanted Ken Adam, a divergence Tony considered rather too wide and consequently withdrew. Before that happened we had lunch with Rudolf Nureyev in the White Elephant in Curzon Street. I had just been shown some very rickety film of Anna Pavlova as a dying swan and Rudi asked what I thought of it.

" Oh I think we can do a bit better than that. "

Because he was as blind to photography as I was to dancing he thought I meant Madame Pavlova's performance and was greatly horrified. Tony needless to say was delighted.

Yet another large-scale project of Tony's at about the same time was H.G.Wells' 1909 epic about the advertising business, *Tono Bungay*. It would have made a great movie, but at this stage I can't recall why it never got anywhere, apart from the obvious problem of finance.

Lastly, with Tony, there was a musical that would have renewed my acquaintance with Twiggy and Tommy Tune, *My One and Only* - a show however that contrived to miss all its opportunities. In the first place the stage production was to have been directed by Peter Sellars. He had finally persuaded the musical rights out of Ira Gershwin (something which no one else had ever been able to do) but, despite being the raison d'être for the whole idea, he was fired at the last minute; a minus for Broadway but a plus for the opera houses of the world. Everything was in place for Tony to direct the film version at the end of the New York run, but it never went ahead.

Rusty Lemorand, who had been Barbra's amanuensis on YENTL, asked me out to Los Angeles for a remake of Verne's JOURNEY TO THE CENTRE OF THE EARTH. At the planet's core in this rather camp version, we were going to encounter the earth-mother herself in the person of Hermione Gingold. She was by then about ninety years old, lived in New York, refused to fly and so had to trundle across the continent by train. Just when she was about to leave, her 24 year old boyfriend (and chauffeur) had, like many an explorer before him, run into the unexpected. Going through a bureau he came across a copy of her will; what he did not come across was any reference therein to himself. Irritation at this failure to round things off properly caused him to leave abruptly in search of somebody who paid better attention to detail, and she arrived in LA in a state of utter distress. Rusty tried to calm her down but after a couple of days she got back on the train and went home. Remembering those London revues watched eagerly from the gallery in my first year of freedom, just out of the army, I was disappointed for myself and very sad for her.

I did not feel entirely compensated by a visit from Michael Jackson. Conversation was affable enough but never really got off the ground due to one half of it having to be conducted through a surgical mask covering his nose and mouth. There was a very beautiful young friend with him and I quietly hoped that Michael would manage better than poor Hermione.

Another camp lady missed by a hair's breadth was Mae West. My initial response to Los Angeles on CATCH 22 was to regard it as a cross between a bypass and Hampstead Garden Suburb, and so I spent most week-ends up in San Francisco, staying overnight in a bathhouse - cheaper than a hotel and a lot more amusing. Thus I was out of town when the invitation

"Why is there only one word for Thesaurus?"

to tea with Miss West was extended, which was a pity - she would have rivalled any bathhouse.

It may have been at the suggestion of Eddy Fowlie, who by then was producing for him, that I was asked to go and see David Lean. In his eightieth year he was planning to do *Nostromo*, a vast undertaking even by his standards. I took the first edition from the shelf where it was standing the right way up (unlike the prop books on film sets) though it was probably upside down when Conrad picked it up because he has inscribed the rear end-paper instead of the front, and set off for Narrow Street, Wapping.

What I remembered from my early days in London as a Thameside warehouse was now an apartment with a splendid view of the river. David was very gracious and talked fluently at some length. He had an excellent grasp of the book and I was struck by his observation that Mrs Gould was the only good person in it. It was all very interesting, although one of his ideas surprised me; he wanted the silver hoard to glow. This seemed more appropriate for a production of Wagner but I suppose if anyone could carry that kind of vulgarity off it was probably him. When he had talked for a while I started to tell him some thoughts that I'd had. He listened attentively enough but after a minute or two I knew for a certainty, without him saying a word, that whatever I said would make no difference at all - a polite solipsist. Lunch was excellent and I left about tea-time having spent four or five hours with him.

The next thing was to test two artists down at Shepperton, the girl playing Mrs Gould and an actor for *Nostromo*. The young actress was excellent, and it was fascinating to watch David, though I was a bit startled when he drew me aside at one point and confided that what he really wanted for Mrs Gould was Celia Johnson!

From my side everything was normal, he left me alone and I lit the two scenes in the way I thought best. When the time came to move in for a close-up I took a quick look through the camera and said that I was ready. "But this is when I go away and think about the scene for twenty minutes."

The atmosphere on set was a sort of calm intensity, but it was good and as usual I was enjoying myself. Later in the day he said, "Well at least you make me laugh."

The labs must have had a bad night of it because the rush prints were some of the worst I've ever seen. Nothing was said afterwards, and in a situation that is entirely a matter of first impressions it would make no difference anyway.

A day or so later Eric Rattray, the most gentlemanly of production managers, phoned up.

"We want to shoot some more tests."

"I'm not surprised."

"No, no, David wants to do some more work with the actors ; he'd like you to call him."

This promised to be interesting and I was not disappointed.

" Nobody does that kind of lighting as well as you do it; but you know Noel Coward used to say to me 'always come out of a different hole and surprise em'. Will you do that for me - come out of another hole? "

" I'd be happy to. "

" You're a good chap - see you Friday. "

It was something of a shock getting asked to do this by someone who had been coming out of the same epic hole for a good many years now, and I wondered how long it would take for me to know him well enough to be able to say so.

There was a very good man at that laboratory (appropriately named Peter Bath) so I asked him to reprint all the first lot of stuff, and booked a theatre at Shepperton for David to see it when he arrived. Afterwards he came to me on the stage and said very generously that he would not have thought it possible for two such different prints to come off the same negative, that it was all fine and I should not change anything. I told him the other hole was already dug, not as good or I'd have done it that way to begin with, but since these were only tests why not leave it - I might learn something.

I was away for the next two weeks and did not see the result but when I got back Eric phoned to say that the picture was put back a year; but also that David felt he would be more comfortable with someone who worked in the ways he was accustomed to. Whether that meant the lighting or the amount of time taken to do it I was not sure, but I didn't mind; it would not have worked well between us, whereas now I can always treasure the days I spent in his company. Perhaps if the backers had let him go ahead then *Nostromo* might have been made. Sadly they spent another two or three years debating about his age and by the time they decided that he wasn't too old - he was.

At least with David I'd managed a couple of days test-shooting. The next encounter with a mythical giant from the past I didn't even get to meet him. I admired Michael Powell because he was vividly original and years ahead of his time. I also felt that I knew him already from hearing accounts (amazingly consistent) from people who had worked with him in the past. He had not directed a picture for many years. THE UPSTART CROW was about the life of the young Shakespeare and the title had been his friend Ben Jonson's name for him. Everything was going extremely well when a diligent lady screen-writer discovered an "off, off Broadway" production having nothing to do with our subject apart from its title (which was after all a 300 year-old quotation) and served the poor little company with a writ (if Ben Jonson had slapped on an injunction it might have been understandable). There is nothing like a hint of legal proceedings for driving backers away from films, and by the time the dust settled on this one three years later, Michael had died.

Mention should also be made of an unlucky group of films (larger than anyone would imagine) that have been completed successfully, and even reviewed with enthusiasm, but whose owners have chosen to bury (in common parlance: not bother to show), either because it was not their project in the first place (as when a company changes hands) or simply because they've thrown a hate on somebody. So much for the profit motive; it may be ludicrous economics, but it has happened to at least three of the better movies I have worked on.

There are treasurable sequences (some possibly still lying in vaults) that got left out of the final edit, usually to shorten a picture that was over length. A matchless scene in THE CHARGE OF THE LIGHT BRIGADE, with a young officer being fitted for his first uniform by Wilfred Lawson's brother (uncannily alike) that opened with Vanessa's great line, "Why are all tailors hump-backed?". Another gem, in HELP, featuring Frankie Howerd with the Beatles had to be lost because he completely up-staged them. This is to name only two, but when I wanted to include them in a talk at the NFT in 1997, the cost of digging them out and obtaining permissions was prohibitive.

Roles that miss actors are another tantalising part of what might have happened (I've already explained why MADEMOISELLE had to manage as best she could without Brando). Rex Harrison for Lucan in CHARGE, and Peter Sellers as the Underwater Vicar in THE BED-SITTING ROOM were each discarded by directors (who knew them well) as likely to be too "difficult". Since the Underwater Vicar was only one day's shooting that tells us something about Peter Sellers; I wasn't bothered about missing him but it would have been interesting to see what Rex made of Lucan.

Hugh Hudson had wanted Ralph Richardson for the Master of Caius opposite Gielgud in CHARIOTS OF FIRE. Unfortunately Ralph was playing in the theatre at the time and Hugh thought he'd give Lindsay Anderson a try. Things looked to be OK on set, but the screen was another matter - there, with a great actor, a thousand colours appear out of nowhere. Lindsay was fine until you put him next to the best there is, with the sad outcome that some of their scenes together were cut down in consequence.

There is a moment in MEMPHIS BELLE where the Commanding Officer hands the Air Force's PR man, John Lithgow, the letter of a bereaved parent; as he reads it Michael Caton-Jones wanted to put Jimmy Stewart's voice-over. I don't know why it didn't happen, or why they didn't at least get Michael Jayston to mimic him. Again, this story of an American Flying Fortress crew only came about as an alternative. David Puttnam had originally wanted to make a film about the RAF, but in Thatcher's Britain nobody would give him the money for it.

MEMPHIS BELLE was also the occasion of a purely photographic "might have been", or "near miss" is perhaps a more suitable category, because although carried out successfully, it never reached the screen.

Towards the end of my time at British Transport Films, Edgar ran a Polish documentary that he suggested, in his best laconic manner, "..might be worth taking a look at" - and indeed it did contain one unforgettable night sequence. An empty screen to begin with, momentarily relieved by a tiny figure in the far distance lit in the surrounding blackness only by the flash of the spot-welder he is operating - like the first piece of a jig-saw puzzle on an empty table top. As he lifts off the electrode he falls back into the night, though in other areas similar fireflies are now flickering in and out of the dark. Then, in an explosion of light from every corner of the screen, we see finally where we are - inside the hull and ribs of a gigantic ship with a veritable army of welders at work in her. The scale of it and the ever shifting light patterns were breathtaking - like Canterbury Cathedral over again; and achieved with no lighting of any kind apart from that thrown out at random by the work itself.

Abstract technical ideas should be kept strictly in the back of the mind unless and until there is a valid use for them and that use did not suggest itself to me until twenty eight years later. There was a scene in the script of MEMPHIS BELLE where Matthew Modine walks away from a dance taking place in an aircraft hangar to the neighbouring maintenance hangar for some brief dialogue with the chief mechanic, and thence outside to engage in a mawkish soliloquy with his B17 on the tarmac. I remembered my Polish shipyard and it seemed a perfect contrast with the brightly lit party. I do not know to what extent shot-up aircraft were patched together by welding (having regard to the amount of aviation fuel about), but everybody seemed prepared to allow some licence in this regard so we went ahead and distributed, I think it was eight, arcs throughout the vast shed, reversed their polarity and choreographed the length of the scene. The result was certainly a knock-out but I was not all that surprised when David Puttnam phoned up during the editing stage to say that the scene had been cut because it held up the story. Nothing is more vital than the pace of a movie, and Jim Clark was the best of editors, so that was fine by me. What was not fine was to retain the shot where Matthew walks towards his plane, because he is now coming from the wrong hangar and where he has just left a party there appears to be an electric storm in progress. Needless to say no one seems to have noticed. The documentary, that can now rest unplagiarised, was NARODZINY STATKU (Nativity of a Ship) directed by Jan Lomnicki and photographed by Jerzy Goscik in Szczecin shipyards, Poland in 1961 ; produced by Warsaw Documentary Film Studio.

When we shot THE BOYFRIEND in 1971, I wanted to use the extreme width of the anamorphic system in a similar manner to the half-diopter trick described in chapter 13, but this time in order to poke fun at the 1930's convention of diffusing the faces of leading ladies (an example of sex discrimination if ever there was). The picture had a sentimental duet for Twiggy and Chris Gable, where I wished to put a hefty gauze over her every close-up, leaving his all clean and sharp, and ramming the point home by cutting off the diffusion half-way across the screen in the two-shots. It never got done because Ken Russell, reasonably I suppose, didn't want me larking about during his love duet.

Another technical non-finisher involved the most basic ingredient of all, the film that goes in the camera. When I began in this business there were no reflex finders, but because there was no opaque backing to the filmstock, it was possible on some cameras to see the picture on the film itself through the celluloid. To this end certain cameramen wore a patch over one eye, like a pirate chief, thereby keeping the iris open sufficiently to discern the rather dim image well enough to operate by.

In a chance conversation with Gerry Fisher, he suggested that this translucence of the stock must have contributed to the romantic glow early movies of Garbo and suchlike had about them. Light entering the lens passed also through the film and, there being nothing to stop it, a little would bounce back out again giving a luminosity to the faces. Highlights were most affected where there was a practical light source in the shot - a candle flame always had a halo around it. To placate the more prosaic users of their product, who were offended by this sort of behaviour, the manufacturers slapped a black anti-halation backing onto it that put a full stop to everything. It would be nice to return the element of choice to where it belongs, and easy enough because the backing is put on the base before the emulsion is; all that need be done is coat some of a given batch onto a clear base instead of an opaque one.

Before bothering Kodak I enlisted Les Ostinelli, then at Technicolor, who agreed that as the backing was water-soluble (indeed the first job when the film goes in for processing is to wash it off) he would rig out one of his drying machines as a dark area and clean 400 feet of unexposed Eastman Colour for me.

The result was ravishing so I tackled Kodak. They said, quite correctly, that their backing had a secondary function; being composed of carbon particles it prevented the build up of static electricity. Why then had static not mattered in Garbo's day? Well I already knew the answer to that one because a former focus-puller's father had worked in their factory at Harrow - close on the heels of the new backing had come an American efficiency expert with orders to speed up the coating process so as to make twice the amount of stock, and a corresponding twice the amount of money. That speed of manufacture would itself be enough to cause static unless there were something to prevent it so I explained to them that apart from being pulled about at a high speed the only causes of static were dryness and extremes of temperature. The stock was wanted for a studio picture (YENTL) and there would be a temperature-controlled darkroom with a humidifier in it. Furthermore my loader was not in the habit of yanking the film about, neither was Les Ostinelli; the only risk of static would be during manufacture and could they slow down their machinery for an hour or two? When it was found to require rather more than that, the idea had to be abandoned; later on, when I hoped Agfa might be able to do it for me, they had a different problem - their anti-halation screen was incorporated between the emulsion layers and therefore impossible to remove. It's a bit of a shame; photography creates images of extraordinary beauty when given the chance.

One chance it never got, due in part to my inadequacy, was an idea of David Hockney, whom I came to know when I used to stay with Tony Richardson in LA. At the time he was interested in grouping polaroids together to give a sense of movement, and his studio was packed with a variety of these assemblages (a better description than collage I think). One I liked was where someone had taken a series of David walking down a path in his garden. It conveyed movement quite as well as any movie shot and, what was great about it, he made no attempt to match either the background, which was allowed to overlap from picture to picture, or the density of the adjacent polaroids. David wanted to know if the idea could be applied to film.

We had done something along these lines for the opening of THE MUSKETEERS where Richard Lester had wanted to start with a swordfight - the sweep of the blades captured in the same way as those multiple exposures one sees of ballet dancer's limbs against black backgrounds in coffee table books. We'd managed this well enough by step printing first two frames together (like a double exposure) then three and so on up to about half a dozen; then on the next frame leaving off the first of the series so that there were a progressing six staggered images of the moving blades on each succeeding frame. I'd hit upon a good lazy way to achieve the necessary dark background by kicking the swords as hard as I could and stopping down to f.16 - then as we slowly opened up to f.2 (the correct exposure) the actors and the set would gradually appear. This had the added advantage that when asked for the stop by my focus-puller, Frank Elliot, I was able to say it was anywhere between f.2 and f.16!

However it was a long way from what David was after, and on thinking hard about it for a couple of weeks (probably the mistake) I told him there might be amazing possibilities but they refused to present themselves.

Back now to 1950. I had just started as a supernumerary on my first real film down in Southampton, when it was decreed that the picture was grand enough to have a continuity girl - a grade not normally found on documentary units. I had heard all about these legendary all-knowing and unassailable ladies, and when she arrived abstracted and confused I was rather surprised. I now suspect that putting her with us was one of Edgar's inconspicuous acts of kindness, as only a week or so earlier she had been the lonely companion of Humphrey Jennings when, on a recce in Greece, he fell a mere three or four feet from a rock and was killed. Had he lived it is hard to imagine that he would not have done something for Edgar in which I might have been involved and I've allowed myself to be fanciful to this extent because if I had any such thing as a favourite film it would be LISTEN TO BRITAIN (a predilection shared with David Puttnam) and because over a long time I witnessed the truth of Dai Vaughan's loving description of his editor Stewart McAllister - "the desolate survivor of twins".

Bob Payntor, the camera assistant on FAMILY PORTRAIT, once shared a room with Jennings in a hotel in Sheffield. It must have been quite late when Humphrey came in, as Bob was already asleep. In the morning there was a straight line of clothes along the floor from the door to the bed. Bob got himself dressed without disturbing his roommate but finally gave him a nudge and said they were shortly due to leave the hotel. Jennings promptly got out of bed, followed the line of clothes to the door putting them on as he went, and joined the unit for breakfast. Perhaps the same thing had happened the day of the National Gallery concert.

There is one last reference to what might have been. I have indulged from time to time in imagining what we might have seen if intermittent photography had been invented a couple of centuries earlier: Mozart, Voltaire, the French Revolution, Kean and Garrick in Shakespeare, and perhaps in my home town the scene in the music room of Brighton Pavilion when, at a concert of his music for George IV, "... Rossini, though only a musician, had not the slightest hesitation in taking a seat uninvited by the King's side ... an act that greatly displeased Lady Granville". I'd have been tempted to keep the camera on Lady 'G' rather than Rossini ; George it appears didn't mind in the least.

Indulging in this sort of idle speculation one day on the set of HAMLET I asked the designer, Dante Ferretti, if he would make me a drawing of an 18th century film camera for this book, which thanks to his kindness, has managed to escape the customary photo-frontispiece of the author.

"Why is there only one word for Thesaurus?"

Truth

" Beauty is truth, truth beauty, -" that is all
Ye know on earth, and all ye need to know.

to quote one little cockney boy.

18

Teaching children to tell the truth always seemed misguided to me; some may be natural liars, but most are not. The former are unlikely to change, and the latter would be better off being advised not to emulate their grown-up associates. By the time an acquaintance of mine, raised as a Catholic, fell due for confirmation (a sort of Christian Bar Mitzvah) at about twelve years of age, he had developed a roguish habit of thinking for himself and, unable to credit such an improbable scenario as organised Christianity, had declined to continue with it. This proved a short cut to the headmaster's study.

" Now Michael, why won't you be confirmed in our holy religion? "

" Because I don't believe in it. "

" Well yes, but now you've learned it, at least why not just fall in with the others? "

" Do you want me to pretend then? "

It took a bit more than twelve years for me (always a slow developer) to discover that telling the truth is remarkably effective. I claim no virtue for adopting this practice, it is much harder work being a liar and I knew from the start that I was far too lazy to be any use at it. Veracity certainly simplifies life in the camera department; "It was me", although regrettable from a grammatical standpoint, removes at once all the frustrating and costly delays identifying a fault that could be the camera, the filmstock, or the laboratory. Also the people who matter most of all, your own crew, are never fooled for one moment. One notorious "alibier" was a camera operator named Frank Drake; not only was he the worst operator in the world but whenever he went wrong someone else, usually his focus-puller, "had got in the way". Filming THE MUSKETEERS in Madrid it was necessary to get an extra operator out for a few days so I mentioned his name, merely as a joke, whereat the Spanish crew we were working with got very excited and threw their hands in the air crying,

" No no, not Fran Dray, not Fran Dray. He always wrong and blame us. "

" O dear, that'll be the second Frank Drake to upset you. "

If they got the point of this they certainly weren't going to show it, but for the rest of the day they went about happily chuckling among themselves over Fran Dray.

Here is as good a place as any to go into some detail about the camera crew. In descending order from myself, who does very little, are the operator and the focus-puller (normally called camera assistant or "focus"), who do an amazing lot.

Ostensibly the operator's job is to keep the camera aimed in the required direction (for the most part towards the actors) but that is the easy bit; his most important function is to see things - both what is there and what is not, and most of all what lies hidden among the endless possibilities that there are. That is why I have only known a handful of supremely great operators in my life, amongst plenty of others who have been merely competent and good to work with. He is at the same time my link with the director and, as it is senseless to keep a dog and bark yourself, I expect him to do a lot more talking and conferring with him than I do (in this sense he is the one person on the unit who belongs to two departments). This leaves me unfettered to do my own job which is to think about how the picture is going to look. He is to some extent my link with the actors also, as he will know them inside out long before I do; naturally enough because they help each other all the time. For example an experienced film actor getting up from a sitting position will signal with a slight lean forward as he starts to move (unless of course it happens on a given line of dialogue in which case no signal is necessary). A few practitioners (Orson Welles springs to mind) if unhappy with their performance, or with someone else's because it is outshining theirs, will do the lean and then delay getting up so that the camera goes without them, and it looks as though the operator has screwed it up. This is where a director who knows the ropes can easily nip such tactics in the bud -

" It's OK - no need to go again, I'll be on someone else for that. "

At least the operator and I can both see what we are dealing with, but in a very real sense the focus-puller has to keep track all the time of an invisible point in space (it is interesting that the French name for the job is "pointeur"). On a film set actors and cameras are in ever changing relationship to each other and as the distance between them alters the lens setting needs to be adjusted accordingly - otherwise the picture would appear blurred or "out of focus". The longer the focal length of a lens i.e.

"Why is there only one word for Thesaurus?"

the more like a telescope it is, the shallower this little zone of sharpness becomes. When a shot is lining up, the assistant uses a surveyor's tape to measure his distances, and puts small marks on the ground - not to pin the actors down but to give himself something to go by, so if someone stops short of their mark by three inches he quietly lengthens the focus by that amount. Like the operator he will accustom himself to the mannerisms of each actor - for example some always shift slightly towards camera as they start getting into a scene; and not only actors - on a beer commercial I once saw an assistant nudge it forward when the head overflowed and ran down the front of the glass. It calls for feline alertness, instantaneous judgment of distance, and the reflexes of a racing driver. On top of which both these technicians look after me like a fifteenth nanny and will wake me up if they think anything needs my attention.

Everyone is able to do the next job up from his own and, whenever it was thought desirable to have two cameras on something, we used to take care of it ourselves. The production, saved the expense of hiring an extra crew for an odd shot or two, made a gracious donation of £100 per set-up which was divided on a democratic basis between the five of us, i.e. we got £20 each. The athletic sequences on CHARIOTS OF FIRE were promising moments in this respect. Noticing the clapper-boy setting up yet another tripod, I needed to know which lens it would be.

" What's this then? "

" Another twenty pounds. "

The loader on THE BOYFRIEND had to work rather harder for his £20. It was a dance routine on the stage of the Portsmouth Theatre Royal, which has quite a steep rake. David was in one of the boxes, on the long end of a zoom which is the very worst place to be (the zoom not the box). Very carefully he put small pieces of black camera tape on the floor to mark his distances from mid-stage to the orchestra pit and returned, confident of fulfilling his task, unaware that Ken (Russell) had stacked the back of the stage with dry-ice machines. As soon as the music started this billowed up in grand style and, being heavier than air, rolled down the rake covering up all his marks well before the dancers got to them.

One of the best operators I ever worked with was Alan McCabe (already mentioned) and, as with all good crews, it was a partnership founded on honesty. He once told me that he started work when he was sixteen in Ealing Studios, loading for someone who, although eminent in the profession, belonged to the school that have never quite finished lighting, and between every take will dart in with an extra flag, reset a lamp, or move a Charlie bar. Right from the start Alan was beset with constantly recurring "hairs in the gate". Spending his evenings vacuum-cleaning all his magazines and every corner of the dark-room was of no avail and he ended up getting fired from the studio, a severe set-back in those days. It took him a year or so to recover and then by chance he found himself on a job with the same focus-puller he had been with at

Ealing.

" You know you weren't to blame for what happened, there never were any hairs in the gate. If --- wanted to go again because he changed something, he'd just make a sign for me to say there was. "

The likelihood is that the cameraman in question never knew his weak subterfuge had got a sixteen year old sacked from his first job; he probably didn't even notice there was a different loader on the crew.

It was on a picture with Alan that I once found myself on the receiving end of this kind of trick. During one lot of rushes I was (unusually for me) feeling pleased with a particular scene. This is rare because rushes normally consist of a continuous array of ones own mistakes, though most of them are mercifully invisible to everyone outside the camera crew. To my astonishment the director declared the scene was unuseable because of the lighting and would have to be .reshot. Now it has never bothered me if something isn't liked, provided I can understand what the matter is. Putting wrong right is easy enough but putting right right is impossible. When I asked what ought to be done differently on the reshoot there was no coherent answer. I told Alan I was perplexed.

" Do exactly the same again, you'll find when we come to it they'll stage it differently, and probably the dialogue will be changed. "

This proved exactly the case, with the altered direction and dialogue my faulty lighting (about the only thing that wasn't changed) suddenly became OK. Other directors when they've not thought out what to do with a scene will find fault with the costumes; it gives them time to get their end right. I just happen to prefer saying "I'm not ready yet"; it's a lot simpler and you are left with the single task of solving your problem without the burden of having to sustain whatever pretence you have set up. The Rubicon for me came when I asked for a number of large lamps on one job and then found that it would look more interesting with a single small one. Just for a moment I was tempted to use what I had ordered but quickly realised that it is better to look good on the screen for the next thirty years than good on the set for five minutes.

I had already been given a useful lesson about false modesty at the age of about ten by one of my brothers (the fast bowler) who was studying to be an architect. Utterly hopeless at any kind of drawing, it had struck me in my enthusiasm for railways that as a locomotive is constructed entirely of a combination of straight lines and bits of circles this might be an area worth exploring. My brother kindly lent me his drawing-board, T-square, pens, indian ink, compass etc. and after a lot of care and effort I was able to show him a passable result. He said he thought it was very good.

" Oh not really. "

" All right it isn't then. "

It seems only sensible and healthy to form an honest appraisal of what is good, just as much as what is bad, in yourself; though it often causes surprise when you are paid a compliment and promptly agree with it.

Self deception is a handicap one travels faster and farther without. For instance what usually follows getting an ideal take on film is to do it all over again for safety. Safety from what? If a professional camera crew say that all is well and the gate has been checked the only things left to go wrong will do it in the laboratory, and whatever form disaster takes there it will not stop short neatly between takes. The only way that "going again for Lloyds" makes any sense is to do it on a separate roll of film and not send it into the labs - and nobody ever does that. Even sillier, it often happens that the safety take is not good and so more attempts are made at it, by which time everyone has forgotten that the shot that will actually be used is already in the can. It will be lucky for the schedule if this ritual does not waste more than half-an-hour.

Another form of self deception is the use of diffusion to get rid of lines on faces. The only way to hide lines is flat lighting. A line on a face is exactly the same as a valley in a landscape, only smaller (in most cases at any rate). Light across it and there will be a shadow ; light straight into it and there will not. Diffusion only gives you a diffused shadow, and where is the point in having the best lenses with the best film behind them only to spoil everything by hanging an indiscriminate blanket in front? There is a lot that make-up can do, there is a lot that lighting can do, there is something that wardrobe can do. After that it is foolish to pretend to be able to do any more. It will not get better between the dark-room and the screen. The use of diffusion in the first place probably arose more from its efficacy as an alibi than as a cosmetic. If someone comes up in rushes looking like an old boot you can then say "well I used a number four Harrison on them" and walk away from it.

Quite early on in my career in features a new lens became available. It was not the sort of thing one would use very often, it might never come out of its box at all, but on the other hand in the right place it might transform the whole look of a sequence. It also cost eighty pounds a week at a time when all other lenses were about ten. I was starting a picture with a director I did not know, but by now Richard Lester had become a friend so I phoned and asked him what he thought.

" Have you any idea of the cost of mineral water on a picture, and the audience doesn't see a drop of it? You have your lens."

In the early sixties an enterprising engineer in California, Bob Gottschalk, bought up some of the best cameras ever made (Mitchells) and, using their well nigh perfect mechanisms as his starting point, built a new generation of cameras that in almost every respect were the best available. By far the most comfortable ride for the technicians who had to use them, they quickly became very popular. As the gentleman's business instincts ran parallel with his engineering ones, he fitted them with his own lenses; unfortunately the design of the reflex shutter meant that nobody could use his cameras with anyone else's. I did not care for this very much myself though nobody else seemed to mind.

While doing CATCH 22 I was told Bob would like us to have lunch together. We met in Oblatt's and, as he was paying, I let him finish his soup before saying I thought his lenses were rubbish. It was just as well I'd waited - otherwise he might have choked. His immediate response was to produce out of his wallet a piece of graph paper with some curved lines on it to show me just how wrong I was. I asked if he intended these to be handed out to the audience as they entered the cinemas, since otherwise they might look at the screen and agree with me. We went on to have a pleasant lunch together and the next day he confided to one of my crew that he liked me personally but had never met a DP with so little technical understanding. He was probably right but the trouble is that the audience hasn't much either and only sees two things - the lens and the film behind it (the rest of the camera is merely a device for moving celluloid along while keeping the light out). They certainly don't see the camera crew having an easy time. It is so quickly forgotten that the sole reason any of us is on a film set at all is to put pictures onto a screen that people can go and look at.

CATCH 22 was shot on the anamorphic system, an optical catastrophe that I have taken pains to avoid ever since. Stephen Grimes and I managed to talk Sidney Pollack out of using it for OUT OF AFRICA. He went on protesting throughout the shoot, but nobody has ever suggested to me since that the picture would have been any the better for it. It is claimed of course that it opens up more space; perhaps it does longitudinally if you are willing to overlook the true fact of the matter which is that there is merely less top and bottom.

Bob's normal, or spherical lenses as they are called, seemed nearly as bad to me as their anamorphic counterparts. Peter Macdonald, who operated for me on YENTL, was surprised that I would have nothing to do with the wretched things. He had been Geoff Unsworth's operator for many years and apparently Geoff had always used them because their inferior quality meant that they would match perfectly with the zoom lens. He was right of course, but I personally prefer that there should be one or two lousy shots in among all the good ones rather than adjust everything downwards. Zoom lenses by their nature cannot compete optically with primes, so they should only be used if the shot cannot be done any other way - and it is surprising how seldom that is the case. In CHARIOTS OF FIRE there is only one shot on a zoom lens. There is no mystique about this, all you have to do is shoot a direct comparison, but there is a surprising disinclination in this business to doing anything of the sort.

All manufacturers of new film stocks behave very unscientifically, in my humble opinion, by shooting their demonstration footage in conditions so favourable that the worst film in the world couldn't help looking decent. They then invite every cameraman with nothing better to do to come and view it over cooking sherry and smoked salmon sandwiches. If they stretched the film to its limits and did the same with a comparable existing emulsion there would be a lot more point in it for their guests - though possibly not for them. Again I think they could save immense sums by simply changing the name of their product every couple of years rather than the film itself. The stock could then stay the same and everybody would be happy; indeed when Agfa altered theirs, I tested it with the nicest possible outcome - there was no perceivable difference.

Honesty is so fundamental to good work. When Toscanini came to conduct the BBC Symphony Orchestra for the first time in 1935, Adrian Boult introduced him to the orchestra using the word "great". At this the Maestro gave him a hearty thump on the shoulders,

" No, no, no, no, no. Not that at all ; just an honest musician. "
He was right, but I don't think he was being modest.

A working habit of facing up to things may explain that healthy irreverence for solemnity of any kind that crops up from time to time among some of my distinguished colleagues. Ted Scaife was always noted for his colourful and expressive use of words, as to one American director sporting a crew-cut and an eyepatch, with whom he had grown disenchanted -

" You're a scrub-nutted, know nothing cunt. Isn't he? "
The interrogative was addressed to an embarrassed clapper-loader (probably as part of the lad's training in tact and diplomacy). Ken Hodges, shooting a film in Malta at a time when the prime minister of that island, a certain Dom Mintoff, had adopted a severely anti-British stance behind his pebble glasses, was confronted by two men in dark suits who stepped out of a black limousine, Chicago-style, and asked for him by name. Taking him to one side they then explained,

" We have a serious problem; when our Prime Minister speaks to the nation on television all that can be seen is a reflection of the studio lights in his glasses. You are a very famous cameraman, can you advise what we should do? "

" Yes there are two things - " they began to look pleased,
" - smash his glasses or hold an election."
He none-the-less found time to go and arrange some lighting for them which was apparently kept exactly in place for as long as Mintoff remained in power.

How often do we think up an ideal response a fraction too late to be able to use it, but that was seldom a problem for Gerry Fisher. He was shooting with Otto Preminger (not the most ingratiating of directors) in the crowded lobby of a West End hotel. Suddenly somebody put their head inside the door, yelled

" Otto Preminger is a fucking cunt! "
and disappeared into the street again. Otto couldn't believe it.

" Who is this man - I don't know him? "
" Well he obviously knows you. "

Another operator seldom at a loss, Freddy Cooper, had one waist shot where the boom, with a uniquely maladroit technician on the end of it, was put in from below. It rose steadily throughout the take until it must have been well in shot. The instant we cut, the wardrobe mistress, who had noticed a faint grease mark on the actor's costume, rushed in a great flurry and asked if it would show.

" Don't worry, it was hidden by the microphone in that take. "

Freddy also operated Stanley Donan's STAIRCASE (one of many pictures the Inland Revenue successfully steered away from these shores so that it had to be shot in a Paris studio). Two rather straight actors, Rex Harrison and Richard Burton, played a gay couple and were both a bit edgy about it, particularly when, during a scene in bed together, they noticed a guest of Stanley's, the Duke of Windsor, sitting quietly in a corner of the set. The camera had been mounted on a board at the foot of the bed and a sudden nervous movement from one of them sent the lot crashing to the floor.

" Don't you worry your highness - we'll get it! "

It was someone on the unit of the Crown documentary THE INSTRUMENTS OF THE ORCHESTRA who gave Malcolm Sargent a nickname so apt that he was known as Flash Harry forever afterwards. This has been attributed to Beecham, who certainly made good use of it, but he didn't invent it - that was one of the film crew, and if not the camera department was probably electrical. Sargent certainly behaved in ways that, whatever the response elsewhere, caused him to be regarded as a bit of a prat by film crews. Before any recording sessions of film music for example, he would always insist on playing the National Anthem, which is like having prayers before shooting a steady test! (He'd have hated Tom Heritage's cinema coach).

Even producers are amusing once in a while. When Tony Walton stuck to building a set on the orientation his director, Richard Lester, had asked him for, Mel Franck put a kindly arm round his shoulders,

" Tony my dear, when will you have a mind of your own and listen to me? "

Camera crews are also among the world's most ardent gossips and the invention of the fax machine has greatly increased their range; that operated by the discreet Laurie Frost at Shepperton (see YELLOW DOG) serving them as the equivalent of Reuters. Every production office has its fax and a camera operator falling off the crane, or a focus-puller getting his leg over an actress (quite common - the event, not the actress) instantaneously warms the hearts of his colleagues across continents and seas.

A useful start towards making the most of our talents, whatever they are, is an open mind. Thanks to a poor record for doing what was expected I've sometimes followed alternative paths that suited me better. Recounting them here is not to suggest them to others, but they have become too well known to be left without an explanation.

Once Ritchie's maxim to "... make sure you've done all the right things..." has been observed, it is best for me to detach myself from the proceedings to some extent. Apart from the temptation to mess things about after they should be left alone, it helps no one to tire yourself unnecessarily. The day's work may be long, and periods of activity and concentration will certainly be interspersed with much longer ones when there is nothing to do, so I sometimes put these to constructive use by going unashamedly asleep - the only activity after all that makes one less tired. It may occasion surprise when people are not used to it, especially in the USA where, as we've seen, they're more concerned about appearances.

Another unorthodox approach is to be sparing of the time spent looking at the script. A lifelong practice of reading tends to place film-scripts a fair way down the list of literary delights, but again there is a positive reason for abstinence. Ideas with any go in them always spring from a first encounter; familiarity may breed contempt but certainly not an original idea. However a determination to read a script no more than once runs into a difficulty right at the start - when to do it? Throughout the preparation period and (except for a few people like David Lean) during much of the shooting as well, scripts undergo a continual metamorphosis. They will either hand you a new one to start all over again, or there will be pages of amendments, each series on different coloured paper.

" Are the orange pages the last for scene 89 ? "

" Eau de Nile, I believe. "

If read too early on it may bear no relation whatever to the film you are making, so it is better to borrow somebody's polychrome copy just before shooting starts. All that I need to know can be found out anyway by asking one or two questions, though of course nothing is entirely secure if a director is determined to score points.

In the aftermath of an atomic war some of the survivors in THE BED-SITTING-ROOM undergo certain mutations: Ralph Richardson into the bed-sitting-room itself, Arthur Lowe into a parrot etc. Having "done all the right things" for one scene and watched a couple of rehearsals, I retired to my private world while they got on with shooting, only to be disturbed by Richard Lester.

" I want to see Mother clearly in this. "

" But she's not in the scene. "

This assertion was unfortunately assailable because Mona Washbourne had by now mutated into a wardrobe and was standing against the back wall of Ralph Richardson.

More recently I was expecting the director of a forthcoming picture for lunch at Shepperton and only remembered the day before that he had written the script himself. Isobel, the obliging wife of my camera operator, made a précis for me by the following morning, on two sides of a post-card, so lunch was able to go off without embarrassment.

One ceremony always to be avoided is the production meeting. If you have told your own people what you want, where's the sense in sitting endlessly while hair and make-up discuss the heating in their trailer and whether the honey-wagon should be parked next to it or not? USED PEOPLE, although shooting in Canada, had a three week location in the Big Apple requiring a recce with my New York crew. The only place to hold a meeting afterwards was in the departure lounge of La Guardia airport, where, if I was to catch the plane back to Toronto, I could hardly avoid being present. With a reputation to keep up I distanced myself from the proceedings by lying down on a bench and feigning slumber. After a while I could hear my key-grip struggling with some absurd irrelevance and sat up long enough to clear it out of his way. This charitable act caused inordinate delight to all the New Yorkers who, claiming that thereby I had attended a meeting, became clearly impatient to get away and tell their friends.

My youthful antipathy towards exams extends naturally to the daft ritual of interviewing people; it discovers nothing - but after half a day working with someone you'll know. Given a chance most genuine technicians will manage to say the wrong thing at interviews; the phoney ones never do. I was asked by a young director about to embark upon yet another remake of BLACK BEAUTY how I felt about photographing a horse. Naming a couple of well known actresses I assured her that after them no horse was at all likely to be a problem. Happily this sober observation was mistaken for a frivolous one and I was not offered the picture.

Occasionally, in the hands of a master, the interview may afford entertainment of a kind. When setting up his first Hollywood movie Tony Richardson asked to meet with the continuity girl. Meta arrived wearing white elbow-length lace gloves. Without troubling to ask about any of her previous films or directors, Tony went at once to serious matters.

" Why are you wearing those long white lace gloves? "

" Ah always wear long white lace gloves when Ah come to see people like you Mr Richardson. "

I would have been an average cinema-goer up until about 1950 after which, as I became properly involved in the making of films, this fell off to a great extent. This wasn't calculated in any way; it came about because there was now much less time for what I enjoyed most, music and books, and they sometimes reveal elements that are fresh to what I am doing, whereas the cinema merely demonstrates what has already been done. Music in particular gives a sense of spanning the dimension of time (play loud to start with and you can't make a crescendo) and with it an escape from the temptation to make every shot as beautiful as possible; it may be

"Why is there only one word for Thesaurus?"

more interesting to play a sequence down to start with so that the emphasis when you choose to make it will have more impact. A strong advantage for me in not seeing films is that it's easier to carry out an idea without being put off because someone's already done it, with the added prize that when asked to make some commercial look like such and such a film, I honestly don't know what they're talking about.

Most of my knowledge of other films is gathered from the conversation of people on the set, and I was agreeably surprised at one stage to hear a great deal of an actor quite unknown to me, one Sylvester Stallone, who had made a hugely successful movie about Rimbaud. French poets, however abandoned their behaviour, had not hitherto made it very strong in Los Angeles and there was no reason to suppose they were any better acquainted with young Arthur than they had been with Tchaikowsky before Ken Russell came along. It was nevertheless encouraging; that is until I enquired in all innocence about others in the cast, and who had played Verlaine? Years afterwards Hollywood finally discovered the author of *Une Saison en Enfer* and *Le Bâteau Ivre* and chose young Leo di Caprio to play him, though there is nothing in the film's title TOTAL ECLIPSE to suggest whom it is about; that would be confusing.

When a film has finished shooting there is a long interval while they get on and edit it. At this stage the negative is stored exactly as it was when it passed through the camera, the editor using the original rushes for his "cutting copy" and ordering further prints as he requires them. The sound, on the other hand, will be on several separate records or tracks: dialogue, music, and any number of sound effects each having a track to themselves. When the final edit has been decided, all these separate tracks are run with the cutting copy in a dubbing theatre, short sections at a time, where the balance between them is set. They are then all recorded onto a single track which will be the sound-track of the film. When that is done the negative is taken from the vault and cut to match the cutting copy; it is the point of no return because every time that you join two shots together, one frame is lost from each of them.

As soon as the picture is "neg-cut" I get involved again and "grade" a print that will hopefully be the final standard for all that follow. Normal practice is for the cameraman to run the cutting copy with the grader in the laboratory and indicate how he wants it to look, but that is like reading the script too often. The corrections necessary in the first "answer print" will be obvious to any grader so I let him do that on his own; then I can see it with him with fresh eyes, giving alterations as to density (lighter or darker) or colour as we go along. He then makes a second print and we do the same thing again, up to a third, by which time there should be few if any changes. I won't carry on beyond the third print because one's visual sensitivity is a finite thing and it gets used up. On the fourth answer print of Terry Donovan's YELLOW DOG I gave the grader an alteration; he hesitated a moment and then said that he would do it of course, but hoped I didn't mind his pointing out that when it was made the shot would be back exactly as it had been in the first print.

Our American cousins have, sometimes, a perverse notion that rendering this service should be its own reward. Making a negative is merely the first half of the process. That the second half, making a print from it, takes only the same number of days as the former took weeks, seems hardly a reason not to pay anyone. It has been put to me that it is in my interest to have the movie look good (as if I'm going to be watching it over and over?). That's like telling the captain of an ocean liner he's only paid up to mid-atlantic, after which it's in his own interest to carry on for free - a degree of longitude at which it would seem entirely reasonable to drop the anchor and put everyone in the life-boats.

I always had a disinclination to joining things. The only exceptions, both of them unavoidable, were the British Army and the ACT (trade union). My father was surprised when I stubbornly refused to join the boy scouts, and he was quite likely right for once - I might not have had to wait half so long for sexual enlightenment. I did hesitate when the Royal Photographic Society suggested I should submit a print of THE KNACK with a view to being offered a fellowship. They are serious people and it was nice of them, but I soon felt that once I could sit down and earnestly write letters after my name something would be lost for ever. Honours are even worse, being primarily a means of paying off civil servants, and I really think it a mistake for creative people to accept them.

I paid a visit to Charles Potter shortly before starting this book. He had been Edgar's right-hand-man at Transport for years and when Edgar (who had landed an OBE in 1969) retired, Charles was the logical choice to succeed him, but for whatever reason, and I would not hazard to suggest one, he was passed over in favour of someone else. Charles was then tossed an MBE -

" They keep a certain number each year for that sort of thing. Anyway I thought I might as well take it. "

So at least they are distributed evenly enough - some for getting the job and some for not getting it! But the British Empire (founded upon the odd notion that other people's countries somehow didn't belong to them) is happily a thing of the past so how can anyone be a member of it? (The case with the OBE is slightly different as my mother's private interpretation, "Owing Bills Everywhere", may now apply generally). At the time of writing one noteworthy Dame of the British Empire is a former card-carrying member of the Nazi Party and although there's nothing inconsistent about that, it does further the view that in accepting these so called honours people may place themselves in rather doubtful company. When they bestow posthumous honours on Alan Turing it may be time to reconsider. As fewer than one in a hundred readers will know who he was, a mention here may lead a few towards finding out. To help them solve this little enigma - he did more as a single individual to save

"Why is there only one word for Thesaurus?"

this country in World War Two, almost than Churchill; though he was not rewarded in quite the same way.

At the handing-out ceremony, Elizabeth is said to average a hundred in an hour, and afterwards you may purchase an overpriced video of your personal 36 seconds; they will also sell replicas of the medal to give to any aunts or cousins you want to impress. Perhaps Brighton Pier would be a more suitable venue for this sort of fairground activity.

Away from work I had adopted a non-standard approach to the matter of pensions. No sooner was I earning my own money than my father explained that everyone had to have life insurance and the best thing for me would be an endowment policy with the Edinburgh Life. I discovered later on that he was an agent for them on commission, but I won't blame him for that. After a few years, times got hard, I surrendered the policy and got back considerably less than the total amount I had paid in, and I wouldn't blame anybody for that either. I did resolve though, when things improved, not to get caught again. Rather than some unreadable document with a red seal to it I was going to have a civilised library that would enhance my life, and if the need arose I could simply re-read *Mansfield Park*, sell it, and carry on. At least the misery of being hard up would be mitigated by becoming well read - "... it looks like a lean time ahead, better get started on Gibbon." The extent to which any departure from accepted norms upsets the establishment is astonishing. The Inland Revenue thought dreadful things were going on when they could not find any substantial insurance policies, and spent a couple of years of their seven-hour days looking for an explanation.

Once, the library succeeded in counterattacking officialdom. In the early days of VAT, a man from Customs and Excise came to the house for a check on things. He was nice enough and before he left I said he must see one of the books. Lifting down the first volume of Samuel Johnson's Dictionary I laid it open before him at -

EXCISE n s (accijs, Dutch; excisum, Latin) A hateful tax levied upon commodities, and adjudged not by the common judges of property, but wretches hired by those to whom excise is paid.

Shakespeare named it for all time "... the insolence of office ...". Vested authority always gets carried away with itself whether it be a high court judge or a parking attendant - there's not really a difference. My earliest lesson in ways to confront it was at the age of about ten years when my father had a brush with a policeman outside our house.

" ... remember that I pay your wages! "

This, though undoubtedly effective at the time, is rather too direct for modern use. The more deft approach of one assistant director addressing an obstructive member of the force was to insert a brief pause between the first two syllables of the word "constable". For this a certain amount of care is necessary, and I would recommend some quiet practice beforehand; a semi-quaver rest is all that's required - a minim will get you arrested.

"Why is there only one word for Thesaurus?"

The Heel of Achilles

One section that deserves a chapter to itself is the art department, and that is because it's the only one that can really screw things up for me.

19

The first danger is that starting, as they do, ahead of everyone else, they may make justifiable inroads into the funds that there will be attempts to repair by subtractions from the rest of us, (though it is not their fault when budgets are unreal and it would be worse still to start a production off with inadequate sets).

It is an interesting relationship, me and the art directors (now called "designers", the same as lighting cameramen are now called "directors of photography", both examples of inflated nomenclature). If they build a rotten set and I manage to light it passably, they will probably get the credit; on the other hand should they provide a splendid one, the world will declare how clever I am - not that either way matters.

Sometimes their work has a kind of magic to it. The exterior of Elsinore in Franco's HAMLET was Dunnottar, a castle two miles south of Stonehaven, on Scotland's east coast. Its last occupant, George, tenth Earl Marischal of Scotland, had "come out" in 1715, and, although this did not mean quite the same as it does today, neither sense has ever been popular with descendants of the House of Hanover. They took the roof off his castle, and it has presented the aspect of a ruin ever since. That is except for three weeks in the summer of 1990.

By cleverly exploiting the presence in the neighbourhood of helicopter pilots, so accustomed to placing ungainly objects on North Sea oil-rigs that dropping bits of timber onto an old castle on dry land was child's play, our Art people put the clock back two hundred and seventy five years - and a watcher at the northern end of the bay might gaze on outlines that had disappeared forever in 1717.

Their department seems to have changed more over the years than others. When I first came into the business they were all attached to the major studios and were completely professional, their sets planned with built-in perspectives that took your breath away, and nothing ever begun without making a proper projection beforehand. This has now given way before an onslaught of alumni from art colleges and television, where it is clearly never explained that no one is ever going to set eyes on the sets they build. What *will* happen is that some people come along with a thing called a film camera and take photographs of it, and that is all an audience will see. So any set, however wonderful in other respects, that is impossible to photograph properly is a waste.

Then there is the vexed question of glass, particularly in picture frames, because as soon as the camera operator gets a reflection he will simply angle the offending prop until it looks as if there were none (sometimes a very obtuse angle indeed). On location there will obviously be glass in the windows for practical reasons, but on a stage it is nearly always unnecessary so long as the backing is balanced properly, and I always ask them not to use it. They never take any notice of course, glaze everything in sight and show their handiwork to the director; then I come along, take it all out again, and everyone's honour is satisfied. When one gentleman went so far as to double-glaze a set of large proportions I asked for every pane that had to be removed to be dumped on the production manager's desk. That request was also ignored, either because the desk wasn't strong enough or perhaps because, apart from the time wasted, the unused glass had cost something over two thousand pounds.

Next to contend with, is a widespread love affair with egg-shell paint, which will end up sprayed with anti-flare or covered with flour and water paste (both time consuming) until it looks exactly like the matte stuff they could have used in the first place. Not to mention the walls that don't float any more. It costs twenty percent extra to build for every wall in a studio set to float (ie. remove, either to assist the camera positioning or the lighting, and when so built it takes little more than ten to fifteen minutes to clear away). Economising with that facility, on a recent picture, cost an entire extra day on the shooting schedule, so one wonders who is being clever ? Come to think of it, they could have made up their twenty per cent by sparing all the glass I took out of the windows !

Quite the nastiest of all hindrances to decent photography is the trans-light backing, an American plague that has nearly eradicated the invaluable craft of the scenic artist. Somebody takes a still photograph and an enlarged transparency is made from it (perhaps art directors in Hollywood cannot draw very well). Photo-backings cost a lot, consequently they are always made too small, and because of that are always positioned too close to the set; when I pointed out to one translight-lover that if we moved the camera as little as three feet we'd be off his backing he replied that all we had to do was move the backing across as well. This was true of course, but it would make tracking shots a bit of a problem, except perhaps for the final scene of Macbeth.

On the same level of ineptitude, one Hollywood team arrived at our location when we had finished for the day, to make transparencies for a backing in the studio. The result was realistic enough, featuring as it did all the 2ks and pups we'd left in place for the following morning. Nobody seemed to care, as I think they would have done had I left lamps standing about in any of *my* pictures. Translights also require twice the studio space; you can place a painted backing against a wall of the stage but with a transparency you have to position their lighting behind them at a distance approximately equal to their distance from the set. This at a time when real film studios with proper stages are being abandoned in favour of cast off industrial buildings with all the wrong proportions.

Slackness in one department is usually covered up by the resource of another, but always at the cost of time just when that commodity is most expensive - during shooting. It has often taken me ten minutes to light a set-up and then anything up to an hour trying to make some hopeless backing work. That such novelties as translights and HMIs get away with not doing the job properly while actually costing more than before is puzzling to begin with, but accountants are not concerned about excellence; and extra cost, provided it is expended on machinery rather than a livelihood for human beings, doesn't bother them either.

It stands in sad contrast to the quiet little man who came to the MEMPHIS BELLE set in Pinewood at the end of each day and re-painted the clouds on the sky panorama surrounding the vast stage, so that every morning they were fresh and new. Trans-lights would have had our actors flying alongside the same cloud all the way to Bremerhaven.

A sample of Camera fishing Art out of trouble (and also of what can happen to the latter when they don't make projections) is provided by THE BOYFRIEND, where Christopher Gable puts a record on a wind-up gramophone and he and Twiggy start dancing to it. Then, by the magic of the cinema (and the whim of the director), the little portable machine becomes a giant turntable with a double revolve on which, as they continue their dance, they are spun clockwise, surrounded by a corps de ballet doing their best to resist centrifugal force in the opposite direction. At this point it became the single most expensive prop in the picture (because quite a lot engineering was needed to balance it properly). A second and very specific whim of the director was that the outer circumference of this device should exactly fit top and bottom of frame.

Everything had been built and paid for by the time the rest of us arrived on the pay-roll. When we went up top to make a preliminary survey it was found that no lens in existence could be induced to accommodate the contrivance without first taking the roof off the studio. This embarrassment came upon the Art department because somebody had innocently believed all that was required to work out their dimensions in the first place, was to climb into the roof with a toy viewfinder and gaze through it. In the end my crew calculated that by shooting on 70mm stock and reducing back to 35mm it would all come right (don't ask me how) so a 70mm camera was flown in from California and, after a section of steel girder had been cut out of the roof, we got the shot. All the proper stages at Elstree have now ceased to exist and I suppose our little bit of girder was one thing less for the entrepreneurs to knock down. Destroying the nation's cultural assets for a quick return is deplorable though hardly surprising when selling off the family silver was government policy for almost twenty years.

It is fair to say that Art is probably more at the mercy of cost than other departments. For the underwater vicar in THE BEDSITTING ROOM Assheton Gorton had to build the dome of St Paul's Cathedral sticking out of the waves engulfing a flooded metropolis. He worked out a clever scheme for floating the set on the lagoon that lies between the coast and Chesil Bank in Dorset. Unfortunately the cost of this ambitious set (one third actual size) soared upwards, like the dome itself, until it exceeded its estimate by rather a large amount. Richard's remedy for this was to recoup the money by finishing shooting a week early; this because of an interesting deal he had struck with United Artists: they would let him make his films the way he wanted them without interference, and he for his part would never take them over either schedule or budget. Unfortunately after a week of Richard (a fast worker at the best of times) in overdrive, the remedy backfired because now Assheton had run out of finished sets.

One bad day on Chobham Common the balloon featured in the picture went out of control, nearly collided with an electricity pylon, and was forced to abort, putting the crew in hospital. There was nothing to do except pack up and go back to Twickenham, where on walking through the main gate I ran into Assheton.

" How did it go today? "

" A disaster, we nearly killed the balloonist. "

" Oh thank heaven; that'll give me a chance to get the next set finished."

Well he *is* the son of an Archbishop (C of E, so it's all right).

I have left Ken Adam till last because he will eventually conduct us into another world; the world of coincidence, of Aunty Gipsy and the seaside photograph, but transmuted to tragic dimensions.

We had both been around for a good many years before finally coming together on Norman Jewison's BOGUS in 1995. When we met I said we had already collaborated in a manner of speaking, on his film GOLDFINGER, and while I was at it told him also about the near miss with Tony Richardson, Harry Saltzman and Nijinsky.

Ken is German by birth, his family left Berlin in 1934, and he spent the war flying Typhoons and Spitfires in the RAF. For his fellow pilots, to whom he was always "Heinie", baling-out over occupied territory probably meant spending the rest of the war in a POW camp; for Ken, who to this day still has traces of a German accent, the consequences do not bear thinking about. He of course never alludes to any of this, so I had the chance to like and respect him for himself and his work alone, before finding it out.

A lady who has been a good friend of mine over many years was blissfully married to a young pilot at that period - all too briefly because he died as a result of being shot down by the Americans. I was telling Ken about this one day and he said that the same thing had nearly happened to him,

" ... they were always doing it."
(Eduard Graftiaux would endorse that)

"I was only saved because my supplementary fuel tanks had not been fitted properly. We had crossed the French coast when I switched over and the engine coughed. The squadron commander told me to go back, use minimum revs, and try to glide into Manston. I had just turned away when the American planes swooped down. I heard it all on the intercom."

A day or so later I was chatting to Betty over the phone and asked her the name of her husband's squadron.

" 609 Squadron, Pat Thornton-Brown. "
When I told Ken he was quiet for a moment.

" He was my Squadron Commander. I was flying number two to him. It was he who ordered me back to Manston. Everyone else was lost. He saved my life. "
So I met up with the last person ever to speak with Betty's husband, fifty two years afterwards.

I hope it is clear by now that I am not ill-disposed towards art departments; like the little girl with the curl, when they are good they are very very good, and with people like Assheton, Lila de Nobili, Derek Jarman, Stephen Grimes, Jocelyn Herbert, Stuart Craig, and Ken Adam - I've had more than my share of luck.

"Why is there only one word for Thesaurus?"

More Commercials

In the intervals between features my time was spent happily doing commercials.

20

One of these, on J stage at Shepperton, was to advertise cigars; the director was Richard Lester and the actor an elderly Groucho Marx, someone who had been as much a part of childhood for me as Peter Pan or Long John Silver.

A Madeleine was a small French cake the taste of which, in Proust's novel, used to evoke long forgotten memories of childhood days, and, like a bespectacled Madeleine, Groucho unlocked Mr Shotter from the recesses of my mind. Mr Shotter owned the barber's shop, just up the road from "El Donnée", where we were sent for haircuts. He boasted an assistant and we always carried an extra threepence with which to tip him; however we were told that it would be most insulting to tip the proprietor himself, and so the game was so to manage things that Mr Shotter cut your hair and you could keep the threepence. One method was to be exceptionally polite and allow some unmotivated grown-up to take your place, or else bury your head in a magazine when the assistant called "next please". Success in this manoeuvre meant a ninepenny instead of a sixpenny seat at the pictures and I had already learned that they look much better from further back.

I'd taken great pains over the lighting so that nothing would be reflected in the famous glasses. Groucho came onto the stage with Richard and they stood talking for a while; he was wearing gold rimmed spectacles. After a bit Richard called me over to introduce me and while Groucho was telling a story about W.C.Fields I stole an occasional glance at them to see how successful I'd been. He obviously noticed (he didn't miss much) and when the time came to start shooting looked up at the lighting, gave me a nice smile, removed his gold frames and drew the legendary horn-rims from his pocket - there was no glass in them.

The Billy Fields story was about how they had both been working at the same studio and Fields suggested they went back to his place for a drink at the end of the day. Throughout his life W.C.Fields was very insecure, and this led him to behave in an unusual manner; wherever he happened to be he would open an account in an assumed name with the local bank and to this day there are unknown sums lying hidden in lost bank accounts all over the States. They reached the house, went upstairs, and Fields cautiously unlocked a door which opened to reveal a room filled from floor to ceiling with bootleg whisky.

" But Billy, prohibition's finished. "

Fields waved a confident arm over his store.

" They can bring it back. "

Our shooting commenced and at the end of the first take Richard said that we would go again.

" You're going to tamper with perfection? "

I think the truth is that on this one occasion Richard felt that Groucho had landed a margin short of perfection, but the reply itself was unquestionably perfect and if I were an actor it would certainly be in my repertory of stock answers.

Another one day advert featuring a great comedian, English this time, was with Kenneth Williams, and that strangely sad man cost me my lunch; I sat next to him and was unable to eat anything at all for laughing. He had a serious love for the English language that I shared, and an anxiety about sex that fortunately I did not.

A director in Madrid had the uncommon name, for a Spaniard, of Eduardo McLean. Naturally I asked how he came by it and so got a glimpse of the patchwork of history that all of us carry about unawares. Scotland had clung tenaciously to the old religion long after the Reformation and Eduardo's great great great great great great great great great great great grandfather was its most renowned shipwright at a time when Philip and the Jesuits (an Iberian Heavy Metal Group) were making arrangements to go on tour. He packed himself off to Spain to build a large number of ships which Fran Dray the first promptly set about sinking. Eleven generations had reconciled things somewhat and Eduardo had an English wife.

In Paris the historical associations were more recent. We were shooting on that grand eminence that looks out from the Palais de Chaillot across the Seine to the Eiffel Tower. At our feet, cut deep into the granite, was an inscription which, translated, said that on a certain date this spot with its splendid prospect had been dedicated by President Mitterrand "... to the freedom of mankind of all Nations".

" Was that before you sank the RAINBOW WARRIOR? "

Weak smiles all round,

" Oui. "

The set for a commercial featuring the French mime artist Marcel Marceau was a completely empty cyclorama painted, I think, a light grey. It seemed obvious to light this without any shadows at all so that there would be nothing to interfere with the outline of the artist. It does not appear to have been obvious to anyone else because Monsieur Marceau became very excited when he arrived and declared that this was the first time he had ever seen lighting that properly suited mime. It is always nice to make people happy; I was happy too since there was now nothing further to do other than cast an occasional eye at him to see that all was well. That was easy enough because he proved to be riveting to watch; most of all during a break in the shooting when he quietly tried something out for himself. He sat at a piano, went through some elaborate preliminaries and started to play. After a few bars the keyboard cover came down trapping his fingers. He pushed it back up again and played on but finding one note that continually refused to sound, stood up, leaned over and peered inside the lid which at once came down and hit the back of his head. All this on an empty stage - though it could have been no more real had there been a Steinway D standing there.

French governments, unlike their Britannic counterparts, are able in some way to recognise their artists; they had allotted a very adequate sum for him to make a film record of his work and he said that he would like the director and myself to do it with him. His aspirations may perhaps have been a bit grandiose for so simple an art as mime - nothing less than the history of the world, or of mankind, I forget which. After a couple of trips to Paris the director decided it was pretentious and made his excuses. Perhaps it was; he certainly knew all about pretension, having his own eye securely fixed on Hollywood, the path to which does not lie through anything as subtle as a mime artist, however eminent. I never heard any more.

Twice during my commercials career I've had to help out with a live facsimile of a well known painting, one here and one in New York. The English job was, predictably, *The Haywain*, and the location people and the art department found a perfect duck pond with the right orientation for light. The only difficulty experienced was in persuading the dog to adopt a Constable-like stance.

New York wanted a Degas, with the usual little ballet girl (what with him and Lewis Carrol) and thanks to being in a studio with a meticulous set provided by the art director it was all rather easy, my contribution being little more than the application of common sense. There was an excellent Skira reproduction beside the dolly, and looking through the camera was quite a shock - there you were inside the painting. However, as so often with advertising people, they wanted to go one better and I was approached to put in some more lights which, as it would have destroyed everything, I declined with the best of excuses,

" Don't ask me, ask Degas. "

Tim Guinness, my New York gaffer with ears all over the stage, came up a bit later on and told me they were all saying that I had attitude. Notwithstanding, shooting appeared to be going on happily enough and at the end of the day they came and asked to be photographed with me. After obliging I quietly asked Tim why he thought they wanted to be photographed alongside somebody with "attitude", at which he very unquietly addressed his answer to the world at large,

" Cos you're a classy act and they're used to bums in the Park. "

I wondered if the agency people had asked for a photograph with Orson Welles after the voice-over session he did in London for frozen foods.

Orson (cozily)

" We know a remote farm in Lincolnshire where Mrs Buckley lives; in July peas grow there. "

Advertising person

" Could you emphasise "in", "*in* July" "

Orson (for real)

" Why? That doesn't make any sense. Impossible, meaningless ... show me how you can emphasise "in" at the start of an English sentence and I'll go down on you. "

I was asked to do a commercial in Cape Town for the Halifax Building Society. The director Richard Loncraine usually worked with another cameraman, Peter Hannen, but that gentleman declined to visit a country whose politics he thoroughly disapproved of. I said yes straight way, not so much from being more unprincipled than Peter as from a belief that you can knock something more effectively the closer your acquaintance with it, and went along harbouring more misgivings about spiders than about racial bigots. I had decided to make use of the trip to finally get to grips with Meredith, an author I have never managed to like, and long before touch down was wishing I'd brought something more amusing. However South Africa is the only place in the world, so far, where the immigration people have asked to see what books I'd got - so I probably have dull old George to thank for not being arrested. A good job I'd not brought Anna Sewell - *Black Beauty* with those nice white children and their horse *was* a banned book.

The local contact was a gentlewoman with an extremely posh accent, complete with tweeds, Lisle stockings and sensible shoes. Driving to lunch after a recce the first morning, somebody noticed an animal leaping about in the scrub and enquired if it was a springbok. She very much doubted that it was, as they were become very scarce. We had clearly hit upon her pet subject, if not indeed her pet animal; and she went on to tell us at length about their efforts to prevent poaching and preserve the species. A single pink gin over lunch was sufficient to bring about a startling change. The headmistress of Roedean gave place to the

"Why is there only one word for Thesaurus?"

commandant of Ravensbruck, asserting apropos of nothing at all that the thing to do with the entire native population of the Continent was to machine-gun the lot. There are two possible responses, one to be angry, the other to laugh at her. I chose the latter,

" Isn't that a bit inconsistent with what you were telling us on the way here. One minute you're worried about the bok and the next you want to shoot all the poor old blacks? "
It wasn't much but it shut her up.

My next job with Richard was in Italy (I don't think Peter had any objections to that country - he was probably on a picture at the time). It was for Kleenex paper handkerchiefs and there was an old woman sitting at a kitchen table peeling onions and crying her eyes out. A very diminutive boy, full of grandfilial love, runs out to the shops, returns with a box of the product and puts it triumphantly on the table-top. After the first take he absolutely refused to go again, was offered more money but being below the age when mercenary considerations carry any weight, declined it. Finally the tearful child was taken aside for a brief word with the director after which he ran up and slammed the box of tissues down on the table with a big smile and for as many takes as were wanted. When we had finished I told Richard I was impressed by his ability to handle the younger sort of actor and he explained. The old woman smelled rather badly which was the reason the child had thrown a hate on her and refused to go near again.

" What made him change his mind? "

" I told him she had a weak heart and if he slammed the box down hard enough she'd probably have an attack and die. "

Sometimes I would be asked for a show-reel of my work on commercials. For a young cameraman making his way in advertising a show-reel is very sensible but I had been fortunate enough (since the Paddington Station film) never to need this, and had drifted into the habit, whenever asked, of suggesting they look at my most recent feature film. Not long after the MUSKETEERS had opened, I was in Richard Lester's office in Twickenham Studios when a call was put through for me from somebody's secretary asking about a show-reel. I politely explained that the current show-reel was running at the Odeon Leicester Square. When I'd replaced the receiver Richard seemed more amused than this mild pleasantry warranted.

" It's been moved to the Haymarket. There's a Gerry Fisher picture at the Odeon; he's a good cameraman - you should get some work. "

It was the case at one time that to get the best results on the screen one put Kodak negative in the camera but printed onto Gevaert positive stock - it just looked better that way. It had been going on for a long time and was common practice with a lot of people. A job came along in Miami for Kodak Instamatic cameras and on arriving there I was immediately set upon by a group of the very worst type of PR people from the advertising agency and also from the client.

" This spot is all about photography and what you do represents our product. That's why we got someone like yourself all this way so it can look as good as possible. "

" Do you honestly mean that - as good as possible? "

" Sure we mean it. "

" Then we'll shoot on your negative and print it on Gevaert. "

I was left in peace for the entire ten days of shooting.

There was one commercial for a French mineral water that finished up in mid-air, quite literally, on the top of Mont Blanc. It was a spot way above the téléphérique and only reachable by a hair-raising helicopter voyage following the path of the glacier through the mountains. There were two actors, one a six year old boy and the other a tame eagle. The eagle's job was to perch on an outcrop of rock and then fly off it into the sun, mine was to keep him in picture while he did so, and whatever the six year old boy had to do I've forgotten. The eagle and I had just managed to get it right when our Alpine guide said there was a storm coming and we must all get off the mountain as quickly as possible. The first trip down, the chopper carried the boy, the eagle and myself (clearly regarded as the three beings most undesired in a storm on a mountaintop). The boy sat in front next to the pilot, and the eagle and I side by side behind them. As we lifted off, it struck me that that although for the child and myself this was a fairly novel experience, for the eagle it must have been quite astounding. After all he was accustomed to doing this sort of thing far better on his own and with a lot less fuss. Indeed all the way down he divided the time between peering out of the side window and directing critical glances at the pilot, like a wary instructor with a maladroit learner-driver. This is the only time I've sat next to a bird in an aircraft.

Back on firm ground a call for a British Rail commercial shooting on the concourse of Waterloo station aroused fond memories of "temps perdu" and several times during the day I thought how delightful it would be to hear Bobby over the public address inviting his young sailor over from platform 9. But it was a different railway now, where there were no passengers any more, they were all called customers. The reason for this finally became apparent when my train back to Brighton was forty minutes late. The word passenger had carried too clear an implication of people being transported successfully.

Sometimes I am asked to work on a commercial as a director. This is really enjoyable because having no wish to build a career at it there is no need to put up with unreasonable interference from the agency. I lay stress on *unreasonable* because of course you are only there at all to give them what they want, and it would be very arrogant and stupid to forget it. The charmed life I have led as a director is entirely owing to the kind and wise producers who have looked after me, and on my part to an honest approach to people. I was once asked to meet an agency person in New York about a job for American Airlines. His very first words were,

" We're looking for boundless enthusiasm here. "

I quickly assured him that if I felt any enthusiasm he would be the last to know about it, and of course did not get the job - it would have been disastrous if I had. Professionals always care about what they do and don't waste time wagging their tails over it.

I did land a Yoghurt film in Munich though. A group of Germans of all ages and sizes, wearing folk costume and each waving their own pot of the product, was going to sing a Bavarian chorus in praise of yoghurt. The set was a theatrical cut-out of rolling meadows, and the blue-screen was involved because behind the distant mountains, instead of the customary sun, a yoghurt logo would rise in its place. I took two people with me from England, an operator and Dennis Bartlett, the best and nicest blue-screen technician there is. When we arrived I was introduced to a young American in his early twenties who was to be my first assistant director and interpreter combined. He was a pleasant lad but a trifle too pleased with himself after his two years in Germany. There was only one master shot with the crowd and I told him to keep them off the stage, in the dressing-rooms and corridors, until everything was ready; then we could get them on and do the shot while they were still interested in a new environment. No sooner were they all in place than a girl addressed me in German. I looked at my interpreter.

" She wants to go to the toilet. "

" She's only just got here; five minutes and we'll be finished - that is unless we start *literally* pissing about. So ask her to wait. "

He did this in his best German whereat she threw her pot of yoghurt at him, missing by inches, and flounced off the stage. I now understood that one of the perks attached to being a director is that when you say they can't go to the toilet they throw the yoghurt at someone else. The rest of the crowd stood aghast at such unteutonic flouting of authority, so to make them feel more at ease -

" Please tell them to be patient and as soon as we have done this they all have my permission to throw their yoghurt ..."

(he looked alarmed)

"... not at you or me, but at those people standing over there. "

A large body of agency people quickly left the stage, everything went splendidly and we finished the job early, but I have not up to now been asked back.

The Compleat Tourist in Bavaria will remember the pair of lions either side the entrance to the Residenz that faces the Feldherrenhalle. During the Third Reich they were deemed inadequate by the SS, who had offices inside the building, and they were supplemented by two younger lions belonging to a Mr Himmler. The two bronze guardians have bright shiny noses because Bavarians down the years have always touched them for good luck. I believe no one touched the noses of the two SS guards, nor do I think they would have had any good luck by so doing, but every passer-by was required to salute them and yell "Heil Hitler" into the bargain. However at the back of the Feldherrenhalle is the Viscardigasse, a passageway through which, with a bit of a detour, the nuisance could be avoided. It became popularly known as the Drückebergergasse, or Shirker's Alley, and I like to think that my young yoghurt-thrower may have derived her independent spirit from parents who regularly used it.

Some films in Washington DC had the oddest idea behind them. They were to advertise a local bank and each was restricted to one 30 second shot of some idyllic scene in the contemplation of which the beholder would somehow decide to move his account. Thirty seconds is an eternity on the screen and even my slack principles would not permit of taking their cash for supplying a batch of picture postcards, so I had to think a bit, and the job is only of interest now because it sparked off one original idea. I gathered together two good assistants I knew and an elderly NC Mitchell camera having (along with other refinements no longer available) a variable shutter from 180 degrees to zero that can be altered while the camera is running. It was summer and among the locations there was a meadow adjoining a paddock with a chestnut horse trotting contentedly round in circles. I set the camera down on the top-hat with a longish lens and arranged some wild flowers in the foreground; behind them in the middle distance were some azaleas, beyond those a clump of silver birches, and finally in the background the horse. By moving the focus front to back each would become sharp in turn, but in normal circumstances the foreground and middle distance would become progressively blurred. To prevent this my two assistants lay either side of the camera, one on the lens iris and one on the shutter. Starting with a stop of 2.3 and a 5 degree shutter I gave them a count every five seconds and as one lad closed the iris his companion opened up the shutter, thereby keeping the exposure constant. It meant that at the start there were only wild flowers against a clear background and then in their turn azaleas, then the birch trees, and then the horse were etched into the picture as if out of nowhere, all in focus together.

It is fairly safe to assert that this was never done before or since, there'd be no occasion to for one thing; it will also hardly come as a surprise that nobody will ever see it. When a VHS copy eventually arrived in Brighton, the editor, true to form, had cut off the whole shot and held an entire thirty seconds of the camera run-out at the end of it. Of all the obstacles a visual idea has to surmount on its way to the screen, the cutting-room is the steepest.

After a span of thirty years my TV commercials, apart from a few delightful encounters with old freinds, have virtually come to a halt. This is understandable for two reasons, film-school alumni are content with a bit less money, which is excellent (whatever may have been going on at

"Why is there only one word for Thesaurus?"

their Alma Mater they can only learn the job by going out and doing it). The other attraction to producers is less happy - they will take a long time over it, which impresses the advertising people no end, who think that if a thing is done at a smart pace it can't be any good, especially the revered pack-shot. Here, unfortunately, the brighter newcomers find themselves at a disadvantage since they will soon get their lighting time down from an impressive three hours to a more sensible ten minutes (there are after all only three places to put a lamp) and once you have become accustomed to lighting everything in your head before saying a word to your electrician it is difficult to take much longer. I think I've stopped at the right moment - there are only happy memories, and of those a great many.

"Why is there only one word for Thesaurus?"

Studios

Originally each of the great studios had its own camera department able to supply every need,

21

but on the documentary side all equipment for freelance work was hired at random from a few individuals who had their own Newman Sinclairs or Eyemos, at varying stages along the road to being worn out. Some, though not all, were cameramen and often managed to get themselves hired into the bargain.

One of the most distinctive of these gentlemen was Oliver of the Topical Press Agency. The first time anyone set eyes on him they were in for a mild surprise, because Mr Oliver always wore a wing collar, a frock coat green with age, and a bowler hat. The sight of this quiet little man standing behind a film camera thus attired would astonish almost anyone and it certainly did me on the day of the opening of the Liverpool Street to Shenfield electrification. It was also the only time I ever saw an Akeley in use. The Akeley was a shallow drum-shaped object with a crank-handle in the middle of it, and looked very much like one of Mrs Beeton's patent knife-cleaners. This one, with a bowler hat attached to it, flashed past me, sticking out of one of the carriage windows of the first train as it sped away from the platform. There were half a dozen cameras at this event but the next day in rushes Oliver's material stood far out beyond the rest - it was simply beautiful. I don't know what lenses were on that old Akeley but, though I continued to smile whenever I saw old Oliver, I also had the greatest respect for him.

The first thing to be done after hiring a camera was to shoot a test on it, then the next day you would know whether it was steady or not and if it was going to scratch the film. It was just as necessary to go through all this even when the camera came from one of the small repair workshops, like that operated by Bert Kingston. His domain was a Dickensian basement in Charlotte Street where the area steps led down into a Fagin's den littered with dismembered parts from every camera you could think of. (It was here years afterwards that I unearthed some of the Ross Xpress lenses used on THE CHARGE OF THE LIGHT BRIGADE). Bert was an amiable man and a good mechanic, if a little rough in some of his ways. I once had to take him an Eymo to look at. After he had made tea for me, he laid the camera on his work bench, carefully undid each of the retaining screws and removed the plate covering the mechanism. He secured the spring and then picked up the body, turned it over and shook hard. A medley of cogs, bearings, and washers scattered in all directions and unfortunately one of the lenses on the turret, not wishing to be left out of things, dislodged itself and flew into the air. Bert, knowing that lenses are never any the better for being dropped on the floor, managed to prevent this from happening by kicking it back up into the air and catching it.

" Saved that one didn't I! "

After this display of combined soccer and cricketing skills Bert, well satisfied, set to work. I am sure by the time he'd finished with it our Eymo was in a better state than when I had taken it in, but it can well be seen why testing before use was unavoidable.

Then, in the midst of all this muddle, an enterprising freelance cameraman, Sydney Samuelson, saved up and bought himself a couple of cameras which he then maintained to a very high standard. Slowly (like birds in a garden growing accustomed to feeding out of your hand) people realised that they could hire Sydney's cameras without having to shoot tests every time. It must have been a similar experience taking off a hair-shirt. His business expanded rapidly and, as Sydney was endowed with brothers on an Old Testament scale, it became a family one. In a remarkably short while the whole pattern of the industry changed and nobody thought about hiring equipment from anywhere else.

They took a just pride in their cameras and each one had a plate attached to the side engraved with the name and year of every film that had been shot with it; a harmless but unnecessary measure since it made no difference to anyone what the apparatus had been pointed at in the past other than to suggest, as the list lengthened, that it was getting worn out; and on one occasion at least it was not quite accurate. Just before THE BED-SITTING-ROOM started I was out of the country, and arrived back on the first day of shooting to find there'd been a last minute change of camera. Samuelsons had modified a BNC Mitchell to give it a reflex finder, a praiseworthy ~~worthy~~ attempt to add to its virtues that had only succeeded in removing them altogether. This was soon apparent and the offending machine was returned by ten o'clock the same morning without so much as a foot of film passing through it. The entire picture

"Why is there only one word for Thesaurus?"

was then shot on a standard BNC out of Shepperton Studios. A couple of years later I walked onto the set of a commercial to find the modified BNC carrying the usual plate with "THE BED-SITTING-ROOM - 1968" at the top of its list. In the cause of historical accuracy I wrote "for 45 minutes" on a piece of camera-tape and stuck it alongside - but I don't suppose it stayed there for long.

While all this was happening a parallel situation developed on the lighting side. Once again it was brothers, this time only two of them. John and Benny Lee had both started as sparks on the rail at Pinewood; something they never forgot, remaining quite unchanged by fortune, and that is rare indeed. They began in the same manner as Sydney, saving their money, buying a few lamps, and providing a worthwhile service. There was a minor setback when a couple of lamps they had purchased were alleged to have fallen off the back of a lorry (if so they must have been quite badly damaged) but the enterprise went ahead and prospered the same as Sydney's. The day came when the pattern of the industry changed for them also, and nobody thought about hiring lamps from anywhere else. It was rather like the Garden of Eden, especially as to the good part being short lived - Samuelsons acquired a small lighting firm that was in difficulties and began to expand it.

Once the camera firm had acquired a lighting side it was natural that it would affect the sort of arrangements they made with customers; it was also quite inevitable that the lighting firm would now get itself a camera interest pretty fast. From here on I think rivalry took the place of sense, and finally, at almost the same moment, two great enterprises that for a quarter of a century had been controlled by men who understood and loved the film business (even if they did not always love and understand each other) came under the control of financial institutions where such passionate involvement is less apparent.

An aspect of our nature from childhood on is to want things only after we have been deprived of them, or as is more often the case, when we ourselves have thrown them out of the pram. We have learned to protect buildings of beauty and worth whose functional days are at an end, but we seem less concerned about others that are still uniquely suited to the use for which they were built. The Carnegie Hall in New York is one of half a dozen concert halls throughout the world that has well nigh perfect acoustics. Though in the end it was rescued from demolition by a determined violinist, a replacement had already been built and donated to New York's orchestra by the philomusical millionaire Avery Fisher.

From the street this unfortunate legacy looks like a municipal swimming bath, and it comes close to sounding like one when you get inside. It is a harsh acoustic and I wish an enterprising orchestra would give half a concert in there and then invite the audience to walk down to 57th Street and hear the other half. When I asked Mark Niekrug how he liked the place he told me he always spent at least an hour on the platform before a recital, playing as quietly as he could (very hard work).

"It is impossible to play soft in there, or develop a beautiful tone; and the hall does nothing to help."

Shortly after this the City of Toronto then commissioned the same people to build the Thompson Hall. That edifice bears a strong resemblance to an airport terminal (one expects to go through passport control any minute), again with matching acoustics. When it first opened there was a general outcry in protest. Now no one seems to mind; with no more concerts being given in the old Massey Hall there is nothing to compare it with - people just got used to bad sound. Human adaptability can be a mixed blessing, though I think it is true to say that if someone built an art gallery without any lighting people would be less tolerant; most of us respect our eyes more than our ears. One day on the set of USED PEOPLE there was a man in a well cut suit talking to Shirley Maclaine. Her hair-dresser whispered in my ear that he was the designer of the Thompson Hall.

" You can speak up - he won't be able to hear you. "

When, in the late 1800s, the stout burgers of Amsterdam wished to build a concert hall worthy of their great city they were I believe wiser, if less adventurous, than the elders of Toronto. In those days the Leipzig Gewandhaus was regarded as the finest hall for sound in existence. The Amsterdamers sent to Leipzig for a set of the plans from which they built an exact copy down to the smallest detail, thanks to which, when our own Mr Harris flattened the Gewandhaus the beautiful hall is still preserved for us in Holland. Apart from the auricular considerations there is another that, for me at least, is immeasurable - on the same platform in Vienna's Musikvereinsaal Brahms stood and conducted, in the Concertgebouw Mahler and Mengelberg, and Tschaikowsky in Carnegie (Tschaikowsky was never in Avery Fisher and I am glad for him; he had troubles enough already).

The Kingsway Hall in London was used a lot by record companies because of its near ideal sound conditions, and in the early 1970s something rather interesting happened there. One company, unable to complete a recording in the time allotted, were delayed several weeks (due to artist commitments) before returning to finish it. On getting the second session's tapes back in the editing room the engineer was disconcerted to find that the sound did not match that of the first session by miles - the same venue, the same orchestra, the same conductor, the same microphone placement. Puzzled, he got on a bus to Kingsway and as soon as he walked inside saw clearly the one thing that was different. They had painted it. The old surface of grime had caressed what the new hard gloss bounced straight off again. It is amusing that shiny paint, that renders a set a nightmare to light because of unwanted reflections, screws up the sound as well, and for the same reason.

When London's Festival Hall was being built just across the road from my first job, there was a great deal of pride expressed by the architects because some acoustical engineers had spent a day firing revolvers and measuring the reverberation time. Now almost the only sounds that are certain never to be heard in a concert hall (unless an assassination attempt is in progress) are gunshots. Had the time been spent listening to a violin with musical human ears there might have been something to boast of, even perhaps a better concert hall.

The film studios that were built in England in the 1930s were as perfect for making films as the Concertgebouw or the Musikvereinssaal are for making music; cathedral-like spaces where you can do things that are impossible anywhere else. There was some daft inverse snobbery at Woodfall, the self appointed guardians of realism, who held that everything done inside a studio must be artificial. As I don't like my friends to be stuck with nonsense, I offered Tony to light any authentic location he gave me so that it looked like a bad set, but he enjoyed his prejudices as much as we all do and never took me up on it. In fact the two approaches have drawn closer together since - just as boys a year or two older at school who seemed part of another world then, will be close contemporaries in adult life.

When speculators are allowed to turn the great stages of MGM and Denham into frozen store rooms, and to demolish Wembley and Elstree to make way for shopping malls, they are never replaced by anything that can be taken seriously. Musicians are occasionally better served; the new Philharmonie in Berlin is a superb modern hall (perhaps the Allied Control for Berlin would not allow the German acousticians to fire any guns inside it).

At the same time that the Carnegie Hall was undergoing a very public restoration in New York, a more private affair was taking place three thousand miles away in Middlesex. In 1972 a City entrepreneur bought Shepperton Studios, sold off half the land for housing; he was then, in his turn, bought out by someone else. I think he was hard done by, with this level of behaviour he should have finished up with at least a knighthood. One of his business associates was Secretary of State, first for the Environment and then for Trade and Industry, which is a fair measurement of the Tory Party's interest in a British Film Industry. The whole apalling story can be found in *Shepperton* by Derek Threadgall, published by the British Film Institute in 1994.

By the time the bleeding remains got back in the hands of people interested in making films, even the cabling between the power-house and H stage had been ripped out because of the value of its copper core. Were someone to buy the Tate Gallery, put all the Turners into Sothebys, rip out the floorboards and take the lead from the roof prior to selling what was left back to the nation, I should like to think that it would raise something of an outcry. Is it so absurd to compare a film factory with a concert hall or an art gallery, or are they not all part of the cultural life-blood of a nation? The cinema may be an indecorous step-child of the arts, but when we have flung it out of our pram for the last time, we may find ourselves crying to have it back.

John and Benny Lee bought what remained of Shepperton in 1984 and set about restoring its former glory. For the first time since it was built they put money (and cabling) in, instead of taking them both out; and the whole place breathed optimism and good sense. They succeeded beyond hope or expectation and it is a sad irony that after years of unequalled contribution to this industry their loss (shared by all who care about how films are made) came about over rivalry in an area where they had no contribution to make.

Pinewood has hopes of lasting safety thanks to the care and foresight of J. Arthur Rank, who left it in trust that it should never be used other than for making films. The place has a history of its own with a boardroom (and part of the dining room) that crossed the Atlantic to New York hundreds of times as the first class lounge of the old *Mauretania* ; and in the bar there is a lighter patch on the fireplace where, for some reason, a plate has been removed that recorded the signing of the Irish treaty there in November 1921, when the house was known as Heatherden Hall.

Elstree is gone now, and I wonder if the Greasy Spoon is gone too. The Greasy Spoon was a café opposite the studio gates where the electricians and riggers would go for breakfast in preference to the studio canteen, and where I often joined them for a cup of tea. One morning the place was even busier than usual and the poor girl taking the orders hung about the table while six electricians ran through the permutations of sausages, eggs, beans, tomatoes, bacon and toast, deciding which to leave out. Just when they'd made up their minds she darted off and by the time she came back they'd forgotten again. This happened a couple of times and as she moved away towards a more decisive table one of the lads observed,

" That girl has hairy legs. "
I thought I would amplify this,
" Hairy legs and no patience. "
" That sounds like you governor. "
This was the second time my gaffer, Brian Kemp, left me incapable of an adequate response, having already challenged my total of fourteen nannies by laying his own claim to be the fifteenth.

I am sometimes drawn to walk alone onto a stage where I have just spent weeks - perhaps months - in the most amazing and wonderful sets, the mirrored room in Oz or the great hall of Elsinore, and stand in the vast empty space with the lonely chains hanging down from the grid thirty five feet above, waiting for the next company of ghosts to arrive. It is as much a tragedy as any, that the great studios are becoming as ephemeral as the sets that stood inside them.

The American Film Theatre

In 1972 an American gentleman, Eli Landau, had an idea : to make a series of films of the best contemporary theatre with as far as possible the cast, director, and designer of the original productions, and to show them throughout the USA on a subscription basis.

22

The American Film Theatre would bring Broadway and London to every town in the States with separate performances and advance booking through American Express (with whom he had some arrangement). As he never came back to make any more I suppose it was not profitable enough, which is a pity for generations of late-comers; imagine well made films of Mrs Patrick Campbell in Shaw, or Gertrude Lawrence and Noel Coward together. I was lucky enough to work on two of their productions: Harold Pinter's THE HOMECOMING, directed by Peter Hall in Shepperton Studios, and Edward Albee's A DELICATE BALANCE, directed by Tony Richardson in a house at Crystal Palace.

The Pinter was first. There is a quite different feel working with a company of actors who have played together over a long period, a sort of half-way between the theatre and the cinema that I had not experienced since MARAT SADE. Part of it is perhaps that everyone working in much longer paragraphs, like deep breathing, makes for calm and relaxation; I was glad to be back.

Some subjects more than others gain from a visual style that is appropriate to them and helps hold things together. Others may be quite ordinary by nature and the best thing then is to be ordinary along with them; there's nothing bad about that, it's just sensible, and good ordinary work is better than pretension any time. Sometimes one knows perfectly what to do, or it may occur from a chance remark of the director's. If I don't know I will ask him; what shouldn't happen is for any effort to get into the process. Ideas that come of their own accord will be alive - those that have been laboured over will not. This isn't to suggest sitting idly back without thinking, only that one should ponder with curiosity and a light heart. I didn't have to do much pondering over THE HOMECOMING however, it sprang up armed to the teeth, like Minerva.

My chief electrician was one of the two senior gaffers at Shepperton, Bill Chitty, and he ran his department the same as a sergeant-major runs a company. He was very exacting but he managed it, as had all the sergeant-majors of my experience, with style; it was also amusing. Though he would never gaffer for me again it was the beginning of a long partnership.

One thing I knew I wanted with THE HOMECOMING was for *everything* to be held in good hard focus, not only on wide lenses but on the long ones as well. This would mean small apertures which in turn would require a huge amount of light. Because lighting is really a matter of balance you are governed by how strong you are able to make the brightest source. The day scenes were not really a problem but the night interiors were dependent on the intensity of a large standard lamp which had, at the same time, a symbolic importance for the mildly eccentric family that the play is about. Most opportunely a new development in the manufacture of tungsten light bulbs had just taken place, which was the replacement of a glass envelope with one made out of quartz. The new arrivals were much smaller and flatter in shape, so that a 5k bulb now took up no more space than had hitherto been necessary for a pup. Setting these at 45 degrees to horizontal so that the filament was facing downwards would result in quite a bright lamp; the stand itself could be made out of metal and the shade out of a fire-blanket, so I asked Bill how many of the new bulbs he thought we could get away with. Two he thought.

" Make it four. "

Bill had his doubts, but I don't like to give up too easily and then of course I realised that neither did he - it was the moment that we recognised each other.

We had now got ourselves a 20kw standard lamp. Throughout the play it stands sentinel behind a large wing chair, territory of the family patriarch. As 20kws is the equivalent to ten two-bar electric fires it was a bit warm for the actor sitting underneath, but Paul Rogers put up with it day after day without a murmur. Vivien Merchant on the other hand, as a result of the briefest of sojourns, subsequently chose to decline my services on a later film. You can't please everyone. One day Eli visited us in person; he was obese, perspired continually, and sat in the most comfortable looking chair. Ian Holm offered me money to switch on.

I remember being mesmerised by Harold's surrealist dialogue, and then being shaken out of it by suddenly hearing one of Max's lines spoken by John Gielgud,

" You've had a poxed-up old scrubber in my house all night. "

I looked around but there was no sign of John G., only Michael Jayston. A surprising number of familiar voices on TV commercials would turn out, given close examination, to be Michael.

Mimicry after all, is part of an actor's equipment. Tony Richardson had always an uncommon and quite distinctive manner of speech. Two days after his death was announced, Mary North, who had worked at Woodfall over many years, picked up the phone to hear her old boss say how it was all a total mistake and that he had set Oscar Beuselinck to sue everybody concerned he could think of, on and on for several minutes before the startled girl remembered one actor (*not* Michael Jayston) who had so mastered, not only the voice but every way of putting words together, pause and inflection, that she knew whom she was listening to. It is not chance that over the years "acting", "mime" and "playing" have stood for the same thing, nor that the French vernacular for an actor whether playing Lear or Bottom the Weaver, is "comedien".

Peter Hall had been the first to stage Samuel Beckett's WAITING FOR GODOT and I was not going to miss the chance of saying that to date it was the most depressing evening I had ever spent in a theatre. He seemed genuinely surprised at this.

" Why? It's such an optimistic play."

" Because Godot never comes. "

Peter's eyes lit up -

" Ah, but he *might*! "

Which I suppose is the basis of most religions. Peter Bull's response was a bit more rational. He had been the first Pozzo, and while we were doing JOSEPH ANDREWS together I asked him what he thought.

" I never understood what any of it was about. "

When Tony told Eli he wanted me to do his picture he was advised it would not be possible because THE HOMECOMING would prevent my attending the rehearsals.

" Attend rehearsals? He won't even read the script! "

A lady in Upper Sydenham answered her door at seven o'clock one morning to find an easily recognised film star on the step asking if they might come inside and take a bath, adding in an equally recognisable voice that it need only be a cold one. Katherine Hepburn, on finding that the bath had been removed from the empty house hired by the company to shoot A DELICATE BALANCE had simply walked next-door.

Once again I was working with someone who had been familiar to me since the days of Mr Shotter and the ninepennys. I'd met her a couple of times during preparation and she walked over the first morning on the set,

" You're a very charming boy" (she is probably the last person to ever call me that) "but you won't be able to do anything about my neck. "

I had failed to appreciate, because she had such good features, that she might be sensitive in other areas; it now became clear why she always wore high necked dresses. She went on to say that at the time of THE AFRICAN QUEEN, when she was more than twenty years younger, Jack Cardiff artlessly proposed consultation with a surgeon.

" Well I can't promise you a lot but I won't be as rude as that. "
Tony had overheard this exchange and joined us.

" You're so vain you actors, worrying about your looks when it's your talent that matters. "

" But Tony, it's really vulnerable being an actor. "
I sought to be very gallant,

" Oh only if you're a bad actor. "

" That's worse than Jack Cardiff! "

For the part of Claire, the alcoholic sister, Tony's original casting was a bit too authentic for Kate, who knew all about this sort of thing from looking after Spencer Tracy over the years. After a few rehearsals she put her foot down firmly and the actor had to go. In the telling of this Kate was alluded to as an interfering old bat, which is Tony's way of accepting that someone who has disagreed with him was right. He later admitted that indeed the film might never have got finished, but added that the lady was a marvellous actress and her few rehearsals had taught him a lot about the part.

For a scene of the family at dinner I thought of a lighting arrangement to simulate a chandelier hanging over the centre of the table. The instant it went up I understood two things, first that it was quite useless for my purposes and second that it would completely screw the sound department, who had problems enough already. Being on the top of Sydenham Hill, we had Kate's cold bath on one side of us and the BBC's transmitter on the other; whenever they extended the Fisher boom it became an aerial and Edward Albee became engaged in a losing battle with "Dad's Army".

Unfortunately before I could get a word out Tony saw all the implications of my bad idea and, being Tony, insisted on carrying on with it.

" It's wonderful I love it. "

" Tony it's terrible. "

" The trouble with you Mr Watkin is you never know when you've *really* been clever. "

In vain the sound crew tied a white handkerchief to the end of the boom (it had so many uses on this picture), Tony would not relent. He could embarrass me and aggravate them at the same time, and that was irresistible. Admittedly he had a score to settle with them. It was at the start of his affair with Griselda Grimond (daughter of the Liberal Party Leader) and one of the sound crew had greeted him the first morning on the set,

" You've changed your politics then? "

Very likely he had already decided to loop the scene in any case, he often preferred it that way, believing that he could improve performances. Actors who went along with that idea were more likely to be influenced by other considerations; Olivier, whose fee for a day's looping was immense, would get quite cross if a mixer managed to record too many clean tracks.

Kate was a wonderful person, always direct, always positive. A director I worked with subsequently, told me that during adolescence he had been rather overweight. One evening he was standing in the wings when Kate was playing *The Heiress* in St Martin's Lane. She walked out of her dressing-room and stood next to him waiting for her cue; when it came she looked at this boy, a complete stranger,

" You're too handsome to be fat. "

and walked onto the stage.

She never had any problem of that sort, luckily for her as she is one of the few people I've met more addicted to chocolate than I am. On the table for the dining-room scene just mentioned was a silver tray piled high with Fortnum and Mason's truffles. I felt entitled to one or two on the ground that they would have come from Audrey's in Brighton, who've supplied Fortnums with chocolates over many years, but Kate had no such excuse.

It was invigorating to work with her; she knew everything that was going on and, the best kind of busybody there is, actively helped to make it all work. After a couple of sneezes a mountain of vitamin C tablets appeared on the camera dolly and I was instructed to swallow the lot. If there were any kind of problem her, " *Think* about it" would remind those who rely on habit, that thinking usually works better.

Tony was an even match for her, given the occasion. We went a little late one evening, till about half-past seven.

" I hope you're not going on much longer, I've a dinner engagement that might lead to a wealthy marriage. "

" Really - who with, Cecil Beaton? "

" WHAT? "

" Oh I just thought you might be carrying on where Garbo left off."

I always hoped to meet with her again. It has not happened, but fresh in the mind's ear is the inflection, and that voice.

"*Think* about it."

Terence Donovan.   *Photo: Terry O'Neill*

 "Why is there only one word for Thesaurus?"

Yellow Dog, Black Cat

Donovan, Bailey, and Duffy were the three outstanding photographers of the sixties.

23

I photographed a couple of commercials for David Bailey, and hundreds for Donovan who had his own production company. He had a sense of proportion to go with it and it was not uncommon to finish a thirty second film before lunch (I remember an 11-30am wrap at Alexandra Palace). This shouldn't really surprise anyone, considering that a feature director who didn't manage two and a half minutes screen time a day would be in serious trouble. His producer often pleaded in vain for one shot to be left until after lunch so that the agency would feel they were getting value for money, and I shall always remember Terence explaining to one bunch of advertising people that there is no ratio between the excellence of a photograph and the time taken to get it.

Terence wore a charcoal grey suit, a Turnbull and Asser shirt and a Rolls Royce with much the same timeless inevitability as Mr Oliver his wing collar, frock coat and bowler hat. He was also a judo Black Belt, and when he decided the time had come for him to direct a feature film, his interest in Japanese culture led him to commission a screenplay from Kurosawa's scriptwriter Hashimoto, and to cast Jiro Tamaya as his leading actor. Just before shooting started, one of the backers, perhaps through a too literal interpretation of his role, backed out. Terry confided this to me and said he intended to carry on, using his own resources until he could not afford to pay the crew - and then he would stop.

After the first week of working in the most delightful atmosphere, as it always was with him - quick, economical and acute, I asked if the money was sorted out.

" Not yet. "

" How on earth can you be this relaxed and focussed on what you're doing?"

" Tell you the secret - never pick up a telephone. "

And so he directed and completed THE YELLOW DOG quite happily. It is the best example of cheerful self reliance I know, and sets him apart as a very remarkable man. Since then of course the cellular phone has made film directing more difficult.

Our continuity girl was Maggie Owens. She had undergone major surgery and on that account it was often assumed that it was not sensible to employ her. She was a sturdy, courageous, jolly person, and extremely good at her job. That was enough for Terry, and any commercial with him I knew I would be seeing Maggie.

He used to give me a lift out to the location, a roughish neighbourhood in the East End of London. Walking away from the Rolls Royce one morning we met an electrician,

" Better not leave it there, Guvnor - they might put a scratch down the side. "

" Can't think like that - it's only a tin overcoat. "

Our Japanese actor was very intelligent with perfect manners and intensely serious about his work. He had a big following back at home, which I only discovered when we met with some Japanese tourists who all stopped dead in their tracks and gazed at him as open-mouthed as oriental good manners would allow.

It happened we were in Kensington at the time of the motor show and one morning our star from the East asked the camera crew if it was close enough for him to go along during the lunch hour, so my clapper-loader, an obliging youth, offered to take him. One hour is not much but it was time enough for Jiro to buy the most expensive car in the show (I forget what) and a London taxi as well. At the end of shooting, young Laurie Frost paid a return visit to collect his commission, shedding glory on the camera department and earning considerably more that week than I did.

Jiro was constantly attended by his personal servant, a sweet little man called Yoshi, and their double-act together was an endless delight to the unit. One day I was having lunch with Jiro and as usual Yoshi sat at the next table, where he was just about to have his first experience of "Spotted Dick" when he was prevented by a sharp command in Japanese from Jiro, who had made the mistake of choosing rhubarb crumble and decided he didn't like it. A quick exchange was effected and what was left of the offending crumble was meekly eaten by Yoshi.

Years afterwards I worked on a commercial for a Japanese product and at lunch was surrounded by its native representatives. Conversation was none too brisk; I searched desperately for any topic we might have in common and finally thought I'd found just the thing in one of their top actors.

"Why is there only one word for Thesaurus?"

" I made a picture with Jiro Tamaya called THE YELLOW DOG. What's he up to these days? "

There was a slight pause.

" He aah - Hara Kiri, last week. "

This effectively put an end, not only to Jiro but also to the conversation, and I sat quietly wondering what had happened to Yoshi.

Berry Gordy is someone who has made the transition, rare in human affairs, from being one of the least privileged to one of the most, and he deserved it - bringing together a collection of artists like Motown was a considerable creative achievement. Our meeting came about in an odd way. Tony Richardson had just had a project shelved and was at a loose end at the very moment Berry was looking for someone to direct a picture with Diana Ross. Rather than sit around, he agreed, for the first and only time, to work as a contract director for a set fee.

Filming was to start in Chicago but before I had even left England the Hollywood syndrome cut in. Neil Hartley, Tony's producer and an old friend, telephoned in the middle of the night to say that "they" did not feel that I would know how to photograph black people. We had a laugh and I assured him that, unlike South Africa and the Southern States of the USA, silver halides and D76 were not stupid enough to make distinctions about race, sent Tony my love and forgot all about it. Next night an embarrassed Neil called again. Did I realise that Diana had to have a pink filter in her keylight? And what's more Billy D. Williams, her leading man, had to have a purple one in his? Like spots in a case of measles the symptoms were now out.

" Neil, would you get them to enquire wherever all this is coming from (I'd a fair idea) if there was a scene with a platoon of commandos setting out on a night raid, at what point, when the men start blacking their faces, should the pink filter go on the keylight?"

That did the trick all right and I heard no more.

We started off, with Alan McCabe operating, and with Tony in splendid form. Between them they devised a mechanically elaborate shot inside a tenement block in Chicago's black ghetto, starting with camera and elemac on a narrow landing at the top of a flight of stairs, up which Diana and Billy D. are staggering after an evening out. He fumbles with his keys, opens the door, switches on the light, and they start to dance. The camera follows through the doorway and they perform an intricate "pas de trois" round the apartment, at the end of which Billy D. scoops Diana up in his arms and carries her into the bedroom. The camera, needless to say, follows, and finishes up close as the two heads land on the pillows. With a shot like that there are a number of things that can easily go wrong - the light-change mis-timed, an actor stumbling over a line or the elemac stumbling over a sound cable; but everyone knows that, sooner or later, there will come the one take when everything starts to flow naturally, and all will be right. By a mischance, when, after several

A Little Transistor radio.   *Photo: Chris Mullen*

false beginnings, it was finally achieved, Diana and her lover were found to be sharing the pillow with my Jaro foot-candle meter. This was even worse than sun-visors intruding upon the battle of Alma. Alan carefully locked off the camera and looked grimly around for me, but was forestalled by Tony,

" Don't make a fuss, Alan - it's a little transistor radio."

At the end of one long night of exteriors in Chicago's black ghetto I was faced with a problem. Billy D's hair was disappearing into the shadows and needed a backlight to pick it out. However we were covering a wide area and a long cable run was involved, by which time it would be daylight, so I chose to live with it rather than risk not getting the shot; it wasn't the end of the world. Towards the end of the second week Neil came and said there were a few shots that Berry was not happy about and would I view them with him on Sunday morning? After making the right amount of fuss I agreed to go along. In the theatre three shots came up, two of them bad prints and the other - Billy D's disappearing hair.

" The first two are just the print; the other is down to me, and it won't happen again. "

" Right" said Berry and left the theatre.

By this time Tony had problems also, and more serious ones. Berry was having evening rehearsals with Diana and Billy D. in his hotel room, which meant that Tony had to undo everything the next morning before he could work with them. By now I had come to like Berry, he was completely straightforward in all the dealings I had with him, and Tony, I think, felt the same. But there cannot be two directors and it would have ended quite simply with Tony resigning, except that of course if he did so he would not get his fee. In the friendliest way therefore he suggested that Berry should fire him, take over, and direct the kind of film he wanted. It took a day or two but finally Berry did fire him. I thought it was right that he should have a DP of his own choosing rather than Tony's, and told his factotum that I would tide them over until they found someone else and then go. That caused another phone-call in the middle of the night, this time from Berry himself.

" Why're you going, d'you hate me? "

" No. Actually I like you very much. "

" Come and see me. "

" How about in the morning? "

"Why is there only one word for Thesaurus?"

In his suite Berry was wearing a most beautiful burnous, just what Joseph's coat must have been like.

"... with most people out here, that morning in the theatre would have taken four hours."

I stayed and finished his film for him.

The lawyers started to argue about Tony's money, and as Neil said, it would have dragged on for ages and their fees would have swallowed up most of it; but not with Berry around.

" The guy's a friend. I like him - I fired him - pay him. "

"Why is there only one word for Thesaurus?"

Franco

The start of 1974 was a bad time.

24

A friend of mine, we had lived together for twenty one years, died in April. I had turned down Franco Zeffirelli's JESUS OF NAZARETH because I could not be away for any length of time. Now everything was suddenly changed. Things had changed for Franco also; he had just started shooting when his cameraman, Armando Nanuzzi, was offered an Italian feature to direct and asked if he might leave in order to do it. I flew out to Tunisia and plunged into things.

Apart from the Bartleby syndrome on CATCH 22 I cannot remember any instance of being asked to alter the lighting on a picture (commercials are another matter, and with them it's of no consequence - I'll leave the lens cover on if they want) until Franco did it on JESUS, and with him there were two things you could depend on, his taste and his honesty. If his idea is better than mine everybody has gained, and if it is not he will be the first to say.

For the night scene inside the Sanhedrin I had a simple arrangement of two 8ft square gold reflectors at different angles to each other above the set, each with a 10k aimed at it. They created two pools of light, similar in feeling to Rembrandt's painting of the Circumcision (sorry but that's the best way to describe it) and it was ready by half past eight. Franco then arrived with a preconceived idea of his own, very much the opposite, with tiny points of light from endless oil lamps.

" It'll be ever so fussy Franco, and take until lunchtime. "

" Never mind, I'd like to see. "

At midday I sent for him.

" Na, na, na, don't like it. "

I turned everything out and switched on the two 10ks which I'd been careful not to move.

" Lovely darling - we shoot. "

then he added

" You're just like Lila. "

" Not exactly - she doesn't like to be paid. "

" That's where Lila's stupid and you're not. "

This happened on our first day with Laurence Olivier, who had been called at an early hour for make-up and to wait around in the Tunisian heat wearing a heavy costume; he was unwell at the time and understandably displeased. I was told later that he said to the Italian producer that a cameraman who took as long as this ought to be fired (I would agree with him). I also sympathised with the Italian producer who had just had an unsuccessful run in with my clapper-loader, due to the Continental nicety about early morning greetings already described re MADEMOISELLE.

" You're a very rude boy - you don't say good morning. "

" It's half-past two. "

" That doesn't matter. "

" Good morning then. "

to me " You should fire him. "

Franco came over,

" Don't worry Barry, when I get my yacht you can be my cabin boy."

There is an account of the business with Larry in Franco's own book that, by an oversight, fails to mention the reason for the delay. The next time I stayed in Tony Richardson's house in LA I told him the story knowing it would amuse him. A few days later at about six in the evening I was reading in my room and heard Tony greet someone who had obviously just looked in for an evening drink. Then I was called for,

"David, come out here, there's a friend of yours."

and there indeed was Larry. I guessed what was coming.

"Oh Larry you know Mr.Watkin - the last time you worked together you said he should be fired."

Larry mumbled something about not being able to remember but he'd have done much better to laugh over it. There could never be any back-biting with Tony; he'd wait until he the biter and the bit were together and then repeat every word. It is puzzling that someone who hated pretence as much as he did should have stayed resolutely in the closet to the very end, the more so as everybody knew. When the camera crew on CHARGE OF THE LIGHT BRIGADE told him he had a very camp way of speaking he claimed with all seriousness that it was just a Bradford accent.

While the director was staging Robert Powell being scourged by the Roman Centurions his producer, Dyson Lovel, and I chanced to be high

"Why is there only one word for Thesaurus?"

up on the battlements of an ancient Arab fortress observing the pantomime in the vast amphitheatre below. Franco, showing an extra how to scourge, was demonstrating a stroke that from that distance appeared more like a backhand at tennis.

" Looks like the centre court at Wimbledon. "
Dyson grunted,
" You're right it's ridiculous, "
and hurried off. Minutes later he reappeared below, a tiny figure that approached the director and said something; I couldn't hear what but hardly needed to - with nicely exaggerated mime of a limp-wristed queen wielding a lash Franco went back to his actors, like something from a Jacques Tati film.

Clive Reed, a great first assistant director, told me that when he was preparing a day's work he would try to imagine all the things that could possibly go wrong. Then he would separate them into two categories: what was preventable and what was not. By the time he came to the set he had taken care of the first and had a fair idea what to do if confronted with any of the second. I wonder if he would have anticipated what happened to the Three Kings.

The place of their meeting was a beautiful oasis at the foot of three ridges that lead down from the surrounding heights. Franco had planned for a caravan to descend each of these shoulders in single file. One of white horses with blue trappings, another of splendidly groomed camels dressed with white, while black Balthazar's were a rare breed of beautiful white racing camels dressed with red. Up on the heights we had a wide shot of the three contrasting lines converging down into the oasis. Because of the steepness of the descent it was best for us to follow on down, shoot the scene, then go back up and do the same thing again for the departure when the three caravans go their separate ways.

On arriving below, the camels were tethered together while we shot all the dialogue between the Kings. While we were doing this a romantic liaison began between one of the brown and one of the white camels. Discretion in the conduct of these affairs among camels is perhaps greater than it is where humankind is concerned, because no one was aware of it until, with the camera back on the heights and the diverging caravans climbing their separate ridges, there was a yell from Franco that a white camel had got mixed in with all the brown ones. Camels are as steadfast as the rest of us and it required several takes and a degree of brute force before love was vanquished and symmetry restored. It was amusing, and a bit sad; too like the way we treat each other and God treats us, probably for equally capricious reasons.

It would have been just as difficult for Clive to forsee what happened at the Crucifixion. Franco had decreed rain and storm, so stacks of old motor tyres were burned to windward and the special effects deployed all their usual engines to make everything and everybody wet. It takes a while to reset this each time, so, after take one, the Virgin Mary accepted Saint Peter's invitation to his Winnebago for some refreshment. The single glass of wine he gave her reacted so unexpectedly with some medication the poor girl was under, that in take two the Virgin Mary was to be seen staggering about Mount Calvary apparently pissed out of her brains. Matters grew even worse when Robert Powell was placed in her arms (a tableau carefully arranged to correspond exactly with the Pièta of Michelangelo) when she was promptly sick all over him. This didn't please Franco at all; it didn't please Robert Powell either.

JESUS OF NAZARETH was my second experience of doing a picture with a predominantly foreign crew, French on MADEMOISELLE, now they were Italian; some good, some not. What most of them had in common, I'm sorry to say, was that they were all related to one of our senior technicians.

Their other characteristic was to talk incessantly, regardless of whether we were shooting or not. A red light in Italy can only mean one thing, and it has not to do with silence. One morning we were told that Visconti had died the day before. He had been a close friend of Franco (who had been his assistant at one time) and when he came to the set he at once said we should have "two minutes silence for Luichino". Two minutes came to an end but not the silence - you could hear a pin drop. Finally I could hold out no longer and said to the first assistant that it was a pity one of their top directors had to die for us to have quiet on the set.

Pippo, the first assistant, was a very bright and winning young man whom Franco had virtually adopted some years before. He had taken over when the original first suffered a heart attack at the beginning of the picture, and was very successful at it. One day, however, when there was a large crowd involved, I noticed that Franco was having to do everything himself.

" Where's Pippo? "

" Tummy upset, he's in the hotel. "

It came therefore as a surprise after lunch to see Pippo, bright as a button, running the set with all his usual bounce and charm.

" Glad you're back Pip. "

I was led confidentially aside,

" I wasn't ill darling, it's Franco's birthday tomorrow so I drove over to Sousse to get him a present. "

I was enchanted; I cannot imagine any English first assistant, adopted son or not, leaving his director to manage a crowd of 500 extras on his own in order to go off and buy him a present.

Among the company for lunch in Franco's trailer one day there was one actor who kept up a monologue about himself throughout the entire meal; no one else could get a word in. By the coffee he was aboard time's winged chariot,

" ... we get older every second. Sometimes I want to run round the

"Why is there only one word for Thesaurus?"

house and stop all the clocks! "

His pause to give this its full effect was a beat too long.

" Don't bother about the clocks; just smash all the mirrors. "

As well as self-regarding actors, Franco was also a match for self-regarding conductors (the same thing). During ENDLESS LOVE he kept Herbert von Karajan hanging on the other end of a phone for at least ten minutes, while he played about with the set decorations; all the Americans present getting more and more shocked.

" ... it isn't his secretary, it's Mr Karajan himself. "

" Yes yes, I come in a minute. "

Mr von K was not the first; there was the famous lighting rehearsal for *L'Elisir D'Amore*, one of Franco's early productions at La Scala. He had decided to break with tradition and stage Nemorino's third act aria (as actually makes sense) in a dim light, just as dawn breaks. He was only allowed one rehearsal for lighting which wasn't really enough and was struggling to get everything done when there was a great flurry front of house and in walked Toscanini with a train of attendants, returning to his old theatre for the first time since Mussolini had caused him to leave it. As soon as he saw what was going on he obligingly informed the young director that the whole of this opera had always to be brightly lit.

" I can't see a thing this way. "

" Then consult an optician. "

(This to someone who had to rest a score on the tip of his nose in order to read it). Toscanini promptly left, and Franco got his rehearsal back. As usual where there is directness between good people they got along fine after that, perhaps because the Maestro himself favoured a direct approach, as when he grabbed a full-bosomed but erring soprano by each of her tits during a rehearsal of the Verdi Requiem,

" If only these were brains! "

In the course of the editing a director will often wish there was an added close-up, or that he had staged something in a different way. By then of course it is usually too late and he has to put up with what he's got. However there is an angel of some sort that looks after Franco, and when the final cut of JESUS was shown to the backers (an American manufacturing enterprise which was Jewish owned) their only reservation was that the Jews were "not being nice enough to JC". This was certainly one way of looking at it, and hard to refute; Franco seized his chance at once and undertook to put all to rights provided he was given a crew and a studio for a week. Thus it happened that three months after it had wrapped, the picture was back again - this time on a large stage at Twickenham. There, up until lunchtime on the Monday, we filmed Lee Montague and some bearded extras affably passing the time of day with Robert Powell; for the rest of the week Franco polished and honed away at his film to his heart's content and everybody was happy.

That week in Twickenham, I had two electricians with me named Brian and Peter. Several months later I was again in Twickenham with the same pair, this time on a commercial. Quite by chance Franco was in the dubbing theatre and, hearing that I was on one of the stages, came to see me. When he walked in he noticed the two men.

" Hello Brian; hello Peter. "

Later I said how great it was to remember like that (they had been so pleased) because I am terrible at names. He said that, as a youth at his very first rehearsal, the La Scala chorus, hard-bitten over the years, had given him a bad time. It being a Friday he asked for photographs and names of every member of the chorus, took them home for the week-end and memorised them. By the Monday rehearsal he was able to address everyone of them by name. From then on they would do anything for him.

Those early days at La Scala were recalled once again when we were shooting JANE EYRE at Ealing studios. The set for the long gallery at Thornfield had large windows down one side and there was a scene with two of the principals, Joan Plowright and Charlotte Gainsbourg, both dressed in sober black, and a housemaid in a coffee coloured frock with white lace cap. At the first rehearsal this young lady happened to stand full in the sunlight, which pointed up her lighter costume and lace cap delightfully. Well satisfied I left them to get on with it and only returned for a final look when they were ready to shoot. Much of the zest was now gone because Franco in the meantime had got the girl to change places with Plowright. I reminded him what it had looked like originally (hardly necessary) and, replying that it was Joan who had all the dialogue, he took me aside and told me some more about that first production of his. It had been Donizetti's *Linda di Chamounix*, all the characters in which are Swiss peasants, whose authentic costume for the period was black with a green sash. The first dress rehearsal, Tullio Serafin, while still conducting away for all he was worth, started shouting for Franco.

" Where is Zeffirelli? "

" Here Maestro. "

" Where is the tenor? "

Franco pointed to a gentleman about ten feet away singing at the top of his voice.

" There Maestro. "

" I can't see him. "

Franco led the singer away, dressed him from head to foot in scarlet satin and brought him back. Still without interrupting the music Serafin nodded,

" *Now* he is a tenor. "

When it was fixed for me to do HAMLET I decided to take the play up to bed one evening, and curled up with the fourth folio - which wasn't very comfortable because it is rather a large book. After reading a while it seemed increasingly unfamiliar until I realised that *Hamlet* was one of the

"Why is there only one word for Thesaurus?"

plays first published in quarto in 1603 (the first folio was twenty years later). The two versions are so different that the excellent Nonesuch edition prints both of them and the next day I set out to find one. It is not necessary to house two Shakespeares so I let it be known to the book trade that there was a fourth folio for sale. Soon enough a New York bookseller, Glenn Horowitz, phoned to say he might have a customer and would it be all right to use my name? I said it was fine by me but doubted that it would be any help.

" Well it's someone in your line of business who wants to give a present to --- " (a currently successful Hollywood director).

" Is he literate? "

" If I only sold books to people who were literate I'd be out of business."

Shortly after this I was shooting an artist test for Neil Jordan and told him the story over lunch. He laughed, rather immoderately it seemed to me,

" It's not *that* funny is it? "

Apparently it was - Neil had lunched with the gentleman in Hollywood a few weeks earlier and in the course of it had been informed that *Treasure Island* was a great book.

" Have you been reading it? "

" No, somebody played me the tape. "

The last day of our shooting at Shepperton, Franco was carrying out his customary sensible, if inconvenient, practice of picking up shots for earlier scenes and we came to one where I had had a search-light coming off a mirror up in the gantry. Everything had been struck weeks before and there was not very much that could be done in the time (it was at the end of our final day) to make anything near an effective match. Franco couldn't resist adding insult to injury by telling me that it did not look anything like the rest of the scene; however we shot it and when we had wrapped he said with great kindness and charm,

" You always build the bridge wider than the river. "

" Well I never know when you're going to widen the river, Franco. "

He has written his own book, but excellent though it is, it fails to convey the wicked sense of humour that is never absent for long when you are with him. A young and harassed production manager on HAMLET had just had to alter some hard won facilities at the last moment,

" I'll forgive anyone who makes me laugh. "

"Why is there only one word for Thesaurus?"

Robin, Marian, Swan, and Mr Roguski

Back home after the picture I was on my own and decided, among other positive ways of coping with loss, that I would finally get to grips with a musical instrument and stop blaming my father.

25

A year or two before, my friend had bought a square piano in Bonham's saleroom with the intention of having it restored as a present for me. Nothing had ever been done and I determined now to get on and see to it. Morleys came and looked and went away to quote. Then by a happy chance there was a commercial at a house in Pond Street, Hampstead, which turned out to be the home of a lady music critic. You sensed this on passing through the front door and being instantly surrounded by harpsichords, spinets, clavichords and forte pianos. My own anxiety about overcrowded bookshelves receded and I began to feel better about them. She was a nice lady, we soon got talking and I mentioned my piano.

" Oh there's no question you must get Roguski to do it. "
I did get Roguski to do it; it took me (and him) four years. I would not have had it any other way; restoring a lovely old instrument is life enhancing for you as well, so make the most of it.

On the appointed day Mr Roguski came to the house to look over the piano and afterwards as we sat over coffee he made me a promise that when it was finished it would sound exactly as when it was first made,

" ... what I cannot tell you is whether it will be nice sound, sometimes it wasn't you know. "
I didn't but said I would take my chance and shortly after that he and the piano drove away together. Then the letters began to arrive. One intriguing feature of the piano was that although the satinwood fret bore a beautifully ornate description -

" By the King's Patent FREDERICUS BECK fecit. No 10 Broad

Street, Soho."
yet there was no date given (there is no Broad Street in Soho either, perhaps it was Broadwick).

Dear Mr Watkin,
There is a date on the sound board; your Fredericus was born in 1790...

Dear Mr Watkin,
Fredericus and I have had a good week .....

Dear Mr Watkin,   6th February 1977
    Although very much delayed, I wish you a Happy New Year. Well your Fredericus has been in the shackles for some time and now and then I release him and do more surgery on him each time. I wish you could see your piano in its present state, otherwise you cannot imagine how much has to be done to the little fellow to put him on his feet again.

I soon decided that even when finally back on its feet an eighteenth century piano was not a sensible choice of instrument for a peripatetic cinematographer. There was a lovely shop in Lewes High Street where a fine looking old man sold and restored all the members of the string family. Thinking that it would be the only practical size to take around on location, I went in and said that I wished to take up the violin. The Hans Sachs of Lewes High Street was delightful (working on musical instruments seemed to have an effect on people). He said that if you didn't start the violin as a child the game was up, but how about the cello? He had a good student instrument at a reasonable price that would suit me very well. It seemed fine to me and then I saw that there were quite a few worm-holes so I pointed them out and asked if they had been treated. He didn't know, but I wasn't to worry,
    " They won't stay in there once you start playing. "
Subsequent owners of the instrument have doubtless benefited from my brief custody of it. It must have become a kind of woodworm *Marie Celeste*, and the departing little creatures were followed not long afterwards by any idea I might have had about mastering the instrument; I was even inclined to believe for a while that my father had been right.
    The next film was Audrey Hepburn's first picture after a lapse of six years, which explains, if it does not excuse, Richard Lester phoning to say,
    " Audrey wants to shoot a test. "
    " That won't do her any good, tell her to take her chance with the others."
If she'd been wearing a prosthetic nose or a wig there might be sense in it, but some vague test for its own sake is meaningless. The fact is, in the course of any film there are going to be scenes where the lighting is influenced by the atmosphere of the scene and the nature of the set; you

cannot simulate either beforehand, and it would be silly to try. Nothing happens in a vacuum, even on a test, and every cameraman in the world (including me) will light that the easiest and safest way there is - one in which nobody could possibly look bad. This consequently tells them nothing and nobody gets fired.

The picture was ROBIN AND MARIAN and I set off for Spain, not with a cello but with a set of Proust which I'd succeeded in finishing by the end of the picture (an exercise I hope never to repeat).

At about this time, some laboratories in California persuaded Kodak that to design a new stock that developed at a higher temperature would represent some kind of progress. Certainly the labs could then run their machines faster and process twice the amount of footage every night (and thereby, I suppose, make twice the amount of money) but what could be in it for the manufacturers I have yet to learn. Launched with overzealous haste before it was quite ready, the new "hot stock" landed up with what is called a "red to green cross-over". That simply means that you can never reconcile those two colours satisfactorily; an actor will have a red face and as soon as this is corrected in the print all the shadows will turn green.

Kodak were not the only people with a problem. ROBIN AND MARIAN had a difficulty of its own to deal with. Because the Inland Revenue were demanding ninety eight per cent of his earnings (any sign of a golden egg and they won't rest until they have killed the goose, or at least persuaded it to leave the country) our leading actor very sensibly refused to work over here. This meant that the Revenue got nothing out of Sean Connery at all, and Britain lost millions of pounds because the whole picture went to Spain instead. My part of the difficulty was that Sherwood Forest is expected to be a predominantly green sort of a place and Spain (apart from the golf course at Marbella, which suited Sean at least) is not.

It occurred to me in an idle moment that if we used the new stock so the cast appeared like a row of tomato plants and then corrected their faces back to normal, everything else might turn green. It would only hold good for scenes set in the forest, of course; the rest of the film should be done on the old stock. This preposterous idea worked surprisingly well when tested; in a kind of unconscious collaboration, Kodak had launched their premature stock at the precise moment I had stumbled on the only possible use for it, indeed their timing was perfect - within weeks of our finishing shooting they had the problem sorted out, the crossover no longer existed, and the new film was excellent and remains so.

The unit was still left with long drives to get to locations that were verdant enough (even when assisted by the "hot stock"). This meant very early departures and breakfast on arrival, where orders for boiled eggs were put into very careful Spanish.

" .... tres e media minutos por favor. "

For some reason this resulted in eggs coming up quite raw and the mystery of it remained unsolved until one day someone noticed that all the eggs were placed in a large cauldron of cold water which was then put on the heat. One of the more skittish among us at that hour of the morning asked for a 23 minute egg. Long after this simple pleasantry was forgotten and we were leaving the table to go to work, a perfectly cooked egg arrived.

One of the many pleasures of this film was working with Ronnie Barker. At an al fresco lunch, Sean Connery, a man both modest and quiet, was talking about golf with another actor, who was neither. The latter mentioned some snobbish club in the USA and asked if Sean was a member (obviously hoping that he wasn't). Sean said he was not a member but had once played on the course.

" Oh I'm a member, I'm a member - well I'm only a country member." Ronnie Barker -

" We remember. "

At the end of the film Maid Marian (now in a convent nursing Robin, who is rather the worse for wear after his latest bout with the Sheriff of Nottingham) decides that it has all gone on quite long enough and embarks on a one-sided suicide pact, giving him one half of a poisoned cup (which he doesn't know about) and swallowing the other half herself. When everyone was ready to shoot this, a prolonged discussion took place between the director and Ann Skinner (of the collecting box). It appeared there was no poison available at that period that would act quickly enough for the joint demise to take place by the end of the small amount of dialogue in the script. No one wished to add any more lines so, to help resolve the impasse, I pointed out that suppositories enter the bloodstream very much faster. It met with little gratitude or appreciation, but then there's no point putting forward ideas in this business if you're going to mind when they are rejected.

"Why is there only one word for Thesaurus?"

Ichabod

*For the benefit of my Gentile readers (not to be
confused with the gentle reader always addressed by
Victorian authors) ichabod means "the glory is
departed" and this chapter is about some of the ways it
has done so.*

26

Now if Mr Oliver, like his own frock-coat, presented an air of faded
gentility to the world at large, such was not the case with the
newsreel fraternity, who displayed other qualities of a different nature
altogether. One of these was to take up positions at horse racing and other
sporting events so that they would be facing towards the sun throughout
the day. This was not from any aesthetic preference for contre-jour
lighting but to facilitate the deployment of mirrors that would reflect the
sun back into the lenses of their rivals. If it happened to be overcast less
indirect methods were resorted to; they would hit each other. A leading
figure among these celluloid buccaneers was a cameraman with Pathé
News named Ken Gordon. It was hard to decide whether he bore a closer
resemblance to Mr Pickwick or to Winston Churchill, and indeed he
combined the pugnacity of the one with the charm of the other. This
likeness came to stand him in good stead as he became known to the old
man who, on his first visit to the continent after the D-Day landings, was
sufficiently amused by Ken to give him a lift in his own Jeep. This must
have afforded a greater advantage over his colleagues than any number of
mirrors.

A delightful freelance cameraman from my days as an assistant was Reg
Hughes. He'd been in the RAF film unit during the war, an experience
he had shared with a youth who happened to be, in some degree, related
to William Friese-Greene, ex-Brighton resident and British pioneer of the
cinematograph. Someone at an RAF reception centre recognised the
name in a draft of conscripts and posted him to the film unit, doubtless

thinking they had thereby done a good day's work. Although a most agreeable person however, this Friese-Greene was not only uninterested in his kinsman's invention but was maladroit in many of his dealings with it. One of his duties was to service the 16mm cameras linked to the guns of fighter aircraft, from which he sometimes forgot to remove the lens caps. This frequently resulted in pilots returning from shooting down half-a-dozen Messerschmitt 109s only to find their claims unsupported by anything other than their own memory.

Friese-Greene also fell short of complete success with the captain of a Blenheim in which he and Reg were sent up to do some air to air shooting. This particular pilot was very anti-film unit but, if he had not already been told by one of his nannies that "we all have to do things we don't like", he was so advised by the RAF and up they went. While Reg worked from a blister in the top of the fuselage, Friese-Greene was filming out of an open doorway in the side of it. NC Mitchell cameras have two separate covers to the magazines, one for the feed and one for the take-up. They had just started their filming when Reg noticed a rapidly increasing length of filmstock fluttering in the slipstream. He cut his camera and climbed down to his companion, intently working away while all his exposed film passed straight through the camera and out of the take-up side of the magazine, onto which he had forgotten to put the cover. Reg tapped him on the shoulder and pointed to what was happening, whereat the surprised young man started up and to steady himself grasped the nearest object to hand. Unfortunately this happened to be the handle of a nearby parachute which at once joined the eight hundred or so feet of Plus X outside the plane. This drew the attention (and disapproval) of the pilot, whose flight report must have been a good read, and perhaps helped the RAF realise, as the army had done with me, that not every conscript will fulfil their expectations of him.

After Friese-Greene I must be the most untechnical camera assistant there ever was, having no mechanical interest whatever. Fortunately Newman Sinclairs were driven by two large springs which the camera's original designer had taken out of grandfather clocks. This may have led to unpunctuality in his household but it did produce an excellent camera, with the advantage that if a spring were to break (almost the only thing that could go seriously wrong) you simply went to the nearest clock-maker (there was one in every town in those days) and got him to replace it.

A spring went on me once right at the start of panning a ship into harbour, and I managed to keep running by steadily winding the other one for the rest of the shot without jogging old Ritchie who was operating a slip head. If a motor packed up today that would be that; no ships entering any harbours, captains being an odd lot when it comes to taking her out and in again for a film unit. It is a similar case with arcs, where there is always a light to be got from two carbons by hand-feeding them

"Why is there only one word for Thesaurus?"

(human contact again like Frank Brice on NIGHT MAIL). If an HMI packs up there is no other choice than to pack up along with it.

When fully wound this delightful lens-bearing grandfather clock just managed to run the whole length of a magazine. At two hundred feet this lasts about two minutes; it is not very much and it becomes less still if you dwell too long on the number-board. Accordingly I developed a technique of spinning the inching knob of the camera and catching it again immediately, thereby achieving a three-frame slate. The practice rather irritated the editing department who had to be pretty sharp to catch the scene number as it flashed across the screen in the theatre, though of course they could read it easily enough on the cutting-room bench. An ingenious way to

Two grandfather-clock springs.   Photo: Aardman Animation.

put turbulent cutting-rooms in their place was shown me later in life by a feature crew. The loader stands in front of the camera as usual, but instead of announcing "21 take 1" aloud, mimes silently while someone outside the frame says it a beat later. The lad out front then claps the slate in the normal way and off we go. The cutting-rooms of course link up the rushes to the clap and in the theatre, as soon as the announcement comes up out of synch, everyone is too busy shouting at the editing department to notice that the shot itself is of course OK.

Another task that came easily to a Newman, thanks to the same inching knob, was the elimination of the dark bar that crosses the image on a television screen. This is the TV form of the intermittent, so that if it can be seen in the finder of a reflex camera (i.e. when the shutter is closed), then it will not photograph. The difficulty is to keep it there, because normally it will drift; but with the Newman's amenable clockwork drive, the light pressure of two fingers on the inching knob kept the bar firmly in place. Admittedly this could only be done with wild shooting - the Newman was a "sound" camera only in the sense that it made a lot of it. When I tried the same trick on an Arriflex with electric drive it took the skin off my fingers! Now everything is done electronically there has to be an extra (video) technician with special equipment to lock you in.

An enterprising attempt by the makers to widen the range of Newmans, was their high-speed camera (up to 90 frames per second) and it was hilarious. It still only loaded 200 feet, but as it took about 180 of them to get up to speed it usually ran out just before the shot had started.

In their early days, Newmans had been beautifully handcrafted precision instruments (the Aston Martins of the camera world) but at the start of World War II, the British Admiralty put in a sudden order for about four hundred of them. The annual works output was probably not one tenth of that, but at the commencement of hostilities the Lords of Admiralty were apparently less tolerant than they were to be with me four years later, and the poor little company was told to deliver or get itself commandeered. Just why the British Navy suddenly wanted four hundred film cameras I do not know, unless it was with a similar object to those cameras linked to the guns of fighter aircraft; then if you sank someone else's battleship there would be some visible proof of the exploit. At all events, every apprentice was put on overtime and the Navy got its four hundred Newmans. Unfortunately cameras are particularly vulnerable to holes into which there has not been time to insert every screw. Not only might they fall apart unexpectedly, but before that, light could gain access to the negative without the formality of passing through the lens first. Anyone who hired a camera in those early days after the war hoped fervently that it was not one of those that had been sold off by the RN; and although the post-war Newmans were in fact remarkably good cameras, they never quite recovered from it all. The old man, Arthur Newman, had died in 1943 (perhaps it was the British Navy that killed him) and by the time I came along the workshop was run by an engaging double-act, Ted Hill and Bob Hume. I well remember how they scandalised one camera assistant, a rather more serious person than I was, by claiming that a single stroke with a six inch rasp took off exactly one thou, so there was no need to use a gauge to measure it.

A final story about Newmans is really more about living creatures than about cameras. That in itself is not entirely inappropriate because Newmans, with their simple ways, were somehow closer to living things than any of their successors. I photographed the documentary COASTS OF CLYDE for Ritchie and driving along West Loch Tarbert we saw some seals very close in shore. I stripped off, apart from underpants (always proper), took the Newman with a 75mm and a full magazine, and waded in up to my neck. They were still too far away but having got that wet I decided to shoot something and switched on. In the seal world the sound of a Newman Sinclair across the waters must be equivalent to the song of the Sirens. They looked up and started swimming towards me, and here I was caught. When I stopped the camera - they stopped. When I ran it they swam towards me. If I ran it long enough to get them where I needed them I would be out of film. Taking the magazine off would solve the problem, but you cannot do that, let alone lace it up again, while standing in the sea up to your neck. It was a classical demonstration of man's predicament in his dealings with the Gods that Homer would have

"Why is there only one word for Thesaurus?"

appreciated. I ended up with some reasonable material though far short of what it could have been; yet with an electric-drive camera I would have got nothing at all - the battery would have been under the water.

Intimate contact with the tools we employ and their closeness to everyday life is something that we are losing, and that is a pity. Electronic image manipulation might be *capable* of reproducing the beauty and subtlety of the Ross lenses on CHARGE OF THE LIGHT BRIGADE but how could anybody program it? The Ross Xpress made their own magic as they went along - it couldn't be envisaged before it happened. Computer graphics can only replicate somebody's *idea* of a spontaneous effect, which will always fall short of what occurs when chance is given a free run.

Until 1960 all the scene changes in Brighton's Theatre Royal were carried out by the local fishermen, a tradition handed down from father to son. There was no direct payment, but the men were allowed to use the flies for repairing their nets; to go backstage was to encounter bronzed figures in blue Jerseys plying twine and bodkin with the same artless ease that their wives or mothers at home gave to darning their socks. The beauty of all this was that the theatre became completely integrated with the life of the town; it was *their* theatre. (It would also have made for a cost-saving production of *Peter Grimes*).

In THE CHARGE OF THE LIGHT BRIGADE there is a scene where Lord Cardigan is booed at by a theatre audience because of the "black bottle" affair, and we went down and shot it in the Bristol Old Vic. While all the hubbub is going on in the house an actor on stage is trying to get through the opening scene of *Macbeth*. With an inspired bit of casting they had persuaded Donald Wolfit to play Macbeth. This was another flight back to Mr Shotter for, although I had not gaped at him from the ninepennies, the entire school had been taken to see his touring productions of Shakespeare (productions noteworthy for the care with which, great actor though he was, all the other parts were given to players who would be in no danger of outshining him). Seen close to, his 1840 stage make-up looked grotesquely exaggerated and I made an amused remark to him about it. Thereupon he told me that when he was a very young actor he once shared a dressing-room in the Theatre Royal, Newcastle-upon-Tyne, (one of the earliest theatres in the country), with a very old actor. That takes us back a long way in time. Their room was situated at the top of the theatre and he noticed that all the bricks surrounding the tiny fireplace were worn concave. His companion noticed him looking at them,

" That was the only make-up we had, brick dust for our cheeks and soot for eyebrows and shadow. "
I hope the fireplace is still there.

This isn't a plea for a return to soot and brick dust, or to clockwork cameras; and Brighton's fishermen need all their time to find the few remaining fish that manage to survive our polluting their habitat; but to know these things is to share in a spiritual fund that cannot be overvalued.

Whenever I find myself decrying some new development because it isn't as good as what was there before, I look warily to see if I am getting old (mentally that is) for as an innovator myself, that would be hard to excuse. Of course there are gains as well as losses, but the trouble with the losses is that after a time they disappear completely. There is nobody around who heard Mahler conduct, and there cannot be many cinemagoers who know what a good print looked like with an arc in the projector (it was *etched* on the screen). Of course excellence has been sacrificed to convenience in the past, but only in our day has that been regarded as a virtue.

A useful thing to remember about progress is that it is usually OK provided the target has not changed. All the lamps that were in use when I came on the scene had been designed to help cameramen light their films properly; the target being the best possible tool for the job. If that target is changed to making something as small and lightweight as possible so that it will go on a smaller lorry, the outcome will indeed be a smaller lorry but it will be driving about full of useless equipment. Often the more sophisticated such modifications to film equipment are, the more dire the result.

There is a common failure on the part of mankind to distinguish between cleverness and intelligence, notably with regard to scientists. It is without doubt clever to produce a hydrogen bomb - whether it represents an intelligent use of one's time and the planet's resources is open to question. The kind of stupidity so often lodged in scientific minds was well demonstrated when, during the shooting of THE BED-SITTING-ROOM, I experimented with a specialised stock known as Infra-red Aero. This was a combined infra-red and colour emulsion formulated by Kodak in the first place for military reconnaissance. It had the remarkably vulgar characteristic that it reproduced any form of living chlorophyll (present in all green vegetation) a bright red. Though good at distinguishing a spread of camouflage netting from real trees and grass it was in all other respects an aesthetic disaster, though eventually, with the help of some old black-and-white filters, it did render up some haunting-looking landscapes, which came in useful on THE BED-SITTING ROOM. The actual point of this story, however, is not the emulsion but the base on which it was coated.

Certain inquisitive Americans started sending rockets out into space with film cameras inside them, and in due course, as happens in less exalted places, a magazine would jam and the film break. The resulting absence of pictures proved so annoying that the scientific mind set to work and, after spending a great amount of time and an even greater amount of money, came up in triumph with a base possessing all the characteristics of ordinary cellulose acetate with the additional one that it had the tensile strength of a steel girder. There can be no question that this was extremely clever of them. Naturally the magazines continued to jam from time to time but the film did not break; it churned on its relentless way rending £40,000 worth of camera to pieces. Any clapper-boy could have told them that to begin with.

One result of this increasing tendency to aim in the wrong place was that I had the original target all to myself; every supplier of lighting equipment had stopped aiming at it long ago. In the circumstances it isn't perhaps all that creditable to have scored a couple of hits. After salvaging Shepperton from the asset-strippers, Benny Lee, at my suggestion, took the opportunity to get hold of Bill Chitty (from THE HOMECOMING) and put him in charge of the lighting workshop. I had only to explain an idea to Bill for it to be translated into beautifully crafted reality. The first was an adaptation of the 1939-45 army search-light. A simple combination of an arc and a mathematically exact parabolic mirror, the light itself was already perfect. It was just a matter of making a cumbersome and noisy device good mannered enough to be tolerable on a film set. The mirror forces light from the arc (the same light source as a brute) into an almost parallel beam in the same way that a fireman's hose does water. In both cases the intensity increases alarmingly; the fireman's jet can knock you over, and 150 footcandles from a brute become something close to 4000.

It has never bothered me if other people adopt ideas or devices of mine, which is just as well, but the searchlight presented a slightly different case because there was a finite number of mirrors and nobody was ever going to make any more. It would therefore be nice if people used them with a degree of common sense, keeping sight of their original purpose - which was to pick out night flying aircraft. By the nature of things these are invariably to be found up and above; provided you are standing on the ground the one place you can be certain of not finding an aeroplane is underneath you. This phenomenon was taken into account by the original designer who reasonably assumed that the light would in consequence be always tilted upward. If you tip a searchlight below horizontal the flame of the arc hits the mirror and smashes it. Should you wish the thing to shine downwards the simple answer of course is to aim the light up into an ordinary flat mirror and set the angle accordingly but, just as the wheel eluded the Aztecs, so one otherwise excellent cameraman (a fellow music-lover, who had solved the problem of a portable instrument for himself by taking up the flute) had destroyed his third mirror by the time I felt driven to phone him up.

" ... suppose I went around smashing up Stradivarius violins .... "

The bull's eye was what has come to be known as the Wendylight. Wendy is a camp name assigned to me back in the mists of time by electricians with a liking for alliteration. It would be nice to point to a literary origin, that Peter Pan lost his shadow and Wendy sewed it back on for him, but I don't believe it was what they had in mind.

Night exteriors always irritated me because they involved a great deal of effort for a compromised result. Light falls off in such a way that when you double the distance from the source you halve the amount; thus a measurement of 100 footcandles at 100 feet would become 50 at 200, 25 at 400 and so on, so that the further you can take a lamp from an actor the greater the area he can cover without getting lighter or darker. The reason you don't get brighter as you walk down the street is because the sun is so far away. The best solution to night shooting therefore is the most powerful lamp at the furthest possible distance. Eventually a film came along with a set of Hanover Square built on the lot at Elstree that included an 80 foot high St George's Church. This would need an 120 foot tubular tower to accommodate the lighting and that was going to cost a lot of money, so I decided to spend it another way. I estimated that 10 footcandles 300 yards away from the source was about the lighting equivalent to breaking the sound barrier (not that I rate myself as a Barnes Wallis). There was a lamp called a nine-light Fay comprising three rows of three flattish 3" diameter bulbs, and I thought about 23 of these ought to give me just that.

The idea attracted a lot of scorn, particularly from Benny Lee, so I asked one of his gaffers to set up a bank of twenty three nine-light Fays outside his office and waited for dark while he and John, drinks in hand, assured me that it wouldn't work. I had to go outside the yard gates and across a side road to get my three hundred yards, but when I held up the footcandle-meter the needle rose steadily to 10 footcandles and stayed there. In the morning I phoned Bill Chitty,

" Bill, can you give me the equivalent of 23 nine-lights but without all the surrounding ironwork? Pack the bulbs as close together as you can - I only want one shadow. Oh, and the lot has to fit on a cherry-picker and go 150 feet in the air."

I don't think I spoke to him after that; there was nothing to add, and you never needed to tell Bill anything twice - in fact it was wiser not to. His design has the simple elegance of a sketch by Leonardo (the great Florentine would have liked Bill). Its first job was a night shoot on an airfield; the line of planes on the runway cast a single shadow, as did the actors in front of them. One hundred and fifty feet in the sky four panels shone with such brilliance that you could not see the cherry-picker arm supporting them; the light seemed to hang in the very air - a slice of Battenburg cake with 196 diamonds in place of the sponge. There was a full keylight at 300 yards, it was another 300 before it was down to half-key and a further 600 before quarter-key. That added up to 1200 yards, on a clear night about three quarters of a mile, and it was coming from the right place - above. It was the same feeling I'd had with MARAT SADE; once again something had taken on a life of its own that was more

"Why is there only one word for Thesaurus?"

exciting than all the expectations.

A strangeness that strikes the auricular alert is that the birds are singing throughout the night. Sometimes it is not only the birds that are deceived. On the second of two summer evenings in St Albans I was getting out of the car when a boy about twelve years old came along on his bicycle.

" Are you going to have that lamp again tonight?"

" Yes, did you like it? "

" My bedtime's nine o'clock so it was still light when I went to sleep; then I woke up and that light was outside the window - I thought it was a UFO."

His pleasure and excitement were enough return for all my efforts and Benny Lee's money; the Wendy was not just useful - it was the best of toys!

Toys are serious, as grown-ups who are wise enough are able to remember. It was now about three years into the Fredericus/Roguski liaison and I was invited to drive to Ely to see the progress so far and clear up a question or two. I'd come to know him fairly well

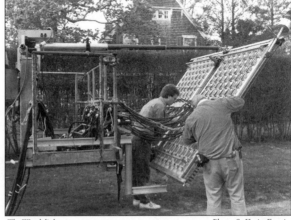

The Wendylight   Photo: S. Karin Epstein

by phone and letter, and one thing that stood out to my mind was that he seemed to have very little interest in music. Settled over tea and biscuits I asked him about this and he replied that I was right; what he had always loved was simply making things. He had escaped from Poland in 1939 and spent the war with the Polish Airforce in England where he met and married a young English schoolteacher. When the war finished he was at a loose end and until he found what he wanted to do for a living he stayed home and kept house while his wife went off to do her teaching. As she had a class of young children for natural history he thought he would make her a working model butterfly that could be used in the school room. He constructed a light skeleton out of wood and glued paper across it, which he painted in watercolour; everything worked, the wings opening and folding just as a live butterfly's would. At this point God took a hand and arranged that among the natural history pupils there should be the grandchildren of Arnold Dolmetsch. They came home full of excitement and told their parents about the beautiful toy they had seen in their classroom, who, in place of the customary "how

Ichabod   237

interesting dear", took the trouble to visit the school and have a look at it.

Bronislav built and restored instruments for Dolmetsch for many years and then, prior to our meeting, set up on his own; a happy man who had found his right place in this world.

Fredericus also is happy with two companions, one of them a modern harpsichord by a designer not only of harpsichords but of a particular method of moving them about between Italy and France. The body of the instrument lay on the floor of a van beneath a mattress on which were superimposed two further bodies, both young and felicitously engaged in either real or simulated intercourse. The entourage would then be waved cheerily through the frontier by delighted Latin customs officials.

None of this amounts to much when set beside the surreal conduct of a beautiful little clavichord (the smallest keyboard instrument) by the great modern builder Thomas Goff. It was loaned to Eileen Joyce and, on hearing of his sudden and unexpected death, that resourceful lady set to and dug a large hole in her garden at Chartwell Farm near Westerham, had the instrument swathed in blankets, sealed in heavy-duty polythene, and under the ground well ahead of its maker. When in due course his estate asked for its return, they were told that it had gone back long since, and after a sufficient lapse of time she disturbed her azaleas once again, and dug it up none the worse (though it may have needed a tune). Perhaps these little instruments are possessed of some arcane virtue that clears away inhibitions, for an earlier exponent of it, Violet Gordon Woodhouse (who also used a Goff), combined performances of Bach and Scarlatti with conducting a "marriage a cinque" in which everyone remained contented and happy under the same roof for the rest of their lives. The technical difficulties implied (and I do not mean Bach and Scarlatti) defy understanding to this day. I've always considered Wanda Landowska the greater musician, but without much question Violet had her beaten in other areas.

Here I will risk an anti-climax by including another story of Eileen and that humble keyboard accessory, the piano stool. Together with Sir Adrian Boult and the LPO, she arrived in Rugby one Sunday lunchtime in 1941, for a brief rehearsal before playing the second Rachmaninov at an afternoon concert. They went directly to the theatre where she found the seat provided for her was not only too high but was lacking the usual mechanism for adjustment.

" I said to Sir Adrian, 'I can't play on this', so he thought for a minute and turned round to the orchestra - 'Somebody get me a saw'. Eventually someone brought in a saw, Sir Adrian took his coat off, turned the stool over, and cut off four neat little bits. Well the next day there was the most awful row; the Lord Mayor was there and everybody, and poor Sir Adrian had to buy it (he asked me if I wanted to buy it first, but I had no money). I don't know where it is now; with him I expect. "

This article of furniture should not be underestimated. Steinways built one for Artur Schnable that incorporated a back-rest of his own design; Eileen, who had studied the *Emperor* concerto with him, owned it for a time, and eventually I bought it myself. Naturally I have examined it for saw marks, but it seems not to have been interfered with; neither is there any evidence of interment, though the poor thing doubtless echoes the heading of this chapter - with my technique the glory has certainly departed.

As for Eileen, she was perhaps fortunate to have been with Boult and not Sargent on that occasion, Sir Malcolm having advised her to leave the Brahms and Rachmaninov alone as they were men's concertos! (Feminist admirers of Flash Harry please note).

Since being able to play I have discovered a remarkable affinity with the instruments. They are almost like people and I cannot resist a strange piano; every one feels different and sounds different, even the worst old dog is fun for five minutes. Pinchas Zukerman gives his Giuseppe Guarneri "del Gesu" a holiday every so often - relaxes the strings and leaves it in peaceful surroundings while he plays on something else for four weeks. It's obvious if you think about it - mutual respect, shared not only only with a fine instrument but with a genius whose products were none the worse because in his leisure hours he was known to be something of a local terror, or in the language of the time, "engaged in dissolute behaviour". Come to think of it the "del Gesu" would probably get on rather well with my Michael Thomas harpsichord.

Photo by kind permission of Cinecentium GmbH, Hamburg.

"Why is there only one word for Thesaurus?"

Chariots of Fire

Almost the first thing I did after leaving British Transport to freelance was a 16mm sponsored film about making food containers out of compressed waste paper (principally in the form of egg boxes).

27

It was a beginning also for Hugh Hudson, who had just formed his own production company. Hugh first endeared himself to me while we were set up on a production line in a factory in East Anglia. From the long procession of egg boxes he lifted one out, wrote "Fuck Off" inside the lid and set it back on course for an ultimate rendezvous with one of the country's drooping housewives, to brighten the day for her.

At another location on a wharf in Chelsea, rubbish was loaded into barges for dumping in the North Sea as part of a routine pollution exercise. Here, having given them a stop that should keep them happy for a bit, I was following my usual practice of nosing about looking at all and sundry. A bank had obviously had a clear-out of its vaults and there were cancelled cheques lying about all over the place. I picked up one of the cleaner ones and saw that it was made out to Aspreys in 1934, in the sum of £10, by Anthony Asquith. This was a bit like Auntie Gipsy's photograph all over again. True I had not known "Puffin" to speak to, and he had never refused to give me half a crown, but we had exchanged the occasional nod and smile at Rymington Van Wyck where we both bought our gramophone records. I had also seen him presiding at union AGMs where he was rightly one of the most universally liked and respected men in the industry. Hugh suggested that it was in payment for a present to some boy; entire speculation of course, but it is a happy thought - ten pounds in 1934 would have been a nice present. Twenty years after letting me do his first short film Hugh threw caution to the winds a second time and offered me his first long one.

Something that may be counted upon in a film about athletes is that the director will sooner or later want to shoot bits of the action in slow motion. This is a customary resort and I'd a fancy to do some of that stuff another way. The exposure time in the cinema is 1/48th of a second. If you took a still photo of a racing car at that shutter speed the resulting image would be a blur; at 1/800th on the other hand it would be quite clearly defined. You can do the same thing in a film camera by closing the normal 180 degree shutter down to 10 degrees (at any rate one used to be able, most modern cameras in the way of progress have not the facility any more). The best illustration of what happens is a fountain of water, because when every drop is separated in outline it looks completely different. With someone running it would mean that their hair and limbs would be better resolved, nothing as noticeable as the falling water, rather the audience senses something unusual without knowing what it is - a much more attractive possibility. When explaining the idea to Hugh I said the only snag was that it needed always to be fairly clear behind them (like a horizon or the sea's edge) otherwise the background would strobe.

" But that's exactly how they did all their training - along the beach at Broadstairs. "

While on the subject of shutter openings the opposite idea, that of a

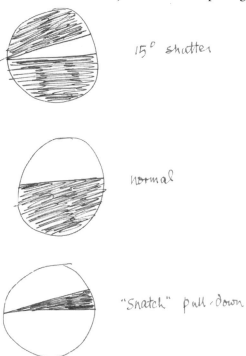

deliberately long exposure so that any movement will be as blurred as possible, is a lot more tricky because the longer the film rests in the gate getting exposed the less time there is to move it down to the next frame. Instead of dividing your 360 degrees (of a circle) into roughly 180/180, as it is for normal filming, you'd want something like 340/20 and that requires what is graphically described as a "snatch" claw mechanism to pull it down fast enough. In my early years in the business I had taken a camera up to Newmans for some repair or other and found them putting the finishing touches to a one-off job for a teaching hospital so they could film surgical operations from a primitive and very dim TV tube (rather than keep on dropping number boards and bits of chalk into the patients). By the time I had a use for this (a scene in a jazz club where the relatively static behaviour of the instrumentalists would contrast with the wild gyrations of the clientele) Newmans no longer existed and the camera had probably long been junked.

With CHARIOTS OF FIRE I was nearly back in my first lit interior, King's College Chapel in Cambridge, but things had changed since 1955. The busy schedule of sight-seeing Japanese coach parties left no time to spare for film units. Furthermore the University authorities refused to allow us to film inside Trinity Great Court, where the original "beat the clock" race had been run, nor would they let us inside Caius; all this because they felt the script suggested that they were anti-semitic. Hugh agreed it did suggest that, and in 1924 they certainly were; moreover if they wouldn't let us make a film about it now, then nothing had changed. Most of the Cambridge material was consequently shot at Hugh's old school, Eton.

He wanted to do a scene in the college library, one of the finest in the country. While he and David Puttnam were talking with the Provost, I got chatting to the librarian, Paul Quarrie, about some of their books, *Roister Doister* for one. It is the first known English comedy and they have the only copy of the earliest printing of it, found in a second hand bookshop in Eton High Street by an old boy of the school who loyally gave it to them. This was uniquely appropriate as the author, Nicholas Udall, had been a master at Eton until compelled to leave under a cloud and take up residence in the Marshalsea prison. I'd often wondered about this (there was one explanation that sprang to mind) and I asked if they knew what had happened. It was like the chemist shop in Harrods all over again - they knew but they weren't saying. I asked if I might see another book.

" Yes it's over there; just look at anything you like except..."

(he indicated two small sections)

" - they're the burglar alarms. "

When Hugh and David finally called me over they said that we would be allowed to film inside the library but that we must not bring in any lamps. Before I could say anything Mr Quarrie looked up from some incunable he was examining.

" Oh it will be quite all right for this gentleman to have what lamps he needs."

This advantage apart, it is fortunate that Hugh didn't want to shoot anything in the other well known library housed nearby inside Windsor Castle, where there would have been difficulties less easy to surmount. A leading authority on Charles Dickens, permitted to view the assembled material of that author in the Royal library, was disconcerted to find his approach to the shelves impeded by a model of a Spitfire aeroplane suspended from the ceiling in front of them. It was explained to him that it hung there at the express wish of Prince Philip, ".. so that he has something to talk about when conducting people through the library". (He couldn't talk about Dickens?). In another part of the room a glass show-case containing a Caxton original stood next to a similar case housing a pair of gloves. They seemed too well preserved to be Caxton's gloves and the visitor cast an enquiring eye at the Royal librarian,

" They are Prince Andrew's flying gloves, placed there at the desire of Her Majesty. "

Well you could hardly expect Brenda to talk about Caxton, I suppose. Perhaps the books should be removed to the RAF Museum at Duxford.

Eton is an interesting place. I looked at Shelley's name where he'd carved it in the woodwork of the upper school but I was even more charmed by Shepherd. A part of the system for brutalizing our ruling class, was a tradition that you must carve your name somewhere on the place and then get thrashed for doing it. Shepherd was a pupil in the nineteenth century who decided to make a name for himself, literally, by carving it in four inch letters deep into the outside wall of Henry VI's chapel. While engaged in this task one night, he was disturbed putting the finishing touches to the letter P by one of the masters. This led to his being flogged in front of the whole school including the statue of the offended gentleman who had built the chapel in the first place, like the Commendatore in the last act of *Don Giovanni*, except that instead of getting dragged down to hell by demons this victim was thrust upwards to the top of Lupton's Tower and secured therein to await the arrival of Mum and Dad in the morning, to remove him from Eton for evermore. In the night he escaped through a window, climbed down the outside of the tower (no mean feat), and finished what had been so rudely interrupted, SHEPHERD.

A criticism levelled at CHARIOTS is that sometimes it redistributes the facts a little. I have a stong attachment to the truth, but there are times when too strict an adherence would result in there being no film at all; not because truth is dull (it is usually the reverse) but because, in an account lasting a mere ninety minutes, it is sometimes diffuse. In a play or a film something else is at work, less exact but just as valid - call it honesty to the subject. The handing of the note to Liddell at the start of the 400 metres is exactly what happened except that it was given, not by Jackson Scholz (though it was Scholz who told us about it), but by someone else who does not appear in the film. It is a good moment but it would have been greatly weakened if it had merely involved someone who was a total stranger to the audience. Often these things are done in the most delicate of ways so that (like the 10 degree shutter) though the audience may not know what they are, yet their presence invests the film with truth.

The main line of the Great Western Railway from Paddington to Bristol was built by Isambard Kingdom Brunel, an artist among engineers. An outstanding feat in its construction was described by an opponent as "the monstrous and extraordinary, most dangerous and impracticable tunnel at Box ", between Chippenham and Bath. Years after Brunel's death somebody noticed that about a mile before entering the jaws of danger and impracticality the line, which has run virtually straight all the way from Paddington, angles slightly and then a similar distance after leaving the tunnel returns to its original bearing. If you have to blast your way through nearly two miles of solid oolite a few degrees make no difference at all. There seemed to be no explanation until, after much pondering, the answer came to light in every sense. The tunnel runs dead straight east to west and on one day in the year the rising sun shines directly through it; that day is Brunel's birthday. The point is he never mentioned it to anyone.

In CHARIOTS Liddell preaches from the pulpit of the Scottish church in Paris. There is a line of half a dozen people listening to him and the right hand figure in that line is an old lady. She is Jenny, Liddell's sister (played in the film by Cheryl Campbell), but that old lady is the real Jenny, though like Brunel with the Box Tunnel, the film does not tell us.

Brunel may have been lucky that none of his people wrote memoirs to give the game away. Sadly the real Jenny betrayed less interest in her brother than concern about the image of herself as a bit of a spoilsport, which she probably was. It is surprising what people care about when they find themselves depicted on the screen. Michael Caton-Jones told me that the only objection that Christine Keeler ever raised over her portrayal in SCANDAL was that she herself had always patronised a better dressmaker than was implied in his film. Neither of these is quite in the class of Lord Alfred Douglas' answer to John Gielgud. John was playing in a revival of *The Importance of Being Earnest* and, realising that Bosie had been in the St James's Theatre on 14th February 1895, seized the chance of an eye-witness account of the original style of acting it; what could Douglas remember of that first night?

" No one paid any attention to me. "
No wonder historians have a hard time.

An earlier instance of someone hidden in a film without anybody knowing who they are is Humphrey Jennings' FIRES WERE STARTED. A girl in a control room passes messages to a young man standing in front of a wall chart, who has one of the better lines in the movie,

" Ten fire-engines ? He's got a hope... "
It is a considerable improvement on the words that had once made him a household name and might have led one to expect him to turn up in the air force rather than the fire service - the first chorister ever to make it to the top of the charts (with Mendelssohn's "O for the Wings of a Dove"), Master Ernest Lough and the Temple Choir. The only accounting for the strange success of this Decani Pop Star must be a puritan English reluctance to allow themselves to idolise a choirboy unless he is extremely

unattractive. I'd have used the wings of a dove to get as far from the gramophone as possible, and to my mind FIRES WERE STARTED was a much better achievement.

There are photographs of the finishes at the 1924 Olympics, and for each race the actors practised until they could always run the final stretch in exactly the same positions and postures as in 1924. Harold Abrahams' 100 metres, when he wins the gold medal, is seen twice in the film, one is in slow motion but the other, by means of careful editing, is on the screen for the exact time to the split second that he took to run it. These instances are not remarkable except as examples of good craftsmanship, as is the bevy of attractive young secretaries in the wake of Lord Birkenhead as he boards the steamer for France (he was apparently noted for them). Sadly they got rather lost, partly in the editing but mainly because of the steadicam, a device that can do little more than dangle the lens under an actor's nose and thus not high enough to see anything beyond him; an unsatisfactory outcome for us all, except for FE's descendants who had a restricted enthusiasm for us as it was.

A bizarre fact disclosed about the American team, again by Jackson Scholz, was that their coach had proscribed the having of wet dreams while they were at the Olympics. Knowing next to nothing about sport I am unsure which way the advantage lies but it may be that our present obsession with testing athletes for drugs has allowed easier means of cheating to be overlooked. We actually shot a piece where Dennis Christopher gets hauled out of bed in the middle of the night and held under a cold shower by his companions, but it was not used.

We did the mid-channel scene between Liddell and Birkenhead in the wardroom of the *Discovery*, berthed at the time in St Katherine's Dock. Nosing my way around as usual I wandered into a small but nicely appointed cabin, sat down on the bunk and asked the RNR officer who was one of the caretaker crew, if it had been Scott's.

" Yes. "

" What do you think of Scott? "

" What would *you* think of someone who had to be rescued every time he sailed any further than the Isle of Wight? "

This was an agreeably candid reply in place of our usual habit of turning any really outrageous fuck-up into an heroic achievement. The whole of Antarctica has been allocated to Scott, as the smaller but warmer Khartoum has to General Gordon; we even started a war to justify his lunacy (though only against Blacks with spears). The charge of the Light Brigade belongs to the booby Cardigan, and the *Titanic* to the unhappy Captain Smith, who knowingly drove her flat out into a field of icebergs on a pitch black night. As GBS observed at the time, there is nothing heroic in being drowned if you cannot avoid it, especially when you drag other people along with you. In this respect Captain Smith was no innovator, an earlier and if anything more polished seafaring demonstration was afforded on the 22nd of June 1893 by old Etonian Vice Admiral Sir George Tryon on his flagship *HMS Victoria* (our top battleship at the time) conducting manoeuvres with the Mediterranean fleet off Tripoli on the coast of Syria. To countermand an incorrect course he had signalled, after his attention had been drawn to it by a subordinate, was as unthinkable to him as to disobey it was to everyone else; so on a calm sunny day he and the captain of *HMS Camperdown* (our second top battleship) stood on their respective bridges as they steadily converged and collided, sinking the *Victoria* and 358 unfortunate sailors for whom he was responsible. Sir George nobly accompanied them down to the depths, but to quote Shaw again "so did the cat". The event was hailed, needless to say, as a shining example of discipline and obedience to orders, though if that is the case it would surely have been been even more glorious if the rest of the fleet had continued the manoeuvre and sunk each other.

I told my Naval friend about a project that Hugh wanted to do - Shackleton's *South*. That is a truly heroic tale but no one was interested in making it, perhaps because Shackleton never lost a man, a serious oversight if you want to become a legend.

An adequate crowd for the Olympics themselves was well outside the scope of the budget so somebody had a clever idea. A Bank Holiday Sunday was chosen and the event advertised over the whole Merseyside area. The location was a stadium at Bebington on the Wirral peninsular. Everyone when they arrived was given a numbered ticket and although they were not paid there was entertainment laid on to fill the time spent by the unit in lining up and preparing (always intensely boring for watchers of film units). The main inducement was a raffle that took place every hour throughout the day, the prizes getting progressively more valuable the longer people stayed. Fiat cars, for whom Hugh had made a number of commercials, gave one of their latest models for the last prize of all - so if you wanted to win a car you had to stay until the end at about six o'clock. Because some people would be leaving before then, there was one necessary rule that was explained each time a raffle took place; a winner must claim the prize within ten minutes, otherwise it would be put up again. The idea was a huge success and a crowd of about nine thousand behaved with remarkable good nature all day long. A possible exception to this was a gentleman who, in parking his car, reversed a little too close to a grassy bank and broke off his exhaust pipe. He spent the rest of the day complaining to people, who passed him along to others equally unable to do more than sympathise (there being no provision made for broken exhausts). His annoyance had increased to such an extent by six o'clock that he failed to hear an announcement that he was the winner of a new car (complete with exhaust) and as he didn't claim it the vehicle was put up again and a lady won it. I don't know whether he found this out but he drove home in such a rage that he got done for speeding.

There is a certain fitness about a film expressing such affirmative values getting itself made because of a collaboration between the Jews and the Egyptians (in the guise of 20th Century Fox and Dodi Fayed). It is true that the joint venture nearly came apart at one stage when Fox got alarmed about the cost and wanted to close us down. We were rescued by the "lazy and inefficient" who offered to buy them out, whereat of course they at once changed their minds. This remarkable collaboration is mirrored in the film's story where Harold Abrahams has an Arab trainer, so that both his success and that of the film came about because Jew and Arab were working together. I came to like Dodi, a quiet and kindly man, who was charming to everyone on the crew. He certainly spent more time with us than Fox did.

While still shooting the picture we stumbled across another collaboration that was rather less admirable. An hotel where we stayed in the north west of England, a grotesque Edwardian-baronial country house on which no expense was spared, had been built as the home of a newly married couple in about 1911. They were the son of Armstrong (of Armstrong Whitworth) and the daughter of Alfried and Bertha Krupp von Bohlen. Armstrongs had patented a design for a detonator which was fitted in every shell fired in the 1914-1918 war, and the happy couple were able to live in style (if that is the right word) on the royalties that were regularly paid them by both sides in the conflict. One ought not be surprised or shocked at this as it is merely the ongoing reality of civilised society; one may however be surprised and shocked at the vulgarity with which they spent the money.

When the picture was ready for release David Puttnam wanted the distributors to send it out with Humphrey Jennings' LISTEN TO BRITAIN as a supporting short film. It was a piece of inspired programming and I asked him why it had never happened.

" Everyone looked at me as if I was mad. "

Isaac Bashevis, and other Singers

In 1981 something happened that was almost too good to be true; I was asked to go to Vienna to film an opera.

28

The director was Jean-Pierre Ponnelle and the piece Rossini's CENERENTOLA. Apart from two small sets in Wienfilm, our studio was a derelict and cavernous locomotive factory in the suburb of Floridsdorf. The place had had an extensive additional complex built by the Nazis and opened with a speech by Dr Goebbels one morning in 1943. He had rather a wasted day because it was then completely flattened by the American Air Force the same afternoon. It was still flattened when we drove through the gates 38 years later, but the old part of the works remained standing with its vast sheds and overhead cranes - a strange place for Rossini's fairy tale opera.

There is a storm in the second act. Lightning effects in films are often simulated by reversing the poles of an arc so that it won't strike up properly; this, however, only works when the shot is confined to a small area, otherwise whatever is closest to the source will be too bright compared with everything else. For wide shots the best way is to light for a very small aperture, close the lens down and simply jerk the iris open and shut now and again, thereby overexposing everything equally, for a split-second. Rossini's storm has every streak of lightning written into the music, thus calling for an uncommon degree of flash-precision that had to be managed on this occasion by my focus-puller getting himself "conducted" with taps on the shoulder from Claudio Abbado's assistant.

Among the good things is to be visited by ideas (uninvited of course, when delightful guests they are), provided we ensure they behave themselves and that means, as mentioned earlier, they must wait until

Jean-Pierre Ponelle   Photo: Unitel

genuinely called for; nothing is worse than thrusting an idea where it doesn't belong. One that had been waiting around for a good many years was to do a scene entirely in silhouette (the real black paper cut-out sort). It never got anywhere, naturally, because with actors it is necessary for the audience to see their expressions, however, this shortcoming for actors might be perceived, in some quarters, as an advantage with opera singers. I spoke to Jean-Pierre and he took to the idea, saying he could use it for the sextet in the second act. Thanks to his staging of it, the scheme worked well enough, with the six figures waving their arms above their heads and looking lost and confused (which is exactly what they're singing about).

When everything was finished with the artists there was a week or so gap before a final day's shooting in the empty house at La Scala. This fitted in with a recce to Prague for the next picture and when that was done I travelled direct from there to Milan. It was my first visit behind the Iron Curtain, and afterwards, sitting at dinner overlooking the Piazza Duomo was like a return from death to life.

That week-end should have seen (and heard) the fourth performance of one of Donizetti's operas sung by the great soprano Monserrat Caballe, but here things went a bit wrong. La Scala had been trying for some time to entice the lady and finally offered to mount a new production of any opera she cared to choose. She decided on *Anna Bolena*, a very taxing role and a loaded choice into the bargain, not only on account of it being the last part to have been sung at La Scala by Maria Callas, but because that lady had modestly averred at the time that after her no one else would dare attempt it.

The day of the opening, Madame Caballe had a tummy upset and the performance was cancelled. Next morning the Italian newspapers carried

"Why is there only one word for Thesaurus?"

on their front pages the profiles of Callas and Caballe facing one another above captions which suggested that Maria, from beyond the grave, had interfered with her rival's digestion. This was small encouragement to the poor woman who then cancelled the second performance. The third came to grief because the Italian stage hands considered they were being messed about and went on strike. By now, the fourth performance had become the first and so there was no chance at all of getting a seat. Precautionary rehearsals had taken place during the day for a young singer with a beautiful voice and a slim figure, so perhaps Madame Caballe ought to have been more concerned about a live understudy than the dead Callas. At five o'clock in the evening the conductor still didn't know if his prima donna would put in an appearance; Jean-Pierre said we could either watch from the wings or have dinner in the Galleria. While we enjoyed our meal, the lady came on, sang her single performance of *Anna* to a surprised house, and flew back to Spain the following morning.

Now for a singer of another kind - to the Berkeley Hotel one evening to meet Barbra Streisand, here to make a film and for the first time direct it herself.

" They tell me you always get the seven o'clock train to Brighton. "

" For you Barbra, I'll make it the seven-thirty. "

We were off to a good start. She went on to tell me how she could not be photographed on one side of her face (I forget which since I never took any notice of it) and her keylight must always come from the same angle so that on a moving shot it had to be carried around the stage with her by a suitably agile electrician. I was expecting to hear about a pink filter any minute, except of course that she was Jewish instead of Black. (Come to think of it the pink filter seems to have got itself attached to the wrong minority group anyway).

" .... it's the only way I look any good. "

It was sad and at the same time wicked - for twenty years they had been telling the poor girl she had a problem when there was nothing of the kind. She has in fact a wistful beauty that is quite personal to her, and it is stupid to complain because it is not commonplace. I said that everybody had two sides to their faces, it was what made them real, and there was nothing whatever the matter with either of hers. In any case we were talking about the wrong thing. What must come first is the scene; once we have got the right style and atmosphere for that, then, if she didn't look good, we'd take one step back at a time until she did - then we'd have both her looking good and the scene right. If we started the other way round the film would look boringly the same, and she'd be walking through it in a mask. If she had not liked this analysis we could never have worked together, but apparently she did and from then on everything was fine.

Whenever I have been told someone is impossible to work with and I'm in for a dreadful time (the two obvious examples being Barbra and

Ken Russell) the result has been the exact opposite. An inability to suffer fools with joy is a reason *for* working with someone not against. In fact when the English press started to print nonsense about Barbra the entire unit wrote a joint letter saying how great she was, which everybody signed. In Hollywood that sort of thing would be more than suspect, but English crews never flatter anyone.

My operator for YENTL was Peter MacDonald (a sort of Heifetz of the Chapman crane) who at the very start landed me with some rather elaborate choreography, one moment over her shoulder into a mirror, then swooping up in the air as, singing away, she throws herself backwards on the bed. For quite some time the camera continues to behave like a hawk after a partridge, finally coming to rest in a close-up. When it had been rehearsed to everyone's satisfaction Renata was asked to fetch a hand mirror "to check the lighting". Renata is a warm and delightful Polish/American girl devoted to Barbra in much the same way as Yoshi had been to Jiro (though not to the extent of rhubarb crumble, that would be needless as Barbra would enjoy *both* desserts). As soon as the glass was held up all the lighting changed of course because the mirror was now reflecting some of it back into her face. I stole a glance at Peter doing his level best not to laugh and Barbra, who didn't miss much, quickly said something else to Renata who scurried off again. She returned after a minute or two and handed me a by no means recent 15x12 studio portrait that had been carefully retouched.

" Why can't I look like that? "
You'd go to Lewis Carroll to find anything as silly.
" You may not be able to remember back to when that was taken but I'm sure that you and the camera weren't hurtling around the room together. They're not called moving pictures for nothing you know. "
She laughed, I handed the 15x12 back to Renata for the next cameraman, and we made the shot.

Working with her in a film as opposed to recording studio it is easy to forget what a good musician she is. One of the pleasures of sitting next to her in rushes was to hear her quietly singing improvised duets with herself. There were other delights. It is customary to carry each shot the whole length of a scene so the editor has his choice of which bits to use. Thus a close-up may run on for four minutes that will end up in the finished film for a mere fifteen seconds. Print six takes and it remains stuck on the screen for 24 minutes (by which time any shot has passed its best). This happened one morning and I sensed a growing unrest in the next seat.

" Oh come on Barbra there's nothing wrong with that; I wish *I* looked like that. "
" Well you almost do. "
The six weeks in Czechoslovakia was amazing. Prague is a beautiful city, the people lovely, but everywhere the most profound and widespread

unhappiness it is possible to imagine. At that time there was no hope; all the younger people could think about was escape. The large generators which had been driven out from England are sound insulated by means of an inner and outer shell; between the two is a space about 18" wide. Some of the young Czech electricians pleaded with our lads to seal them inside for the journey home. It would be an unpleasant death if the generator were started up, which was just the sort of thing the border guards would have done.

The cutting room was inside something like an old church hall where Terry Rawlings had installed his Steenbeck, a sophisticated descendant of the black moviolas of my youth. On the opposite side of the room there stood, of all things, a beautiful Steinway D grand, but all my pleading with Terry to change "ee" to "ei" and "beck" to "way" on his equipment list and take a beautiful piano home instead of an old editing machine, fell on deaf ears.

It was absurdly easy to spot the party men; better dressed than the others, they never ever smiled. One of them was the location manager and we ran up against each other on a recce in a place called Zatec. There was a night scene to be done in the town square adjacent to the cathedral and I wished to put a small source inside the baptistry to simulate a sanctuary lamp. The party member said it would not be possible as there was only one key and the caretaker had taken it with him on holiday to Moldavia. Recces are tedious affairs so I wandered off aimlessly and chanced to push against the baptistry door which swung open to reveal a party of Russians on a guided tour. I headed back, pointed this out and of course had my lamp inside the church. For the rest of the time there I began every request with "If the keys are not in Moldavia I would like ..." to the immense delight of the Czechs. It wasn't much to do for them but better than nothing I suppose. One wonders what that man is doing now.

Zatec had its lighter side, however. In Europe, particularly the eastern countries, they have a quite different attitude to the cinema. There are many students of it and it is taken rather more seriously (whether this is better I can't say - it's never good to be too in earnest). At the end of a day's work in a street market I was talking to Barbra and noticed a young man with steel-rimmed glasses waiting for an autograph. Now Barbra does not enjoy giving autographs and has made a deal with herself that if she can avoid eye contact (and anyone who has ever tried to get the attention of waiters will know all about this) there's nothing doing. If on the other hand you succeed in catching her eye, she will stop, maybe talk with you, and sign. After a while I felt the game was up.

" He won't go away you know. "

She nodded, so I stood aside to let him approach.

" Would you sign this for me please, Mr Watkin? "

I said I'd be happy to and when it was done he thanked me, bowed politely to her and walked away. She was delighted.

" I don't know what you so dislike about it, I quite enjoyed that. "

" You don't ged as many. "

Not everyone would have felt the same; there is no pleasing some people, like the lady who complained to her hotel manager about a crowd of autograph hunters in the lobby, only to become far more annoyed when it was explained that they would not be troubling her because they were in attendance on the Atlanta Braves (an American baseball team), who were also in the hotel.

Barbra has an endless (and quite endearing) curiosity over food; if you order a different course from her in a restaurant she will almost certainly ask for a taste, which gets a bit complicated if there there are more than half-a-dozen of you. When the electricians sent down to the East End for some authentic eel pie and mash, where I personally draw a line, she insisted on joining them.

I have been asked once or twice if Barbra actually directed the film herself (as if I'd have anything to do with it) to which the answer must be that if she didn't no one else did. One of the distinguishing marks of a great operator is his skill as a guide without ever himself being obtrusive, and in this regard Peter was wonderful. Halfway through laying out a long camera move she would suddenly realise she was on the famous wrong side of the face.

" That's all right Barbra, we can go back and line it up differently --- but you do know the reason we've done it this way is because it plays best for the scene. "

" Well, I wouldn't do it for any other director. "

I have only happy memories of her and will end with one of them. Back in Wembley Studios she came to me one morning,

" I've a great idea - let's do one of my numbers in silhouette. "

" It's a splendid idea Barbra but *you* won't like it. "

" Sure I will, it's a great idea. "

By an odd chance I was in the process of grading CENERENTOLA in the evenings, so I phoned the laboratory and asked them to send over reel 4 (the sextet). Then I booked a theatre, sent her in to see it and got on with the set till she came back. When she did she came straight over.

" I told you it was a great idea - but I'll have to have a light. "

"Why is there only one word for Thesaurus?"

Out of Africa

YENTL was shot entirely on a new filmstock; so good was it that it had to be hastily withdrawn and replaced by something else that I didn't much like, though when I complained I was told that everyone else loved it.

29

That came as no surprise. Years before when I was assisting Ritchie he started getting odd printer lights from the labs which told him in effect that his negative had insufficient exposure. Always sure of what he was doing Jimmy got onto Kodak; was anyone else using the same batch? Yes, Jeak was on it (Adrian Jeakins was a taciturn and therefore highly respected cameraman). Jimmy phoned him up. Yes the stock appeared to be losing speed by the day. What had he done about it? Well when it got bad enough he doubled his keylight and carried on. Jim wished him luck, hoped he would finish his picture before the keylight doubled too often, and got back onto Kodak. It transpired that the batch was faulty and rapidly deteriorating, Jim had saved them much trouble and expense by enabling them to call it all back in before any serious harm had been done. They were much obliged and would like to do something for him, how about some free stock? When 100,000ft turned up gratis at British Transport Films the only thanks he got were angry expostulations from the unit's chief accountant.

" .... how am I going to bring it onto the books? Never do this again please!"

A quarter of a century on there were obviously some of Jeakins' successors about and it got to resemble the story of the Emperor's new clothes, with myself cast as the small boy pointing out that the new stock was not all that nice. What had happened was that the tonal range of the emulsion was reduced, as if someone had disconnected an octave at either end of a piano keyboard; you would play merrily on until suddenly you hit a note that was no longer there.

By this time I had started shooting WHITE NIGHTS in Elstree Studios and one day at lunch in the studio restaurant I noticed the stock manufacturer's representative "entertaining" a group of cameramen at the next table. On his way to the cold buffet he called gaily across -

" How are you getting on with our new stock now? "

" Much better. I've stopped using it. "

" Well you must have been over or underexposing. "

All for the edification of his guests of course, so I explained, also for their benefit, that the elements from which a photograph is built up fall into two groups: some are overexposed and are called highlights, while the others are underexposed and they are called shadows. It is on combining the two together that all hope of the audience recognising who it is on the screen must rely, and the usefulness of a filmstock that could not handle either was a bit restricted; why on earth had they changed?

" One reason is that our new stock has a much longer shelf life. "

I was not going to argue about that, and assured him that so far as I was concerned his new stock would have a very long shelf life indeed.

When WHITE NIGHTS finished I was to go to Kenya to photograph the story of Karen Blixen. I had never been on the equator before and was giving occasional thought to ways of dealing with the harsh lighting conditions that might be expected there, when Agfa, with convenient timing, introduced a brand new negative material. They were strangers to me but I asked an assistant to run a test, which he did and said it looked interesting, and so we took some with us; the upshot was that apart from a very few scenes the whole of OUT OF AFRICA was shot on it.

For the next decade I enjoyed myself to the full with one of the most beautiful filmstocks I have ever known. But I should have remembered that where you are dealing with true excellence it won't be long before someone comes and puts a stop to it. As a result of the 1979 silver crisis (a massive leap in the price of silver, the raw material of photography) a giant drug corporation had gained control of Agfa Gevaert. In December 1994 they suddenly decided not to make cinema negative any more; just like that. It is no lighthearted game to change over to a new stock even if it is as good as the old one (and that can't be counted on); getting to know a filmstock is like getting to know a person - it takes a long time to be sure how either is going to behave in varying circumstances. That, however, is insignificant beside the human cost, throwing aside people who had dedicated ten years of their lives to something so good that they were able to believe in it. AGFA came in with OUT OF AFRICA, and was used for the last time on Norman Jewison's BOGUS; not a bad entry and exit.

On the assumption that all Scandinavians have blond hair, Sydney Pollack suggested to Meryl Streep that she should dye hers. From having his ideas about anamorphic lenses opposed by Grimes and Watkin he now

"Why is there only one word for Thesaurus?"

came up against Meryl's concern for accuracy and research, which had revealed that in fact Karen Blixen's natural colour and her own happened to coincide. She consequently told him that he'd got one blond too many as it was. This was a reference to the actor playing the part of Dennis Finch-Hatton. Whatever hair that old-Etonian was able to show the world (he was prematurely bald) had been dark. Robert Redford was not making many concessions to that, but though his appearance may not have been close to the original his combined charm and cynicism probably were.

When it comes to taking exposure readings stand-ins do not always have corresponding flesh tones with whoever they are standing-in for. One does not like to bother the actors so I often take spot readings from my hand. Meryl was lighter than Bob and so I used to read the sun-tanned back of it for him and the inside of the palm for her. He noticed this and asked what I was doing. I told him and ended by way of explanation

" ... so the back of my hand is exactly the same as your face. "
The blue eyes lit up.

" Not quite - one has more talent than the other. "
He was not saying which.

After Bob's rhapsodic shampooing of Meryl's hair to *The Rime of the Ancient Mariner*, it was decided to ram home Dennis's poetic nature by having him declaim *Kubla Khan* in front of her living-room fire. I arranged everything satisfactorily and withdrew to a far corner of the room for a quiet doze. This for some reason I was not able to do, something kept nagging at the back of my mind. Then I realised what it was. Kubla Khan was one of those things (along with guess what poem by Rupert Brooke) that I'd had to learn by heart at school. It is not the clearest of poems but the jumble that was being recited at the other end of the room, with complete lines missed out at random, made no sense whatever. I roused myself and, like my predecessor from Porlock, interrupted them.

" Excuse me Sydney, but that doesn't make sense. "
Bob threw another smile across -

" Not to me at any rate. "
Somewhat anxious, I began, "In Xanadu ..." but the Jesuits were right; what is drummed into a child's mind stays there. When I'd finished there was silence for a moment and then, with commendable caution, Sydney sent away messengers to the four winds and in a surprisingly short time one of them returned from some college in Nairobi with a copy of the poem that was found to correspond exactly with my recitation of it. This engendered a degree of respect in some quarters that had not hitherto been accorded to my photography, a step forward for the English after 1969; when Mike Nichols' camera crew of "Brits" pointed out that a section of dialogue in CATCH 22 would be quite incomprehensible to an

English audience, they were told,

" England is zilch! "

(which added to my vocabulary at least).

My driver in Kenya was a young Masai. Bar Mitzvahs, Confirmations, and such like, vary from one people to another, and with the Masai it consists of killing a wild lion with a spear.

" Have you killed your lion, Richard? "

He looked rather embarrassed and admitted that in Nairobi they had now given up the practice. If this confidence was passed on to the lions they declined to give it face value. The animals used in the scenes with Meryl had actually been born in Los Angeles and were now on their fourth visit to the African continent. Their trainer was a German called Hubert Wells and one thing that impressed me about Hubert was his refusal to allow any guns, other than props, on the set. His reasoning was that by the time a lion is at all impressed by a gun it will be dead and of no further use to Hubert, also in all the excitement it could just as easily be an actor or even the director that gets shot. He had his own inducement to good leonine behaviour which was nothing more lethal than a fire extinguisher (which the animal could experience without incurring any drop in value); and of vital importance, an insistence that no one ever moved after the animal had been freed.

The first day with the lions, Sydney Pollack and I walked over to the trailer behind Hubert's Land Rover where a very amiable beast awaited us. While we were chatting to Hubert he observed a small group of Masai about 60 yards away and, telling us to " Watch this", he beckoned them over. These tribesmen lacked Richard's urban gloss but not his good nature and they stood around laughing their heads off, unlike the lion which as soon as they approached went literally roaring mad. The trailer bounced up and down on its springs like a toy and had it not been for the Masai giggling away the scene would have been terrifying. Hubert thanked them for their trouble and they loped off still full of their laughter, whereupon the lion instantly reverted to being as nice as pie. We appeared to have a racially predjudiced creature on our hands and I was just about to suggest that perhaps it came from Pretoria rather than Los Angeles when some Kikuyu arrived to take a look at it. The Kikuyu are farmers, have no cattle to protect, and do not molest lions. Peace reigned and I asked Hubert what this was all about.

" The Masai have been killing lions for 2,000 years and the lions know about it. "

" *Californian* lions know about it? "

I felt we had witnessed something very old and wonderful, beyond ordinary understanding; but perhaps that is only because we underestimate all living creatures other than ourselves.

In fact the next living creature to be underestimated was not far away. A veteran Hollywood cameraman who specialised in wild life photography, named Jack Couffer, was just about to start a week of night-shooting, with a double: all the action material of the lion attacking an ox inside the boma. In this scene the intrepid Karen drives the intruder away from the boma with a whip, but in reality it would be almost impossible as well as extremely dangerous to do this if the lion was occupied with an actual carcase. Therefore a carefully cleaned ox skin, stuffed with whatever is most unappetising to lions, is used instead, but with a piece of the real thing about the size of a Sunday joint carefully placed so as to engage his interest. Then, when approached by a stunt lady with a whip, he will (unless he is an S&M lion) be only too ready to oblige by running off with it in his mouth in order to eat in peace - just as you or I would were the Savoy Grill to be suddenly invaded by ladies with whips half way through the chocolate soufflé.

When Jack had finished all the wide shots with the double, we'd come along with Meryl and do the close stuff. We were shooting during the day at the same location and I stayed behind the first evening to set the lighting so that his material would match ours. When it was finished, I explained what I had done and went on to suggest a way for his light readings to correspond with mine, using the spot meter on the back of my hand. Then it occurred to me that he might be used to a different method so I asked him.

" What meter've you got? "

" A leg of lamb. "

This non sequitur had me completely lost until it was explained later by Jack's clapper boy, who was obviously brighter at that time of the night than I was. Apart from the crew lamentably calling my meters every butcher's cut to be found in Mrs Beeton's Household Management - "get the guvner's loin of pork for him", a feeble game that took longer to die than it should have, no harm resulted; but it would have been suchlike misunderstandings that caused the powers that be to regard Jack as a "bit of a clunker" and replace him with Simon Trevor. It was about as valid a decision (or not) as Donald Taylor's had been about me on SPARRERS ; they were as good as each other to my eyes. Nonetheless there was a nice irony attendant on Jack's departure because his boma rushes were being viewed at the exact time that their author was boarding his flight back to LA. It was very exciting material and it took quite a while, with all the "oohs" and "aahs" and "wow look at that", before I was able to get in a word.

" You realise of course that you've just fired him. "

It was not easy to assemble enough old carriages to make up the train that is seen in the film and so, together with some others, the notorious Tsavo carriage was taken out of the museum in Nairobi and put on the track again. There was a particular reason why it was impossible to resist having a lie-down on each of its four bunks. It had been used as a dormitory for the site engineers and foremen during the construction of the line from Mombasa to Nairobi and at a place called Voi in the Tsavo district they met with a bunch of lions that soon acquired a taste for the labourers working on the line. As these were all black, the management might not have minded all that much had not the lions displayed such healthy appetites as to actually slow-down the work. So a guard was set on watch throughout the night with instructions to shoot any lion that turned up. One evening only three out of the four bunks were occupied and, on hearing of this, our sentinel decided to vary his routine by climbing into the fourth for a night's sleep.

These carriages had no doors at the side and were entered through a single sliding panel which gave onto a veranda at the tail end. When a lion arrived and set his paw on the step he was heavy enough, being a very large specimen, to tilt the vehicle on its springs sufficiently for this door to slide open; construing this as an invitation, he entered the carriage. The first irony is that if he had approached the train from the opposite side that same tilting would have held the door shut. The second irony is that on entering the carriage he selected the very person whose job it was to shoot him, picked him off the top bunk and exited through one of the side windows, treading on the occupant of the lower bunk on his way out (which must have been uncomfortable). It is all recounted in a book called *The Man-eaters of Tsavo* which I had read years before and it felt strange being so closely confronted with the very same carriage so long afterwards.

Africa was such a good experience that I suggested to two of my friends that they come out for a couple of weeks each. In Llewellyn's case there was an added factor because, whatever his name might suggest, Llewellyn is black and it would be fun for him to see where he originally came from. He was a bright lad and one of the best features of his encounter with the continent was, like Cawdor's life, the manner of his leaving it - he discovered a use for apartheid. The British Airways flights between Nairobi and London originated in Johannesburg and were well patronised by South Africans because their own airline, not allowed to overfly any black African states, had to make a wide detour out over the Atlantic. Llewellyn boarded at Nairobi and finding himself seated between two Boers spread himself comfortably, lightly brushing his neighbours white hands, on their arm-rests, with his own black ones. As soon as the aircraft doors closed both representatives of the superior race fled to other seats and, the arm-rests having served their purpose, Llewellyn pushed them up out of the way and stretched out across three seats for a comfortable night's sleep.

Before getting too smug at the expense of South Africa there is the question of the ears. When Karen Blixen was in Kenya the natives used to wear cylindrical ornaments about an inch in diameter through the lobes of their ears. The practice had been long discontinued so the make-up department devised plastic lobes which, when glued on, looked exactly

"Why is there only one word for Thesaurus?"

like the real thing. They stayed in place for about three weeks after which, as new skin grew, they fell off harmlessly of their own accord. Extras who wore them were paid something more for putting up with the encumbrance. The make-up girls wanted to put a pair on Llewellyn to go home in, and at first he was delighted at the prospect of being met by his mates at Heath Row wearing his new ears; but knowing from past experience that Customs and Immigration officials apply different standards of toleration to the likes of Llewellyn, even without enlarged earlobes, he sadly decided not to risk a hard time from them for the sake of a bit of fun. As well as earlobes, the girls had made a splendid job of the ulcerated leg for Kamante, the little goatherd who became Karen's cook. One day a very old man with white hair came to the set and Sydney asked to see the scar; it was still there all right but, needless to say, it was on the opposite leg.

We made a trip by helicopter into remote areas to find locations, and while Sydney was doing the things that directors always do on such occasions, I wandered towards a group of Masai huts surrounded by its thorn enclosure. There were only a few old men about and they and the women stood calmly looking on while all the children came running over to me. A boy who might have been ten years old took hold of the situation and my hand at the same time and led me towards his home. They are a very tactile people and communicate by the one thing that we have grown unable to do - they feel you. I think I was the first white person this child had ever encountered because he was absorbed and fascinated by my hands, feeling over and around each fingernail; I remember being thankful that they were clean. When we entered it, the inside of his house, made of dried cow dung, was equally so.

Only connect.

Karen had two love affairs in Africa, one with Finch Hatton and the other, probably more overwhelming, with the African people. I came away with the same feelings, of love and admiration for their timeless patience, good nature, and serenity. Eight years later I was back, this time in Zimbabwe, where a different tribe, the Shona, quickly cast the same spell. To start with (literally) when a child is born, instead of calling it after the usual old saints, names can be chosen from all the words that there are. Some reflect feelings or circumstances prevailing in the family at the time: Blessing, Never, Shame and Givemore - rather on the same lines as the angels of Mrs Melrose Ape. The film we were making, about apartheid, also got its name from a prevailing circumstance - BOPHA meaning arrest; it was directed by Morgan Freeman.

We shot in a township for three weeks and within a few days each inhabitant knew the first names of everybody on the unit. Whenever I sat down I'd be surrounded by children and asking them *their* names was a good way to start a conversation. Imparting this information was a serious matter, and they were always very solemn about it (almost the only time they ever were).

" My name is Newton. "

The same solemnity also extended to any further personal information.

" I am eleven years old. "

Talking to Morgan while a new scene was being prepared, I noticed the first assistant had placed two kids on a see-saw as part of the background action.

" If you look down there Morgan, you will see Newton testing the laws of gravitation. "

In the North African countries I have visited, Morocco and Tunisia, there would be plenty of children running after you asking for cigarettes or money, which is understandable; but here they will come to you with their hands out because they want you to hold them and be friends. All the time I was there I was never asked for a thing. That is not entirely true; one day I was stopped on my way to lunch,

" Mr David, I have a problem. "

" Dear me, what is it? "

" I have no friend in England to write to me. "

I added his address to a growing list, to each of which I was careful to send a few lines when I got home. Among the replies there is one that deserves quoting in full.

Dear Friend   27 November.
Firstly I would like to ask you if you arrive very well.
Here we are all right. How are others there in England.
I hope they are all right.
I would like you to send us this following items
1. Three bicycles
2. Three pairs of sports shoes.
3. And a television set.
I hope you are going to do so before 25th of December.
Your friends Jonh, Shame and Vivian.

Obviously they could adopt a different code of behaviour once you were no longer a guest.

Morgan liked to work with a sketch artist, not to lay down set-ups for the camera (a rigid way to carry on unless you're Hitchcock) but just to help him to visualise the completed scene. We were filming a football match. All the action was concentrated at one end of the pitch and after a while I strolled over to the other side of the field where the goalkeeper, a boy about fourteen years old, was crouched down in his deserted goalmouth drawing an elephant in the dust. He was drawing it very well. Reassured that my own attitude to football still had its adherents, I wandered off to find our sketch artist and tell him he had a rival. Keith took his pad and made a drawing of a goalmouth, a boy, and his elephant, inscribed it "to a fellow artist, Keith" and gave it to him. The lad thanked him and asked to borrow the sketch pad and pencil. Keith passed them over and came away. When he went back some time later he was handed a charming sketch of a man drawing a boy drawing an elephant in a goalmouth "For Keith, from Maxwell, Zimbabwe".

In the script of BOPHA there were two church interiors. From a scene of the "special services" torturing a victim, cut to a white Lutheran church with the pastor reading some benevolent utterance of old Jehovah consigning the sons of Ham to be bearers of water and hewers of wood, cut again to a black church where everybody is singing. I said to Morgan that if he shot the Lutherans on wide lenses only and combined this with completely flat lighting the result, however formally attractive, would be utterly souless,

" ... then when we get to the black church I'll ravish you. "

" No, that is not what I want. You and I may not like what they believe but they are sincere in it. Make them both as beautiful as you can. "

It seemed a bit magnanimous. I did what he wanted of course but I needn't have worried, the singing in the black church far outshone anything I could have done with a bit of lighting. As with Maxwell's drawing these musicians grew out of the very earth they stood on, the basses dead in tune, the high voices just slightly sharp; African ears are, as the Americans would say, "something else". There was another reason I needn't have worried - neither scene was used.

With any crowd of extras it is not long before they become bored and restless, wandering off to play cards behind the set or bandy the names of "stars" they have "worked" with. The African crowds stood where they were placed, serene and happy all day long. Even when it rained - by the time they were persuaded to take cover we were soaked ourselves. When, in May 1994, I saw an aerial photograph taken in South Africa of an endless line of people, like a great river, calmly waiting to vote for the first time in their lives, I knew I had seen them before, their patience and the knowing how to live in this world.

OUT OF AFRICA had an Oscar nomination for photography and, as at the time of the presentations I was in LA in connection with another picture, it was easy enough to go along. I stayed as always with Tony Richardson and on arriving at his house was confronted with a massive basket of unripe fruit from the reigning head of Universal Pictures.

Any prepared speech from me would always ring false but if there's a possibility of having to say a word or two by way of thanks for something it is sensible to have a rough idea in one's mind beforehand. I meant to be brief and did not intend to thank any of my forbears, lovers, Sydney Pollack, or worse still Universal Pictures (who should have been thanking me, and indeed they seemed to be doing their best, if the Farmer's Market was anything to go by). At the time of the premiere of THE THREE MUSKETEERS at a theatre on the Champs Elysées, I had been in Paris working on some commercials with Don McPherson, who was a cinema enthusiast. Most directors *are* of course, though a good many confine the enthusiasm to their own films. Large action pictures often have a second unit who go quietly away on their own for days on end and take all those shots of horsemen riding across cornfields into the setting sun. Each time one of these came on the screen, Don leaned across and told me how clever I was; it was enough to fall back onto if the need arose, although I did not think that it would, if for no other reason than what I will call the affair of the snow-covered log (an example of the detrimental effect of a large budget).

OUT OF AFRICA opens with a pheasant-shoot in Denmark and we set off to do this in a Norfolk field under January snow. After two days of more general stuff we came to the crucial part of the scene, between Karen and Blor, where their marriage of convenience is agreed on. For this we moved from the open field into a small copse where the two actors were seated upon a snow-covered log. Sydney was expecting to fly out to Nairobi that same evening and a helicopter was standing by to ferry him and Meryl to Heathrow. With plenty of daylight left and only half the scene completed it was decided to leave the rest to be done with front projection at Shepperton at the end of the African shooting. My suggestion that it would be a lot better to get on and finish it (as we should certainly have done on a picture that could not afford helicopters to fly directors to airports) was quickly dismissed and the second camera was left to shoot the background plates while the rest of us came home for a few days before travelling out to Kenya.

The gentleman who was left behind made a miscalculation over his exposure levels. This was not a disaster in itself - they could have gone back and done them again. The bad mistake was that when the cutting-rooms received the lab report they did not bother to tell anyone, so that five months later we arrived in Shepperton to find background plates that were heavily under-exposed. There is a dearth of snow in Norfolk in July and a number of desperate expedients were resorted to, including getting an artist to paint a snow-covered log and filming the result. We ended up using the original plates that were about three stops under, and looked it. I was philosophical - we all have a snow-covered log or two in our lives.

Inside the Dorothy Chandler Pavilion I was seated next to a tall, dark-haired woman wearing a black evening dress. The Oscars is a protracted affair and I was not at all surprised after a couple of hours when she got up to go to the bathroom (as it is called out there). I was, on the other hand, very surprised indeed when she returned in under a minute, swathed from head to foot in a new creation with every colour in a peacock's tail. I was just recovering from this shock when I received another and had to go up and collect my statue. When, after going through all the press interviews, I finally returned to my seat there she was, to my amazement, back in the black dress. It was explained afterwards that, because the entire proceedings are televised, a number of extras is hired to stand about ready to spring to life and prevent anything as unedifying as an empty seat from being seen by the outside world; rainbow-frock had been one of them.

My speech briefly recounted the story of Don and the second unit, explained, in order to avoid similar misunderstandings, that the flying had been done by Peter Allwork and the animals by Simon Trevor, thanked the Academy, and that was that. Characteristically the BBC at home cut out everything original (including the reference to two other Englishmen) and transmitted the only two words that were entirely predictable -

" Thank you. "

We left the Pavilion to walk the gauntlet of crowds and cameras just behind James Garner (an unsuccessful nominee that year). At one point he was hailed by an excited member of the public,

" Mr Garner, Mr Garner we liked your last movie so much we named our new dog after it. "

" That's average. "

When I got back to Tony's place there was another basket of fruit from Universal (we could have set up a greengrocer's on Sunset) and a message asking me to break my homeward journey in New York to meet with Herb Ross about a film he was going to make there with Michael J. Fox called THE SECRET OF MY SUCCESS. Together we recced all locations, I gave my gaffer a complete rig for the main set in the Astoria studios, agreed a deal for the job and came home, only to receive a desperately embarrassed phone-call the next day to say that Universal didn't want me to do the picture after all. Clearly somebody had decided to fly in the face of over a hundredweight of grapes and bananas! It was neither the first time nor the last, but a good fairy has always seen to it that I never really believe success and so constantly experience mild surprise (only mild) that people should actually want to work with me; this makes it much easier to handle when all of a sudden they don't.

After that Academy Award there were plenty of offers. Any that were worthwhile I should have been asked in any case, and all those that were made solely because of it were not worth doing. Far and away the best aspect of it all was the mass of letters and telegrams from people out of the past, some long forgotten, whom I might otherwise never have heard from again. That part was better than Xmas and only surpassed when I came to do this book, in which both dead and living friends are around once more.

"Why is there only one word for Thesaurus?"

New York, New York

Hugh remarked good humouredly, after CHARIOTS went on to get an Oscar for "best film", that for the best film not to have been made by the best director implied a breakdown in logic.

30

If logic and Hollywood were ever connected it would surprise me; it is the one place in all the world where values are so confused that what is said counts for more than what is done. Like anywhere else there are good people but in Los Angeles they must work in an environment that accepts the bogus as the natural order of things.

Removal from this artificial support system has its attendant problems. A well known "star" on his first day in an English studio walked up to the camera operator and told him in front of the whole unit that he would not go again if the camera crew made a mistake.

" Just to let you know - I'll only do it once. "

An announcement, routine for brow-beating camera crews on the other side of the Atlantic, was met on this with Peter MacDonald's friendliest smile,

" Better know your lines then. "

One Hollywood picture had two weeks shooting in central London where the location was an extensive area on the first floor of a building in Mayfair. The American cameraman went along with Len Crow, a Lee's gaffer, and said what he wanted in the way of lights. Len sought out the caretaker of the building, asked if he might draw a certain number of amps from the mains, and gave him a fair consideration for being so helpful. This meant that the £60 allocated for diesel to run the generator could be shared out among the electricians. On the morning of shooting the Hollywood sound mixer put on his act and solemnly removed his headphones after the first rehearsal.

" You're gonna have to move the genny down a block - it's real noisy. " Len took the producer by the hand, led him down to the street, stood him two feet from the generator (which of course was not running) and waved an arm towards the first floor windows, ablaze with light,

" There you are Guv'nor, the quietest generator ever; specially designed for the West End. "

After Hollywood, New York is another world altogether, and a much more real one. In fact New York has got one foot in Europe, and, as themselves say of the rest of America - " If you can't see the Empire State you're camping out". The first time I worked there in 1980 it took remarkably little time for us to settle into a mutual respect that has lasted ever since. The crew could not have been better, in particular my gaffer, Frank Schulz. He cared for me on my first four pictures, until he gave up gaffering to be President of Local 52 of the IA. Always so expert and so nice, Frank had a personal early warning system to prepare me for anyone that I need be wary of.

" Will Rogers never met this art director. "

Will Rogers was an American actor of the thirties who used to maintain that in all his life he'd never met anyone he didn't like.

I've already said that sometimes progress makes things worse than they were before, and a good example of this is the switch that was made from DC to AC, from the misguided notion that large HMI lamps are in some way an improvement on arcs. This fathered a disastrous breed of bi-sexual generators designed to supply both, but adequate for neither. The Wendylight draws 1100amps and at home a Rolls Royce 1000 amp set was happy with this load all night long if required; the new sewing-machines were reliable only in one respect - they were certain to break down at least twice in the course of a night's work.

Salvation for New York came, by way of the Kriegsmarine of the Third Reich, in the person of Johannes Weber, a U-boat diesel mechanic who settled in New Jersey after the war and decided to build his own generators. Here is a kind of link with Frank Brice and the engines from the R100, a sea change from the world of submarines and airships to that other world of the cinematograph. Germany is the only place up to now where wooden tracing-paper frames, when I asked for them, arrived dove-tailed at each corner; and John Weber built his machines in the same spirit. They were as rugged and as unperturbed as he was, what's more they were nearly always available on account of his refusal to budge from a strict price of a dollar an amp a day. They were worth every cent of it, taking into account not only their reliability but also the ease with which they stood up to what with lesser machines is called overloading. In the fish-market area of Manhattan I was compelled to put the Wendylight further away than was comfortable and when the time came to take readings Frank could tell by the way I was acting that there was not really enough. He called up the genny driver on the radio and asked me to wait

"Why is there only one word for Thesaurus?"

and read it again when he told me to. People on holiday (also on film units) sometimes enjoy a brief, joyful affair together; so it was with my light and John's generator. It was her best moment and she will never burn as brightly again. Standing beside Frank on that warehouse roof it was as easy as bringing a photoflood up on a dimmer and when he told me to read it again there was exactly what I wanted.

The following evening the electricians turned up in a high good humour. They had met a friend of theirs during the day who had also been up the night before working with Conrad Hall on a film in Brooklyn. As they were about to roll, a bright light came on in the middle of their shot, so an assistant was sent to get it switched out. On learning that it was on the other side of the East River they decided to alter their line-up to take advantage of a splendid backdrop of Manhattan (lit by us). It took an hour or so but finally they were once again ready to shoot. At this point we broke for our evening meal and the light went out!

Excellence is seldom prized. John Weber is dead, his generators dispersed and his story at an end. At its beginning, just after he'd established himself in the States, he was on location in the neighbourhood of the Hamptons. Asked by his new- found and houseproud colleagues if he had ever seen this part of Long Island before, he had pointed seawards,

" Only from out there. "

This was not in fact the exact truth and John later confessed that U-boat crews, from the Kapitan down, had all been very young (and sensible), and having found themselves a pleasant spot out of sight of the coastguards (somewhere around Amagansett), parties on hot summer days used to row ashore in a rubber dinghy to swim in the surf and sunbathe among the dunes.

All lighting comes down to two simple requirements - make it go where you want it to, and stop it from going where you don't. It is the second of these tasks that the Americans manage a thousand times better than we do. That is because they allot a specialised crew of "grips" for the job and equip them properly to get on with it. In England both jobs are done by the electricians as best they can; there is only one "grip" on an English crew and he's there to move the camera about. In practice it boils down to my not asking people here to do things that would be a matter of course out there. Ritchie, my "key grip" would take the sun off a whole street if I asked him to.

The common device employed to restrict the passage of light is a black rectangle called a flag. These come in a variety of names and sizes, with the largest of which we run into a question of some philological interest bearing on the absurdity of taboos. D.H.Lawrence (and for once I agree with him) asserts that a word itself is always innocent ".. but the mind calls up some repulsive emotion. Well then cleanse the mind, that is the real job." (from his introduction to the privately printed edition of *Pansies*, June 1929 - recommended reading for everybody over the age of eight). Despoiled over many years by some subhumans in the Southern States of the US, a beautiful latin word meaning black became taboo that side of the Atlantic, and later in this country also. But throughout my early years in the business a large flag was a "nigger" and on first going to America on CATCH 22 I caused quite a disturbance by asking for one. Later on, in New York, I learned that there the article in question was always known as a "Bobby Royal", and after calling for hundreds of them over the years, I finally got around to asking why they had such a jolly name.

" He was an electrician. "

" Who was? "

" Bobby Royal - a big black guy. "

After Frank left nothing changed much since all his people were good (because he had chosen them well) and I have been comfortable with them ever since. Theirs is a tight-knit, knowing community. Tim Guinness would always disappear briefly during the morning with the result that when lunch was called (whatever part of the city we happened to be) a local restaurant was organised: instant service, no delay, and back to the set on time.

The Teamster drivers, whatever their reputation elsewhere, were always delightful characters, though I was a bit surprised when Tim told me that one of the milder ones, who had driven me on an earlier film, was the brother of the man who shot Jimmy Hoffa. Out of respect they buried him in a brand new Cadillac, in the foundations of the Giants Stadium in New Jersey (he was a baseball fan).

One evening, while we were filming in a restaurant in the Italian part of town, Frank informed me that this was where they "iced" Joe Gallo. Uncertain whether it was a wedding cake or a champagne bucket they had upset over the gentleman, I asked him to be more specific. It was then explained that "the mob" had in fact entered the restaurant and fired guns at him. Had this been from caprice, or was there a reason? Well apparently the mob at that time adhered to a strict moral code of their own: protection and prostitution were OK but the more lucrative dealing in drugs was not. Mr Gallo's conservative inclinations resisted any expansion into that area and the more liberal elements had come to regard him as an obstacle to progress. When I sought verification of the facts (as has been done wherever possible, this being a serious book) there was some confusion among my crew as to whether it might not have been another gentleman, Fat Sam Costellano, who had undergone similar treatment at an adjacent establishment. It all hinged on which restaurant we had filmed in, and once it had been determined it was "Umberto's" the matter was cleared up to everyone's satisfaction; Fat Sam had been iced in "Spark's". What may also be safely asserted is that anyone intent on proposing to his girl over a quiet dinner would be better advised to do so in an Indian or Thai restaurant.

"Why is there only one word for Thesaurus?"

I'd been lucky my first time in the States to have the support of excellent laboratory people in California, and in New York it was the same. Technicolor there was run by a glorious Italian named Otto Paoluoni. There was a notice on the wall immediately behind his desk that read - "Everyone who comes to this office brings joy; some when they enter, others when they leave". Will Rogers couldn't have put it better.

Both Charles Dickens and Frances Trollope left two volumes apiece of impressions of America (the lady in particular left a lot of extremely cross Americans as well). I should like to avoid making even one cross American (if any have read this far) but it is a sad fact that quiet good sense, of which they have as much store as the rest of us, does not make for an interesting read. Good sense is as a rule also missing from any encounter with their government officials. Beyond asking for declarations that three year-olds are not communists, the application form for a working visa enquires amiably whether or no the applicant is an international terrorist. I don't know if anyone has ever put "yes" to that, but it is said that when Gilbert Harding in the 1950s replied to an earlier form of it - " Have you any intention to overthrow the President or the Government of the United States?" by writing down "Sole purpose of visit", they still let him in. Never having arrived in the UK as an alien I have of course no idea what idiotic questions we ask them.

The US is without any question a country of superlatives. The captain of the *Queen Elizabeth* at Southampton all those years ago, told us of a lady at his table on one voyage who referred so often to his American ship that he was unable to forbear any longer,

" Madam, you are in a British ship. "

" But isn't it the biggest in the world? "

" Indeed it is. "

" Then it's American. "

It's a pity that she (the *Queen Elizabeth*) wasn't around in 1620 when the Puritan Fathers and Mothers decided to leave us in peace. If it is our misfortune the *Mayflower* was not large enough to take them all, it is certainly America's that it didn't sink on the way over. For a film in Cincinnati, one of the straight-laced capitals of the world, we had to build our own red light district - there wasn't even a dirty bookshop. There was a couple of the ordinary sort, though I cannot imagine they ever sold very much as all the houses we went into in three month's filming contained one volume only - the Bible. There might sometimes be a reproduction secretaire bookcase but the shelves only carried china knick-knacks, or more often family photos in silver frames. Once there was an exciting moment when I spotted *two* books and dashed over to find that the second was titled *How to have a Powerful Vocabulary in Thirty Days*. Perhaps by buying some more books?

Getting back to the superlatives, the most inattentive concert audience belongs without question to the Hollywood Bowl. Somebody must have told them about the Glyndebourne picnics. Seats are arranged in separate small enclosures of four or six and a couple of hours before a concert the front two or three, as the case may be, are turned around and a table-top placed between them. In a landscape of hampers, matching candles and table linen, the evening meal begins. Unfortunately in many cases it doesn't end before the concert starts, so that, on the evening that I went along, half the audience sat munching away throughout Hindemith's Weber Variations with their backs to the orchestra.

By Paganini's D major concerto most had got themselves correctly oriented and were happily rustling away in the programme advertisements, while the lady next to me struggled with the spirit burner of her coffee percolator. I closed my eyes and tried to make the best of it along with the soloist, and we were both doing well enough when there occurred one of those changes, instantly perceived, when an audience suddenly becomes involved. After their previous inattention it was almost distracting; it was also puzzling since the performance, not surprisingly, was hardly on a high level of inspiration. After a minute or so, however, all was as before and I could hear coffee being served. In the interval I asked my two companions if they had noticed.

" Oh yes, that was when a raccoon got onto the platform. "

As a nation they have certain minor eccentricities, writing the date the wrong way round, calling the ground floor the first; they are obsessed by middle initials, and will put their own address at the top of the envelope instead of at the head of the letter inside it, so that when the time comes to reply you've thrown it away. And they use "momentarily" when they mean "soon". This irritates the rest of us, and leaves them without a word for "momentarily". But if a good fairy (and America has lots) were to grant me one wish for them, it is probably that they should pronounce van Gogh to sound like a Dutch painter rather than somebody dismissing a pantechnicon.

Colloquial differences are usually good for a laugh. I first met one of my finest operators in a situation that well illustrates the value of one other Brit on pictures in the US, if only to share things with. Cary is Gerry Fisher's son who, having married an American girl, was living in New York at the time. There was a film called MASQUERADE that he came onto as the focus-puller. In it a young actress, Meg Tilly, starts off a dialogue sequence by calling out to Rob Lowe, playing a yachtsman,

" Hullo Sailor! "

I looked around the set for Cary and found he was already eyeing me.

" Do you think we ought to tell them? "

Just in time, I remembered - that "England is zilch".

To relate all the warmth, good sense, and kindness encountered in this extraordinary country (unable to make either tea or coffee for itself), where a Jap is noways oriental and a service apartment sounds like a contraceptive, would fill more pages than Dickens and Mrs Trollope put

"Why is there only one word for Thesaurus?"

together. There have been so many delights, not the least to stroll on set the morning of July 5th and ask what all the fuss had been about the day before?

Tim   and   Ritchie   Photo: Takashi Seida

"Why is there only one word for Thesaurus?"

K 466

*Music can do a lot to help photography get away with it
(did not Vaughan Williams act as St Christopher to my
own first efforts?) but it is a one-sided affair, for there is
nothing that can ever be added to music.*

31

Visual records of artist's from an earlier time are, however, of great
interest, except for the oldest of them all, some film of Nikisch,
meaningless on account of being silent. With the coming of sound in
1926, much might have been done, but apart from some tantalising
fragments it wasn't. The earliest survival of an entire piece by an artist of
stature that I know of had to be rescued twice from oblivion; the second
time by me.

In 1941 Humphrey Jennings included a short sequence of Myra Hess
playing a Mozart concerto at a National Gallery concert, in LISTEN TO
BRITAIN. Five years later he went back there and filmed her again,
Beethoven this time, for A DIARY FOR TIMOTHY. Although he
wanted only about thirty seconds, he naturally covered the whole of the
first movement to give himself a choice. In the cutting room a young
assistant named John Trumper, shocked at seeing everything dumped in
the waste bin, stayed behind at night, scooped it all out again and put it
together. In 1995 I made enquiries and found that his one-reeler still
languished in an NFTVA vault as a single nitrate print, in which form it
was likely to finish up either as a pile of dust or an explosion. After a hard
slog and signing the official secrets act, I was allowed to recover Myra
Hess playing the first movement of the *Apassionata* from an interment
almost as final as that of the lady herself. What a pity John was not around
in 1941 - we might have had the Mozart as well.

Jean-Pierre Ponelle asked me to light a series of films with Daniel
Barenboim and the Berlin Philharmonic orchestra playing the Mozart

concertos, and for three years running I spent two weeks every January at the Siemens Villa in Berlin, normally used by the orchestra for rehearsals.

At the same time each year Daniel did a concert with the orchestra in the new Philharmonie. The first programme included a concerto with Itzhak Perlman as the soloist, and sitting there with two Jewish musicians playing Beethoven, there was a grim satisfaction imagining how it would have annoyed the squalid old Nazi who ended his career in a bunker a few hundred yards away. Itzhak suffered polio as a child and consequently walking onto the platform is laborious for him, though possibly less so than it looks. This meant that the ritual at the end, when the soloist returns to acknowledge the applause and continues back and forth for as long as they keep it up, grew steadily more absurd. My neighbours on either side were meanwhile casting horrified looks in my direction - I think because they believed I was laughing at the poor man's disability, which was certainly not the case. English and German senses of humour do not always coincide.

There is another difference between the Germans and the rest of us, entirely to their credit. At the end of a piece there is a pause of several seconds before any applause starts. Silence is as much a part of music as the notes are - and never more so than at the end of it; a luxury that sadly may not be enjoyed outside Germany and Austria.

The Austrian camera provided (Movicam) was unfamiliar to English crews at the time and the first day, just as we were about to start, Freddy Cooper's assistant began fiddling with it.

" What ' you doing Mike? "

" If I don't fix this you won't be able to tilt down. "

" Unless he falls off the piano stool I won't need to. "

All I set out for was a clear and unobtrusive record of a great artist and orchestra, that is the only value, and to impose nothing. This said, there are always exceptions, and K466 was even an exception for Mozart, being one of only two concertos that he wrote in a minor key. K466 is in D minor and I thought to use light from one side only and suppress any but the smallest amount of reflection back from anywhere else. When I spoke of it to Jean-Pierre he understood at once.

" Ah, the Don Giovanni light! "

When the time came there appeared to be a problem and the principal oboe, who was spokesman for the orchestra, asked if I would allow some light to fall on the shadow side because while the players were watching Daniel there was so much brightness behind him that on looking down again they could not see their music. I had already noticed this man not only because he played with lovely tone and phrasing, but did it on a beautiful rosewood instrument the like of which I had never seen. Explaining that were I to do what they asked it would upset the balance (as important in lighting as it is in music), I suggested that the piece might not be improved if the present two oboes were augmented by a further eight. This got a smile out of him and when I added that they seemed to know the work by heart anyway, he said that of course they did. It did not make it any easier for them though, and on that account not for me either. The result, on the other hand, was breathtaking and it is the only time I've felt that lighting has made any positive contribution to the work of musicians other than the utilitarian one of allowing you to see them. Sad, therefore, that it is unlikely ever to reach an audience.

Here we come up against what appears to be a fundamental difference between photography and electronics. With the electronic process, definition or sharpness, is capable of improvement by increasing the number of lines that go to make up the image (high definition or HDTV) but in the quite separate area of tonal rendition (the ability to reproduce detail in both very light and very dark areas) the range is badly restricted and there is no prospect of any real improvement. It is difficult to put this into exact figures for the two systems because of the difficulty in defining ideal viewing situations for either of them, but it is safe to say that film's capability is at least twice as high. Photography is a simple process constantly taking place in nature - every time you sunbathe you take a photograph, or rather your swimming trunks do (if you're wearing any). A cathode ray tube doesn't manifest itself as naturally in any way that I can think of; it certainly lacks the immediacy, range and subtlety of light upon silver. In terms of pure expression we are apt to forget just how different the two forms really are. Almost no bad situation is without some concealed advantage and it is likely we owe the present existence of print stocks of delicacy and finesse, more to this video inability than to the taste of stock manufacturers, who seem to have inherited from Natalie Kalmus the view that colour should be as vivid and vulgar as it is possible to make it.

Back in England some weeks later a cassette arrived and I put it on the video machine. On seeing the brilliant high key lighting I naturally expected to hear the opening of the E-flat major, which we had filmed at the same time, but alas, nothing of the kind. Video electronics are able to distort what they cannot get right and they had certainly done wonders,

if that is the right word, with my poor negative of the D minor Mozart. Not long after receiving this shock, David Puttnam phoned up with another.

" The Japanese are ready to present the first ever world premiere of a feature

Photo: Metropolitan

movie on HDTV and have asked for MEMPHIS BELLE. "

" Well you oughtn't to let 'em have it. "

He didn't.

While the cameras were reloading, Daniel would launch into one of the Brahms concertos, quite strange in the middle of Mozart, and once into the opening of the *Kreutzer*, where he was joined by the leader inside two bars, to make you wish for a crew that took longer to change magazines (as I had with that silent pianist, Marcel Marceau). It is yet another advantage that film holds over tape, as well as the contrast range, that every ten minutes there's an interval for improvisations. In the reloading time on one commercial shoot the Spitting Image puppets had Thatcher and Princess Diana in a fight pulling each other's hair out, with Imelda Marcos throwing shoes at them and Reagan yelling,

" Go on fuck 'er, give 'er one! "

- unforgettable.

When Jean-Pierre was not able to continue the remaining Berlin sessions they were shared between two directors who could not have been more different from each other. Klaas Rusticus was a meticulous character who marked every slightest camera movement and cutting point in the score (there should have been an extra stave to accommodate him). I liked Klaas, but I adored George Moorse and you will see why in a minute. I doubt if he could read the score and he certainly didn't write anything in it. We were getting to the end of a session and I had mentioned a couple of times that we had not yet done a close-up of the conductor/soloist. It is not usual for me to remember such things as whether we have done close-ups or not, neither is it to stay anywhere near the camera while shooting. However on this job Daniel's close-ups provided an excuse to stand in the very center of the orchestra where it's not just hearing any more - you can *feel* the sound; it's the ultimate "trip". Standing next to Covent Garden's understudy Wotan on Peter Brooks' little film with Zero had been awesome enough, but the Berlin Philharmonic was a great deal more than that. Quite apart from these considerations, with only ten minutes left of our final session, I thought I had better draw his attention once more.

" Are you worried that the film police will arrest us for not doing a close-up? "

Perhaps I should have adapted G.K.Chesterton's defence of Penny Dreadfuls to reassure him - "Bad story-telling is not a crime. Mr Hall Caine walks the streets openly, and cannot be put in prison for an anticlimax."

When all was over and we came to say goodbye George gave me a friendly smile,

" See you in the film gaol. "

I hope he contrives to stay out of it - I would so love to work with him again.

"Why is there only one word for Thesaurus?"

Censors

Censorship is an ongoing advertisement of its own weakness; people who are secure in their beliefs are not in the least concerned about ideas expressed by others, though they may be interested in them. It is called an open mind, and it is a great deal better than a closed one.

32

We are lucky that in our society half the censorship we are subjected to, the moral and religious half, is now merely ridiculous. It was not always so when religion and politics were in close association together, and it is not so today in those countries where they still are.

Richard Lester once told me he had spent a morning working on separate versions of one of his films for two different States in the USA. In one of them it was allowed to show pubic hair but not violence, while in the other violence was all right but no pubic hair. For my part I am on the side of pubic hair, but I am wary of deciding for anyone else. There is a general acceptance of quite horrific violence (people hating each other) as opposed to relentless strictures about sex (people loving each other) which stems from moral and religious influences. The righteous do not have a history of being kind to those holding different views from themselves and, after torturing and killing more people than all the wars in history, are not so sensitive about violence as less ardent souls. Censorship is itself an act of violence aimed at suppressing some aspect of truth or other; no one has ever bothered to suppress lies which are easily disposed of simply by standing the truth alongside them. Thinking men and women are their own censors and it is pretty arrogant to set up as a judge on their behalf.

Long ago our own establishment evolved an education system designed to prevent any independent minds escaping into the community, but as some invariably do, there is constant pressure towards more control. To keep that menace at an arm's length, the cinema adopted its own system of shuffling films into a set of categories according to the degree of disapproval they are considered likely to attract. In the days of Mr Shotter there were three - U, A, and H. The interesting one out of those three was the "A" (adult). "U" (universal) was OK for children, "H" (horror) was likely to scare them out of their wits, but "A" was in a class of its own. It decreed that it was OK for children provided they were accompanied by an adult. Just how whatever a child might see or hear inside a cinema would be modified because they were sat next to a grown-up is unclear. The children themselves however were not unclear; if you wished to see an "A" picture you simply accosted the first likely looking cinemagoer and asked them to take you in with them; I did it myself many times. I cannot believe that it benefited anyone at all, except that it became a lot easier for the nation's paedophiles to make contact with kids. Since those days several more letters from the alphabet have been enlisted. While we were shooting CATCH 22, Mike Nichols asked the film's producer John Calley what certificate he thought would be allocated. John said he imagined a "Z" most likely (he pronounced it "zee" of course).

" What category is that? "

" Restricted to Helen Keller only. "

An author whom I cannot place dedicated one of his books to "the child who asks why", and how right he was, for "why" is arguably the most important word in the language.

" You mustn't masturbate. "

" Why not? "

" Never mind why not. "

" But ... "

" Don't contradict. "

And there you have it; moral censorship is the ultimate dog in the manger.

Richard Burton (the explorer not the actor) was a renowned scholar of Hebrew and Arabic whose translation of *The Thousand and One Nights* remains to this day the only complete and accurate one. On its publication in 1885 he was threatened with prosecution for obscenity. Before the case came to court he let it be known within the confines of his London club that he intended to give evidence on his own behalf and that, after taking the oath, instead of returning the Bible to the usher he would hold it up before the court and explain,

" You've just asked me to swear on a book from which, as it is sacred to you, you will not object to my reading some short passages; however it will soon become clear that if my book is obscene, then so is this one. "

The prosecution was quietly dropped. I wonder which pieces he would have taken - there is quite a choice. Have many sermons been preached successfully on Genesis XIX 32-38, for instance? (Lot's daughters, and you can hardly be rude about incest after what *those* girls got up to on Jehova's instructions!). Then there is the somewhat insanitary passage in

Ezekiel IV 12 enjoining the children of the Lord to eat one another's excrement. That might be expected to rule out marmalade entirely from episcopal breakfast tables, but in this instance our privatised water authorities appear to be outstripping the hierarchy in obedience to Divine precepts. Or how about Leviticus XXI, always good for a laugh, "For whatsoever man he be that hath a blemish, he shall not approach: a blind man or a lame, or he that hath a flat nose or anything superfluous, or a man that is broken-footed or broken-handed, or crooke-backed or a dwarf, or that hath a blemish in his eye, or be scurvy, or scabbed or hath his stones (testicles) broken ... that he prophane not my sanctuaries." In other words, kick the spastics out and show your bollocks to the church-warden on the way in.

Then there are some precise instructions in Numbers XXXI 13, "... kill every male among the little ones, and kill every woman that hath known a man by lying with him; but all the female children that have not known a man by lying with him keep alive for yourselves." That also seems fair enough - butcher the boys, massacre the mothers, and debauch the daughters. It was only by including the Jews themselves among his victims that Hitler stepped out of line with Holy Writ, and Pius XII certainly didn't consider *that* worth making a fuss about. I will bring this short catalogue to an end with the seventy children's heads in two baskets, lovingly described in the tenth chapter of the second book of Kings, though not because I regard the Bible as ideal reading for children; but it is the only book to have been prescribed for them by law in this country.

How many of the world's religious, one wonders, have actually comprehended all the cruelty and barbarism to be found in the "inspired word of God"? Not that I blame the Almighty for any of it, as John Lennon said of the Complete Oxford Dictionary - "Some feller wrote that". In fact it was a lot of different fellers, some of whose contributions, as we have just seen, are not very nice. What is more, in 1546 another gang of fellers got together at Trent in the Italian Tyrol to decide what to leave in and what to sling out. They must have got bored fairly early on to have overlooked the coprophagy, unless of course they had a taste for it. In any event it is hardly fair to drag God around with them.

If there is any case at all for censorship then the H.Bible should be at the top of the list; slavery and its kid brother apartheid are justified within its pages, two of the three religions founded upon it have inflicted countless wars and persecutions on mankind and still cause more human misery than any other agent. The more closely people stick to this book, in fact, the worse their behaviour gets and the relative benevolence of the Church of England only comes about because they left off taking it seriously years ago (the one place in the British Isles where they've persisted, Protestants are less benevolent than anyone). Still, however pernicious it may be, whoever wants to read it, or make epic films for that matter, should be allowed to.

Sticking a copy in everyone's hotel bedroom on the other hand is something of an intrusion. I once indulged in the lighthearted pastime, somewhere in Middle America, of throwing the Gideons into the waste-paper basket every morning before going out. Each evening it was back sitting next to its relatively harmless companion the telephone directory. After a couple of weeks I gave up and threw out instead an idea that had suggested itself of placing a copy of "Lady Chatterley" inside everyone's room, an altogether more innocent alternative unlikely to lead to anyone getting killed, except possibly from boredom.

A bookseller of my acquaintance with an orderly cast of mind, having ranged his entire stock of religious volumes in the mythology section, kept them there in face of all protestations. His firmness may have been underpinned by sound marketing considerations, since the only way the devout could dislodge the Virgin Mary from the embraces of Dionysius would be to buy her.

At the outset of World War I in 1914, when it might be thought there were other things to upset him, the then Pope saw fit to ban - wait for it - the Tango. It's OK to kill each other but they mustn't dance. Formalised insanity on this level often passes unchallenged although Samuel Johnson had, in a previous age, known how to deal nicely with it; when a busy lady approached him shortly after the publication of his dictionary,

" Oh Doctor, I am gratified there are no lewd words in your book. "

" Alas Madam, that can mean one thing only - you've been looking for them. "

In the long run we usually end up with what has been so sedulously hidden from us, truth being fortunately a robust commodity, but it can take a long time. I was never keen on the admonition of most of the fourteen nannies that "you'll enjoy it all the more for having to wait".

" Thence by water ... to Trinity House ... Mr Batten telling us of a late trial of Sir Charles Sydly the other day, before my Lord Chief Justice Foster and the whole Bench -for his debauchery a little while since at Oxford Kates, coming in open day into the Balcone and showing his nakedness - acting all the postures of lust and buggery that could be imagined, and abusing of scripture and, as it were, from thence preaching a Mountebanke sermon from that pulpitt, saying that there he hath to sell such a pouder as should make all the cunts in town run after him - a thousand people standing underneath to see and hear him." (I'm not surprised) "And that being done, he took a glass of wine and washed his prick in it and then drank it off ... to the King's health."
That entry in Pepys' Diary for the first of July 1663, took 308 years to get published (in 1971).

The sad part is that the things which moral guardians are most keen to conceal are often those which, with the advantage of hindsight, reflect the most credit on the people concerned. George II and Queen Caroline were the most touching love affair to be found in the long saga of British

"Why is there only one word for Thesaurus?"

Royalty, and not at all with the respectable (almost Victorian) tedium of George III and Charlotte. The second George was a rough enough character married to a cultivated, intelligent and refined lady who made everything work for him. They adored each other, but there was a constant feud between their eldest son, Frederick Prince of Wales (who did not live to be King) and his parents, which led to his behaving unspeakably towards them and also to being nasty to poor Handel, who was a friend of theirs.

The best historical source book for their reign is the Memoirs of a rather camp courtier and friend of the Queen's, Lord Hervey, which were first published (after undergoing a seeing-to) in 1848. They include an account of the birth of the first Royal grandchild, in which the Princess of Wales, whilst she was in labour, was dragged out of bed, bundled into a coach, and driven through the night from Hampton (where the court was in residence) up to St James' Palace, for no reason but to annoy the King and Queen. After a day or so Her Majesty pocketed her pride, went up to St James' to see the baby, and was treated with consummate rudeness by her son.

" It is easy to imagine, after such a reception, that the Queen made no more of these trips to St James'".

There the account ended until an edition of the full surviving text, limited to nine hundred copies, was published in 1931.

" ..and the King told her she was well enough served for thrusting her nose where it had been shit upon already."

Prior to reading this I had never thought all that highly of George II; now, though admittedly not quite in the Sir Charles Sydly class, there was all of a sudden a real human person to deal with.

The other side of censorship, that stems purely from political motives, is less amusing. When it was nothing more than a poor little script, *No Language but a Cry*, Group Three's serious treatment of delinquency in Liverpool, was stopped in its tracks by the British Censor, the "nicotine-stained watery-eyed" Brooke Wilkinson (Paul Rotha's description of John Trevelyan's predecessor).

" In my opinion, films of this kind about such problems as we are facing in Liverpool merely exacerbate the problem and do nothing to alleviate it. I will not guarantee a certificate if you make it. "

That was the view of one established old bigot and it was enough; the picture never got made and Liverpool was swept beneath Mr Brooke Wilkinson's threadbare carpet, a fairly crowded place as the entire country's unemployed were under there already, a film called LOVE ON THE DOLE (an honest attempt to face up to this immense national tragedy) having been blocked by the gentleman on two separate occasions. The plight of the unemployed was not permitted to reach the screen until 1941 (by which time of course there were no unemployed left).

During the 1930s my old boss, Edgar Anstey, was with THE MARCH OF TIME, an American news/documentary magazine that had a production team over here. The Conservative government of the day wanted to remove from all prints shown in this country anything that was unattractive about Mr Hitler's Germany (which must have meant it got precious little coverage) and here our Mr Wilkinson proved every bit as assiduous in protecting other people's bad behaviour as he was our own. Edgar was concerned enough to show an uncensored print to Winston Churchill,

" Mr Anstey, I can tell you that your film should be seen by every man, woman and child in this country; but I am powerless to help you. As you know, I am out of office and have no standing or status at the moment. " Churchill himself, of course, was not always the champion of freedom of expression; in 1956 he urged the owner of a manuscript poem by Kipling to destroy it because it was unflattering to Woodrow Wilson. Not to mention his pyromaniacal wife's attentions to Graham Sutherland!

The Americans may have been allowed to see THE MARCH OF TIME complete with students burning books and stormtroopers maltreating Jews, but when the war was over they were not going to get *The Execution of Private Slovak*. The rights to that book, which tells of the only soldier shot for desertion in World War II, (by the Americans), were owned by Frank Sinatra who was going to make a film of it; that is until he was "leaned on" by Joe Kennedy. because the screen-writer was black-listed as a Communist.

Back to England in 1939, where the egregious Mr Brooke Wilkinson was still busy preventing the Boulting brothers from making a picture about Pastor Niemoller - because it was anti-Nazi.

" How dare you argue with the board ... you will never make that film while I remain secretary. "
Shortly after September 3rd the Boultings set to work, although Mr Brooke Wilkinson (having done his level best for Dr Goebbels) "remained secretary" until 1948.

With a possible eye on the demise of the Lord Chamberlain the British Board of Film Censors no longer behave quite so arbitrarily, which only means that now our rulers have to do the dirty work themselves. Just before a film that included details of some indefensible behaviour (to put it mildly) by the Northern Irish Constabulary was to be shown on television, the police in the "mother of the free" raided the studios and destroyed it. The preparation of another project, which might have glanced at some characteristically shabby and disreputable behaviour by the Duke of Windsor, was interrupted by people's homes being broken into with nothing taken, apart from copies of the script. I've not seen a script yet that was interesting enough for any honest burglar to bother with.

When I asked Michael Caton-Jones if SCANDAL covered the whole of

"Why is there only one word for Thesaurus?"

what had happened he replied simply,

" No, we were not allowed to. "

I did not press him further - if he'd wanted to tell me any more he would have.

The extent to which people mind the incidental behaviour of one drab family in particular is curiously overestimated. British royalty are a sad lot, like the three monkeys with hands on mouth, eyes, and ears, who sat on every mantelpiece when I was a child; not allowed to mention AIDS, see the homeless on our streets, or hear a land mine blow a child's feet off.

On the other hand, who can forget those quiet September days, when this nation, in one of its better moments, demonstrated the admiration and affection in which it held a Princess of Wales who had consistently defied everything the frowsty Palace establishment stood for?

Thirty years earlier, in 1967, when practically everyone agreed the time had come to do away with that anachronism, the Lord Chamberlain's censorship of the theatre, the Queen brought all her influence to try and preserve it, because she was petrified that someone would put on a play about Philip; her only ally, the Prime Minister, was not at all bothered about Philip. His concern was that *Mrs. Wilson Diaries*, about to be staged and of which he had seen the text made him out a complete mugwump. The Queen needn't have worried, nobody cared enough; Mrs Wilson had the distinction of being staged by Joan Littlewood and ran for nine months at the Criterion. It's all in *Crossman's Diaries*.

A journalist beleaguered by gagging orders, or "public interest certificates" as they are called by the civil service, (presumably because they are slapped on top of anything the public would find interesting), remarked that "News is what some powerful person does not want you to print - the rest is advertising". In the end we would all like to ban whatever we ourselves disapprove of. My own dislike of violence would make me an unsatisfactory censor of it, and at one time, given the chance, I'd have obliterated BIRTH OF A NATION (which would've upset a legion of cinema enthusiasts). But it would have been doing Griffith too great a favour; to his everlasting discredit that film will stay, a reminder of what he really amounted to.

There are quite enough instances of individuals appropriating censorship into their own hands. Lady Burton incinerated her husband's diaries and last book, and Thomas Moore burned Byron's diaries in the fireplace at John Murray's in Albermarle Street still there to this day. For Moore to do that is a little surprising because it was of one of his own works that somebody wrote-

LALLA ROOKH
Is a naughty book
By Tommy Moore,
Who has written four.
Each is warmer

Than the former,
So the most recent
Is the least decent.

When Turner died his paintings were left to the nation. There was a huge number of them and who better to catalogue the bequest than that pinnacle of authority on beauty and taste so revered by the Victorians, John Ruskin. While carrying out the assignment he came across some sketch books containing a series of nude drawings. An item of considerable interest no doubt but one nobody will see ever; our stunted arbiter of art destroyed the lot.

An insidious form of censorship, much in vogue, is the law of libel. In a society free of hypocrisy it would be well nigh superfluous. If a thing is true why not just admit it, if it isn't true it can't possibly matter. I have racked my brains to imagine what anyone could print about myself that would get me out of my pram for a moment. If somebody doesn't like me it is their affair not mine, and there's nothing I'm prepared to do about it. However the gross cost of litigation renders it the private reserve of the rich and powerful (whose forerunners framed the law to suit themselves in the first place). It still serves as a shield for millionaire newspaper proprietors raiding their staff's pension funds; also for venal cabinet ministers, since the instant an action for libel is started everybody is frightened into silence. With adequate funding this state of limbo can be kept going almost for ever - certainly until everyone has got bored and lost interest.

Most cynical of all instruments of censorship is the Official Secrets Act; seldom invoked for any genuine protection of the realm, it is everlastingly exercised to protect the wrongdoing of politicians and civil servants. It was a bright day when an English jury refused to convict Clive Ponting and, of course, Thatcher took immediate steps to prevent them ever doing anything like it again.

In all the years that I knew Tony Richardson, the subject of censorship was never talked about, so that when recently I was shown a clip from an interview with him filmed in 1959 (while I was still at British Transport) it came as a reassurance from an old friend.

" Certain films people might want to make might require scenes in them which couldn't possibly be shot under the present circumstances and I think that's a bad thing, because I think you should be able to say or do anything on the screen. I don't believe in any form of censorship whatsoever. I mean with all the dangers that it might expose people to I still think that films should be made so that people can see anything that they want to see. "

Joan Littlewood put it differently,
" It's a matter of taste isn't it? "
and Gavin Ewart perhaps best of all,
" Paint me a riot or battle scene, with all its pitiful dead

"Why is there only one word for Thesaurus?"

And all its violence, so crude, obscene, and far from the comforts of bed.
Paint me a murder or two, and tortures - ancient and modern as well -
Paint me the millions dead of starvation, and the cities modelled on hell.
Paint me some capital punishment, some hangings, some racks and a wheel,
And the floggings that for Tory ladies never lose their appeal.
Paint me no more. For there you have it - two galleries that show plain
How even the lowest of sexual pleasure is higher than virtuous pain,
And censors are idiots who hardly ever, though perhaps they can read,
Are capable of distinguishing between the word and the deed -
Not to mention love, a threadbare noun, but at least it doesn't kill
In a world where murderous monsters have always been run of the mill."

"Why is there only one word for Thesaurus?"

Journalists and Critics

It may seem ungrateful, but were I capable of a rough response it would probably be to being told what to think, and I can't for the life understand how so many don't appear to mind it.

33

I might glance at a review of a concert I'd attended just to see how someone else enjoyed it or didn't (more an assessment of them than of the concert) but to swallow another's opinions about a play I have not seen or a concert I have not heard seems ridiculous. For a start, most of these people cannot perform whatever it is they are writing about (I don't know what sort of a critic Godard was, but he had the good sense to give it up and make films himself) and down the years they have steadily failed to recognise anything really significant when confronted with it. As Corno di Bassetto even GBS merely penned amusing twaddle. Try him on Brahms (18th June 1890) one is not annoyed since it is Shaw that looks silly, not Brahms. Even so, Sibelius' comment that "nobody ever put up a statue to a critic" seems inappropriate; we put up statues to the biggest idiots and villains and I'd have thought that critics merited several, and are hard done by.

This chapter follows naturally upon the last because the subjects of it sometimes, though not always, play the role of censorship's little brothers. HOW I WON THE WAR was released to a chorus of outrage from the great and the good, and Richard Lester was confronted on the tele with an indignant military gentleman whom he disposed of quietly and effectively. This was not at all what the programme controllers had in mind, so at the end of the recording, (to forestall any outbreaks of honesty, these programmes are always recorded beforehand), Richard was told that the tape had been "accidentally" wiped and the interview would have to be done again. This time of course the old duffer was fore-armed and it was Richard who came off badly. Serve him right in a way; I know he wished to defend his film, but he should have just said "oh what a shame" and left them to it.

Professional critics spend a good part of their working lives writing about other people, so they ought not to object to being written about themselves for a moment. First an observation about that interesting phenomenon, the comfortable situation occupied by cinematographers. It may sometimes be reported that some film or other has been beautifully photographed by such-and-such-a-body, but I never heard of a case where anyone was held to have photographed a picture badly. It may be that by the time he has finished with the actors, the writer, and the director, any critic will have run out of ill nature, or possibly cameramen are just not interesting enough to slag off. I have no idea what a DP would need to do to provoke some adverse criticism (short of writing a paragraph like this perhaps) but I am not complaining. Cinematographers come into their own as victims where other kinds of reporters or journalists are concerned, especially the ones that do interviews. Stretching back to the four evangelists and doubtless beyond, this body has never been at ease with accuracy. When a stressed-out pianist threw the score of a Mozart concerto at Mahler's feet during a rehearsal, the press all wrote that he'd hit him on the head with it (and I don't blame them, it's much better). I suddenly twigged, when an interviewer became disconcerted because his leading questions were getting nowhere, that he had already decided what to write and was merely trying to get me to endorse it; that he failed of course made no difference, he simply went away and wrote what he'd decided to in the first place.

Reluctance to print anything resembling what has been said to them is not always consciously deliberate - in fact if a child persistently grabs the wrong end of every stick, parents should be aware that a successful career in journalism probably lies ahead of it. The worn old precept not to believe everything you read in the papers is wide of the mark, you shouldn't believe *anything* in the papers. There is no single instance in my own experience, where I have been close enough to a reported event to know the truth about it, that any press account has been accurate.

For an example let us quote the *New York Times* in the autumn of 1997, on the subject of a new fashion for Hollywood people to make gifts of antiquarian books to one another with, of course, flattering implications of intellect on both sides.

"David Watkin, a cinematographer who is in New York shooting Sidney Lumet's remake of GLORIA with Sharon Stone, wandered into Argosy Books on East 59th Street recently to buy a rare book as a gift to a major figure on the set, said Judith Lowry, the store's antiquarian specialist. She declined to name the intended recipient."

In fact, the major figure on the set was none other than Jonathan, a bright and courteous little seven year-old stand-in; and much as I ended up liking Sharon, I have no occasion to give her a $40.00 reprint of *The Jungle Books*. Nor do I think that Judith ever misled anyone; as she put in a note to me, "... the real story is much better".

A favourite question of the press is always what problems have I got on a picture?

" None. "

" Come now, you must have *some* difficulties. "

" Not really - either a thing's possible or it isn't. If there's a way to do it then it's not difficult, and if there isn't a way it's not difficult either, 'cos then you don't have to do it. "

The other stock query - which is the favourite of all your films? - is harder to deal with because one doesn't think of them enough to have an opinion, and turning it around to give them the least favourite doesn't help either - one thinks of those even less. It is far more about whom you were working with and how much fun was had; what lands up on the screen is partly in the lap of the gods anyway (and several other laps before it gets even there). Tony Richardson said that a film took over his life while making, and when finished was gone forever.

The present use of small Walkman recorders in the place of shorthand notebooks may have unlooked-for consequences. I was once shown a lengthy "interview" in a women's magazine, of which I was certainly innocent, and on reading it realised that it had been cobbled together from an old interview given to someone else years before. The girl who talked to me then had obviously kept all her old tapes and sold them off to someone else after a year or two. I hope she got a new hat out of it; it did me no harm.

The trouble with the critical branch of the faculty is that often harm *does* come of it, usually in the form of a film not getting distribution (tough on the people who want to see it) and the director not getting the chance to do another (tough on the director). The critics are not alone to blame for this. We all love saying what we think and everyone who sees a show becomes a critic of it by the nature of things. But whereas we can all indulge ourselves without upsetting anyone's apple cart, distributors do the critics, and the rest of us, the disservice of taking notice of what they say.

Really smart people manage to pick their way around these oracles on occasion. David Merrick, the Broadway impresario, once had on his hands a production so bad that the response when it opened was in little doubt. He therefore set the office staff to comb through the telephone directories of every State in the Union for people with exactly the same names as well known New York critics. The staff did an excellent job and a number of individuals were brought in from remote areas (or boondocks as they are called) to the Big Apple for the first time in their lives, installed in the best hotels, wined and dined in style and taken to see a dress rehearsal. Before going back home they were asked to write down what they thought of it all, and the next day all the hoardings carried ecstatic quotations from every top theatre critic in town.

Tony Richardson's way of dealing with the London film critics was more direct and less successful. There is a long- standing practice of showing a new film to the critics on the Thursday morning before it opens. After the running there is plentiful champagne and smoked salmon provided for the audience who then go off and write their bad reviews. Tony decided for THE CHARGE OF THE LIGHT BRIGADE to ignore this ritual and said that they could of course write whatever they pleased but would have pay to see the film like everyone else. This caused an almighty uproar and at its height I remember seeing the tail-end of a TV interview with Tony and an aggrieved representative of the critical band who had just explained that the Thursday morning junket was important to him and his kind because they prefered to sit in their own select company than view a film surrounded by a pack of Yahoos. Tony had the last word,

" Well unlike you Mr --------, I've never thought of a cinema audience as Yahoos. "

Needless to say, he never got a decent review from anyone after that, and, although there were other factors, it had much to do with the sorry neglect of a good director over the last two decades of his life. The last movie I did with him, THE HOTEL NEW HAMPSHIRE, got given a hard time (because its subject was an innocent love affair between brother and sister) by people who would doubtless regard an evening at *Die Walkure* as a cultural night out - which indeed it is. Innocent doesn't mean they don't get into bed (some people are more innocent there than others would be inside a cathedral) but they're not raising a family for goodness sake and, although I never fancied any of *my* siblings, sometimes it happens.

To be fair, as in every métier, there are noteworthy exceptions - Harold Hobson and Kenneth Tynan in the theatre; Caroline Lejeune and Dilys Powell for the cinema in earlier days, and Barry Norman in our own, manage to be both perceptive and entertaining. They also actually like the cinema. In so far as awards matter, The New York Film Critic's citation is usually more informed and less political than the American Academy. I do not write this because they've given it me twice already, being entirely without vanity in these affairs.

A friend of mine who is an opera-singer asked me, shortly after YENTL, how Barbra, whom he admired, reacted to assaults by the critics.

" She doesn't like it. How about you? "

" Well I ask myself - how can they be so sure? I am full of doubts (on stage no doubts) but off stage always doubts. "

That was Claudio Desderi, Figaro and Don Alfonso in Mozart and a splendid Falstaff in Verdi, and it is the sensible response of an intelligent and modest man. Some may prefer the more robust attitude of the great

"Why is there only one word for Thesaurus?"

German conductor, Hans Knappertsbusch,
  " Well a church doesn't notice when a dog pisses against the wall. "

"Why is there only one word for Thesaurus?"

A Brief Excursion into Politics

Just before the 1979 General Election I was asked to photograph some TV spots that were being directed by Piers Haggard for the Labour Party.

34

The first of these was an interview with James Callaghan, but as the date coincided with a previous commitment I was not able to do it; the production company therefore got hold of someone else and my first politician, a day or two later, was Shirley Williams.

I had barely stepped inside Transport House when a group of party managers came up and said they were all going to be very unhappy if she looked like Jim Callaghan. I said that I had never thought there was a resemblance, unless they had photographed Big Jim wearing a frock in which case they should speak to the wardrobe people. Piers quickly took me to one side and produced a clipping of the Prime Minister and Leader of the Labour Party looking like a fiend from Hell; it was quite an achievement and obviously my substitute (who had better be nameless) was a keen Tory supporter. Seeing that their concern was now reasonable enough, I did my best to calm them down and said not to worry. This failed to reassure them much and they kept coming back every few minutes as anxious as ever.

" Will she look all right? "

" Yes. "

" You seem confident. "

" Well Vanessa Redgrave never complained. "

This reference to the Worker's Revolutionary Party inside the orthodox precincts of British Labour effectively shut them up, so far as I was concerned, for the rest of my time there. As for Shirley Williams she not only looked all right she was all right. A bright, alert, delightful little woman - much too good for a politician, which is perhaps why she didn't get elected.

The next candidate, David Owen, combined a high manner with inability to comprehend the fundamentals of film editing. When we had covered his speech on a 25mm lens, we switched to an 80mm and Piers asked him to do it again.

" Why? "

" Well we cannot cut two bits of the same shot together, there'd be a jolt; so we do it again on a closer lens, then we can go smoothly from one take to different one - either to shorten the thing, or perhaps you may be better in one place than another. That way we can use the best parts from all the different versions. "

A clear answer to a perfectly reasonable question; but questions grow less reasonable when they are repeated over and again (which this was) for the rest of the day.

He was not alone in having difficulty over the rudiments of film-making. The editor's main implement is not, as might easily be thought, a pair of scissors; it is a wax chinagraph pencil. He runs each shot backwards and forwards through the moviola and marks the frame where he wants to make the cut with a cross; it is his assistant who comes along afterwards with a joiner and film-cement. Because our stuff was being transmitted the same evening, they had to work fast and one of these crosses did not get properly wiped off. This caused a gigantic outcry from the Conservative Central Office that the black arts of subliminal persuasion were being exercised on an unsuspecting electorate.

There was not much in the way of ideas about and most of our time was spent waiting around to find out what the other side was up to.

" What has she said? "

("She" being a lady who'd started by taking away milk from school-children, and finished up years later selling them cigarettes, a commodity barely less lethal than the merchandise with which her son was making a fortune).

It was not an uplifting experience; allow a handful of noble exceptions and politicians seemed a second-rate lot; if that is what Labour were like I should not care to be anywhere near the Conservatives. From this point, the lady in question started her adherents down a path between personal and corporate greed on one side, and arrogance and contempt for truth on the other, towards their ultimate disrepute.

We have at last witnessed a massive repudiation of it all, and may entertain guarded hopes; but there remains always the "permanent government" of civil servants, (a further example of something named by its opposite - they are not civil, nor are they our servants), which to this day is recruited from the cadre of a small number of public schools (here we go again: an adjective meaning exactly the reverse) where hauteur and beatings, double standards and insolence to inferiors (that means the rest of us) remain the basis of the curriculum. That will be a lot harder to change than the House of Commons; any establishment sets about regenerating itself, like Mr Orwell's pigs, and the most we can do is see them for what they are, and put all the ridicule their way that we can.

Actors are told their first time in front of a camera that they must never look directly at it. To do so is to make eye contact with each person in the audience, and that instantly shatters the very illusion upon which the cinema is founded (in the theatre an actor could look at only two of the audience at a time, and to do even that he would need to be cross-eyed). Once, in the last days of live interviews on television, John Lennon broke the rule in mid-sentence and looked straight into the lens,

" You're all governed by idiots. "

then picked up instantly where he had left off.

An example of government by idiots so far as our industry is concerned, happened at a time in the 1970s when London was virtually the film capital of the world. Major tax concessions for foreign nationals were swept away overnight and within a single year a shocking number of international film-makers left these shores for ever. To be exact, our people were only partly to blame - unfortunately the very moment they chose to remove fiscal incentives the Americans decided to provide them. The next James Bond movie, MOONRAKER, (they had all hitherto been based at Pinewood), went to France, and the centre of gravity swung back to Hollywood for the first time since their own brand of idiot politician (McCarthy) had sent every worthwhile creative mind in the business heading for Europe nearly twenty years before. Allowing that most fiscal lunacy is dreamt up in the first place by the Revenue people themselves, it is still unfortunate that the silliness of imposing taxes you are never going to collect (because the investment will simply go elsewhere) should not appear to those ultimately responsible. After a decade of comparatively harmless neglect, the Thatcher administration took a renewed interest in us and the same thing happened all over again, although this time from more sinister motives - now the idiots were vicious. Since British film producers left off portraying the police as a family of uncles all played by Jack Warner and were turning out films like SCANDAL, IN THE NAME OF THE FATHER, DEATH ON THE ROCK , and LET HIM HAVE IT, they were certain to become the target of a government that took so much pride in being economical with the truth. Although DEATH ON THE ROCK is the odd one out here, being a television documentary not a feature film, it is a good example nonetheless of what was happening.

If inaccurate, Thames TV might have been in some trouble, but nothing to the trouble they found themselves in for getting it right. When the time came to sell off the TV franchises (a splendid way to take money out of the arts instead of putting any into them) the auction was set up so as to make virtually certain that Thames would not get a look in. It is true that DEATH ON THE ROCK *was* shown, and no one from Thames disappeared into a death camp, so we still had some way to go.

They could not destroy our independence by implanting their sympathisers, as they did the BBC's, but an alternative way of killing a cat is to starve it, and the Eady fund, which for years had helped to sustain home production, soon went the same way as the children's milk allowance. Incentives to outside investment fell not so much from taxing the profits of foreign companies as by insisting that huge sums be put up in advance of any such materialising. The vast BATMAN set that had been left standing on the outside lot at Pinewood for shooting the sequel was taken down and the whole movie ended up being made in California.

Films are the Americans' second largest export (after aeroplanes) and are, quite rightly, taken seriously by them. So it is nice to have a friend come along and strangle one of your main competitors for you (part of the special relationship perhaps), it must also have been doubly attractive for Thatcher working off her grudge against us and helping her crony (the bad actor) in the White House at the same time. She could hardly have done more damage, "the removal of mechanisms like the Eady Levy and capital allowances really upsets the equilibrium of the entire industry by removing the incentive to recycle revenue as future production capital" (letter from David Puttnam to the author). A British film can be as big a hit as it likes, and scoop all the Oscars there are, nothing will accrue here to support British production. The investment will have come from outside, which is where the returns will follow and any tax revenue from them, wherever else it goes it will certainly not be towards assisting our own industry.

It may help to bring home the nature of the disaster, to give a personal illustration of it. Paramount had a fund of UK profits allocated for the production of short films as a way to bring in new talent. Don McPherson (the MUSKETEERS second unit enthusiast), after years of persuading, was finally given the go-ahead by them to direct a series of short films based on the Saki stories (*Gabriel Ernest, Sredni Vashtar*, etc) which they planned to put out as a package with their main features. The day following the British Government announcement, Jeffrey Katzenberg, the head of the studio, personally phoned Don and explained sadly that in the light of such sweeping changes they had ceased all investment in English production. The loss isn't just some films of the Saki tales, but a director who would most likely have gone on to do other things here. At this time France was subsidising its industry to the tune of £83 million a year, with Germany and other European countries not far behind, all of them without the advantage we have of a common language with the world's largest market. (A single town, Munich, now spends more on the arts than the whole of the British Isles).

As window dressing while this removal of funding was going on, an official body was set up to promote us all. Given their derisory budget, about the best they were able to do was send out a brochure illustrating locations in Great Britain that were deemed capable of being passed off as somewhere else (Camber Sands for the Sahara Desert provided you stick to the long end of the zoom). This was intended to inspire foreign producers to flock over here, cheerily flinging advance sums in lieu of possible profits into ESCROW on the way in. A gathering at which technicians were invited to suggest locations that could be used in this way went much better than expected thanks to one young man,

" I know a film studio that's just been made into a supermarket."
(it was Elstree)

In all fairness the first Films Commissioner, Sydney Samuelson, was a truly dedicated man, as well as a friend, and they *have* been able to do some valuable work in helping foreign film-makers address practical problems when shooting over here. Still, if someone cuts off your legs and then gives you a walking stick, it may be a very nice walking stick, but it is not a substitute for legs; and it is not wise to forget whom it came from.

Until rescued by the National Lottery, a robust industry that had survived every world recession in the past found itself (at a time when cinema audiences were increasing) dominated by countries such as Australia, Ireland and fellow European nations, who encourage their industry properly. Films by English writers, with English directors, are being made in English studios, but often with *French* technicians, for the good reason that the French have put up the money. One young friend of mine, directing his first movie, was last heard of fending off a Gallic principal actress; so if a Shoreditch girl turns up on your screen with a French accent, you'll know how the picture was financed. I don't blame the French, good for them - at least they know what to say to American Presidents who ask them to nobble their own industry! All we do is make other people's films for them. I've had a busy enough time of it myself, but for several years past, never in my own country, (except with an Italian director).

I get an average of two letters a month from young people who want to work in films and where possible they come down for lunch; not that I can do much more than encourage them, and it is sad that as things are they are often regarded as a pool of cheap labour. There is somewhere between allowing unions to be protection societies for tenth rate people, and clobbering them altogether so employers can run a sweat-shop culture to undercut the rest of the world; neither makes for a healthy industry.

The fashionable mode of official subsidy for the arts is to replace a scene painter with an accountant. Arts Council money now goes on sending teams of them into our theatre and opera companies to advise about "stabilisation" i.e. making profit the *only* criterion of worth. In this they reflect the alarming change that has taken place in the US - the new power of frigid accountants and lawyers. The old movie moguls may have been brigands but at least they were brigands with a showman's instincts. I suppose frigid accountants are not quite a novelty, bearing in mind how John Davis dominated Ranks until the Torys helped the film industry for once, by taking him away for a politician, but that was an individual not a general blight.

There is one particular that I am able to impart from personal experience of this philistine and unpleasant man, which is that he was hard of hearing. At the premiere of THE CHARGE OF THE LIGHT BRIGADE at the Odeon Leicester Square the sound was so deafening that Tony sent Neil Hartley to the projection box to ask them to turn the level down a bit. This met with a flat refusal and Neil was asked what business it was of his?

" You are showing Mr Richardson's film."

" Perhaps, but it's in Mr Davis' cinema."

Having seen out the cinema documentary it now feels like Louis XVth a second time round - "Après moi le deluge". But then I have just remembered that I am writing this on Mozart's birthday, and look what he had to put up with.

1995 brought a return to the hustings in the slightly odd setting of someone else's elections. Germany's Social Democrats chose a Swedish director to make their campaign films, while he in his turn took along an English cameraman. I am very pleased that he did because Daniel Bergman is a delightful person and the whole thing was a splendid success, except alas, politically, as the SDP didn't get in (perhaps with my success record at elections I ought not have turned down a request from the Tory Party in '97, although happily they managed to lose without my assistance). The speeches, being in German, were obviously less boring than if I'd been able to understand them but I still withdrew sometimes to take a nap, which led Daniel to lament that I had never worked with his father,

" He'd go absolutely mad if anyone yawned on the set. "

" Then I'm sure we'd have got along fine, people only yawn if they're trying to stay awake. "

To cheer him up though, I told how part of SIX SIDED TRIANGLE was banned in Sweden for piss-taking.

I almost forgot to mention a rather jolly commercial featuring Denis Healey. We had already met some years before when I discovered him on hands and knees examining the lower shelves of the local antiquarian bookshop.

" Well I can't imagine finding Mrs Thatcher on her knees in a bookshop."

This time I took with me a print-off of this chapter and gave it to him, together with a copy of his own book, *My Secret Planet*, for him to sign. At the end of the day he handed me the book with a smile,

" I'm not sure if I've got the noun right. "

 "Why is there only one word for Thesaurus?"

The art director was Roman Voytek, an amazing man, the same age as myself, but who had spent his adolescence rather more heroically as a member of the Warsaw Resistance. The three of us sat down to lunch with my two companions exchanging some words in Polish together. I said to Denis that I was impressed.

" When I was a young party delegate after the war we all learned two sentences in every European language. The first "I greet you on behalf of the British Labour Party and hope you have a good Congress", and the second "Dear Lady, I love you". It was important not to get them confused. If you say to someone you've just got into bed with "I greet you on behalf of the British Labour Party ..." - it's too formal. "

When I got home I opened MY SECRET PLANET -

" With best wishes to David Watkin - a literate socialist - from another such! "

He *had* got the noun right. As for Thatcher, her mark on England was epitomised by an Irish poet two hundred years before she left it -

" Ill fares the land, to hastening ills a prey,
   Where wealth accumulates, and men decay. "

"Why is there only one word for Thesaurus?"

Settling Accountants

At British Transport Films we used often to find ourselves up in Scotland, presumably because persuading people to travel as far as possible from the capital would bring in more money.

35

I don't recall our making any films to promote Southend. The unit accountant was a nice enough man named Walter Keegan. Actually you've already met him at the start of chapter 28 where he got very put-out because an enterprising cameraman had managed to get 100,000 feet of free stock out of Kodak. Something else that upset him was a union rule that, rightly in my view, required that anyone travelling *in charge of equipment* should be paid overtime at the full (instead of half) rate. As we always went to and from Scotland by the night trains this meant in practice that I went to bed in a first class sleeping compartment, with the Newman Sinclair on the luggage rack, and got paid double-time after midnight while fast asleep.

One evening in the Kyle of Lochalsh, our assistant director was called to the telephone just as he was about to have his dinner and did not return until the rest of us were on to our coffee, having been kept on the line for over an hour by Keegan in London arguing over a petty-cash form for 1s-6p. Always quietly and neatly dressed, he was unfailingly pleasant towards me (perhaps he saw something amusing) and there was certainly that about Keegan which prevented my looking too far down my young nose at him, though I could never make out what it was. Then one day I was in his room collecting some taxi-fares (real or imagined); there was a wall calendar with a picture of that apotheosis of mountains, the Matterhorn, and I facetiously expressed a hope that there was enough room to stand up on the sharp point at the top after all that climbing. He turned and glanced out of the window,

" About from here to the corner. "

" How d'you know that? "

" I climbed it. "

I recalled being hauled like a sack of potatoes up the side of Sron na Ciche in the Cuillins for a film called SCOTLAND FOR SPORT and saw our unit accountant with fresh eyes.

The next accountant in my life was rather different. When the time came to leave Transport and become a free-lance I went to see Rosser-James (you could never refer to him as Mr Rosser-James, for he was far above that). He was with a long established and respectable firm of accountants called B.Davis and Co, who occupied imposing premises on Sloane Street and specialised in the world of entertainment. Rosser was quite the most urbane person I've ever met and in a way he set the seal on my new life after the somewhat dowdy world of superannuated clerks from which I had just escaped. When we had exchanged formalities he launched straightway into an explanation,

" I have an excellent understanding with the Revenue and there are two courses open to you. You can record exactly what you spend and keep hold of every bus ticket, that way you will incur slightly less tax (though you will be paying us more for the extra work involved) or I will put in a reasonable amount for allowances in which case you will pay a bit more to the Revenue but you won't have to bother keeping expenditure accounts. "

Paper that isn't used to enshrine human visions and ideas (even when expressed in the worst of sonnets) is of greater benefit to mankind left as a tree, so I chose the second alternative. Indeed, in the very opening chapter of his autobiography, James Callaghan, one of our ex Prime Ministers, who started off as a tax inspector at Portsmouth in the 1930s, tells us that it was instilled into them as a matter of pride that the same care must be taken to see that nobody paid any more than their due, as was devoted to ensuring that they did not pay any less. If that were true today there would be a legion of unemployed accountants, which is not the state of affairs by any means. Now it may be that Mr Callaghan, who is after all a politician, is not telling us the truth; but I don't think that is the case. For a good many years I was left quietly alone to build a reasonably successful career for myself and pay considerable sums to the revenue, which I certainly never begrudged them. Rosser alas, retired from the scene and his place was taken, though never filled, by another. Then all at once everything changed and I was asked to supply not only bus tickets but a lot more besides.

" Don't they realise that if we do all this they will end up with less money?"

" They don't care. "

Keegan would have understood.

Authority having woken up to the fact that people had been using initiative and common sense in a branch of the civil service, set about putting things to rights and a collaborative attitude was replaced by an adversarial one.

A bizarre scenario in my tax-paying life took place after finishing ENDLESS LOVE in New York. There is a double taxation agreement between us and the United States so that if you are working there and they withold 30%, that amount is offset against UK tax. "Make sure you get a certificate from them", said Pam (my lady accountant), and I duly returned home clutching the document and sent it off to her. At about this time the British and American tax authorities were engaged in some kind of lover's tiff, and a demand arrived from our people for their customary 70%. Even my mathematics could add 30 and 70 together and deduce that I had just done four months' work for nothing. After eight years of futile effort on Pam's part I gave up. It was so ludicrous the best thing to do was laugh at it; the worst, to let it interfere with enjoying my life. So long as one is earning it, money can be kept in its place; when one is not is another matter.

It is also inadvisable to consider what happens to the money once they've got hold of it. Charities may allow a degree of choice in which areas contributions are to be spent but no Establishment would countenance the Arts, or even a hospital, nosing ahead of their cherished plutonium factory at Seascale, where dwellers in the adjoining Lake District live in hopes that Wordsworth's clouds will manage to float on high o'er vales and hills without dropping strontium 90 on any surviving daffodils. In that event the names of their villages would be changed overnight, confusing the children and wasting all the headed notepaper.

At one time our mine-sweepers in the Persian Gulf must have outnumbered the fish, and the hair-dresser on a commercial I was doing remarked that, as he had paid for at least one of them, he ought to be allowed to have it painted pink and manned only by nice-looking sailors. This seemed very reasonable, and would certainly make the Navy more interesting. I thought I might have apple green for mine and piano lessons for the crew, pretty or otherwise.

Neither Simon nor anyone else questioned that it was right and proper for us to sweep away mines - as one of the world's leading arms suppliers, we had probably sold them in the first place.

Helen Mirren   *Photo: Terry O'Neill*

"Why is there only one word for Thesaurus?"

Actors

Jessica Tandy was once asked by a young actor who had just got an Oscar,
" Now I'm a star, people come up to me in the street and I don't know what to say to them; how should I deal with it? "
" If you were really a star, dear, you wouldn't be able to go in the street. "

36

There hasn't been much about stars up to now because this isn't that kind of book; also I haven't met very many. Most turn out to be actors, far more interesting people; for actors are about the only reason that any of us is there at all. What is often regarded as a sort of dabbling in makebelieve is actually a formidable task that makes relentless demands on those who do it, for delicacy at one moment, strength at another, and always for inexhaustible energy, concentration and sensitivity. I was made to realise this by Tony Richardson during my first film with him. He had one actor who was sadly inadequate and Tony's patience had been extraordinary. When we were alone together I made some slighting remark, I don't remember exactly what it was, and he said,

" Yes, but you must remember that it is they who have to carry the whole thing in the end; especially in the theatre where there is nothing between them and the audience. They may get the adulation when things go right but they have the most terrible time when it goes wrong, usually through no fault of theirs."

I knew while he was speaking I would always remember it. I also knew that I had heard him pass entirely devastating remarks himself on occasion and, unable to resist the chance to make a point, said so; however it was never easy to score off Tony,

" But I say it with love. "

He always was splendid with them. At the end of THE HOTEL NEW HAMPSHIRE Rob Lowe encounters Matthew Modine (Chipper Dove) on Fifth Avenue.

" We should have a great fight and I could throw him across the street."

" This isn't a Charles Bronson movie Mr Lowe. "

" But the audience would love it. "

" Well they're not going to get it. "

Alfred Hitchcock is supposed to have said that ".. actors ought to be treated like cattle", but if that is so then what Paul Wilson told me about his patience and kindness to a young and nervous actress during the shooting of FRENZY is curious (perhaps he'd only met considerate dairy farmers).

" Don't worry about any mistakes my dear, that's why we use film - so that if any of us gets it wrong we can simply do it again. "

Ritchie Guinness, my key-grip from New York, said there was a thing that he had seen only twice in his career, both times on a picture with me. I wondered what on earth was coming, but it was simply the director sitting by the camera watching his actors - anticipation, smiles, tears, heart in mouth, completely involved with them (this sort of director doesn't need a video playback to know what to print). That it was all quite normal to me shows just how lucky I've been; for someone who has done as many pictures as Ritchie to find it unusual is sad indeed. The directors were Norman Jewison and Sidney Lumet.

For years Hammer Films specialised in the production of an endless succession of horror movies, of which the only one I did for them, TO THE DEVIL A DAUGHTER, proved to be their last (for which I take neither praise nor blame). The principal source of amusement on it was Richard Widmark, quickly known to the unit as Bismark. I rather liked him myself - he was an actor without pretensions who knew the business, did not suffer fools, and was completely dependable. There was a scene where he has to turn a large wheel controlling a sluice, and when we moved closer on this the continuity girl told him he was doing it the opposite way from the master shot.

" No I'm not. "

She was young, but she didn't give up; so he insisted on betting £100 (a small fortune for her) that the next day's rushes would prove him right. This they failed to do and he quietly handed her a bundle of notes, which she gracefully declined saying it really didn't matter.

" Take it my dear, I'd have had it off you if I'd been right. "

Another feisty old actor turned up on Beeban Kidron's USED PEOPLE; a great star of the thirties, this was Mr Shotter with a vengeance. Sylvia Sidney, just past her eightieth birthday, was the best fun, getting away to a splendid start by refusing to wear a hat at a Jewish wedding.

" If you ain't nice to me I'll *die* before you can finish my scenes. "

Jessica Tandy confided to me that she didn't like *her* hat but was not making a drama of it, by which time Beeban had decided to risk death and of course ole Sylvia wore the hat.

Sitting in hair and make-up one morning, she was accosted by the usual television crew preparing to do interviews with the cast.

" Miss Sidney, what is your preferential lighting? "

" What?!! "

" Well Miss Sidney, all the big stars have ways in which they prefer to be lit. "

" Bullshit! "

She then went on to indicate a couple of younger colleagues to whom she considered "preferential lighting" would be of no avail. All very refreshing, but I wondered if she had been quite as carefree about her lighting in the 1930s.

Sidney Lumet told me he once played a scene with her when he was a child actor. When it came to his close-up she'd disappeared but, good for him, he had her brought back to give her off-lines. She returned, carrying a ball of wool attached to an unfinished garment, and sat dutifully beside the camera. I am told the click of knitting needles may still be heard behind his dialogue.

To a point, it is only sensible that actors be concerned how they look (they have a livelihood to protect after all), and beyond that point anxiety usually stems from insecurity rather than vanity. Directing his first picture when little more than a youth, Norman Jewison got himself landed with a leading lady whom he thought unduly sensitive in this regard. He chose a confidential "between us" approach,

" You know Dear, you don't really need a make-up person, you could do it yourself if you had a mind to - same with hair. You could also design your own wardrobe - you don't need any of these people. And as for lighting .... "

" What are you saying? "

" I'm saying dear, that we have the best cameramen, the best make-up artists, hairdressers, and costume designers, in order that you can get in your limo at the end of the day and never think about any of it. "

If vanity ever arises it has usually more to do with status than appearance. One actress decided to adjust what she perceived as an unwarranted discrepancy between her fee and that of her leading man by demanding gold embroidered silk undergarments (which the audience would never set eyes on). This was going to put the wardrobe somewhat over their budget and I happened to be standing by when the producer was apprised of this.

" Keep the lady happy. "

It was fine by me, that is until some months later I was invited back to grade the print (which an audience certainly *would* see) gratis. I had to explain that this proposal was unattractive; it was not simply a question of working for nothing - by turning away other work I'd actually be paying for the privilege and my disinclination to this was greater than my compassion for the studio and the producer, especially when they could so easily recover their outlay by auctioning off a some second hand knickers.

Size of camper has been known to cause as much dissension as size of fee and Leo di Caprio at 16 years old already had the wit to make fun of it,

" Why is my camper smaller than Ellen's? I'm the title role - it *is* called THIS *BOY'S* LIFE y'know not this mother's. "

If someone likes what you do it is nice if they tell you so; communication should be reciprocal, but unfortunately the case with all good things is that sometimes there is too much of them. Barbra's delight the day in Zatech when her autograph was passed up in favour of mine may have been sharpened by an event that had taken place a few weeks before. When YENTL was still in the planning stage it had not been decided whether to shoot the location scenes in Prague or Budapest, so she had set out on a reconnaissance trip to both capitals. As a single flight on Czechoslovakia's OK Airline (the name was really not appropriate) had done nothing to dispel her strong dislike of flying, she insisted against all advice on travelling between Budapest and Prague by road. When she and Rusty Lemorand reached the frontier their passports were taken from them and they were left, without a word, to sit in the car for an hour and a half. It took a lot less time than that for Rusty to get upbraided because they should have gone by air (which of course he had advised in the first place). No one spoke a word of English, so it was impossible to find out what was going on, and it is perhaps difficult to imagine, now that the iron curtain is not there any more, how alarming their situation must have been. Finally, after things had become very tense indeed, their passports were handed back and they journeyed on to Prague, where an interpreter was able to talk to their driver. What had happened was that one of the frontier guards had been on the phone to his wife. "Who d'you think *I've* got sitting outside?" He was thereupon told to keep everything as it was while the good lady fetched out her bicycle and pedalled over from a nearby village to see for herself. Barbra shrugged shoulders,

" That's what you get for being a star. "

It wasn't all you get.

As a result of Larry de Waay, her producer, telling me over lunch that his house in Hertfordshire had been the home of William Penn and that in fact the founder of Pennsylvania had married his second wife in Larry's living-room, I said it would be nice if he had an autograph letter and set out to find him one by putting word around the book trade. Somehow Barbra got wind of this and her secretary asked me, if one came up, to let her know without saying anything to Larry, because Barbra wanted to give him a present at the end of the film. A bookseller friend of mine phoned from New York a few days later to say he knew of a colleague with a good ALS, and that it was twenty five hundred bucks.

" Add something for yourself then. "

"Why is there only one word for Thesaurus?"

" No, it isn't mine and you're a friend. "

" Jim, I think the person who's buying this can afford you a modest profit."

" Who is it? "

" Barbra Str--- "

" Thirty five hundred bucks. "

A recce to Liverpool one Sunday, for the final song on board the ship, was almost as hazardous for Barbra as the Czech/Hungarian border. For some reason we picked up the Liverpool train at Watford and were duly assembled on the down platform when Barbra, employing an American euphemism, wanted to go to the bathroom (I have not myself been inside the ladies' convenience on Watford Junction but I doubt if it was the sort of thing she was used to). American trains may present streamlined exteriors that suggest they would not wish to be seen doing less than 150 mph but they have to content themselves and their passengers with ambling along at about thirty, due to the shocking state of the permanent-way. Here at home "125" means just what it says and there are conspicuous yellow lines three feet from the platform edges on all through stations, inside which it is injudicious to stand on account of getting sucked in by trains not scheduled to stop. I just managed to grab her back in time to prevent this happening as an express with its heart set on Crewe zipped past us.

" Different from Amtrack isn't it? "

Finally arrived at the Prince's Pier, Barbra was timing her number, hurtling along decks and down companion-ways with an assistant carrying the tape-player struggling to keep up. Below on the quayside a group of adolescent Beatles gazed up at her,

" Hey Ba, give us a wave. "

Choreographing musical numbers for the camera requires a degree of concentration that did not allow for this.

" *Wave* yer big-nosed kike. "

She was splendidly unperturbed.

" Liddle mother-fuckers! "

When a friend visiting the set of HAMLET remarked on the pleasant atmosphere and how nice everybody was, I was surprised for a moment; one gets so used to it. It is usually safe to say that people are disagreeable in inverse ratio to the amount of talent they have. I've led a charmed life and, though I couldn't go quite as far as Will Rogers, most actors that I have worked with have been unselfish and helpful not only to their fellow actors but to everybody on the set.

In the THREE (or FOUR) MUSKETEERS there was a scene between Charlton Heston and Michael York with the camera set up on a wide lens at one end of a long refectory table with the actors in the foreground facing each other across it. They began to walk away from the camera with Chuck talking across the table to Michael until they reached the far end. After the first rehearsal, Simon Kaye, the sound mixer, removed his headphones and looked so awestruck that I asked what had happened. When Chuck had reached the point on our lens where he knew the microphone could no longer follow without coming into picture he had gradually raised his voice so that Simon had not needed to make any adjustment to the recording level. No one had asked him to, he had simply, as Katherine Hepburn would have said, "thought about it". The poor man did fail rather miserably with Ann Skinner, however. When a few of us were remarking what a nice person he was, she surprised us all by dissenting strongly. I asked why,

" He goes out of his way to be liked. "

" What's wrong with that?"

" Well nobody could say that *you* go out of your way to be liked, but I prefer you to Chuck Heston."

Another actor in the MUSKETEERS was Faye Dunaway, who took the part of a beautiful but extremely malevolent and dangerous character called Milady. When I came to her first close-up it struck me that if it could be managed somehow to have no highlights whatever in the eyes it might imply, on a subconscious level, the presence of evil without detracting from her looks. Eyes, being shiny convex things, always reflect any light source that hits them, and so it was not at all easy. I remember thinking it would all go for nothing anyway, although Richard Lester liked the idea. Over twenty years afterwards someone showed me a passage in her autobiography where Fay was kind enough to say that I was a very good cameraman - except that I seemed unable to get highlights into people's eyes. So at least it didn't go quite for nothing.

A Mr Stanislavsky is credited with having introduced what is called method acting. I am unqualified to say any more than that it does appear that his precepts are open to misinterpretation by some of his followers. There was one who hurtled around like a scalded rat to such an extent that he finished up performing for all he was worth not only off the set but behind the camera. We had to stop and explain. Another was asked by the camera operator to change his position slightly,

" No, no, I *feel* it will be better here. "

" Perhaps you're right - you're just outside the edge of frame. "

It is at such times that I think with affection of old Esmond Knight. As a young RNVR officer on the battleship *Prince of Wales* he had been blinded by a shell from either the *Bismark* or the *Prinz Eugen*. One of the last things he must have seen would have been the destruction of *HMS Hood* minutes before in the same engagement, a sad final image for a quiet sensitive man whose great love was watching birds. I was lucky enough to work with him twice. He came to the set knowing his lines; one careful walk with his wife through all the positions, and the only difference between him and the rest of the cast would be that he never went wrong.

"Why is there only one word for Thesaurus?"

It is said that when Laurence Olivier was asked by someone, who expended a great deal of effort working himself into the required state for a scene, how he managed the same intensity merely by laying down *The Times* crossword and getting up from his chair, Larry replied, "I pretend". Well pretend he certainly could. The same afternoon he arrived in Tunisia for JESUS OF NAZARETH we had to shoot a clip of him saying "thank you" for some award or other being presented in absentia; it would then be screened during the ceremony. This was several days before we were to start shooting on him for the movie, so it struck me as odd that he should do it all got up as Nicodemus, but then I didn't know Larry. Still more odd, when we turned over the camera for him to say his piece, the affable business-like individual Franco had just introduced disappeared suddenly into a soapy character ladling out emotional effusions in the worst of taste. Thankfully the instant we cut, the original sharp minded person reappeared like a conjuring trick.

And sharp he certainly was. On one of his pictures, at a time when his illness was more burdensome than usual, he had to work an extended day, due to the inadequacies of a fellow member of the cast. By the end of it he was quite exhausted, and the director's personal assistant, a very sweet lady, was taking him back to the hotel. On the way he was so bad they had to stop while he vomited at the roadside. Finally he dragged himself back into the car.

"Oh Larry, I'm so sorry."

"Think nothing of it my dear, it would happen to anyone who'd played a scene with --------"

Tony Richardson used to say that the trouble with Larry was that he was too good a faker but, to quote Sidney Lumet, there is nothing about acting to suggest that it can withstand endless repetition night after night in the theatre - or take after take on a film set (with some directors). Faking gets over the barren moments; if Larry was the best faker Ralph Richardson was certainly the worst, which is why he was the most moving actor of them all - but on the rare occasions when inspiration deserted Ralph there was nothing.

The set for the Sanhedrin in JESUS OF NAZARETH had wide and lofty windows filled with carved alabaster, like three fretwork screens. For the day scenes this meant that with an open arc outside each of them a lace-like pattern of light was projected over the entire set. Larry was playing the scene in constant movement, all over the place, and I noticed in the first rehearsal that wherever he had a line or a reaction his eyes were always lit. Somewhat relieved I went over to him,

" I don't have to worry about you then? "

He looked up and smiled, a tiny patch of light once more exactly in both eyes.

" I think I know how to find the glory. "

I now understood why he'd made his "thank you" speech in his costume.

While on the subject of actors, an interesting digression may be made into the conduct of the mothers of some of the younger ones. One noteworthy solved the problem of chaperoning her daughter by diverting all the available young men into bed with herself; even to the point of driving away from the studio with a youth who already had an assignation with the film's director. When the poor man entered his house to spend the evening on his own he was handed a message which read,

" Ladies first - better luck next time. "

So far as screen mothers go however, she by no means heads the list; that pre-eminence resting securely with the mother of Vivien Leigh. Tony Richardson finding himself seated next to this partial matron at a screening of GONE WITH THE WIND felt obliged to say when the lights went up that she must be very proud of the film. Well yes, but it had serious shortcomings. Tony asked what they were.

" All those shots of other people! "

Of course some screen mothers were less doting. That great lady, Eve Arnold, had photographed Joan Crawford on a number of occasions and when we were together on WHITE NIGHTS I questioned her,

" Was it really like the daughter said - you know, all that stuff in *Momma Dearest*? "

" No not at all - it was *WORSE*. "

Far from Hollywood, in London's West End, one old actor's way of calming any nervousness felt by a young actress, in a play where they both made their first entrance on stage together, was that each evening as they stood in the wings he would ask her "Anything today?" and she would recount some triviality that had happened, like getting out of bed and stepping on the cat. In turn she would ask him "Anything today?" to which he might reply that his motor-bike had been difficult to start (it was Ralph Richardson). Then one evening when she enquired

" Anything today? "

there was a pause,

" I went to my brother's funeral. "

" Oh I am sorry. "

" Yes, he burned to death. "

" How dreadful, you must be ... "

" Well it won't happen again. "

and she had the wings to herself; he was on stage.

Another routine enquiry before going on had been

" Anyone out front? "

" Aunt Maud is up, from Carshalton Beeches. "

She in turn would ask if he had anyone and became more and more surprised at the number of times Mr Gordon had been in the audience; he must be an obsessive theatre-goer. Just before curtain on the last night a bottle of gin was delivered to her dressing room, "with the compliments of Mr Gordon".

Peter Hall once sent Ralph a play that he wanted him to do and after a day or so hearing nothing, paid him a visit. Ralph handed out a large tumbler full of whisky and launched into a discussion of a number of topics unrelated to the theatre. After some considerable time he suggested taking Bessie for a spin, stuck the director of the RSC on the back of his motor-bike, like one of my nannies, and zoomed up the M1 with him. When they got back Ralph took off his helmet and goggles,

" Great ride; *terrible* play. "

The first time I met him was on Chobham Common at the start of THE BED-SITTING-ROOM. When Oscar Lewenstein took me over to him Ralph went to shake hands - then, realising that this would be awkward for me, and also for it, returned the white mouse he was holding to his overcoat pocket and all was well. Richard Lester told me that his first meeting was in Ralph's flat in Regents Park. He had looked up when Richard was ushered into the room.

" I feel that we are all God's bees; do you? "

Richard did not say exactly how he had dealt with that (at least he'd escaped the M1) but I was glad to think that most of God's humans had more fun out of sex than his parthenogenic bees did. Perhaps Ralph made it a habit to introduce the animal kingdom into his first meetings with people; there was not much vagueness about when you got to know him. Six years after THE BED-SITTING-ROOM Franco brought him across to introduce me on the set of JESUS OF NAZARETH,

" No, no, we're old friends. "

"No, no, we're old friends".

I loved him for that.

There wasn't anything vague about John Gielgud either; the faux pas for which he became noted were always quite deliberate so far as my experience of them goes. During one of the Superman films, because a shot had to be done immediately after the break, Richard Lester, to save time, asked Christopher Reeve if he would mind keeping his costume and make-up on over the lunch hour. Walking into the restaurant with his vivid companion, Richard noticed Sir John sitting at one of the tables and took the young actor over to him.

" John, I'd like to introduce Christopher Reeve. "

" Delighted to meet you, dear boy. Now, tell me what you're up to here."

Dear John. Someone who had trained as an actor and later diverged into the career of schoolteacher was intending to portray Lear in one of his end of term productions (ambitious, you may think, but I am told it was done very well). As he knew John G. slightly he decided to write and ask for any insights he could offer into the role. John replied very kindly though the advice was brief - make sure you have a light Cordelia. That was John all right, bless him.

The lovely thing about the play of minds is the picture we get of the owners; you didn't need to meet Noel Coward to guess what he was like. After a performance of ENTERTAINING Mr SLOAN at the Royal Court he went into Beryl Reid's dressing-room with a bottle of Scotch which, in the course of three hours chatting together, they managed to dispose of. By this time the theatre was locked-up and everyone had gone, apart from the fireman who remains on duty throughout the night. Picking her steps with care to the stage-door she called out,

" Good night, Fireman. "

" Oh Beryl you're so wonderful - you know everybody's name. "

It was during a rehearsal at the same theatre that someone came into the auditorium and announced the suicide of a person known to the cast as of somewhat restricted intelligence,

" So and so's just blown his brains out. "

" He must have been a very good shot. "

Among the many songs written by Coward there was one that exhorted a Mrs Worthington not to put her daughter on the stage. It has been called an overcrowded profession. Admittedly it is crowded, but with people who love what they do. A friend once put it that he would rather be unsuccessful at what he cared about than successful at what he didn't. I think that actually turns him into a kind of success. Certainly the drama schools will never be short of applicants. I had lunch with Tony Richardson and his second daughter Joely shortly after she had been accepted by two drama schools at the same time, RADA and Central. She asked his advice as to which she should choose.

" Neither will make any difference. No one can teach you how to act - well, they can show you a few tricks - but either you have a talent and will work it out yourself, or you haven't a talent, in which case nobody can do anything."

After the actors, a word or two about those important ancillaries, their

"Why is there only one word for Thesaurus?"

stand-ins, important to me at any rate. Their job is to help the crew by going through all the moves and positions during the lining-up (preparation for shooting) because it is not a good idea to have the cast hanging around for the purpose - they might lose their edge. I have not read any books about the cinema, and indeed have done my best not to write one, so I don't know if they've been written about already; but I rather doubt it.

The first misconception about these people is that it is necessary for them to resemble the actor they are standing-in for. Quite early in my career, on THE BED-SITTING ROOM, due to a temporary indisposition, I was given Arthur Lowe's stand-in for Rita Tushingham; but apart from my surprise when the actors finally took their places, nobody was any the worse. It is much more important that what they are *wearing* should bear some relation to what is going to turn up later on; lighting a person in black denim who is then replaced by someone swathed in white satin wastes time. Height is important for the camera operator, not so much for me; as to the actual features of people, however close the resemblance, they will always be different. One memorises one's actors lineaments as far as possible but if there is a problem it can only be solved by working with the person himself.

What *are* important are brains and interest; the first guarantees the second because the job is in fact quite absorbing. When I started in features there was a professional stand-in, a man in his sixties named Jack Dearlove. I can remember walking across a set and glancing up at the gantry on the way, something that any good gaffer electrician would interpret without my saying a word, but it was Jack who said,

" It's all right, I'm never going to be there in this scene. "

The good watch every rehearsal and know the mechanics of the scene far better than I do; the bad don't even know why they are there, and might as well not be. One Anglo-Saxon lead in a movie was given a stand-in of remarkable outward likeness, but very limited understanding. There happened to be a dance routine in the script, and when the day came to shoot it I was approached by an apologetic first assistant,

" We need to have someone who knows the dance, but he doesn't look at all like our man. "

I'd already noticed a nimble Afro-American gentleman moving around the set like the title of a Firbank novel.

" Is he intelligent? "

" Yes. "

" Can we please keep him for the rest of the picture? "

Michael Sundin

"Why is there only one word for Thesaurus?"

And the Band Played On

Michael Sundin, Ian Charleson, Brad Davis, Derek Jarman, Tony Richardson, Denholm Elliot, Ron Vawter

37

... not just a group of gifted men whom I knew professionally; I am haunted by them and by many brave and sunny people in other walks of life linked together by an illness that, avoiding the sanctimonious, singles out the kinder and life-embracing among humanity. It is scything down many of the most promising talents in the liberal arts and we are all impoverished by their loss.

A person's sexuality is of supreme unimportance to anyone but themselves (and those hoping to get off with them); even so, before any conclusions are jumped at, it should be said that not every one mentioned above had the same inclinations. However its original focus on the gay community, the strange suddenness with which it appeared and the convenient timing of that appearance suggest, to a mind that has finally lost its innocence, origins that owe more to Auden's good family men -

" and so, in secret regions,
good family men
keep eye, devoted as monks,
on apparatus
inside which harmless matter
turns homicidal."

than it does to a capricious nature saying "let's have a new disease for a change"; the moment was too apt. With the long overdue liberation (sexual and otherwise) of the 1960s there was a fair amount of excessive behaviour on a scale not seen in England since the Restoration. This natural reaction after a prolonged period of puritanical repressiveness, was over and out the way in something like record time, and by the mid 1970s all ordinary sensible people had settled into a happy tolerance of each other. Then, to rescue the old ways, there comes a strange and wonderful sickness confining itself to decimating homosexuals and drug users and bringing along with it a narrowness of fear and selfishness that put the clock back twenty years.

While the Vatican was busy helping to spread the epidemic by banning every sensible attempt to educate people, as well as any practical means of controlling it (apart from fatuous advice not to have sex), there was a Jeremiad from the righteous in every quarter pointing to the wrath of the Almighty. The Chief of Police of one of our great cities coined the memorable aphorism "they are drowning in a cesspool of their own creating". This casting back to the mediaeval witch-hunt proved no obstacle to a subsequent knighthood for the gentleman (a fair example of the sort of company you will get into by accepting these trinkets).

Suggestions that any human agency might lie at the back of it all were dismissed with that swiftness which only increases suspicion. It took forty years to admit that myxomatosis was manufactured in a laboratory and human beings will have to wait a lot longer than rabbits before they are allowed the truth. It could be that nuclear radiation triggered some viral mutation to add to the other benefits provided for us by that branch of science, or the virus may have originated in a bacteriological-warfare laboratory. In the latter case it might have escaped by accident; but it might equally have been seen by some as a weapon for moral rearmament - certainly secret and intelligence services such as the CIA and FBI have enough prejudice and skewed morals between them not to rule it out. Nobody would question their secrecy but intelligent, definitely not, and the likelihood of bi-sexual individuals in society diverting it outside the target area would be unlikely to occur to them.

In 1994 the Clinton administration disclosed that during Eisenhower's presidency American scientists had fed plutonium in milk to mentally retarded children, and apart from the obvious mistake in placing the adjectives (mentally retarded surely applies to the scientists), the facts remain clear enough. Such people would be unlikely to demur at feeding a virus to their sexually unco-operative fellow beings. It is now known that parts of Africa where the epidemic is supposed to have first appeared were used by the Americans for experiments they preferred not to conduct closer to home, and scientists are seldom endowed with the common sense to worry about losing control of what they create. Mary Shelley hit *that* nail on the head ages ago.

Realising that by now I will seem like an hysteric to many readers, I gave this chapter to some honest people in the medical profession, doctors and bio-chemists (I have a wide diversity of friends), who assured me that it was a view held by quite a number of them, though they keep it to themselves, being rightly more concerned with finding a cure than a culprit. Of course this is speculative, among other theories equally so, but it derives from some understanding of history and of a society that has not changed since I've been in it. You can never be definite about the fuck-up to conspiracy ratio, although the latter will always be ahead if only because a calamitous or expensive fuck-up is immediately followed by a conspiracy in order to hide it. The third possibility - of something beyond any human agency - is the least likely.

From having been the unwitting first couriers of the disease to the rest of the world, the Americans have ever since refused entry (even for a holiday or a visit to a lost aunt) to anyone unlucky enough to have caught it from them, which must take the shutting the stable door after bolted horse exercise to the power of a hundred.

In the Lawrence A. Wein Center rehearsal rooms in New York there is a board across one wall carrying seventy carefully arranged white cards each with the name, some well known - others not, of people who once used these rooms and have since died from AIDS. It calls to mind those war memorials in every town and village of England listing the victims of a different antagonist who, without bigotry and greed to begin with, might equally never have been there.

In the mid 1980s I was in a mini-bus carrying an American crew with whom I was to direct some commercials. It was early morning and we had not yet met each other so I sat quietly at the back, while they talked about a case of two children who had contracted HIV from blood transfusions. When their misfortune became known they were turned away from school - the parents took the matter before a federal court and the school was ordered to allow the kids back in, whereupon their house was promptly burned down. The discussion in the mini-bus was concerned with the confrontation on TV the evening before, between the parents and the leader of the Catholic Women's Guild. The latter had apparently declared that arson in this instance, although regrettable, was quite understandable, and went on to advocate tattooing the letters HIV on the faces of everyone diagnosed positive. One of the crew remarked that it did not strike him as a very Christian way to behave, and I thought it was time for them to meet their new director.

" On the contrary it's exactly the way Christians have been behaving for nearly two thousand years. "

It is very strange how the word Christian is still used to imply some kind of superior decency. In my lifetime the two best efforts to exterminate an entire section of their fellow humans was carried out by Christian Germans and Christian Serbs, while three centuries before that, the Christian Spaniards did a thorough job on the Aztecs. I'm not suggesting that Jews, Muslims, and others do not behave badly; nor would I pretend there is no competition from places like Cambodia - but they will have to work hard to catch up. The all comers record for genocide will still be held by Christian society for the lifetime of the youngest person to read this. As Graham Greene postulates at wearisome length - it doesn't matter how badly you behave provided you're a good Catholic. Christian is perhaps the best example of them all, of a word that means the exact opposite of what it is supposed to.

"Why is there only one word for Thesaurus?"

BBC

Until recently the BBC and I had managed to stay at an arm's length from each other.

38

It was always a love/hate relationship on my part; where their music programmes and orchestra (prior to the silly removal of Boult) could never be valued highly enough, what they did to my other great love, the English language, could only be deplored. The trouble is that when you have power enough to be a good influence you also have sufficient to be a bad one. They steadily ironed out local dialects as though they were creases in a table cloth (to speak BBC English when I was a boy was a synonym for talking posh). When our speech had been well and truly gelded, they allowed in one or two voices that combined condescension with insipid regional accents, but by then the flavour of the language had disappeared along with a lot of other flavours (try some organically grown vegetables and you'll know what I mean).

Ken Russell told me that when he was making his Monitor films there was an assertive virago head of programmes called Grace Wyndham Goldie, who decreed that no word shall be included that is not readily understood by 90 per-cent of the population (a great way to expand our vocabularies). She may be gone by now but the same bovine patronage is still doled out, alongside arrogant tamperings with pronunciation. To make quite sure that the great 90 per-cent know what we're talking about the accent on the first syllable of "comparable" has been moved to the second (same as compare - get it?). It is ugly to listen to, and extended to other forms of the poor word becomes an incomparable embarrassment. Closer to home is their irritating short o in homosexual (nobody ever talks about hommo sapiens) but the explanation here is different, mispronunciation being a way of expressing dislike without laying themselves open to a charge of prejudice.

The widely accepted notion that it is ill mannered to use unfamiliar words in general conversation and even worse to correct others who use them inaccurately, is ridiculous. It is how we all learn to talk in the first place and humanity would have ended up mute long ago were it not for people bad mannered enough to pass on the ability to talk - given there will be certain individuals of whom we might wish their parents had been more polite. I may hesitate to correct a total stranger, but anyone who can put me straight (philologically at any rate) is more than welcome to. The real bad manners consist in imagining we have reached a stage where there is no more to learn. After a couple of pictures together my electricians have better vocabularies than most producers and certainly use them more amusingly.

With the arrival of television in the 1950s it was impossible for the BBC to crew from among the existing body of technicians, there simply were not enough of them and in any case in those days they were all working. So television set about creating a new hybrid with the emphasis on electronic engineering, admirable in many ways but hardly a formula for visual excellence; added to which there was no tradition behind them, and the stimulus to create one would be quickly stifled by any expedient-loving administration. In those days nobody was going to see it on anything larger than the cover of Country Life in any case. So we went down separate paths, with one or two of the more enterprising TV cameramen crossing over to films, where, after getting used to things for a bit, some of them have thrived happily enough.

One day in 1990 I had a phone-call from a director and good friend who had written and was directing a story for the BBC, there would be no argument about money within reason and would I do it? What had happened was that the BBC had got into collusion with a Hollywood independent producer and were putting in 20 per-cent of the budget. In real terms this wasn't costing them anything since it comprised the provision of a crew and the studios at Ealing - both of which they had on their hands in any case. Thus I came finally into contact with the other side, where strangely enough it was the oldest member of the crew who was the most open minded, and indeed was the only one I would be happy to have with me on any other film. He was my chief electrician, a very good and experienced gaffer who in all his years had never worked outside television. His name was Ted Turpin.

I had not thought that I would ever find myself working in Ealing, that great studio started by Will Barker in 1902 and carried on for so long by Michael Balcon; where in 1948 I had seen Will Barker in person, then eighty-one years old, and attended a lecture by Max Greene (of which I did not understand a word). Here were the stages where they had shot SCOTT OF THE ANTARCTIC, preserved, in spite of years under BBC ownership, like Pompeii beneath the ashes of Vesuvius.

Our principal set was a large one and I knew when I walked onto it for the first time with Ted that the lamps I should want for the backing had for many years been "non grata" with the authorities. They are called sky-pans and the name derives from their sole employment in lighting backings - quite useless for any other purpose, they are simple affairs consisting of a white enamel saucer about three feet in diameter with an open 5Kw bulb where you'd put the cup. It was the open bulb that upset the BBC hegemony, regardless of the fact that nobody is ever going to be anywhere near it when it is burning.

" Fourteen sky-pans on the backing, Ted. "

There was an agonised silence and then the poor man tried to explain that such lamps were regarded as wicked and evil by his masters and that itinerant sky-pans seeking admission were always turned away at the studio gates. With genuine unconcern I carried on giving him all my other requirements, cutting short every attempt on his part to get back to sky-pans. Finally, at about five o'clock in the afternoon, he asked me if I would speak to the safety officer of the BBC who was on the telephone.

" Mr Watkin, do you realise that if someone stood in front of one of your lamps they could be badly injured by flying glass? "

I did my best to visualise the important official at the other end of the line

" I certainly do, but before that something *far* worse would happen. "

" What?!! "

" There'd be a shadow on the backing. "

The next day Ted was like a child on Christmas morning and fourteen sky-pans were lighting the backing. In addition the set itself had a fair number of lights rigged including some arcs, and to supply it all the original power-house that had stood unused for years was brought back to life. Its beautiful marine diesels, out of an old destroyer, were going to be taken away in a few weeks time and though I don't pride myself on very much it will always mean something to me that I was the last person ever to use them. When at the end of shooting Ted took me inside to look at them, gleaming and silent at the end of their life, I knew he was expressing his thanks for the fresh air I had managed to let into his work. It was a splendid repayment.

"Why is there only one word for Thesaurus?"

Coda

39

My first experience of this was seeing the delight of two kids in front of me at a running of THE THREE MUSKETEERS, and as their enjoyment was not confined to the second unit material, it became clear they were not, as I'd first assumed, nephews of Don McPherson. Sometimes there is more even than a good laugh to be had. A student at the university in Belfast was helping to run publicity for an arts festival in which the MARAT SADE was to be shown. The tickets did not sell so he came up with the idea that some students as asylum maniacs (not difficult to arrange) should parade around town and campus in costume with placards bearing the full name of the film on one side and show times on the other. As the full title reads THE PERSECUTION AND ASSASSINATION OF JEAN-PAUL MARAT AS PERFORMED BY THE INMATES OF CHARENTON UNDER THE DIRECTION OF THE MARQUIS DE SADE, there was a fair amount of work to be done and since it was his idea he was volunteered to do it. Seeing a possible diversion to the task, he took the opportunity to enlist the help of a rather nice girl he'd had his eyes on for some time ...

" ... several days (and nights) later I emerged with twenty or so hand-drawn placards, heavy bags under the eyes, and a new girl-friend. We also managed to sell all the tickets. "

So you never know what you're helping to bring about.

I started my career in features by getting fired (off poor Joan's SPARRERS) and since then have repeated the process to arrive at a present total of five, each time with the same circumstance attached - the picture had not yet started. With the last recurrence however there was a difference, I had been given a contract and would have to be paid. My replacement (an American) charged almost twice what I was getting and as his first act on arrival was to double all the lighting and camera equipment we must between us have sent up the cost by quite a bit. I mention these otherwise boring particulars because just prior to my departure there had been a lengthy debate as to whether they could afford a trainee in the camera department or not!

My gaffer, who stayed on the picture, said afterwards what I had already guessed,

" You'd ave lit it better, but 'e *directed* it better than you would've. "
That's for sure. I was glad they benefited from the arrangement because I certainly did; it left me free to work with some of the most fun people I had met in years and began an era of working with young directors who would revive feelings of awe and exhilaration experienced thirty years before when I first found myself with Joan Littlewood, Peter Brook and Tony Richardson.

I had just put the phone down after being told not to leave home for the next ten weeks, except to pay the cheques into the bank, when it rang again. Rainer Mockert is a producer of music films whom I had first met on CENERENTOLA. Rainer, by the way, was a name often given to kids in the immediate post-war era, being unmistakably German without any National Socialist associations (where before Siegfried, Siegmunde, and Gutrune had been the "in" thing). When he and his school-mates asked a new teacher always to call them by their first names she had thought what nice, friendly, sensitive children - until she discovered that in her

class of 23 there were no fewer than 17 Rainers.

" I know you're doing this other movie, but I want to make sure before fixing anyone else for Peter. "

" Rainer, I've just been fired. "
Peter Sellars was a very young American who had so far worked mostly in opera. After a performance of his *Magic Flute* at Glyndebourne he was presented to a famous British orchestral conductor, who upbraided him thus,

" Young man this is disgraceful, an outrage; you must realise that Mozart is a great composer. "

" Mr Heath, thank you. I can see that until now the whole of my life has been entirely wrong, and from this

Peter.   *Photo: Bob Marshak.*

"Why is there only one word for Thesaurus?"

moment I will change everything. "

" Then you will have a future. "

" Coming from someone with a future like yours, Mr Heath .... "

After liberating Mozart from Peter Shaffer, Sellars was about to make a silent movie - or as silent as is consistent with a music score by John Adams. I went out to Vienna and spent most of the day getting acquainted; we didn't talk much about films, always a good sign. There was a performance of *Don Carlos* that evening in one of those stunningly ordinary productions that dog the great opera houses of this world. Peter wished me a pleasant evening.

" Don't look. "

Next morning he kindly asked if I'd enjoyed it.

" It was fine but I made the same mistake as Orpheus, I looked. "

" Ah, but this one was dead to start with. "

THE CABINET OF Dr RAMIREZ was a resiting, in the Wall Street area of Manhattan, of an earlier belonging to a Dr Caligari. Films are a small world and one evening in New York Rainer found himself having dinner with the wife of the director who had just changed his mind about me.

" Please tell your husband we can't thank him enough. "

Peter intended the picture to open at the Hollywood Bowl with the Los Angeles Philharmonic live, and it is a pity that subsequently this did not happen; it would have taken more than a raccoon to divert attention from it. When completed, RAMIREZ got a very brief airing indeed before languishing in a bank vault because, by a regrettable oversight, somebody had forgotten to pay the San Francisco Symphony Orchestra. It is a pity for those who would have enjoyed seeing it.... and perhaps also for those who would not. Peter told me once that in the theatre he feels happiest if half the audience loves it and the other half hates it, if nobody minds either way he hasn't achieved very much.

" If everyone who's going to walk out does so in the first ten minutes, you know you're in for a great evening. "

Four years later it was Peter who pushed the wheel almost full circle by taking me back to documentary, for a workshop rehearsing *The Merchant of Venice*; the first thing of this sort to come my way for ages - the kind of world I'd grown up with in the early years. Lighting Portia's face as I thought best, brought out two pockmarks that in no way

Me and Peter.

detracted from the beauty of it, and recalling how a couple of equally innocuous moles in the same place on the features of one "star" brought yelps of protest from their Hollywood director, I thanked Peter for the freedom to work sensibly. He said that when Klemperer was once asked to re-record a passage where a horn cracked on a note the old man had replied,

" It happened because the player got a bit of spit on his lip. We are all human - I thought that was the object of all this. "

He then added characteristically that anyway, nobody could possibly confuse a recording with music. When computer-graphics become commonplace, as they must, everyone may hopefully remember that the object is to make the imagination work, not to spoon-feed it.

Peter is one of those rare people who, when they enter a room everybody inside it feels better. The last time I was in LA I telephoned his assistant beforehand so as we could meet up, and was told that he had a class of three hundred at UCLA, and at the end of the academic year he always saw each individual student alone for ten minutes - so Tuesday and Wednesday were bad but Thursday would be OK. I speculated what he could possibly achieve in ten minutes.

" Oh, Peter can do a lot in ten minutes. "

I was to find that out in New York at the end of 1997, while shooting

Maximilian Schell - facing self and operator on camera.

GLORIA with Sidney Lumet. The only time we could meet was to drive together to the set one morning. The trouble was I always shared Sidney's transport, and directors like to quietly gather their thoughts on the way to work. The same evening Sidney asked would I please tell Peter what a joy it had been to meet him.

"Why is there only one word for Thesaurus?"

" To tell you the truth, I felt just a bit tired when I left home this morning; but by the time we got to the set I could have dealt with anything."

The Thalia in Hamburg is a theatre with a similar tradition to our own Royal Court, that is, a courageous one. Its director, Jürgen Flimm, had staged a piece, *Through Roses*, by the young American composer Marc Neikrug, about a phenomenon that has afflicted a number of people who survived the Nazi Holocaust. Well enough adjusted, as they hoped, to lead a normal life in the everyday world outside the camps, after many years, with the onset of age the full horror would hit back again and overwhelm them. Jürgen knew all about this because it had happened to a member of his own company. An actor who had been with them for many years came to him one day in a state of shock saying that someone in the night had daubed "Juden Rauss" on his front door. Jürgen dashed round to the apartment, to find nothing, no sign at all. Some days later the same man came again and told Jürgen that other members of the company had warned him to get out because he was Jewish - something none of them would ever have done. The poor man ended up, serene to all appearances, in a countryside home for old people. Always when Jürgen visited him there he would say the same thing,

" I know who you are, but it is too long a journey. "

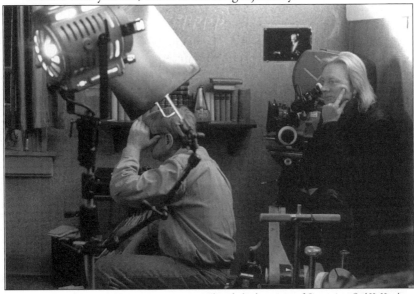

Photos by kind permission of Cinecentium GmbH, Hamburg.

Marc's piece concerns the same point in the life of a violinist who had been in Auschwitz, where the commandant's wife, a frau of horticulture, had made a rose garden at the very entrance to the gas chambers. We shot it in Cologne with Pinchas Zukerman, and that amazing actor, Maximilian Schell. Sometimes, having lit the scene, I'd leave them to it and go upstairs for a piano lesson with one of the finest pianists of the day. The film business has certainly had its moments.

I began life at the sea's side and when you do that you always need it (to look at, not to go on). I am comfortable by the sea as nowhere else. There is great value for humans to have an infinite horizon handy and every day I am calmed and renewed by the sea in all its moods. It is also nice to live in the same town as Hamilton Harty and Max Miller: "Christopher Robin went down to Alice" and "Here we go up to our nuts in May" - to give a rough idea (of Max Miller not of Hamilton Harty). Max was held in such local pride and affection that if ever he was delayed after playing in London, they used to hold the last train out of Victoria until he was on it. He had a house in Burlington Street, and a reputation for meanness. As my local butcher's shop stands on the corner of Burlington Street, I asked if he remembered him.

" He'd come in here and buy half a lamb's kidney; Anna Neagle now, that was a bit different .... "

I can believe it was. A very young Pat Cahill, up to town for some function, found himself sharing a compartment with her on the London train. He had never met her before but they were soon in conversation. At the last minute he had mislaid his cufflinks and lightheartedly mentioned it.

" My dear, we can't have you going about like that; there's a pair of Herbert's in my bag ... there you are. "

Notice how the railway became part of the town's community, especially in the days of its own Pullman service, *The Brighton Belle*, (no stopping at East Croydon for that one!). When kippers disappeared from its breakfast menu, Larry raised them to a national issue by complaining to *The Times* newspaper. The kippers were hastily restored. Just as stepping on a British bound flight from anywhere in the world you feel you're already home, so it is for me on settling into a Brighton train at Victoria. And be it in train or car, I have only to see the outline of the South Downs, to know that it's all been left behind.

Half way through my sixties I finally drew level with Handel in the attic at the age of six, having abandoned the silly idea of carting an instrument around in favour of getting the production to install a piano wherever I was staying. This impressed one Hollywood producer no end.

" *Our* cameramen, Mr Watkin, are more interested in lighting and camera equipment. "

" Oh you mustn't be hard on them, I'm sure they're very good in spite of that. "

At a school location on another picture there was usually a small audience for any practising undertaken during the lunch hour. One attentive 11 year old extra stayed to the end,

" Are you a professional pianist? "

Intuition, always strong in the young, had clearly suggested to her a nicer way to criticise the lighting than is resorted to by mature actresses.

It was good at last to be properly intimate with Fredericus; it was also a kind of postponed reconciliation with my father. He had been right after all; I wouldn't have made any money at it.

It all came about because I got to know the owner of a shop in East Street selling second hand LPs (at the time a source of some music otherwise not available). Getting to know Paul Mathias was to discover one of the best musical minds I've ever encountered. He had at different stages been a teacher, an ethno-musicologist in West Africa, and finally a partner with Eileen Joyce in four-hand piano recitals - until they fell out due to her being a manic schizophrenic (Paul's version, I never heard hers).

Here again was someone larger than life - an Eddy Fowlie of music. Being in East Street one morning I looked in to see him and found only the assistant.

" He's gone shopping, back in a minute. "
Suddenly the door was flung open behind me and Paul, who had just had a set-to with a traffic warden, hurled a carrier-bag of groceries the entire length of the shop with spectacular results, then sat down and talked quietly about Knappertsbusch and Bruckner.

His clashes with the system took on themselves the dimensions of the crusades. When the shop began losing money he didn't have and his landlord refused to co-operate over the lease, Paul moved out.

" He'll find where I am soon enough, and then it's up to him; but just in case he sends in a bailiff may I put a few things in the spare room? "
For the next 18 months the spare room was crammed from floor to ceiling, one was almost unable to enter it, but eventually the "all clear" sounded and I got it back.

Now, for the first time in my life, someone took the musical part of me seriously, and watered the desert,

" Feeling as you do musically you can't go on any longer not able to play. I know if I put you on scales you'll give up, so find a piece that is so good that you'll never tire of it. "
and that was the first prelude of the 48 of Bach.

I'd small hopes of reconciling my desperate fingers with ears that were a lifetime ahead of them and would have little patience with what was going on, but I had not realised the compensations that went with such an imbalance: I would know the instant the slightest mistake happened; and being unable to sight-read meant having to memorise each piece, which in turn meant that playing in six sharps was no more tricky than playing with none at all. I've received many gifts in my life but never before one that would transform every remaining day of it.

He was diabetic, which in the end caused him to go blind, but he was always a fighting optimist. The last time we met he sat at "our" Steinway and played the first of Bach's Six Little Preludes as I can scarcely hope to hear it again. When he died a few days later, I sat up most of the night playing the piano, better than I have ever done before or since.

Lastly, one more young director, Beeban Kidron, who as a photographer went to take pictures of the women laying siege to the atomic missile base at Greenham Common and ended up joining them and making a 16mm film of it all.

Coming up from Brighton to meet her, I suggested as a novelty, coffee at the Ritz - I could walk it from Victoria across Green Park.

" How will I know you? "

" I'll be wearing green sneakers. "

There is no better way of being recognised at the Ritz; Beeban saw me being thrown out and came over. We settled for a tea-room in Piccadilly but I still regret that I had not thought to walk her on a bit further to the Italian coffee shop in Maddox Street where I had spent all those hours with Joan Littlewood thirty years before.

She had been the start of it for me, a precursor to all the others who

Beeban.   Photo: Suzanne Hanover

came afterwards to make the sixties the golden renaissance that it truly was. I know it will come again and hope when it does that we shall not lose it so easily. In the meantime it is as heartening to know that Britain is still turning out artists of truth and originality as it is dispiriting to see that most of them will end up abroad. While shooting JANE EYRE for Franco in 1994 I came in contact with Deborah Warner because she wanted to do a film of *Measure for Measure*. It was put back, so I went onto something else, and when we finally met, over a Glyndebourne picnic, she said she'd given up the whole idea of working in films.

" While I was trying to get that going I did five productions on the stage. "

She is right in a way, as Joan was when an interviewer remarked it was sad that apart from SPARRERS there was nothing to show what her work had been like.

" Don't matter - someone'll come along and do it just as well, I hope."

Yet to have put something on film ... it might lie hidden for years (like

Myra Hess) - but to touch people outside your own time; if only once.

For my own part I have always loved England's language (*all* of it) and its landscape, more than I've hated its hypocrisy and its philistine establishment. As for the people, considering all the nonsense they are subjected to, they don't do badly either.

The thing about lighting is knowing when to leave off; if I've been good at anything it has always been that, and I imagine the same applies to writing autobiographies. Most of my fourteen nannies were strong on the idea of leaving the table while still having an appetite for more, and that is my best wish for the readers of this.

FIN

(Five past four, Saturday 10th May 1997. Time for a cup of tea).

"Why is there only one word for Thesaurus?"

Glossary

40

ACT Association of Cinematograph Technicians. The original trade union of film makers (my no.13831) which, allowing for its quirky ways, served the industry well enough until the advent of television. Then the tail outgrew to such an extent that the dog all but disappeared; large bodies of permanently employed drudges have different needs from freelance craftsmen. There is a natural tendency for unions to decline into protection societies for tenth-rate people (usually the result of hanging on to outmoded seniority rosters), but generally it stays within reasonable bounds. Unions are a traditional and essential part of a decently ordered society; almost the first enactments of both Hitler and Mrs. Thatcher were to cut their balls off.

ALS Autograph letter signed.

ARC the oldest, simplest, and still in many cases the best light source, consisting merely of a gap between two sticks of carbon; runs only from a DC supply.

ARRIFLEX first realistic hand-hold electric-drive camera. Originally made for the Wehrmacht to charge about battlefields with.

BASHER exactly what the name implies. A flood lamp shaped like one of those things ladies sit underneath in the hair-dressers, which is positioned directly behind the camera and "bashes" light all over the place. Having, as an assistant, watched endless cameramen light their shots well enough and then wash away every trace of what they'd done with a basher in a kind of reflex insecurity, I have never used one.

BEST BOY a misleading appellation for the assistant to the chief electrician or key grip; use confined to the USA.

BLIMP relatively sound-proof housing for film cameras.

BLOW-UP photographic enlargement - not a special effect.

BOMA an enclosure surrounded by a barrier of impenetrable African thorn.

BRENDA Queen Elizabeth II (the lady not the boat).

BRUTE the second largest of the arcs, and the the only one remaining in general use. Originally the other members of the arc family comprised -
    65 amp = appx between a pup and a 2K
    120 amp = 5K
    150 amp = 10K
    du-arcs = sky-pans
There were also eight Titans, the only arc larger than a brute. They lived in Los Angeles and I managed to use all eight of them for one shot in CATCH 22. They ate through a pair of carbons every twenty minutes.

BULL, Ole Norwegian violinist (1810-1880)

BUTTERFLY a delicate little silken hoop for softening the sun on close-ups; never large enough.

CAMPER not the comparative of camp, but an excessive American caravan comprising everything short of a full-size billiard table, also known as a Winebago after one of the leading makes.

CEMENT film - actually a solvent (acetone) that was used for welding two pieces of film together, until someone discovered that clear adhesive tape was less messy, and rescued assistant editors from the hazards of glue-sniffing.

CHAPMAN CRANE the Rolls Royce of camera cranes; one of those splendid pieces of machinery that inspires affection in its human users.

CHARLIE-BAR a very narrow flag. In the 1920s and 30s a lady's breasts were discreetely referred to as "Charlies". To increase the allure of actresses

"Why is there only one word for Thesaurus?"

under-endowed in this respect a shadow was often arranged with one so as to suggest what was missing.

CUTAWAY exactly what it says; an insert or close-up that enables the editor to go from one part of a scene to another.

DAY-FOR-NIGHT the technique for shooting exterior night scenes in daylight; when done properly it is indistinguishable, and very often better, than actual night shooting. But the emphasis does have to be on *properly* for once, and every requisite must be exactly in place before shooting. This often causes directors that have got accustomed to sailing along with the wind behind them, to become impatient, and I once suggested to Richard Lester that he was not emotionally equipped for day for night, (which equipped him better than anything else could have done - by making him laugh).

In France it is called Nuit Americaine, I imagine because it was done so consistently badly in Hollywood, whose incompetence in this respect is probably the origin of the absurd convention of printing all night stuff blue - a desperate colour code to signal as a night scene something that doesn't look anything like one.

DOLLY Possibly a corruption of trolley since that is what it is; the device for moving the camera about during a tracking-shot. Another name from my early days, but no longer used, was velocilator.

DRY ICE solid i.e. frozen CO_2 (carbon dioxide) - when immersed in vats of boiling water transforms itself into volumes of the heavier than air white clouds inseparable from fantasy sequences the world over. Legend has it that a director in quest of realism for an Alaskan scene being filmed under more temperate conditions, put dry ice in the mouths of his actors so their breath would condense; I am not disposed to believe this but some directors are silly enough.

ELEMAC a comparatively small and manoeverable Italian designed camera dolly.

EYMO the most compact and beautifully crafted little 35mm hand camera, 100 ft spool loading. Only ran about 20 feet at a wind, but as it was held with one hand either side you could re-wind it by twisting your wrists in opposite directions while running after your quarry.

FILMO 16mm version of above.

FINAL CUT in a directors contract, means that his edit of the film is what gets shown to the public. Increasingly rare.

FLAG oblong-shaped black cloth stretched across a wire frame, used to keep light from going where it is not wanted.

FLAT (noun) large rectangular frame, covered with hessian and wallpaper, used in set construction.

FLAT (adj) lit from the front only, with no modelling; also expressed as "flat as a witch's tit".

FLAT-BED a bench with two turntables and an illuminated ground glass between them, for speedy examination of film without running it through a moviola.

FRESNEL circular ribbed glass in front of all conventional film lamps, that is those which excercise control over light as opposed to sloshing it about regardless. Named after its inventor, Augustin Jean Fresnel (1788-1827).

GEARED-HEAD the pivot on which the camera is mounted, controlled by two crank handles - on the left for lateral movement (panning) and at the back for vertical (tilting). Skill in the use of this, like anything worthwhile,takes time and effort to acquire; but it is by far the best way to be in control. A rod sticking out of the back of the camera (pan-bar) - unless it is a shot of a racing car or a rocket, is a likely sign that the operator is not all that good and you should send for someone else.

GOSSIP a useful antidote to pretension of any kind, also a vital catalytic for a healthy film crew (and, come to that, for anywhere else).

HAIR in the GATE The gate is that part of the camera immediately behind the lens, through which the film passes and is held still at the moment of exposure. Raw film-stock is manufactured in wide sheets which are afterwards sliced into 35mm widths and perforated with sprocket-holes on either side. The cutters that do this get blunt after a time and have to be replaced. Sometimes the last run or two before replacement may result in slightly roughened edges and tiny splinters of celluloid can break off and get lodged inside the frame, where they look like black hairs waving about when the film is projected. After a satisfactory shot has been made, the camera assistant always examines the gate to make sure that this has not occurred; if it has the shot must be done again. In my early days it was sometimes more accurately referred to as celluloid or "cell" in the gate. This has now gone quite out of use, possibly because of the sort of response one impatient director got when I once found an offending sliver and called out - " Cell in the gate. " -
" *Why* is there cell in the gate? ".

Seeing me at a loss Ritchie suggested I should
  " Ask him if he would like to do the next one without any celluloid in the gate."

HMI a bone of contention, see appendix. (A teacher friend tells me the letters also stand for Her Majesty's Inspector - so HMI seems to denote bad news in any walk of life).

HONEY WAGON mobile toilets for film crew.

IA Short for IATSE; International Alliance of Theatrical Stage Employees. The trade union that covers movies in the USA, organised into numerous locals e.g. 644 is Camera NY, and 659 is Camera LA. Fraternal relations between the two last seem to have derived directly from Cain and Abel.

INCHING KNOB for turning over camera mechanism by hand when threading up etc.

INSERT tight close-up of a piece of action the first unit doesn't intend to waste time on. A task for the second unit.

IRISH JIG Wig.

JAP Jewish American Princess.

JARO METER from the initials of the J.Arthur Rank Organisation who, very sensibly manufactured this Rolls Royce of foot-candle meters to the specifications of their own cameramen. Weight one and a half pounds, and dead accurate from one to twenty thousand foot-candles.

KEY-LIGHT principal light source (not necessarily the strongest), hence high-key means an overall bright scene and low-key an overall dark one.

KICK really strong backlight.

LIE main instrument of civil and ecclesiastical authority, although the axiom that you cannot govern without them is probably out by one syllable; you certainly cannot misgovern without them.

LINE-UP the mechanics of preparing a shot - where to put the camera and when and how to move it about.

LOOPING or post-synchronisation, is a remedy for unsuccessful sound recordings. A section of the film is joined head to tail forming a loop (hence the name) which can be run continuously round and round in the projector. The actor sits inside a sound-proof booth and speaks the lines while watching his own lip movements on the screen. Some directors favour this process even when there was nothing wrong with the original track, because by altering inflections et cetera it is possible to change a performance. Some actors favour it because they get paid all over again.

MUCK, Karl The only conductor of Mahler's generation to leave recordings of any real value, most of them made in the first quarter of this century.

MATT-BOX rectangular housing for holding filters in place, immediately in front of the lens.

NATKE National Association of Theatre and Kinematograph Employees (the classically irreproachable spelling of Kinematograph should be noted). The projectionist's trade union. By some graceful oddity the grips were always NATKE members and thus the only camera crew not in the orthographically plebian ACT.

NFTVA "Never Fails To Veto Access", although first intended to stand for the "National Film and Television Archive", a body governed until recently by instincts similar to those of a dog with a bone, (though not entirely since the canine original digs the bone up occasionally). Gratifying improvement starting to appear.

OPTICAL anything made through a lens on an optical printer (as opposed to normal contact printing). Until recently this always involved loss of quality. Now, given enough money, a new original negative can be made by laser-scanning where the quality will be the same as the original.

PACK-SHOT what a TV commercial is actually about i.e. a packet of cornflakes or soap powder. Held in such esteem by advertising agencies that they get upset if you to take less than three hours to light it; on a feature this is done inside ten minutes by the second unit and called an insert. (see above)

PAN-GLASS short for panchromatic (as distinct from orthochromatic) viewing glass, worn round the neck on a piece of string. An instant guide to contrast in B&W lighting (it short-cuts one thought process), it is valueless for colour work. The only use it retains is as something to look through while attempting to augur cloud-versus-sun behaviour, but for that it's a lot safer to use a welder's glass and, better still, hand the lot over to your chief electrician. It is now a badge of office for cameramen wishing to be noticed, some of whom even go so far as to have their

"Why is there only one word for Thesaurus?"

initials engraved on the holder.

PRINCIPAL PHOTOGRAPHY the precise meaning is photography of principal cast, as distinct from action unit, model unit, flying unit, second unit and all the other units.

RUSHES rush print for viewing previous day's work, called "dailies" by Americans who always have to be different.

S.U.P. "Shot under protest" Aggrieved cameramen sometimes put this on the slate when they were overridden by the director. Fallen into disuse from the number of times material so marked turned out to be the best thing in the rushes.

SKY-PAN a white enamel saucer about three feet across, with a naked 2K or 5K bulb in front of it. Used only for backings.

SPECIAL FX (effects). Happenings outside the everyday run of events, that have to be induced by robust gentlemen with gas bottles and sticks of dynamite. Their most arduous assignments however tend to be in TV commercials, where they are expected to ensure that the product works.

STEADICAM gyroscopic straight-jacket for hand-held shooting. Nine out of ten steadicam shots would be much better on a crane; the tenth justifies the device completely.

STOP an occult cipher for regulating the size of the hole in the lens through which light reaches the film. Appears as a disjointed set of numbers based on how many times one lens dimension divides into another - 2.8, 4, 5.6 etc. In practice all you need remember is that each one lets in half the light of the one before it.

STUDIO obviously a place for making films, but also used to denote any of the major production companies such as Universal, Paramount, Twentieth Century Fox etc.

SUPPLY Once upon a time all film lighting ran off 110 volts DC and life was uncomplicated; arcs are by nature DC and 110 volt tungsten bulbs were everywhere standard for film work. With the advent of HMIs a changeover to 220 AC took place bringing with it some serious disadvantages (see appendix). There is one aspect only where AC is vastly superior and that is when dimmers are needed, but it is hardly worth the sacrifice of so much else.

TUNGSTEN the same thing as a household light bulb, inside a housing with a fresnel in front. The family consists of -

"inky-dink"
"pup" (500 watts, nowadays 750 watts)
2K (2 kilowatts),
5K and 10K.

- all exactly alike in principle. A final word of advice from Jimmy Ritchie as I set out for Blackpool with John Taylor in 1955 had been, "Don't be afraid of a brute when the time comes, the only difference between it and an inky-dink is the size."

ULCER as unpleasant as the name implies. A large wooden flag full of holes, to distribute uneven patches of light. Arbitrary and for that reason of little use.

UMBRELLA gadget for keeping the rain off, often mistaken by stills photographers for a light source.

VIDEO ASSIST a device for ruining the optical system of cameras while conveying an image of the frame to a TV screen for an army of people who don't need to see it. I even had to remind a commercial company, when it broke down on a shoot, that the camera would still take pictures without it. A dummy teat for directors.

VOICE-OVER same thing as spoken commentary where an actor's voice is laid over the picture but he is not seen. The opposite of the unfortunate children held up as an example by all my fourteen nannies, who were expected to be seen but not heard.

WILD CAMERA the noisy sort, smaller but not usable for sound shooting.

WORK-LIGHT lamp put on to enable everyone to see what they're doing before starting to light the set.

ZOOM a lens on which it is possible to vary the focal length i.e. from wide to tight and vice versa. Of necessity there is too much glass to compete with any but the worst ordinary lenses; for which reason it should only be used if you can't get the shot any other way - then, like the steadicam, it comes into its own.

Appendix

First printed in EYEPIECE Magazine, Oct/Nov 1992.

41

Having spent years telling anyone who would listen, that large HMIs are no substitute for a brute, I find myself, for the first time, having to shoot a picture with them because there are no brutes in Africa. It is always irritating to be proved right.

Firstly, to define what it is we are talking about, a brute is a simple mechanical device for keeping two sticks of carbon a short distance apart. That is all. There is nothing to go wrong that cannot be repaired on the spot, and at worst you can maintain the gap by hand-feeding.

An HMI, on the other hand, is a large and heavy box of electronics, prone to failure, and unrepairable when it takes place (as it surely will). They are attractive to accountants because, on paper, they might save an electrician's travel, hotel, and living expenses. It is a false calculation because the hire charge is not only far more than that of a brute, but, whereas on a picture I would normally carry two lamps and two spare mechanisms, I should need at least a dozen HMIs - in order to be sure of having two of them working at any one time. This is not in any way fanciful. On a picture called WATER, Dougie Slocombe took twelve to the Caribbean, and ended up with just two that were serviceable.

Apart from such chronic unreliability, the list of their disadvantages is a long one.

1. Having a tiny light source (the crater of one of the carbons - I never know which), a brute, with the fresnel replaced with a clear glass, will create vividly etched shadows. There is no comparable way to do this, and with an HMI it is not possible.

2. The best lightning flash, in a confined area, is obtained by reversing the poles of a brute - far more effective than scissor-arcs. Not possible with an HMI.

3. To situate a backlight on the opposite bank of a river to where you are shooting (essential if you are to see water at night), simply ferry the lamp across, and drop the cable in the water. An HMI would require a separate generator, and a ten mile drive to the nearest bridge.

4. HMIs waste about ten minutes after being switched on, before they are warmed up; then you can't switch them out because they won't light up again! Sophistications, like "instant re-strike" and "flicker-free", only render them more capricious than ever ("flicker-free" I can only assume to operate on the principle that the lamp is never on). Therefore you may not over or under crank, neither can you flash a lamp to see what it is doing in the normal way - a minor disadvantage, but who needs it?

5. They are dangerous to the point of being lethal - imagine working with HMIs in a swimming pool, or in heavy rain for that matter.

6. The worst aspect of all is the Gaderine rush from DC to AC, (an arc runs on DC; an HMI on AC). AC supply is highly dangerous. One electrician has already been killed on a picture in the Philippines, because of three-phase AC in a humid climate. With DC it could not have happened.

7. AC produces a high-frequency hum, even with ordinary tungsten lights. Now that 110v DC tungsten bulbs have been phased out, along with the DC supply in our major studios, there are dire problems for sound. On HAMLET, Shepperton C stage was like the inside of a bee-hive, with hours wasted trying to change the more noisy lamps.

In fairness, the smaller HMIs (up to 4kw) are a tremendous asset for interior/exterior locations, but this is easily managed with a small AC set. It is the abandoning of brutes, and of DC, that is mistaken.

I well understand that, after a certain amount of money has been wasted, there develops a kind of economic momentum that bears down all reasonable argument. I'm putting two fingers up to millions of pounds - but it is time someone pointed out that the Emperor has no clothes.

By the end of two weeks on this picture, four 12kw ballasts have packed-up completely. At the rate of two per week, that sets the level at twenty four for a twelve week schedule. How that is cheaper than two brutes I cannot imagine. The current charge for a brute is £48, as opposed to £150, plus £20 per hour burning time for a 12kw HMI (the latest models incorporate a clock to record this), on account of the high cost of the bulb.

In the same two weeks, the lamps in question caused the loss of six hour's shooting time. If I had not compromised the look of some scenes (in one instance by taking the roof off a building - an admirable technique that fell out of use about 1910), we would have had to shut down altogether. Three hours lost per week adds three full days to a twelve week picture. The cost of a feature unit standing about doing nothing for three days, would pay for a hundred electricians - and that rather offsets the one you are supposed to have saved in the first place.

One excuse offered, is that Africa is hot and dusty; but films are often made in hot and dusty places. A former sufferer apparently resorted to packing the sensitive things with dry ice (perhaps he was shooting a musical), and we are told the latest models will incorporate larger fans (to drown the humming?), and may be painted white (useful as reflectors).

The demand for these lamps originates from television, where nobody knows any better. And why should they? When television first erupted, all film technicians were busy making films; so the TV companies recruited a bunch of electronic engineers who had never set eyes on a film set, and whose ignorance has been handed down ever since. Moreover, the prevailing attitude disposes the younger cameramen to be wary of asking for equipment that may discourage producers from employing them a second time.

Is it really too late to act sensibly over this? The only asset I've been able to discover where large HMIs are concerned, is that there is a deal of comedy to be had from them. I shall struggle through this picture, and the look of it will suffer to some extent. But that won't matter - the big HMIs have survived on the basis that what you don't see on the screen you won't miss.

David Watkin, BOPHA, Zimbabwe.

Dear "Eyepiece" Editors,
I read with interest the well argued article from David Watkin on brutes. One passage totally foxed me, however. His sixth disadvantage, on page 18, mentions a "Gaderine rush from DC to AC ". I have tried to look this up in dictionaries and encyclopedias, but can find nothing. Is it a scientific term, or a film term?

Yours, Brenda Lane, Norwich.

Dear Editors,
What a treat ...... May your carbons burn for ever David!

Expat DoP.

"Why is there only one word for Thesaurus?"

Index

by chapters

"Why is there only one word for Thesaurus?"

"Why is there only one word for Thesaurus?"

"Why is there only one word for Thesaurus?"